THE ECONOMICS OF TRANSITION

The Economics of Transition

From Socialist Economy to Market Economy

Second Edition

MARIE LAVIGNE

First edition 1995
Reprinted twice
Second edition 1999

Published by
PALGRAVE MACMILLAN
Houndmills, Basingstoke, Hampshire RG21 6XS and
175 Fifth Avenue, New York, N.Y. 10010
Companies and representatives throughout the world

PALGRAVE MACMILLAN is the global academic imprint of the Palgrave
Macmillan division of St. Martin's Press, LLC and of Palgrave Macmillan Ltd.
Macmillan is a registered trademark in the United States, United Kingdom
and other countries. Palgrave is a registered trademark in the European
Union and other countries.

ISBN-13: 978–0–333–75408–5   hardback
ISBN-10: 0–333–75408–5   hardback
ISBN-13: 978–0–333–75416–0   paperback
ISBN-10: 0–333–75416–6   paperback

A catalogue record for this book is available
from the British Library.

10   9   8
08   07   06   05

Copy-edited and typeset by Povey–Edmondson
Tavistock and Rochdale, England

Printed in China

Contents

List of Tables, Boxes and Figures

Tables

Boxes

Figures

Preface to the First Edition

Until recently the world was divided into the first, second and third world. The notion of the second world is now losing its substance. What remains is a huge amount of debris and ruins which is a combination of the first and third worlds: by its aspirations and longing to create a democratic political system and prospering market economy it relates to the first world, a part of which it would like to become; however, by the state of the economy and the types of national and social problems it often resembles the third world. (Vaclav Havel, President of the Czech and Slovak Federal Republic, 4 September 1991, Prague, opening speech of the International Forum for Culture and Democracy)

Since the Berlin Wall was breached on 9 November 1989, the former socialist countries have remained on top of the agenda in the Western media, not only because of dramatic political developments such as the anti-Gorbachev coup and the collapse of the USSR in 1991, or because of the lingering state of war in the former Yugoslavia and in parts of the former USSR. Economic developments make headlines as well. The transition to the market arouses public interest out of proportion to the share of these countries in the world economy. Western governments, firms, international organisations and ordinary citizens, are eager to keep informed, to understand, to help, to advise, to trade, to invest, to be involved in one way or another.

At the same time, after several years of transition, frustrations and even a kind of fatigue develop in the West. Though transition to the market is now acknowledged as a longlasting process which might extend to a whole generation, structural transformation seems very slow. While growth has resumed in Eastern Europe, there are only a few signs of the possible ending of a protracted recession in Russia. Along with this gloomy assessment, the West increasingly feels the impact of the East, in many ways. East and West are now parts of the same world. In the past, following the usual international classification, one could divide the world into three parts: the developed market economies, or, in the parlance of the East, the capitalist world; the 'second' world of the centrally planned economies, which used to call itself socialist; the Third World of the developing economies. Now there is just an economic division between rich and poor countries. There is no longer a systemic division. The market economy has won. What is the price of this victory? Will the Western model succeed in the East? Will the rich Western countries be able to go on supporting the South and at the same time pull the East up to their average level of development? What does this imply in terms of assistance, market liberalisation, and increased immigration? Are our recipes and programmes really suited for the transition process? If these programmes do not work as they should, is the model to be blamed?

Much has already been written on transition. Reports, conference materials, collective books, guides for businessmen, and scholarly articles in specialised and non-specialised journals, have flourished. It is fairly impossible to follow this surge in the literature, and to avoid being overtaken by events. It looks therefore provocative to offer a textbook by one single author on such a fast-moving subject. The purpose and the approach need to be clarified.

The author of this book has been studying Soviet and Eastern European economies for over thirty years. Thus, I belong to the professional world of what used to be called 'sovietology'. This profession is feeling very frustrated lately. Since the beginning of the transition many new experts have come into the field, from various backgrounds, mainly from an experience in developing countries. Many of the former 'sovietologists' have lost credibility, because none of them had predicted that the system would collapse when it did, or the way in which a collapse would occur, and also because they were suspected of bias due to their involvement in the study of a now dead system. Personally I do not feel guilty of lack of foresight. We all were wrong: both those who year after year predicted that the system was bound to collapse, and those, more cautious, who thought it might go on muddling through for many years. Many of us believed that the system might last longer if reformed, and we had even devised the categories of 'modified' or 'reformed' planned economies. The sudden end of the system took everybody by surprise, as well as the radical shift to the market, which excluded any 'third way'. Does this mean that we may now dispense with any understanding of the past? The present transition process has no historical equivalent or precedent, such as the situation of the Western European countries after the Second World War, or the evolution in the developing countries. The transition is burdened with the legacies of the past. This past has to be assessed, especially as history is being rewritten due to new information and new statistical data now available. Slowly, 'the figure in the carpet' reveals itself. Knowledge of the past helps to undestand the inertia of the present. History also evidences that the fruit was rotten, through dozens of signs that we know how to decipher only now; thus the present provides us with keys to explain the past.

This book is concerned with economics. Is there such a thing as 'transition economics'? In the past there was a wide debate in the profession as to the relevancy of mainstream economics to the analysis of centrally planned economies. Whatever the answer in theory, in practice it was very difficult to use any sophisticated econometric model for lack of reliable data. Now there seems to be a wide consensus on the theory. In the East, while communism has been discarded politically, and even outlawed in some countries (for instance, in the Czech Republic), economists and policy-makers alike endorse the fundamentals of neo-classical economic science. Their Western advisers eagerly support this attitude, especially as the standard adjustment and stabilisation packages which they recommend are based on the same theoretical assumptions. I believe that the disillusions in the transition process will lead to a more complex approach, closer to the 'political economy' concept. This concept is generally considered with suspicion both in East and West. It is reminiscent of Marx, more than of Ricardo. It suggests at best a reluctance, at worst an inability to use mathematical formalisation. Beyond such simplifying views, one may find an inspiration in new approaches such as the institutionalist one, and in the combination of economics with political science and history. The last chapter of this book explores these alternatives approaches.

This book is also the outcome of a personal involvement. I have been travelling in East Central Europe and in the USSR since 1964. I have witnessed the first year of the transition in Prague in 1990–1. I have many personal friends in all these countries. Therefore I cannot look at the transition from a mere scholarly point of view. I want the transition to succeed, and I sense all the sorrows and pains associated with this process, which looked so exhilarating in the beginning. I have a special thought for my Russian friends. Not only are they facing the damages and losses resulting from the past regime, which they had to bear for so long; and not only, in their own private lives, are they looking back at their wasted years, and anticipating an uncertain and difficult future for their children. But also, they are explicitly or implicitly burdened with a collective guilt for what their leaders have imposed upon others. Their native motherland has vanished; its name is associated with infamy, and glorious memories are wiped out. The 900 days during which Soviet Leningrad resisted the enemy sink into oblivion while St Petersburg is born again. Transition is irreversible: nobody wants the communist past to be revived, but should all of it be doomed?

Finally, let me add a few methodological notes. The book is divided into two parts, the fist one dealing with the past of the centrally planned economies under 'real socialism', the second exploring the transition in progress. Central and Eastern European countries, together with the former USSR, are mainly considered here; other experiences are mentioned but not elaborated upon.

The book is targeted for students in economics, political science, and history of Eastern Europe. Though designed for undergraduates and not requiring a preliminary acquaintance with the subject, it may also be used on advanced courses as an introduction to transition economics. For teachers and graduate students, a guide for further reading provides opportunities for a deeper investigation. The book is also meant for the general public wanting a simple and clear approach to the complex issues of the transition to the market. It does not pretend to convey detailed information on all its aspects for all the countries under review. This is why, contrary to almost all the books devoted to this topic, no country studies are presented. The purpose is to offer basic and comprehensive guidance to the essentials, so that the reader may use what he/she already knows about the past of this area, sort out the huge volume of information brought to him or her by the media day by day, and follow up on his/her own through further reading.

A book on such a topic cannot be definitive. The process analysed is transitory by definition. People and governments in the East have to go through and out of transition; international organisations, states, and experts in the West are busy helping, advising, monitoring, and observing the process. The ultimate aim is not to create a new type of society, a new system. The East wants to rejoin the developed West where it stands. To reconstruct a market economy is, however, a long and complex task: we know where we start from, we believe we know how to get there, but we cannot know exactly what the outcome will be. The story is still open-ended.

*   *   *

I could not have written this book (as well as the shorter French book on which the present volume elaborated and expanded, *L'Europe de l'Est, du plan au marché*) without various favourable circumstances such as fruitful contacts and discussions in several research centres in the beginning of the transition. I would like to acknowledge the research support of the European University Institute (1988), of the Bundesinstitut für internationale und ostwissenschaftliche Studien (BIOST) in Cologne (1989), of the Averell Harriman Institute at the Columbia University and of the Institute for East–West Studies (IEWS) in New York (1990). I had the great privilege of being appointed by the IEWS as the director of its Central European branch, the European Studies Centre in Prague (1990–1), and this gave me the invaluable opportunity of witnessing the first steps of transition in a former communist country, as well as the privilege of working with a team of people enthusiastically dedicated to assisting the transition process. I was asssociated for two years (1991–3) with the Programme for Strategic and International Security Studies of the Graduate Institute for International Studies in Geneva. With the support of the French Ministry of Education and of my university, I organised in 1992 an international 'summer school' on the transition to the market which again allowed me to develop exciting intellectual contacts.

I cannot formally express my gratitude to all the friends, colleagues, specialists and institutions who actually helped me in devising this book, gathering the material, and clarifying my ideas. I earnestly apologise for not mentioning everybody toward whom I have an intellectual debt. Among the few names I want to mention, I shall begin with two dear friends of many years, with whom I have repeatedly discussed the issues of feasible or unfeasible socialism, and who both died in 1994: Alec Nove, Emeritus Professor at the University of Glasgow and father of the British sovietology, and Aleksandar Vacic, the head of the Division for Economic Analysis and Projections at the Economic Commission for Europe of the United Nations in Geneva. Several friends agreed to read the manuscript and to comment; I am especially grateful to Joel Dirlam, Marvin Jackson, Viktor Kuznetsov, Harriet Matejka, and Mario Nuti, for their attention and their remarks. All conclusions and remaining errors are mine.

Pau, France   MARIE LAVIGNE

Preface to the Second Edition

Is it still relevant to talk about the economics of transition when the process is already almost ten years old? When embarking on the update of this book I felt greatly relieved by the statement of Joseph Stiglitz, author of *Whither Socialism?* (1994) and chief economist of the World Bank, upon being asked whether there was such a category as 'transition country': 'Definitely', was the answer (*Transition*, the World Bank's Newsletter, December 1997). True, he said, Central European countries are moving towards less and less differentiation as a category, but many transition countries have still a long way to go.

The approach to these countries has changed. We know increasingly more about them. Attention has shifted away from broad assessments of the macro-economic situation towards micro-economic investigation based upon detailed case studies, often conducted in cooperation with professionals from these countries in the framework of technical assistance programmes. The analyses have focused on branches, regions, enterprises. Large data bases have been constructed and exploited using standard tools. We have now a huge amount of detailed studies, working papers and technical material. It is increasingly difficult to keep track of this information, which is disseminated in journals, conference documents, and updated papers available on numerous Internet sites.

From this increasing mass of infomation, I have tried to extract the basic trends of change in a comparative approach. My aim is to give the clearest picture of what is happening in the main areas of transformation, and to help the reader to find his or her way in the available sources, should he or she want to go further. This is why I have substantially revised and updated Chapters 7 to 9 to account for the progress in macro-economic stabilisation, micro-economic restructuring and integration in the world economy.

I did not alter the first six chapters, because I have not changed my mind either about the main features of the past centrally planned system, or about the causes of the collapse of communism (though some of my reviewers have criticised me on this latter point). I substantially altered Chapter 10, because I have been convinced that there cannot be a 'theory of the transition' (I am particularly grateful to János Kornai for his advice and comments). We are now heading towards the end of transition. The question is how and when.

What we may be sure of is that the end is not going to be as obvious and clear-cut as the beginning has been.

Bagnères-de-Bigorre, France   Marie Lavigne

List of Abbreviations

BIS	Bank for International Settlements
BSEC	Black Sea Economic Cooperation
CAP	Common Agricultural Policy
CEEC	Central and Eastern European Countries (Bulgaria, the Czech Republic, Estonia, Hungary, Latvia, Lithuania, Poland, Romania, Slovakia and Slovenia)
CEFTA	Central European Free Trade Agreement
CIS	Commonwealth of Independent States
CMEA	Council for Mutual Economic Assistance
Comecon	Council for Mutual Economic Assistance
CPI	consumer price index
CSFR	Czech and Slovak Federal Republic
EAs	Europe Agreements
EBRD	European Bank for Reconstruction and Development
EC	European Communities (before 1993)
ECE/UN	Economic Commission for Europe of the United Nations
ECO	Economic Cooperation Organisation
ECSC	European Coal and Steel Community
EEC	European Economic Community (before 1993)
EFTA	European Free Trade Association
EIB	European Investment Bank
EMS	European Monetary System
EMU	Economic and monetary union (within EU)
EPU	European Payments Union
ERM	Exchange rate mechanism (within EEC/EU)
EU	European Union
FDI	foreign direct investment
FTO	foreign trade organisation
FYROM	Former Yugoslav Republic of Macedonia
GATT	General Agreement on Tariffs and Trade
G-7	Group of Seven
G-24	Group of 24
GDP	gross domestic product
GDR	German Democratic Republic
GNP	gross national product
GSP	generalised system of preferences
IBEC	International Bank for Economic Cooperation

IBRD	International Bank for Reconstruction and Development (World Bank)
IGC	Intergovernmental Conference
IMF	International Monetary Fund
MFA	Multi-Fibre Arrangement
MNCs	multinational companies
NIS	newly independent states
OECD	Organisation for Economic Cooperation and Development
OPT	outward processing trade
PHARE	*Pologne, Hongrie, assistance à la restructuration économique*
PPI	producer price index
PPP	purchasing power parity
SDR	special drawing rights
SITC	Standard International Trade Classification
SMEs	small and medium enterprises
SOE	state-owned enterprise
TACIS	Technical Assistance for the CIS
UNCTAD	United Nations Conference on Trade and Development
UNDP	United Nations Development Programme
UNIDO	United Nations Industrial Development Organisation
USDA	United States Department of Agriculture
VAT	value-added tax
WTO	World Trade Organisation

I

The Past: Real Socialism

1 The Bases of the Socialist Economic System

We have chosen to call the former *socialist* countries as they usually called themselves, rather than 'Soviet-type', 'centrally planned', or 'command' economies, or other designations sometimes preferred by scholars. This is not just a matter of semantics. Using the wording 'socialist' may involve the writer into conflictual issues. As does Kornai (1992, p. 10), we have decided to keep the phrase by which the system referred to itself. In this sense we deal with 'really existing', or 'real', socialism (a wording coined by dissidents in the 1970s, such as Rudolf Bahro), as opposed to 'ideal'. Our aim is 'to empirically examine actual economies and their behaviour' (Pryor, 1985, p. 3). Why then keep the word 'socialist' which has been extensively used in a normative sense? Because it is impossible to describe this system without stating its ideological and normative foundations. The task is not an easy one. There has never been an economic theory of really existing socialism, though some definitions have been offered (Sutela, 1994).

Is it possible to define features common to all the countries which belonged to the 'socialist economic system', from the 1930s in the USSR up to the collapse of the system in 1989–90, from Eastern Europe to China and Cuba? Three criteria are usually quoted. First, in such a system, economic life was under the control of a single party, whether or not the party was called communist. Second, the economic institutions were based upon collective, or state, ownership of the basic means of production. Third, compulsory central planning was the main coordinating mechanism, with an increasing but still subsidiary role devoted to market instruments.

From this it is sometimes inferred that the party ruled everything, that people did not own anything, and that the plan commanded all economic decisions. Even in a science-fiction novel, such mechanics are inconceivable. The principles define the foundations of the system, not its real operation. They are intimately linked with an ideology, Marxism-Leninism, which was revised and adapted in each country by the individuals and elites in power. This intimate linkage explains why these principles have been totally rejected by the new governments in all countries where a political 'revolution' occurred at the inception of transition.

THE PARTY CONTROL OF THE ECONOMY

In all socialist countries the party controlled the economy. For historical reasons the party sometimes appeared as the dominant element in an 'alliance' or 'front' of parties. It often called itself communist, but in about half of the socialist countries other denominations were used, such as the Socialist Workers' Party in Hungary, the Polish United Workers' Party, the Party of Labour in Albania and North Korea. In Yugoslavia, to distance itself from the Soviet regime, the party had chosen to call itself a 'league' of communists. These variations made really no substantial difference in the basic concept of the leading role of the party.

The Ideology

Some differences existed, however, in the interpretation of the Marxist-Leninist doctrine, even beyond the Soviet-Yugoslav rift in 1948, or the Sino-Soviet schism in 1961. In fact, the ideology of the 'really existing socialism' had little to do with Marx or Lenin, from which only a few standard quotations were borrowed. It was a set of norms and codes of speech and conduct, which were defined by the leaders, and were not subject to discussion or critique. Any person entitled with some authority or responsibility had to comply with the codes and to refer to the official doctrine. Thus the smallest divergence from the code was significant, and generations of Western 'kremlinologists' became very apt at deciphering the meaning of these variations. Actually, while 'socialism' was still an ideal for the Western left, nobody believed in the ideology of 'real socialism' in the East; moreover, nobody was supposed to believe, as long as the official behaviour conformed to the party standard. Breaches were tolerated as long as they remained hidden, but always remained subject to penal liability. In the economic field, parallel to the 'official economy' described in textbooks, a 'shadow' economy developed, as a safety valve to the official system, but was never officially acknowledged.

Such a status of the dominant ideology helps us to understand what occurred in this field immediately after the transition. There was a massive rejection of the words 'communism' and 'socialism', and of anything associated with these words, such as social democracy (and probably even 'social' security, which is an oblique reference to socialist values: the reluctance to consider it a priority is not only due to the lack of resources to finance it). In some countries not only the communist party but also the communist regime was formally outlawed (as was the case, for instance, in the Czech Republic, by a law of July 1993). The communist parties had to find a new denomination to remain legal; none of them had a clear doctrine other than the opposition to the new majorities – not excluding tactical alliances once back in power.

The Nomenklatura

The leadership of the party was often associated with the *nomenklatura*, a Russian word which became internationally the symbol of communist privileges. In fact the institution allowed the party to control all the high-level appointments. For instance, all executive positions in the economic sphere, from the government members to the enterprise managers, were mentioned on special lists (hence the word *nomenklatura*, coded list). Any appointment on a listed position had to be approved by the relevant party organ, for instance the Central Committee for a minister, the city committee in the case of the director of a local enterprise. The word *nomenklatura* ultimately qualified all the party cadres entitled with political power and economic responsibility, and benefiting from privileges such as the right to shop in special stores.

The party itself was a hierarchy. At the lowest level, in the enterprises, the collective farms, and more generally in all local economic units, the party cells had to ensure that the management was complying with the political instructions from above. The local or regional party authorities had often to settle disputes that occurred between the enterprises, or those that occurred between the enterprise and the state administration, for example a ministry. On each decision level, the party was above all other authority and ruled in last resort. This system was particularly sophisticated in the Soviet Union, due to the immensity of the country and the federal structure of the state. This explains the disastrous disorganisation which occurred there once the party system collapsed. No other authority could any longer keep the economy together. The seemingly powerful state bureaucracy derived its legitimacy from the party alone, and revealed itself helpless once the party was outlawed in the economy.

At the level of the state, the party organs had pre-eminence over the governments and the parliaments in fixing the main lines of economic policy, approving the macro-economic plans, determining the regional or sectoral policy, deciding upon the share of consumption and investment within the domestic product. They have also launched all the economic reforms. However, the party usually had no specific apparatus to deal with economic questions. The only exceptions were the party administration in the USSR under Khrushchev, in Romania under Ceausescu, and the Asian communist parties. The overall party control usually operated indirectly, through political intervention in other bodies.

The Economic Administration

The communist regime is indeed often equalled with a pervasive state bureaucracy. The Soviet model was imposed after the Second World War in Eastern Europe. A large number of sectoral and functional agencies were set up. Functional agencies, such as the Planning office, the office of Prices, the Investment Bank, the Labour office, had to implement the kind of coordination tasks which the market realises spontaneously in capitalist economies. For instance, the offices of Prices were fixing wholesale and retail prices. In market economies, whenever price agencies exist, they do not fix prices; they just have to check that prices are determined by the market in conditions of fair competition. Most typical were the agencies for 'material and technical supplies', which performed the task of linking together buyers and sellers in the production and distribution process. When there is no free inter-enterprise market, the state has to bring together the suppliers of means of production and the users of these goods, and to ensure that the contracts comply with the provisions of the plan, by issuing selling and purchase state orders for machinery, intermediate goods and spare parts. In the USSR, this agency was called *Gossnab* (state supply administration) and employed about one million workers by the end of the regime. Its collapse severed inter-enterprise links before new ones could be established through the market.

Along with these coordination tasks, the state bureaucracy was also managing the enterprises, often exerting a 'petty tutelage' on them. This was done through branch ministries, more or less numerous according to the countries. In the USSR there were about sixty of them in the beginning of the 1980s. In some Eastern European countries the state bureaucracy had been revamped and simplified along with the reforms in planning and management. However, party control remained, in a modified form, as we shall see in Chapter 3.

Local Government

Is a communist system compatible with strong local governments? In principle this should be the case. The USSR was born as the Republic of Soviets, i.e. of elected councils of people's representatives. In fact, the local soviets have always had only limited economic and political power. The big enterprises were managed directly from Moscow, through federal ministries and central party organs. The lack of a genuine economic base in the regions is also an explanation for the chaos in the former Soviet Union. Once the system collapsed, the republics and regions were left with huge unmanageable industrial giants on their territories, which were meant to supply a large range of customers or users all over the country, and operated often with 'imported' labour from other republics, mainly from Russia.

There was a brief attempt at reviving local authorities in the economic field. In the USSR and elsewhere in Eastern Europe, in the beginning of the 1960s, regional economic agencies (called *sovnarkhozy* in the USSR) were set up to break the power of the branch ministries. This was an initiative by Khrushchev to get rid of the Stalinist administration; the outcome was to substitute the 'parochial spirit' of the local administration to the 'petty tutelage' of the ministries, and the experiment was dropped everywhere. In China, however, the provinces had always had extensive economic rights, which were only occasionally cut during recentralisation campaigns in the 1960s and the 1970s.

Self-Management

One should expect a socialist regime to grant large management rights to the workers, who are the collective owners of the means of production. According to the communist ideology, the party itself is merely the vanguard of the workers' class. Actually only Yugoslavia organised all economic activity on the basis of direct self-management since 1950. In other socialist countries formal arrangements for worker participation in management have operated through various institutions and mainly through the official trade unions, which were considered as the 'transmission belts' of the party. This worker participation always remained very indirect. More politically active workers' councils emerged occasionally during periods of crisis, such as 1918 in Russia, 1956 in Poland and Hungary, 1968 in Czechoslovakia, and 1980 in Poland (where they were supported by the unofficial trade union *Solidarnosc*). They have been crushed or rendered ineffective.

The official trade unions had quite significant functions, but not in the sphere of management. They were mass organisations encompassing almost all the workers, unlike the party, which always remained an elite organisation with a membership amounting to a share of the total population comprising between 6–7 and 12–15 per cent. The trade unions were active in guaranteeing job security, and effectively opposing redundancies. In most countries they were also managing social security at large, and hence were perceived as welfare organisations providing, along with social security benefits proper, also free vacations, semi-free housing, gardening plots, etc. In the transition process they were discarded as supporters of the communist party; they have yet to be replaced in their social functions.

Self-management has collapsed as a form of economic operation and as a doctrine. Its weaknesses were patent in Yugoslavia, where it remained in force until the end of the regime (Uvalić, 1992, p. 207). The system led to inefficiencies and corruption, fuelled inflation, and generated disguised private ownership and inequality. In the other post-socialist countries, self-management ideals were soon identified with hidden communism, and workers' participation schemes were rejected as inefficient compared with genuine capitalism. Employee ownership was often banned from privatisation blueprints. The failure of self-management in the East is probably in turn jeopardising any attempts to implement it in the West beyond the existing scattered and imperfect experiences.

COLLECTIVE OWNERSHIP OF THE MEANS OF PRODUCTION

In all socialist countries except Yugoslavia, 'socialist' ownership of means of production was established. Consumer goods have never been socialised, and could even be transmitted by heritage. However, the ownership of consumer goods was called 'personal', as 'private property' was considered a capitalist concept. In addition the access to consumer goods, especially durables, was rationed for economic–systemic reasons, because demand was always in excess of supply, and through administrative regulations.

Socialist Ownership

As a rule in all socialist countries, large-scale productive assets were state property, in industry, domestic trade, and services (transportation, banks, insurance companies), following waves of nationalisation in the wake of the revolutions that had established the new regimes. In Yugoslavia the concept of 'social' ownership was introduced in 1950 as a distinctive feature of the self-managed system. The assets did not belong to the state, nor to the workers, but they were the property of the nation as a whole. This fuzzy concept was never clearly specified and only generated confusion in the legal definition and economic management of property rights in Yugoslavia.

In agriculture, socialisation mainly took the form of collectivisation through the compulsory establishment of cooperative farms. Land itself was seldom nationalised: the USSR and Mongolia were exceptions. In most Eastern European countries only large landowners were expropriated, and their property distributed to the peasants in the early stages of the land reform (see Chapter 2). Land was later turned to cooperatives for an indefinite use period: this emerged as a big problem when transition began and it became obvious that many, if not most, of the potential claimants on land had either left the country or become city-dwellers.

In the USSR the collectivisation was conducted through terror during the period 1928–36 and led to the constitution of *kolkhozy* (from the Russian *kollektivnoe khozjajstvo*, i.e. collective farming), while a part of the agricultural sector was organised in *sovkhozy* or state farms (from the Russian *sovetskoe khozjajstvo*, or Soviet farming). There were differences in principle between these two types. Legally the *kolkhozy* were cooperatives, managed by an elected chairman and a general assembly of members endowed with decision-making and income-sharing rights. The *sovkhozy* were state farms managed like state industrial enterprises, by an appointed director. Whereas the *kolkhozniki* were members of the cooperative and were supposed to divide among themselves the revenue of the farm once all costs were covered and all obligations toward the state met, the *sovkhozniki* were wage-earners like industrial workers. The *sovkhozy* were originally established as technically more advanced, specialised farms, and also as the model of a more socialist type of farming. It was expected that in the long run the *kolkhozy* would transform into *sovkhozy*. This never happened, but the differences between the two types of farming became gradually smaller, especially when both types were merged into large-scale agro-industrial complexes, managed on the model of the big state enterprises.

In Eastern Europe state farming never gained great extension, and large-scale cooperatives were the dominant format. However, like those in the USSR, these cooperatives also evolved toward a state-like management. They were very large units; they farmed between 3000 and 25,000 hectares of land, and they were increasingly involved in industrial activities.

Non-Socialist Ownership

Non-socialist ownership in the production sector was to be found mostly in agriculture. In two countries, i.e. Yugoslavia and Poland, cooperative farms were abolished almost from the outset, in 1953 in Yugoslavia in the wake of abandoning the Soviet model, in 1956 in Poland due to the strong political protest of the peasants. In these two countries private agriculture was conducted on over 80 per cent of the arable land. However it was considered as ideologically inferior to a socialist type of farming. For this reason private farms were discriminated against in terms of severe limits on total acreage farmed and supplies of equipment or materials; they were indirectly controlled by the distribution network. Private farming was managed on a family, non-capitalist type, with backward organisation and low performance.

In all other countries, peasants were allowed to farm a family plot for their own use, and to sell their produce, at free prices, on the city markets which were called in the USSR '*kolkhoz* markets'. They had specific property rights including the ownership of the house and the use of a narrow strip of adjacent land, plus the right to a limited number of cattle, all of which was subject to administrative regulation and political control, and could not hence be likened to genuine 'private' property. The family plot had three basic functions: to alleviate the political resistance to collectivisation; to provide fresh produce and meat to the cities and thus to supplement the deficient state supplies; and to serve as an excuse for the state not to guarantee that people employed in the cooperative sector would actually be paid for their work. In some countries and especially in Hungary the family plot system evolved into a genuine quasi-private system within the cooperative, with extended rights to the peasants based on contracts with the cooperative.

Outside agriculture there remained sometimes a small private sector in the form of small retail trade and handicrafts, for instance in the German Democratic Republic.

Within the state sector, a semi-legal or illegal 'parallel' or 'shadow' economy developed in all socialist countries. This is one of the most harmful legacies of the past, which is heavily constraining the transition process. The shadow economy was based on corruption and pilfering or large-scale stealing of state property. Its operation implied a close cooperation between the 'mafia' and the party *nomenklatura*. It did not encounter social disapproval, first because everybody tried to benefit from its spillovers be it on any small scale, second because despite the ideology, ordinary citizens never really cared for the state property which was rather perceived as belonging to nobody. Sometimes this 'second' economy is now assessed as a valuable experience of the market, and the only one successful, in the former centrally planned economies. In fact it had quite disastrous consequences. It contributed in shaping an image of successful business as linked with crime. It helped the former members of the *nomenklatura* to initiate very early privatisation to their sole benefit. It provided organised crime with power, financial and material means, and networks which established it as one of the main social forces following the transition. Thus, it may be seen as the most damaging outcome of the state ownership based on the political monopoly of the party.

CENTRAL PLANNING

When one does not wish to label 'socialist' economies as such, one generally calls them CPEs, centrally planned economies. The plan is a coordination mechanism opposed to the market. Strictly speaking, a plan is a set of techniques for determining what future action should be taken to achieve given objectives with a maximum coherence and efficiency. In a socialist economy, the plan is mandatory and not indicative. It encompasses the economic activity overall. The decision-makers are political authorities (such as the party hierarchy, and the state administration subordinate to the party). Its implementation is controlled and subject to legal and political sanction; the plan is imposed on a large number of executive bodies such as ministries and departments, enterprises, local agencies.

Defined as a 'mechanism', or as a set of 'techniques', the central plan was considered as an instrument enabling the management of everything under socialist ownership and party control. In the 1960s, when the performance of the planned economy seemed to falter, the party authorities tried to reform the mechanism through introducing some elements of the market. This reforming approach overlooked the point that the market and the plan were not compatible, not just because of their mechanisms, but because of the system of which central planning was a part, based upon the power monopoly of the party.

Planning Techniques

The planning procedures covered different time-spans (five years, one year, one quarter, one month). The most important plan from the point of view of its binding nature was the yearly plan. The planning process went through several stages. Technically the core of it was the drafting of 'material balances'. The method has been developed under Stalinist planning and used in all socialist countries. A balance is a table identifying sources of supply and uses for individual products or product groups. It shows domestic internal production on the supply side, and its domestic uses (intermediate outputs, investment, consumption) on the uses side. As the two sides of this table can only be made equal fortuitously, the balance is achieved through internal iterative adjustments (increase in production, cuts in intermediate or final uses), and only then through foreign trade (imports increase resources on the supply side; exports provide a use for excess production). Table 1.1 gives an example of a simplified scheme of balance. The balances were drafted first for the material inputs (raw materials, fuels, agricultural goods, semi-manufactured intermediate goods), then for machinery and equipment, and finally for manufactured consumer goods.

Table 1.1   *Simplified scheme of material balance*

Resources		Uses	
1. Domestic production	1,000	1. Inputs used for production	500
2. Imports	200	2. Investment	250
		3. Consumption	150
		4. Exports	300
Total	1,200	Total	1,200

These figures are conventional. Data are measures in kind, in physical units such as tonnes, metric metres, etc.

For example, let us suppose that this balance deals with coal. The units would then be (thousands of) tonnes. On the left side, domestic production is calculated on the basis of the capacities of production, such as the number of fields and pits already operated or to be put into operation during the planned period, minus the capacities to be closed during that period. The planner uses technological coefficients to determine how much a given pit may produce during the planned period (year, month, five-year period, etc.). These coefficients are always estimated for optimal conditions of operation, i.e. the plan is 'taut'. Hence, if the possible production has been overestimated, the planned uses cannot be covered, which has in turn consequences on the whole production chain. On the right side, the various uses of coal are estimated for the whole planned period. One may need coal as an input (as fuel for power stations, as material for the chemical industry, etc.); one may use it for final consumption, both collective (to heat hospitals, schools, state buildings) and individual (when coal is bought by the people for heating purposes); one may want to replenish the state reserves in coal. Once this process is completed the balance is adjusted through foreign trade. Here coal is both exported and imported, with a net export position.

In the Soviet Union during the Stalinist period their number exceeded 18,000. The procedure was iterative. Once the planner had finished a first 'round' he had to redraft the whole set of balances, because unexpected users' needs in the manufacturing process led to a reformulation of the balances ahead. The process was never convergent, for many reasons: first, one never had time enough to refine the calculations; second, the methodology was crude; and third, the initial data were always biased.

The last reason is crucial. As long as economic data (such as physical output, capacity of production, initial stocks) are used at a same time as initial information for the planner and as the basis for assigning tasks to an enterprise and for evaluating it, the enterprise, which is the initial information giver, will cheat on the figures. And thus, there will be a cumulative process by which initial biases will propagate; corrections made on the spot will not restore a true picture. In fact, plan orders are largely determined and written by those who are to implement them, but not according to a deliberate process of decision-making sharing. Cheating is a built-in feature of the system.

A Non-Reformable System

Are there conditions under which a central planning system may function efficiently? The answer is probably yes: in a situation of war or similar circumstances. There have to be few key priorities, strictly defined, and the plan has to be implemented under a quasi-military discipline. Western democracies have briefly experienced such situations. The USSR was a comparable case from the beginning of central planning in the early 1930s, until 1945. Even then the planning process did not operate efficiently: not all goals were met, except for a few priority sectors, and the achievements went along with a huge waste of human and material resources.

Later on, when the Soviet economy became more diversified, as the Eastern European economies did after the war, the amount of planned items increased, and controlling of plan implementation became increasingly difficult. The first wave of reforms in the planning and management system followed in the 1960s, so as to improve the declining growth performance of the planned economies. All these reforms failed, because the basic principle of planning remained untouched: the units and agents subject to the planning process had to prove that they had successfully implemented the plan, for which they had provided the data embodied into the compulsory indicators to be fulfilled.

Only after the collapse of the system was it clearly understood that the system was not reformable. It was not a question of decentralising the planning process, as long as there remained a controlling political authority to whom one had to report. Nor was it a question of refining the planning methods. Restoring mathematical methods applied to planning, rediscovering linear programming for the drafting of an optimal plan (i.e. maximising an objective function under constraints) could not improve the outcome because, however loosened, the plan remained a binding order based on political priorities.

This is not to say that the plan could effectively regulate the economic activity overall. Even under totalitarian regimes, the plan was unable to control it in every detail; later on, when most of the centrally planned economies shifted into a bargaining-type, or manipulated, economy, with decentralised units trying to influence the political authorities, central control was less and less effective. However the voluntarist ideology remained. The party still claimed to ultimately keep the economy in tutelage. The combination between such an ideology, and the increasing complexity of economic life, leading to contradictions among multiple target and performance indicators, gradually became unsustainable.

Here again there is a negative legacy. The plan was linked with the party to such an extent that the transition governments rejected any concept of a plan, even indicative, even strategic, even drafted and implemented within decentralised and really autonomous enterprises. 'Plan' will be a dirty word for a long time.

Plan versus Money

In the beginning of the Soviet regime money was considered as an anachronism and a symbol of capitalism. Later, when planning was introduced, the targets or 'indicators' were set in kind. The metric tonne became the most used unit, not only for commodities such as coal, steel, wheat, etc., but also for manufactured goods such as machinery. Money was used when it came to aggregate the material balances into a global macro-economic balance, but only as a unit of account.

Attempts to reconcile money and plan emerged within the reforms aiming at introducing 'market-and-money instruments', to use the Soviet parlance, so as to enable a better fulfilment of the plan. However, though 'market-like' notions such as prices, profit, monetary policy, credit, etc. were increasingly used, the wording was misleading. Money was not playing an active role in the economy: prices were administered, plan targets still privileged the volume of output, the survival of the enterprise did not depend on its profits but on its aptitude to negotiate the plan targets with the political authority. The Central Bank which issued money and which also was the single credit institution – the so-called 'monobank' – performed mainly accounting functions. Its extended network of branches surveyed the implementation of the plan at the enterprise level. Each enterprise had an account in the local branch and had to use it for all its payments. Conversely, individuals could only have a savings account and had to use only cash in banknotes or coins for their payments. Separate circulation of cash and non-cash money allowed for a separate control of enterprise and consumer spending, the ultimate aim being the strict implementation of the plan. Thus, though planning procedures are not technically incompatible with money, the Soviet-type centrally planned system excluded money from any significant influence on the economy. This too has a strong impact on the transition: though there were currencies and banks, the operation of money categories was by and large a *terra incognita* for the new leaders in the transition countries.

2 History

The ideal-type presented in the first chapter was not meant to describe how the socialist economic system appeared and evolved, but to stress its most permanent features which transcended time and space. This chapter will show how it came into existence and extended to a relatively large number of countries.

This book mainly deals with the countries which belonged to the 'Soviet model': the USSR itself and, after the end of the Second World War, the people's democracies in Europe. The latter comprised a sub-set of six countries, from north to south: the German Democratic Republic (GDR), Poland, Czechoslovakia, Hungary, Romania, and Bulgaria. These countries, though applying increasingly distinct models of planning and management, nevertheless remained in the framework of the Soviet model. They formed with the USSR the core of what was called 'the Soviet empire', and belonged to an international economic organisation called Comecon, or CMEA (Council for Mutual Economic Assistance), which embodied the Soviet control on the international economic relations of the area. In Europe, two other countries initially followed the same model, then broke the link: these were Yugoslavia and Albania. Yugoslavia defined itself in 1950 as a self-managed society. Albania chose to join the Chinese camp in 1961 in the Sino-Soviet dispute, and later on, in 1977, also broke up with China. Despite its rupture with the USSR, it remained the last case of the Stalinist model until the collapse of the regime in 1991.

Several developing countries adopted the socialist path: China, Mongolia, North Korea, Vietnam and Laos in Asia, Cuba in America. Mongolia, Cuba and Vietnam joined the CMEA; China and Korea developed a different kind of socialism.

All these countries called themselves socialist and in some cases would deny the same denomination to the others, like the Albanian regime to which the Soviet-type countries were 'ex-socialist' or revisionist. In addition, many Third World countries were at one point or the other engaged on a 'socialist path of development', or 'socialist-oriented'. But they never reached the end of the path so as to become fully-fledged socialist.

Though this chapter deals with history, the purpose is not to add one more assessment of the past to the many existing. It is rather to better understand the present by looking at the past with a new glance. Why did the Soviet model collapse so quickly following the beginning of the transition process? Why is economic transition to the market well under way in Asian socialist countries while communism remains as an ideology and a

15

political regime? Can one derive lessons for the transition from the beginnings of socialism?

THE USSR: THE STALINIST MODEL

There was never in twentieth century history a case of transition to socialism without violence, i.e. without a revolution or a war. In all cases there was a violent breach with the past. The first one occurred in Russia. The October Revolution was for decades celebrated in the communist world as the beginning of a new era which would bring happiness to the world along the lines of Marx in the *Critique of the Gotha Programme* (1878): 'when all the springs of social wealth will flow in plenty and when the society will be able to write on its banners: from each according to his abilities, to each according to his needs'. Such a society was to be built in two stages. The first one was building socialism. This stage was officially reached in the USSR in 1977, for the sixtieth anniversary of the Revolution. The new Constitution which was adopted in October of that year stated that the Soviet Union was an 'advanced socialist society', from which one could move to the next stage, building the communist society. In fact, even the first stage was an ideological fantasy. The shift was from a rather primitive capitalism to a planned partocracy labelled 'really existing socialism' by its dissidents. The stages of this evolution are briefly described in Box 2.1.

The Beginnings: From War Communism to the NEP and from NEP to Stalinism

The November 1917 Revolution (October according to the Russian calendar) brought to power the majority faction (in Russian, *bolshevik* meant those retaining the majority) of the Russian workers' social-democrat party, under the leadership of Vladimir Lenin.

The revolution

Was this first 'transition' inevitable, from autocratic tsarism to communism? In February 1917, another transition was initiated, by the 'bourgeois' Revolution which launched the Provisional government, based on a parliamentary democracy and on a market economy with a strong role devoted to the state, not just to deal with the war, but also to complete industrialisation (which had heavily relied on foreign and state capital until then) and to conduct an agrarian reform, in a country where over 80 per cent of the population lived in the country. Why was is necessary to wait almost seventy-five years to see a pluralistic democracy and a market system implemented?

Box 2.1   *Chronology of the USSR*

- 25 October (7 November) 1917: beginning of the October Revolution (the Bolsheviks seize the Winter Palace in Petrograd); they proclaim all power to the Soviets (the councils of delegates of workers, peasants, and soldiers);
- 26 October (8 November) 1917: the private property on land is abolished; the 'Land Decree' declares the land national property;
- 14 (27) December 1917: nationalisation of private banks;
- 21 January (3 February) 1918: all foreign debts are repudiated (nullification of the 'Russian loans');
- 3 March 1918: the peace of Brest-Litovsk is signed with Germany and ends the war; the treaty will be renounced by Russia in November 1918;
- 22 April 1918: nationalisation of foreign trade, which becomes a state monopoly;
- 28 June 1918: large-scale industry is nationalised;
- 1918–1920: period of 'war communism' (the economy is managed in a military way; cities are supplied by compulsory deliveries imposed on the peasants; money nearly disappears and most of the transactions are conducted in kind);
- 29 November 1920: nationalisation of industry as a whole is decreed;
- March 1921: the New Economic Policy (NEP) is launched: compulsory deliveries of food products are abolished, and replaced by a tax in kind; trade of any kind is authorised; small-scale industry is denationalised;
- 12 October 1921: the State Bank (*Gosbank*) is officially created;
- 30 December 1922; establishment of the Union of Soviet Socialist Republics (USSR):
- 1922–1924: currency reform through nearly two years of circulation of parallel paper currencies, the *sovznak* ruble and the *chervonets*;
- 20 January 1924: death of Vladimir Ilyich (Ulyanov) Lenin, the founder of the Russian bolshevik party; Josif Vissarionovich (Dzhugashvili) Stalin who was secretary general of the party since 1922 begins to build his one-man power on the party and the state;
- Law of 29 June 1927 on 'state industrial trusts', which is the basis of the legislation on state-owned enterprises;
- December 1927: the NEP ends; the first five-year plan 1927/28–1931/32 is launched;
- 1928–1932: mass collectivatisation of agriculture;
- 1935: beginning of the Stakhanovite movement, named after the coal-miner Stakhanov who managed to achieve an output fourteen times greater than the norm;
- 1937–1938: Stalin 'purges' the Army, the Party and the state administration; terror extends to the whole society;
- 22 June 1941: German forces invade the USSR by violation of the Nazi–Soviet pact of 1939; human war losses amounted to at least 20 million people;
- 9 May 1945: the Soviet soldiers seize Berlin; this date is officially the end of the war for the USSR;
- June 1947: announcement of the Marshall plan of assistance to the reconstruction of Europe; participation in the plan is offered to Eastern Europe, which rejects it on Stalin's instructions;
- January 1949: the Council for Economic Mutual Assistance (CMEA or Comecon) is created by the USSR, Bulgaria, Hungary, Poland, Romania and Czechoslovakia;

———▶

- May 1955: the Warsaw Pact is signed by the same states, plus the German Democratic Republic (GDR);
- 5 March 1953: Stalin dies; Nikita Khrushchev becomes First Secretary of the Party;
- February 1956: XXth Party Congress; de-Stalinisation begins;
- October 1964: Khrushchev is ousted and replaced by Leonid Brezhnev as first secretary of the Party and by Alexander Kosygin as prime minister;
- 1965: the Kosygin economic reform is launched;
- 1979: a minor economic reform is launched for industry;
- May 1982: a large-scale food programme is launched so as to restructure the agricultural sector and to provide food self-sufficiency to the USSR;
- November 1982: death of Leonid Brezhnev, who is replaced by Yuri Andropov; a campaign to increase discipline in industry is launched;
- February 1984: death of Andropov, who is replaced by Konstantin Chernenko;
- March 1985: death of Chernenko, replaced by Mikhail Gorbachev, who starts a campaign for economic recovery based on anti-alcoholic measures, a commitment to a sharp acceleration in growth so as to counteract the so-called 'stagnation' of the Brezhnev period; in politics, *glasnost* or 'transparency' of political and public life is proclaimed;
- 1986: launching of an economic restructuring package, called *perestroyka*, which is more radical than any previous reform; private property is indirectly admitted (through the 'leasing', or *arenda*, contract in agriculture, the 'cooperatives' in industry and services); very quickly a general disorganisation develops in the economy and the society, threatening the state institutions;
- January 1991: *de facto* disintegration of the CMEA;
- 19 August 1991: a coup against Gorbachev fails; Yeltsin takes the power in Russia; the USSR gradually disintegrates;
- December 1991: the Commonwealth of the Independent States is established among all the former Republics of the USSR, except the three Baltic States and Georgia; the USSR ceases to exist.

This failure may be partly explained by the weakness of the Provisional government. But the main impulse was the seizure of power by a party organised on a military style and inspired by the communist ideology; the circumstances of the world war and the civil war that followed, and the desperate situation of the economy, helped to strengthen the grip of the party and to develop its monopoly. In the economic field, Marxism revisited by Lenin led to the party taking over the 'commanding heights' of the economy, using the state apparatus. Thus the basis for the socialist ownership of the means of production was set. Land, banks, industry, and foreign trade were nationalised in 1917–18. The third foundation of a socialist economic system was established more than ten years later, when in 1928–9 planning became the main controlling device of the economy.

How should one look at the 'war communism' period in 1918–20 (Malle, 1985)? Some historians see it as at the first experience of fully-fledged communism, when state property was forcibly established along with an overall state control on production and distribution. Others point out that terror and military discipline went along with economic collapse and country-wide chaos, and that the measures taken were a desperate attempt to cope with the situation and to survive, i.e. to ensure food supplies for the cities through requisitioning in the country, which triggered peasant riots. Probably 'both factors played a role and reinforced each other' (Nove, 1992, p. 75). The debate on the nature of 'war communism' is not just intellectual. It has an impact on how the New Economic Policy (NEP) is seen.

The NEP

Was the NEP, or New Economic Policy, launched by the communist party in March 1921, the first experience of a transition from socialism to capitalism? Much later, during the *perestroyka* years (1986–91) the NEP was often invoked as an example. The answer should be no. The transition was meant to lead from a militarised communism to the first stage of socialism, with a strategic retreat during which temporary concessions would be made to the market principles. Thus, capitalism was partly restored in the small and medium-size industry, which was denationalised. Some forms of mixed economy were implemented on a relatively modest scale, such as concessions of mining fields to foreign companies, and leasing of nationalised enterprises to private capitalists. Large enterprises were kept in state ownership, but with a market-type management. They were gradually merged into state-controlled trusts which were the harbingers of the huge industry-wide 'branch' monopolies which developed later. Requisitioning was abolished and replaced by a tax in kind which allowed individual peasants (who provided most of the agricultural production) to retain the rest of their produce for their own consumption and for sale on the urban markets. Finally, over the years 1922–4, the currency was stabilised, which put an end to several years of hyperinflation and flight from money. The currency stabilisation was achieved through a quite unprecedented method. The paper currency introduced by the Bolsheviks, the *sovznak* (Soviet token), had depreciated at an accelerated pace since the end of war communism, and in June 1922 it was decided to introduce a parallel paper currency, the *chervonets*, which was backed by gold and supposed to be equivalent to the pre-revolutionary 10-ruble unit. Both currencies co-existed in 1923 and early 1924, until the sovznak was driven out of circulation in March 1924, and a new stabilised ruble became the sole currency, following an exchange of banknotes. This experience was very often discussed in Russia in 1992 and 1993 as a possible way of ending hyperinflation and monetary disorder.

During the years of *perestroyka*, there was an extended debate on the nature of the NEP. Was it really a deliberate strategic retreat, the ultimate aim being to build full communism? Or could it have been a longlasting process leading to a stable mixed economy? Such questions were hotly discussed by the end of the 1980s. Only if the answer was yes to the second question could the NEP provide a suitable gradualistic model for transforming the Soviet economy. Indeed, some of the fascinating intellectual debates during the NEP could point to such an answer. But again, it was a political move, the seizure of total power by Stalin in 1929, that determined the course of the events by putting an end to the NEP and its promises.

The Stalinist Era

Was Stalin really necessary? This is the title of a famous book by Alec Nove (1964). What would have been the development of Soviet socialism without Stalin? In any case Stalin shaped the system. He had been secretary general of the party since 1922, eighteen months before Lenin's physical death. He ruled the party when Lenin was no longer able to speak and act; he put an end to the NEP after defeating Trotsky, in 1927, and Bukharin, in 1929. From then on the ideological monopoly of the party was blended with the sole power of a leader.

The Stalinist model was based on three principles. A heavy industry base was to be built so as to ensure growth. This could not be achieved without forcibly extracting the surplus created in agriculture, which acted as a justification for collectivisation. Five-year planning was launched as a mobilising force, as well as an instrument for controlling the economy.

The great industrialisation debate

The Soviet industrialisation debate (Erlich, 1960) was in fact a debate over agriculture. Clearly agriculture was the single source of surplus (primitive socialist accumulation, as Preobrazhensky called it). How to increase this surplus through a suitable agrarian policy? How to channel it into industry?

In 1927, the Soviet agriculture was very little socialised. Nationalisation of land was pure fiction. Cooperatives accounted for less than 1 per cent of the sown area. Most of the farms were small in size, and following the abolition of requisitioning peasantry shifted to a subsistence-type economy. The 'right-wing' opposition led by Nikolai Bukharin contended that one should base the development of industry on a political alliance (*smychka*) between urban workers and peasants on which NEP itself was built. Peasants, especially middle and 'rich' peasants (the notorious *kulaks*; see definition in Nove, 1992, pp. 103–4), should be encouraged through market incentives to produce and sell more. The government would thus be able to export grain and to import the machinery needed for industrialisation, while agriculture would provide industry with raw materials to manufacture, and food to process, so as to feed a growing-in-size urban labour force. In turn, industry would help agriculture to modernise, through sales of equipment, fertilisers and industrial consumer goods. Then the conditions might be ripe for the socialisation of the country without scaring the peasants.

The left-wing opposition did not believe in the *smychka*. Its leaders, Lev Trotsky and Eugen Preobrazhensky, advocated a forcible collection of the surplus through taxes in kind, non-equivalent exchange (i.e. high prices for industrial goods sold to the peasants and low prices paid for their produce, changing into deliberate policy the 'price scissors' crisis which had developed in 1923–4), and forced cuts in supplies of consumer goods to agriculture.

For political reasons Stalin used the debate so as to get rid of his political opponents. First the left opposition was defeated in 1926–7. Later the arguments of the left served to defeat the right-wing opposition in 1929, and the collectivisation could be launched (Davies, 1980).

The mass collectivisation through terror

The immediate aims of collectivisation were twofold. The first one was to liquidate the *kulak* as a class, as they could not be won over, and to base the political support of the regime in the country on the poor and middle peasants regrouped in cooperatives. From the beginning of collectivisation, therefore, anyone reluctant to join a collective farm was labelled a *kulak* and deported. The second aim was to increase procurements for the cities so as to force and support industrialisation.

The consequences of this type of collectivisation were manifold. Peasants resisted collectivisation by slaughtering livestock. The Soviet animal husbandry never really recovered, and still in 1940 remained under its 1928 level. Millions of peasants died, due to the physical elimination of the peasants considered as *kulak*, and to the famine which developed in 1933 as a consequence of the forced procurements policy. A large share of these deaths occurred in Ukraine, which still fuels the resentment of the Ukrainians against the Russians.

Finally, though it may seem not so tragic a consequence compared to the sufferings of the people, the mass collectivisation terror led to the political discrediting of the cooperative as an institution in all the ex-communist world: perhaps not for ever, but at least for a long time. People tend to remain in cooperatives for job security and social security reasons; governments want to get rid of them because of political aversion. In transition countries, the only politically acceptable and economically feasible way of agricultural management is thus small family farming, because capital is lacking to develop large-scale capitalist farming. It will take a very long time to overcome this rejection of the cooperative as such, including the various models experimented with in Western countries such as food-processing, marketing or supply cooperatives, which are still unconsciously identified with the Stalinist *kolkhozy*.

In the USSR, mass collectivisation was officially completed by 1935, when the model statute of the kolkhoz was adopted. Before that, the MTS (Machine and Tractor Stations) were set up in 1931, not only to supply the cooperatives with machinery and spare parts but also to control them politically. Though the MTS were turned into repair and maintenance stations after Stalin's death, without explicit political functions, the *kolkhozy* were never really able to control their technical capital, and this also explains much of their inefficiency.

The state sector was made of *sovkhozy* which were supposed to represent the highest model of socialist agriculture. *Sovkhozy* did not develop very much however, mainly because they were costly (the peasants had to be paid a fixed wage, as in industry, while the *kolkhoznik* was supposed to get a share of the *kolkhoz* revenue, if any, once the procurement obligations had been met).

Planning

Already in 1920 a first concept of an all-embracing economic plan had been drafted under the misleading name of GOELRO (State plan for the electrification of Russia), which was in fact a long-term development plan, already using the 'balance' method. This plan was never actually implemented.

Stalin turned planning into a political undertaking, not only by making it compulsory, but also by mobilising all the party propaganda for its implementation. The first five-year plans were meant to achieve a 'leap forward' in heavy industrialisation, through large increases in output of electricity, raw materials, metals and heavy machinery. The first three five-year plans fixed unrealistically high targets which were never met, but there was a dramatic rise in the production of the heavy industry (see Chapter 4). Operational annual planning only began in 1930 for 1931.

The Stalinist model was adjusted to the war effort and post-war reconstruction requirements, by becoming still more dictatorial. Stalin himself decided to theorise it in a series of articles, published in pamphlet form in 1952, as *Economic Problems of Socialism in the USSR*. The pamphlet stressed, among other things, that the Marxian 'law of value' did not apply within the production sector. Stalinism did not disappear with the death of its founder in 1953 despite the ideological 'thaw' which occurred in the late 1950s, and the reforms that followed. It permeated economic activity as well as political life. Among its main sequels in the conscience and behaviour of economic agents one may mention the shunning of any individual initiative, the formal compliance with the political will expressed by the authorities, the cult of the overfulfilment of the plan, and the pervasive cheating and biasing of means and achievements.

Post-Stalinism

Stalinism and the cult of the personality of Stalin were officially abolished in 1956. Three leaders played a dominant role as heads of the party and, since Brezhnev, of the state: Nikita Khrushchev (1953–64), Leonid Brezhnev (1964–82) and Mikhail Gorbachev (1985–91), not to mention the shorter terms of Yuri Andropov (1982–4) and Konstantin Chernenko (1984–5).

In an erratic style, Khrushchev launched economic reforms which were to be extended but also paralysed by his successor. His merits were significant. He put an end to the terror; he denounced Stalin's crimes in his famous 'secret report' to the XXth Congress of the party (1956); he allowed for a cultural and intellectual 'thaw'; he alleviated the situation of the peasants for the first time since collectivisation; he permitted a renaissance of economic thought. He promoted the first economic experiments which were to inspire the Brezhnev–Kosygin reforms. The Western world was sympathetic to these reform ideas, which were expressed in a theoretical form by an economist, Yevsey Liberman, in the famous article published in *Pravda*, 9 September 1962: 'Plan, Profit, Premium'. This article triggered a huge literature, in the USSR and in the West, on the combination plan–market and its viability.

In the next chapter the reforms that followed will be discussed at more length. Due to the action of Khrushchev, the Soviet Union emerged from totalitarian Stalinism. But Khrushchev did not, any more than his successors, breach the monopoly of the communist party which granted him legitimacy. He instructed the other party leaders in Eastern Europe to repress all movements that put this monopoly in jeopardy (in 1953 in GDR, 1956 in Poland and Hungary). He strengthened the role of the party in the Soviet economy by doubling the state economic administration with a specialised party administration at each organisational level. Thus he maintained the legacy of Stalinism while ending the worship of the individual who had founded and embodied this regime.

THE CREATION OF THE PEOPLE'S DEMOCRACIES IN EUROPE

After Europe was split up between East and West at the Yalta Conference (February 1945), Eastern Europe was in the orbit of the USSR. But not only Soviet tutelage and the Red Army established the communist power in this region. The war and the resistance to Nazi occupation had strengthened the local communist parties. In most countries, just after the war, leftist, non-communist movements were struggling in favour of a democratic transformation of their countries. Before the Second World War, only Czechoslovakia was a democracy in the Western sense. All the other Eastern

European countries had been ruled by dictatorships for most of the inter-war period. Czechoslovakia was also a developed market economy, a feature shared with Eastern Germany which became ruled by the Soviets in 1945, until its transformation into a fully-fledged state, the GDR, in 1949. The rest of Eastern Europe was much less industrialised, and had been hit by the pre-war depression and by unemployment. About 60 million peasants in Eastern and Central Europe had been subject to a quasi-feudal rule; after the war they demanded a land reform, expropriation of the big landowners and the redistribution of land among the peasants.

The First Measures

Should these countries have remained in the orbit of Western Europe, one may imagine the pattern of their post-war transformation. There would have been a land reform, most likely nationalisations of industrial enterprises belonging to wartime collaborationists (as in the case of the firm Renault in France), and of 'natural' monopolies such as railways, energy carriers, mines and public utilities; the governments would have been of a dirigist type.

Indeed, nationalisations began before the communists seized the power in Eastern Europe. Even before the end of the war the workers had established their control on the enterprises abandoned by their owners as the Soviet troops advanced, in various self-management experiences. The new governments, within which the communist parties shared the power with others, proceeded to nationalise first the property recovered from the enemy or confiscated to the collaborators, and only then large-scale industry. The former owners, except the collaborationists and the ex-occupying forces, were compensated, unlike what had happened in Soviet Russia. This explains why after 1989 the transition governments which decided to compensate the victims of nationalisations, or to restitute property in kind, chose to include only those who had suffered from communist national-isations *stricto sensu*. Such a principle for establishing compensation rights entailed huge procedural difficulties and legal disputes, which in turn delayed privatisation. In addition this principle virtually excluded Jewish people (or their heirs) from any compensation, as their property had been confiscated by the occupying forces and then nationalised in the first wave.

In the country areas, the estates of the great land-owners were confiscated and redistributed to the peasants, with an extreme fragmentation of holdings. Re-concentration soon began. Cooperatives pooling agricultural labour and equipment were installed, especially in those countries which had already had a cooperative experience before the war, such as Bulgaria, Czechoslovakia and East Germany.

The Shift to the Soviet Model

In two countries, Albania and Yugoslavia, the communist rule was established without the help of the Red Army, without any democratic transition following the national liberation. In both cases the Stalinist model was immediately implemented. Both countries left the Soviet orbit as we have seen (see Table 2.1); Albania was to retain the Stalinist model until the very end of communism.

In the other countries, after the communists seized power, mass nationalisations began and were completed very quickly, in four or five years (1948–52) except in the GDR where a sizeable industrial private sector continued to exist until 1972. In some countries (Hungary, Poland, and the GDR) a small-scale handicraft and retail trade private sector remained. Collectivisation in agriculture was on the whole less brutal than in the USSR. Administrative and police coercion was nevertheless often employed, and the negative impact of these procedures led the authorities to relax their pressure in the middle of the decade 1950–60 – only in Poland did the government decide to stop collectivisation altogether in 1956. By the beginning of the 1960s the collectivisation was completed, and the cooperative was the dominant model of farming. The state farms remained very limited in terms of their share of arable land, which nowhere exceeded 10 per cent.

Planning emerged much later. In fact Eastern Europe had no consistent planning system until the early 1960s. Long-term development was monitored through investment programmes. Current economic activity was politically controlled according to short-term voluntarist policies.

Nevertheless Eastern Europe followed the 'Soviet model' very closely. The communist party had a political monopoly. The authorities controlled the production capacities in a centralised way. The strategy of economic development gave priority to heavy industry, even in those countries which had a diversified industrial structure before the war (Czechoslovakia and the GDR).

Was Yugoslavia a Different Model?

Of all the features just mentioned Yugoslavia retained only the first one. The 'League' of Communists was a communist party. The fact that Tito broke with Stalin and declared the regime non-aligned, and also the economic and social trends in the country, created an illusion of commitment to democracy and to the market. Self-management became a foundation of the regime in 1950. However, the very vague concept of 'social' ownership really meant in practice ownership by the state, though without the legal institutions of state property. This concept only made things more difficult when the transition began in 1990 and when moves were made to privatise what did not belong to anybody; in some cases it was

Table 2.1   *The beginning and end of the socialist economic system*

Country	Beginning of the socialist regime	End of the regime or present state
Russia/USSR	October 1917 Revolution; nationalisations, 1917–18; launching of mass collectivisation, 1927–9; introduction of five-year planning, 1928—→	December 1991: founding of the Commonwealth of Independent States. January 1992: beginning of the transition to a market economy in Russia.
Mongolia	A people's democracy is proclaimed in 1924. 1940–60: nationalisations and collectivisation.	1991: beginning of multipartism and of the transition to the market.
Yugoslavia	1945: the People's Front wins the elections; a Soviet-type economic system is announced. 1946–8: mass nationalisation and collectivisation.	1948: Tito breaks with Stalin. 1950: self-management becomes the basis of the Yugoslav socialism. 1965: instruments of a market economy are introduced. 1991: break-up of Yugoslavia.
Albania	1946: the people's democracy is proclaimed. 1961: break-up with the USSR; Albania chooses a 'Chinese way' of development.	1991: anti-government demonstrations; elections won by the communist party. 1992: new elections; a non-communist government is formed.
Eastern Europe	Between the end of 1945 and 1948: the communists win the elections. Feb. 1948: Communist coup in Prague. Between 1946 and 1949: mass nationalisations; introduction of central planning. 1948: collectivisation begins; stopped in 1956 in Poland.	Poland: first non-communist government in Sept. 1989. Hungary: beginning of multipartism in 1990. Czechoslovakia: 'velvet revolution' in Nov. 1989. Romania: end of the Ceausescu regime in Dec. 1989. Bulgaria: free elections in 1991. 1990–2: beginning of the transition to the market.
East Germany	Oct. 1949: the Soviet zone becomes a people's democracy, the German Democratic Republic (GDR). 1950–52: large-scale nationalisations and collectivisation. August 1961: the Berlin Wall is erected.	9 November 1989: the Berlin Wall is breached. July 1990: monetary and economic union with Federal Germany. October 1990: Germany is unified in a single State.
China	Oct. 1949: the people's democracy is founded. 1949–52: nationalisations, setting-up of people's communes.	During the 1980s: the political line is hardened (massacre of the students on Tian An Men square, 1989) while the economy is moving gradually towards the market.
Vietnam	1945: a people's democracy is established in the North. 1976: the socialist republic of Vietnam is proclaimed following the end of the war and the reunification.	During the 1980s and early 1990s: communist rule remains, a market economy gradually emerges.
Cambodia	1975–6: Khmer Rouge Revolution; the country is renamed Kampuchea. 1979: Vietnam takes control of the country.	1991: an agreement of national reconciliation is signed. 1993: free elections; chaotic development of a market economy.

Laos	1975: founding of the people's democracy.	During the 1980s and early 1990s: same trend as in Vietnam.
North Korea	1948: founding of the people's democracy. 1950–3: Korean war ending with the permanent division between North and South; a Stalinist-type economy develops in the North.	1991: reunification begins to be discussed; no significant change in political or economic trends within the regime.
Cuba	1959: revolution conducted by Fidel Castro; founding of the socialist republic of Cuba.	No evolution toward a pluralistic democracy or a market economy; limited openness toward the world economy.

Sources: For Eastern Europe: Geoffrey Swain and Nigel Swain, *Eastern Europe since 1945*, London and Basingstoke: Macmillan, 1993; for the non-European socialist countries: Jeffries (1993).

necessary to first nationalise social property in order to clarify property rights. Planning no longer existed after the early 1960s, but markets were nevertheless controlled, especially for means of production.

Since the break-up of the country in 1991, the ex-Yugoslav republics have been pitted against each other in nationalistic and ethnic conflicts. The story of Yugoslavia is one of deception. The Western European left was thrilled by the self-management experience, which fulfilled utopian dreams. Third World ideologists valued the non-alignment of the country until it became obvious that Yugoslavia sided with the developing world so as to benefit from commercial and political privileges. Idealists were frustrated, and free marketeers very happy, with the opening to foreign investment, and with the operation of something resembling a wild market economy, at the end of the 1960s. Everybody underestimated the communist nature of the regime, quite authoritarian though localist, and hence necessarily compromised in regional conflicts.

THE VARIANTS OF THE SOCIALIST MODEL IN THE THIRD WORLD COUNTRIES

Why have only a few Third World countries embraced the communist regime? Why did this regime survive much more lastingly than in Europe?

China was the first case. Mao Zedong brought his party to power in 1949. The regime was supported by the USSR until 1961, though the building of socialism proceeded until 1958 slower than had been the case in the USSR; it became more radical in 1958, just when Khrushchev was loosening the system in the Soviet Union. In a nutshell, one can summarise the evolution of Chinese socialism as a series of vacillations. Totalitarian collectivisation through people's communes, and an unrealistic 'Great Leap Forward' in the 1950s were followed by some liberalisation in the early 1960s, then by the fanatical Cultural Revolution in 1966. Less dramatic vacillations followed in the 1970s. The turn towards a more radical reform was taken in 1978, with a specific mixture of an increasingly strong private sector co-existing with a traditional state sector, increasing autonomy to the provinces, macro-economic regulation replacing planning, and all this topped by the unflinching political control of the party (Lemoine, 1986).

The other socialist regimes in Asia have more lastingly remained under Soviet influence, especially in the case of Mongolia which was a landlocked country almost enclaved in the USSR, and became socialist in 1924. In North Korea and North Vietnam, the building of a socialist regime was heavily influenced by war (Korean war starting in 1950, various Vietnam wars from 1947) and by the strong personality of the first leaders (Kim Il Sung and Ho Chi Minh). The militarised economic system established in North Vietnam, based on mandatory planning and the quest for food self-sufficiency, was extended to the reunified South in 1976, to Laos, and to Cambodia which Vietnam controlled since 1979. Like China, the Vietnamese regime introduced a strongly market-oriented reform in 1986 without relaxing the party control on the economy and society.

The Cuban regime was shaped by the leadership of Fidel Castro who conducted the 1959 revolution and since then remained at the head of the party, and by the impact of the cold war and of the US boycott which put the Cuban economy under Soviet sole influence.

Many other countries in the Third World were at one time or another on 'a socialist path of development' after the end of the colonisation era in 1955 (the year of the Bandung Conference). Usually these were countries under a one-party rule, which introduced land reforms, conducted more or less extended nationalisations, mainly to control their natural resources, initiated some planning, and were assisted by the USSR and subsidiarily by the Eastern European countries. An exhaustive list would yield more than twenty countries, most of them in Sub-Saharan Africa but also in Asia (Indonesia before 1965; Burma; Afghanistan after 1979; Iraq; Syria; South Yemen), and in America (Nicaragua in 1983). These countries were called, in the socialist countries' parlance, 'socialist-oriented' (Lavigne, 1988). What prevented them being considered as socialist? The vacillations of the economic policies and regulations suggested that their commitment to socialism might be reversed. The parties in charge almost never were communist ones; Afghanistan is an exception, but in this case the communist party was not credible because it was imposed by the Soviets. Socialist-oriented regimes were often established in Muslim countries. The Islamic doctrine proved to be a powerful barrier against communism, and the fundamental incompatibility between these two ideologies has been later underlined through the emergence of Islamic integrism: a lesson which should be kept in mind when looking at the transition in ex-Soviet Central Asia.

3 The Reforms: Experiences and Failures

How did the one-party, one-property, one-plan system operate in practice? Before Stalin's death the question was hardly relevant. The Soviet Union had been living in war-like conditions, preparing and conducting war, then recovering from it, and was protecting itself against the 'capitalist encircling'. All economic failures could be attributed to these exceptional circumstances.

The political thaw following the death of Stalin triggered a first wave of reforms in the USSR and in Eastern Europe. Another wave followed in the 1960s, to which many supplements and corrections were added, without success. *Perestroyka* in the USSR was the last attempt.

Why did all these attempts fail? There was a widespread awareness that it was impossible to plan and control millions of human activities from the centre, that state ownership had to be managed by people who felt economically, and not just politically or legally, responsible for it and interested in the outcome. Why did it take such a long time to acknowledge the failures? In other words, why was the system non-viable and why did it nevertheless survive for so many years? All these questions are asked and answered for the 'Soviet-type' socialist countries in Europe, excluding non-European countries, and, in Europe, Albania and Yugoslavia.

THE APPARENT LOOSENING OF PARTY CONTROL

As we have seen in the previous chapter, Khrushchev perceived the need for reforms. He tried to relax the overcentralisation of the economy, by replacing the powerful industrial ministries inherited from the Stalin period by regional economic agencies, the *sovnarkhozy* (see Chapter 1). In doing so he merely shifted the 'petty tutelage' of the ministries to the 'localism' of these agencies, and the reform was in fact gradually nullified even before his ousting in 1964. Similarly, in Eastern Europe and especially in Hungary and Poland (already the forerunners) blueprints for a more decentralised management of the economy were developed. When the movements toward political liberalisation were repressed in Eastern Europe, following the Soviet intervention in Budapest in 1956, the reform projects in the economic field were stifled as well. Khrushchev went even so far as to press for a supranationally centralised system of planning in the framework of Comecon in 1962, which could never be implemented due to the active

(Romania) or passive (other Eastern European countries) resistance of his partners.

This first wave of aborted reforms yields two lessons. The first one is that no reform was viable if this led to questioning the leading role of the communist party in each country, and of the Soviet party in the region. The second lesson, which was not so obvious at that time, is that any reform complying with the first principle could indeed achieve a great degree of liberalisation in the economic field, without meaning that the regime was fundamentally modified. The normalisation which followed the Czechoslovak reform of 1967–8 – the 'Prague Spring' – epitomises the first lesson: the experiment was stopped when the Soviet party understood that the Czechoslovak party had lost control. At the same time in 1968 the 'new economic mechanism' was launched in Hungary. It did not meet with substantial objections from the Soviet party leaders, even when it proceeded much further in economic management liberalisation than the Prague blueprint of 1967. Here was the illustration of the second lesson.

New Relations between the Centre and the Enterprise

It was a decline in the rates of growth that prompted the search for a reform blueprint. While in the 1951–6 period in almost all countries there was a two-digit annual percentage growth of the national product (see Table 4.1 on page 45), after 1956 growth rates declined steadily, well into the next decade. A political decision was then made: the enterprises should get new incentives so as to work better, without any altering of the foundations of the system. The socialist enterprise should be induced to implement the plan more efficiently, not by compulsory orders or by sanctions, but through appropriate incentives. This should be achieved without abandoning central planning or central control on the economy.

Almost in all countries these reforms concentrated on the industrial sector, and only in Hungary was the agricultural sector considered as a priority for reform as well.

Obviously, for the enterprise to react to new stimuli, it needed more autonomy and more room for manoeuvre, so that alternative strategies could be implemented. The need for autonomy was amply proclaimed, but never actually satisfied. The enterprise remained in most countries subordinate to industrial ministries; in all countries it was kept under control of the party. There were oscillations in the policy, from more to less decentralisation, and vice versa. There were also conflicts between the party authorities and the enterprises. However one must not forget that the party officials, the high-level cadres of the economic administration, and the enterprise executives belonged to the same *nomenklatura*, and shared the same material and political privileges.

A Limited Autonomy

The reforms shared similar features in all the countries, despite sometimes marked differences in their scope. Officially their aim was to grant more autonomy to the enterprises.

(a)   In Eastern Europe the number of *the branch ministries* was reduced – in the Soviet Union the streamlining of the central administration, though on the agenda, could never be implemented before the Gorbachev era. In Hungary, for instance, the cut went so far as to suppress almost all central ministries. However, the relevant control functions were often transferred to the central departments of the suppressed ministries.

(b)   The *mandatory character of the plan* was relaxed. The number of compulsory indicators was cut, even to zero in the case of Hungary. But the party system remained unchanged, and through that channel the authorities could always intervene in the enterprises' management.

(c)   Only the *large enterprises* got more freedom of manoeuvre. The smaller units remained technical divisions of the big enterprises, and had no autonomy whatsoever. Large enterprises were themselves merged into even larger complexes called industrial associations or unions, which were endowed with some of the functions held by the ministries. In the GDR these complexes were called *Kombinaten* and were vertically integrated, from the raw-material base up to the distribution of the final processed product. In Poland the so-called 'big economic organisations' which were formed in the beginning of the 1970s helped to decentralise the management of the economic units, and later, after 1975, were used to reinforce central control. The Hungarian trusts were also vested with administrative functions, which loosened in the 1980s. In the less reformed countries, the industrial *centrale* (Romania), or state economic amalgamations (Bulgaria), or *koncerny* and associations (Czechoslovakia) retained control functions on their lower components until the end of the system.

(d)   Even in the most favourable cases, the autonomy of decision-making never extended to the *investment* sphere. Here it was limited in three different ways. First, the central plan was always dealing with new investments, in creating new enterprises, and in developing infrastructures such as transport, communications, energy distribution. Second, in the case of investments within existing enterprises, the decision-making power of the enterprise was in fact hampered by the difficulties in the supply of investment goods, which in most cases remained allocated centrally. Finally, in most countries investment was basically financed out of the budget, and the enterprises had very limited funds for self-financing. Long-term investment credit was used in some countries, including the USSR, and developed in Hungary on a large scale. Even in this last case, the process meant that the National Bank of Hungary, a 'monobank' financing all the economic activity in the country, in effect controlled the enterprises.

One may thus question the very concept of 'autonomy of the enterprises'. The enterprises were still obeying orders. True, they were increasingly writing down these orders themselves, and discussing their commitments with the political authority. The command economy was becoming a bargaining economy (Kornai), or a manipulated economy (Fallenbuchl).

These processes have sometimes been likened to the Western lobbying practices. The stakes and the positions of the partners were however totally different. The socialist enterprises, or their coalitions, did not aim to get additional markets or to realise additional profits, like the lobbies in a capitalist economy. They wanted to preserve power positions, which were measured in terms of control on resources: how to get higher allocations of investment goods, how to be permitted to hire more workers, so as to supply a greater volume of output. The party authorities alike wanted to steer input and output flows. This was in essence a Stalinist framework; but now, negotiation replaced command.

The Illusions of Participation

Workers' participation, in terms of power-sharing, was high on the agenda of the reformers. In all countries some scheme was devised to enrol workers into a more active involvement in planning and management. There was a contradiction here: self-management, Yugoslav style, was still considered with suspicion. The party authorities were strongly opposed to that form of self-management, which was again evidenced when in 1980 in Poland the dissident trade union *Solidarnosc* pushed a self-government scheme forward. The martial law in December 1981 put an end to the endeavour.

It was not possible either to resurrect the Stalinist-type of workers' stimulation through Stakhanovite-type policies. The Stakhanovite movement was born in 1935 (see Box 2.1, on pages 17 and 18) when a coal-miner managed to rationalise his work so as to get a dramatic increase in his output. This was a political way of mobilising the workers for a higher productivity; the 'heroes' of such stories were politically selected individuals; their performance was set beforehand, and obtained through better supplies of equipment and through help of aides. The Polish film director Andrzej Wajda showed this process in his excellent movie *The Man of Marble* (1976). In the 1960s, collective performance had to be promoted, not just in output, but in management. In the USSR there were thus 'brigade contracts' whereby groups of workers within an enterprise pledged themselves to achieve a series of performance indicators, both physical and financial, while the management committed itself to provide the required supply conditions for them to be able to do so. Official trade unions took part in these schemes. Hungary went so far as to establish enterprise councils with a large workers' representation, which had to elect the director of the enterprise.

However, all the efforts made to associate unions or workers to the management of the enterprises remained formal. The workers were less than enthusiastic, which is quite understandable: if the enterprise has no real autonomy outside its political links with the authorities, why share this helplessness with its executives?

A DWINDLING OF THE STATE OWNERSHIP MONOPOLY?

'Everything belonged to the state' is a widely accepted cliché, but state (or, in fact, party) ownership was never exclusive. Other forms of collective property were to be found along with it. State property itself gradually eroded in the wake of the reforms. We have to grasp its essence to understand why the transition is nowadays so difficult.

State Ownership

Let us sum up some of the features of the state enterprises. They were managed by members of the *nomenklatura*. They were much bigger than comparable enterprises in the West, in terms of the number of employees for example. Often, especially in the Eastern European countries, only one enterprise or two manufactured a given good. They were subordinate to some administrative body but they could bargain over the directives they received. Finally, there was a hierarchy according to a branch criterion. It was much preferable to be director, engineer, worker, in an enterprise belonging to the military–industrial complex than in light industry. This complex included not only defence industries but almost all heavy industry in general, i.e. the mining, fuel, steel, machine-building, and automotive industries. The privileges of the executives, and the wages and bonuses of the employees were higher. In addition, these industries were advantaged in the planning procedures, and got better supplies, attracted better quality workers, than the light industries manufacturing consumer goods. Three features of this industrial structure have to be discussed at more length.

(a) The standard *industrial structure* in a socialist economy has very often been described as 'monopolistic' or 'oligopolistic'. This is, strictly speaking, a misconception. A monopoly or an oligopoly is a particular kind of market, defined by the number of sellers facing the buyers. Here we have no market at all. Hence we cannot use the same phrases. This is not just a matter of terminological accuracy. Failing to understand how the socialist 'monopolies' worked led to illusions and difficulties during the transition: the illusion that such entities could respond to market signals in ways described by the microeconomic standard theory; the illusion that they might be controlled by some kind of 'anti-trust' policy borrowed from market economy regulations; the difficulties of dismantling these big units.

For the same reason – the absence of a market – one cannot apply standard concentration analysis to the large socialist firms. Only by approximation can one speak of the industrial associations in the East as cases of horizontal concentration, or of East German combines as examples of vertical integration. The socialist 'trusts' were not the result of mergers, or expansion and entry into new markets, as both goods markets and capital markets were controlled. They were the outcome of a political–administrative decision not based on competition or market criteria such as profitability. They were used to relay the central orders to the constituent units. This situation also explains why the conglomerate form of the external expansion of the firm was not to be found in the East. Such a structure did not fit the sectoral division of the economic administration, and would have implied the existence of a fully-fledged capital market. The socialist enterprises were not allowed, even in their limited range of autonomy in the field of investment, to expand in sectors different from their main scope of activities. They were however allowed, and even encouraged, to carry on 'complementary' activities with their 'spare' capital and human resources. This was indeed often the case, in the USSR, in the enterprises belonging to the military–industrial complex, which used to manufacture various consumer goods in addition to their main output.

(b)   In contrast to market economies, there was a *lack of small and medium enterprises*. We have already seen that within the huge state firms and amalgamations the smaller units had no autonomy whatsoever. Outside these firms, there were simply no such units. In this sense, the socialist oligopolies could not be compared to market oligopolies with a fringe of subcontractors, maintenance units or suppliers, such as is found, for instance, in the Western automobile industry. Such activities were 'internalised'. Each big firm or amalgamation developed such units or workshops within its own structure, so as to protect itself against shortages or defects in the supply of these goods and services. There was no specialisation in the supply of spare parts and components; self-sufficiency was the rule, which entailed large inefficiencies. In each enterprise, so-called auxiliary activities absorbed a large share of the workforce, and no economies of scale could occur because there was no pooling of these activities. Thus we may understand why privatisations stalled in the beginning of the transition. It was very difficult to privatise these giant enterprises as they were, and de-monopolisation was required; but there was no clear criterion on how to split them. On the other hand, one could not begin with privatising the small and medium enterprises, as these were very scarce in the industrial sector, the only significant exception being Hungary at the end of the 1980s.

True, there were smaller state units in the consumer services sector: restaurants, hotels, retail trade outlets, repair services, more generally all household commercial services. But very often they were part of chain stores or establishments. They were also totally dependent on wholesale 'monopolistic' suppliers.

(c)   The last feature is the *multi-faceted nature* of the large socialist enterprises. They were not just production and management units. They had political, administrative and social functions. The director was appointed by the political authority on the basis of the 'one-man rule'. This Stalinist principle (*edinonachalie* in Russian) endowed the director with wide powers but ensured that he was politically accountable to the party. The 'red executives' (Granick, 1954) were politically reliable, often technically competent, but had no management skills in the Western sense. They had to perform a number of administrative tasks as medium-level directing organs. They also were the heads of social communities which might compare to the big family enterprises in early capitalism, and they could be likened for instance to the ironworks lords in France in the beginning of the century. They provided their workers not only with a salary and a guaranteed job, but also with a full set of additional benefits such as housing, kindergartens, vacation centres, enterprise restaurants and stores offering staples and various consumer items at reduced prices, and sometimes health care services as well. The official union played a substantial role in managing these social benefits. This amounted to a large social protection system of a paternalist type; the 'father' here was the communist state, above the manager who acted as its representative.

Here is one of the big dilemmas of the post-transition period. The economies in transition need a modern industrial structure with large firms surrounded with small and medium enterprises. But they cannot just keep the ex-communist large firms, simply privatising them and turning them into market 'monopolies' or 'oligopolies' by virtue of renaming them. They must first be dismantled and restructured again, so as to rescind their previous features.

Cooperative Ownership

In the years preceding the transition, the status of the cooperative sector increasingly became very close to that of the state sector, along with the growing concentration of collective farms and their evolution into agro-industrial complexes. The political control on the (formally elected) management was always quite stringent because peasants were traditionally considered with suspicion by the communists. However, like the big state firms, and perhaps even to a greater degree, the cooperatives provided a social protection framework to their workers, taking into account that the social security regulations were extended to the peasantry later, and in a less complete form than to the urban workers.

Within the cooperatives, a quasi-private sector developed, mostly through contracts between the management and the peasants, whereby the latter performed definite tasks for the cooperative, such as fattening up livestock or grow specific produce, while the cooperative would provide seeds, fertilizers, feed, young animals to breed. An entrepreneurship spirit developed in the cooperatives as well as among their members, especially in Hungary where 'co-ops' came to own hotels and night-clubs.

These features explain at the same time why the post-transition governments were impatient to dissolve the cooperatives as strongholds of the communist system, and why the peasants were not so eager to leave the protection which the cooperatives provided, so that even when new legal rules organised the dismantling or the transformation of the cooperatives, they were not applied in actual fact.

Non-State Ownership

This section deals with the legally operating non-state economy. The parallel or shadow economy activities will be dealt with in the next section as it rather resorts to the perversion of central planning by the black market.

The private sector proper remained marginal until the end of the system. It was almost non-existent in the industrial sector, except in Hungary. In this country it was, so to say, incorporated into the state sector, through a specific institution called 'enterprise economic work partnership', established in 1982. It could be likened to the contract system in the agricultural cooperatives: the workers pledged themselves to undertake a specific task for their own enterprise, in their usual workplace and with the regular equipment and materials belonging to the enterprise, but after hours and on a sub-contracting basis. Their firm could thus escape the rather stringent rules on wage increases, as members of the 'partnership' were not paid as wage-earners but as sellers of a service. The experience showed that both productivity and profitability were much higher than in the normal workshop – not surprisingly as the employees were 'hoarding' their forces for these jobs. This form of hidden privatisation was also applied in the USSR under Gorbachev.

The family plot within the agricultural cooperatives (i.e. in the USSR and in Eastern Europe except Poland where there were no cooperatives) was almost everywhere promoted in the framework of the reforms, except in Romania. In 1985 the share of the family plots in total arable land was between 3 per cent (in Czechoslovakia and the USSR) and 15 per cent in (Hungary). Their share in agricultural output was much higher, up to 34 per cent in Hungary; for some products such as potatoes, vegetables, fruit, poultry, eggs, it was much higher still (Lhomel, 1990). The family plots performed apparently much better, which has often been attributed to the sheer superiority of private versus collective farming. This is a misinterpretation. The family plot was a part of the collective farm. It used the cooperative's equipment, seeds and fertilisers, either legally on a contractual basis, or by pilfering. The family plot was labour-intensive at the expense of the cooperative; the peasants spared their effort for their own plot. This was especially obvious in the harvest periods, when urban workers were compulsorily sent to the country to help the peasants and found out that most of the latter were busy on their own plots. This is not to say that the peasants benefited from the system unduly. But if one looks on the family plot as a quasi-private form of ownership, as an enterprise it operated in artificial, non-market conditions. Demand was guaranteed because of the shortage of agricultural goods on the state market, itself due to inconsistent planning and to artificially low prices for food products. The peasants did not have to worry about the usual financial constraints faced by market economy peasants (how to get and repay bank loans for instance). Low public transportation prices allowed them to travel long distances to sell their produce. The case of Georgian producers selling tomatoes and flowers on the Moscow market is well known; true, in this case to get on crowded planes with a large shipment required bribery, and hence strengthened the 'Caucasian mafia' which was later to derive high benefits from the transition. Family plots looked successful, but they were not quasi-markets. The family plot institution partook of the global system proper to Soviet-type economies.

COMBINING THE PLAN AND THE MARKET

In the mid-1960s the phrase 'combining central planning with market instruments' was very popular. The Eastern reformers used it to express their commitment to a greater efficiency of the system, and to some openness to Western concepts. In the West it was hailed as a step toward capitalist methods. The failure of all attempts to 'combine' the plan and the market exemplifies the economic non-feasibility of socialism, which is basically due to its political foundations. Though the principles of the reforms seemed sensible, the implementation led to a stalemate whatever the variants. The only successful outcome was the soaring parallel economy, a perverse combination of black market and central planning.

The Principles

The market was supposed to assist planning by introducing more efficiency. It was understood as a set of recipes which had allowed capitalism to flourish, of which the most successful was the principle of profit maximisation. By reading Western textbooks, open-minded economists found that according to the neo-classical theory, whenever an economic agent maximises his own interest, with all economic agents behaving in the same way on all the markets, one gets an optimum, that is the maximum output associated with the complete utilisation of all available resources. As mathematical economics had been rediscovered, and re-established in the USSR in the late 1950s, under the leadership of Nemchinov, Kantorovich and Novozhilov, this could also be expressed in terms of linear programming, as the solution of a problem of maximising a production function (or minimising a cost function) under input (or output) constraints (Kantorovich, 1959, 1965). At the same time, the procedure allowed the determination of scarcity prices for inputs and outputs.

This indeed looked an ideal world. The idea of reconciling the interests of all members of society with the interests of the society as a whole seemed perfectly compatible with the socialist ideal of increasing the welfare of the people. The mathematical backing of the theory granted it scientific respectability irrespective of any system. A crucial point was however overlooked. It was assumed that the 'common good' of the society as a whole could be defined by the central planner, that is by the party. The law of the market was to be applied, which meant that supply had to adjust to demand; however demand was equated to the needs of the consumers and the producers as they were expressed in the plan.

In the West the reforms revived the discussion over market socialism, theoretical foundations of which will be discussed in the last chapter of this book. The reformers in Eastern Europe and in the USSR did not refer to market socialism (except in the short-lived Prague Spring experience), and following the repression of the Czechoslovak reform after 1968 the phrase remained even taboo almost until the end of the system. However in the West the reforms were hailed as a genuine rapprochement between socialism and capitalism. The thesis of a convergence between both systems was expressed as early as in 1961 by the future first Nobel prize laureate in economics (1969) Jan Tinbergen. Each of the systems would improve in borrowing the best elements of the other; capitalism and socialism would gradually converge towards a mixed socio-economic system (Tinbergen, 1961). Another sign of this misinterpretation of the reform trend was the fact that the Nobel prize in economics was awarded in 1975 to Leonid Kantorovich, though the laureate had always been very keen on presenting himself as a mathematician, not as an economist, and dismissed all perception of his work as supporting the idea of market socialism.

Indeed this misperception was strengthened by the fact than in the East the reformers claimed that the market instruments should be used in two crucial fields, price determination and assessing the efficiency of investment. At first glance one could expect that the two principles to be applied in the management of the enterprises, that is greater autonomy *vis-à-vis* the Centre and profit maximisation, would allow for rational price fixing and investment decision-making. But as we have seen earlier, nothing really changed either in the political subordination of the enterprise to the party authorities, or in the dominance of state property. In such conditions market instruments were stifled.

The Stalemate

Though some progress was made in the way prices were determined, in the incentive system which should have induced profit maximisation, and in the choice of investment criteria, the reforms came to a deadlock because market coordination could not operate.

(a)   In the field of *price-fixing*, prices were supposed to guarantee a 'normal' profit to 'well-managed' enterprises according to the Soviet reform blueprint. The concept of a 'normal' profit was never really clarified, either as to the definition of the profit ratio (various formulas were suggested, the profit being related to full costs, or to wages only, or to the value of productive assets), or as to the magnitude of the ratio. The enterprises were supposed to be 'well managed' when they complied with the plan commands. Even though they were supposed to take part in the drafting of these orders, in form of 'counter-plans' as in Russia, or even when plan orders were formally abolished altogether as in Hungary, the enterprises had always to seek approval from the authorities.

Prices were to be 'liberalised' but in fact remained centrally fixed in most cases. Only in Hungary did liberalisation reach significant proportions, but was never complete. In other countries 'rationalisation' of prices was sought instead. This meant that prices were set by a special administrative agency, according to various formulae based on a cost-plus principle. For some categories of goods, price-fixing was more flexible, and used price brackets or ceiling prices; a very small share of the prices could be fixed directly by the enterprises. This was the procedure for wholesale prices. Retail prices were a matter of social policy and were either heavily subsidised for essential goods, or much higher than the costs of production for 'luxury goods' such as cars, many items of clothing, footwear, and various household appliances. The differences between wholesale prices and retail prices were either covered from the state budget as subsidies or accrued to the budget in the form of the turnover tax, and there was no automatic relation between the two categories of prices.

The resulting prices were not market prices. They were not, and could not be, influenced by domestic competition, not only because the wholesale prices were centrally controlled, but also because of the concentration of the economic units. External prices had no impact either. There was no automatic repercussion on the domestic prices through the exchange rate as the domestic economy was isolated from the outside by a functional autarky, the instruments of which were foreign trade planning, state monopoly of foreign economic relations, and currency inconvertibility (Holzman, 1974 and 1976; also see Chapter 5). In some countries a limited impact of foreign prices was deemed useful and actually organised in the beginning of the 1970s (Hungary and Poland). Even in this case, essential goods such as energy carriers and raw materials were largely excluded from repercussion, especially after the increase in world prices following the first oil shock in 1973, as the socialist countries were wary of importing external inflation.

(b)   The *incentive mechanisms* aiming at profit maximisation were quite soon paralysed. The enterprise could not control profit-making because prices and costs were largely fixed independently of its action. Profit-sharing between the enterprise and the state budget was highly unequal; along various schemes the budget collected 70 to 85 per cent of the total net income of the enterprises. Profit-using was very limited though the need for more 'self-financing' was professed. The enterprise could not freely procure the goods allocated centrally, such as equipment, raw materials. In such conditions, the scope for decentralised investment was very narrow.

(c)   For centrally planned investments, *efficiency calculations* were supposed to help the planners in their choices. Decisions to allocate investments to given branches or regions were political, as well as the choice of the macroeconomic investment rate. Most of the available resources were tied up in such choices. Efficiency criteria were used only for choosing between alternative solutions for getting the same outcome. The main criteria were the minimising of the pay-out period (the period required for returns from the investment to balance initial outlays), and a more refined approach introducing time-discount, along with using an internal rate of return to which the estimated profitability of the investment was compared. In this second approach, any investment with a profitability higher than the reference rate would be selected (see the entry by Ellman in Eatwell *et al.*, 1990). Such an approach is not unusual in Western business practice. But in the West, the reference rate is currently the rate of interest which is faced by the firm on the market. The interest rate could not play such a role in socialist economies. Even when investments were supposed to be financed mainly through bank credit, which was increasingly the case in Central European countries in the 1980s, the bank remained a monobank itself controlled by the authorities. The interest rate was merely an accounting device and could influence investment decisions only very marginally.

Could Any Reform Succeed?

It is only too easy now to answer negatively. Market coordination cannot go together with the monopoly of a party on the economy and the society. This could not be acknowledged openly but was implicitly taken into account. In the 1980s one had thus several variants:

(a)   the *Hungarian* model, which included: a large decentralisation of decision-making; encouragement of private production activities;

price flexibility, coupled with international openness allowing the repercussion of external prices on domestic ones; regulation of the use of material and human resources through interest rates and taxes; some enterprise autonomy (limited by the high level of concentration) in the choice of suppliers and buyers. However the enterprises not only remained subject to political control, but also to frequent changes in policies and rules. This *ad hoc* regulation worked as a safety net as they could always be bailed out whenever the market indicators suggested they should be closed. It also generated a climate of uncertainty in the environment of the enterprise;

(b) the *Polish* variant: it went very far in the direction of decentralisation and liberalisation in economic life, but the reform blueprint initially drafted with the contribution of the dissident union Solidarity was implemented by a military power born of the martial law of December 1981; this impaired the credibility of the reform both in the country and outside it;

(c) conservative (as in *Czechoslovakia*), totalitarian (*Romania*), or technocratic (*GDR*) communist orthodoxy, with lip-service to the rhetoric of reform;

(d) rather erratic economic experimentation with various reformist schemes, very often under the guidance and control of the Soviet Union (*Bulgaria*);

(e) finally, the Soviet *perestroyka*, which went out of control, and which story belongs to the end of the system (Chapter 6).

Were the most far-reaching reforms at least a good introduction for the transition to the market? A full answer can only be given later. In some ways they were: Poland and Hungary immediately emerged as front-runners of the transition. At the same time it is easy to see how these incomplete reforms led to misunderstandings in the West and the East alike. Just because words such as prices, profit, interest rate, efficiency, and profitability seemed to mean something in the East one assumed that once all central controls were removed (which was presumed to be possible overnight) the market signals would lead to market-type automatic adjustments. It was not to be the case, and this would lead to bitter disillusions.

This is not to say that economic agents could not adjust to market-type signals. They could do so in a distorted way, which was the parallel or shadow economy.

The Pervading Parallel Economy

The parallel economy has sometimes been defined as a set of variously illegal or coloured markets, with shades going from almost white (official) to black (Katsenelinboigen, 1977). It ran parallel to the official economy but it belonged to the same system.

(a) The parallel economy was firmly established within the *party monopoly* itself, though the political and legal authorities were waging war against it. The material privileges of the *nomenklatura* made its members vulnerable to corruption as the beneficiaries of the privileges wanted to increase their standard of living; at the same time the *nomenklatura* cadres had the means to corrupt using their power positions. The mafia did not belong to the *nomenklatura* but used to bribe it, through buying judges, police officials, and the civil servants who could give access to any chunk of state ownership. As most of the resources were under public ownership this gave the mafia a much greater scope of activity than that of its Western counterparts.

(b) The parallel economy infiltrated the *state economy*. It would have been difficult to find anybody not practising it on any scale: moonlighting, use of state buildings, machinery, materials for personal needs, use of official positions to derive private advantages. It has to be mentioned that contrary to a rather widely accepted view in the West, the official positions procuring advantages need not be high-rank. A vice-minister could procure seats for sold-out performances in state theatres, but the cashier at the theatre window could do so as well, in a situation of chronic shortage generated by too low public prices.

The sheer mass of people involved in the second economy made it impossible to eradicate. Big crime was in some sense protected by such a number of accomplices. It is easy to see that the second economy, or shadow economy as it was also called, was not generated by the same reasons which explain a similar behaviour in the framework of a market economy. Moonlighting in the West is due to the desire of the employer as well as of the worker to evade taxes or social security payments, or to dodge some legal regulations such as those on immigration and the right to work. Moonlighting in the East was due to the fact that most of the services, though being in short supply when provided by the state, could simply not be offered in a private framework. Even when it was legally possible, the suppliers of services were discriminated against in access to equipment and materials. Remaining within the state sector while filching and stealing was by far the most practical solution.

(c) The parallel economy operated within the *planned system*. Exactly like the official economy, it was an economy without money, or at least where money played a secondary role. The high-level mafia did not hoard money; it hoarded goods, or, what is tantamount in an inconvertibility regime, it hoarded foreign currency, whenever its members had access to foreign trade activities. As a rule this did not lead to ostentatious consumption. In such egalitarian societies as were the communist countries, wealth was immediately identified with 'speculation'; in police-controlled societies, it led to denunciation.

In the production sector, the parallel economy operated as well without money. Many of the operators acted not just in their own interest, but very often in the interest of their enterprise, to avoid deadlocks due to the rigidities of planning. When they acted in their interest it was not mainly to increase their profits or material benefits, but to strengthen their power within the system through overfulfilling the plan, or through increasing their material resources. Thus, in the USSR, emerged large hidden 'commodity exchanges': the directors of the state enterprises would use these organisations to swap equipment or materials so as to avoid the cumbersome official supply system. Later, during the transition, these organisations would come out in the open and merge with the remnants of the official allocating agencies to build rather efficient bartering corporations, which would now be used in the framework of a nascent market economy for 'spontaneous' privatisation.

Again, a parallel with the market economy illegal practices is in order. The parallel economy operators in the production sector did not bother to accumulate money. As there were no capital markets there were no associated economic delinquency: insiders' crimes did not exist in a literal sense, though of course insiders' positions within the system brought large advantages.

Central planning was helping the parallel economy in many ways. It allowed it to avoid the financial constraints of a market economy. The planning system generated the shortages through inadequate supplies and low prices for a range of basic goods. It allowed for unlimited opportunities of wasting and stealing public resources. The development of parallel activities eroded the moral sense of the population. The official ideology was obviously contrary to these activities while its representatives were involved in it. The people became used to a double language, and to a schizophrenic style of life. Everybody paid lip-service to the rhetoric of communism; everybody's everyday behaviour was the negation of this rhetoric.

4 The Performance

Is the overall performance of the socialist economic system to be considered as a total failure? Sometimes the system is credited for having brought an underdeveloped country, Russia, out of backwardness, be it at very high material and human costs. Could not another regime have achieved the same results at lesser cost? In Eastern Europe the Soviet model was introduced forcibly; it was not adapted, in any case, to those countries which were industrialised already before the war. The inefficiencies of the model became obvious as early as in the 1950s, triggering a 'treadmill' (Schroeder, 1979) of reforms. By the middle of the 1970s an open crisis developed and led to final collapse.

This is the story of a failure. It raises many yet unresolved questions. Can one really measure the performance of the system? For years the US Central Intelligence Agency reconstructed the Soviet statistics, considering them as exaggerating growth rates. Now the new Russian statisticians claim that the growth rates were actually lower, and deride the optimism of the CIA. Qualitative features are not easy to assess either. Was the lack of unemployment an advantage of the system or the sign of inefficiency? Shortages were obvious to any traveller. The actual level of consumption in households was much higher, especially taking into account social benefits. Again, was this a plus or a minus? Finally, how can we qualify the rampant or open crises in the socialist countries, which ended in the final crash?

THE STRATEGY OF GROWTH

The Soviet leaders liked to compare the performance of the country to the capitalist ones. Before the Second World War, Stalin claimed two-digit growth rates at the time of the Great Depression. After the war, in 1961 Khrushchev asserted that in the next twenty years the USSR would catch up with the United States and overcome them in terms of growth (XXIst Congress of the Communist Party). Was such a contention just preposterous bluster? We have to consider the aims, the professed strategy, the variants, the actual results. We shall begin with one of the most debated issues: the measure of performance.

The Measure of Performance

In the past, Western experts who used Soviet and Eastern European figures were suspected of lacking critical acumen. These data could only be distorted. When one used other figures recomputed in the West, there were usually large discrepancies among sources: not surprisingly, as the authors started from Soviet (Eastern) figures and derived theirs using different methodologies.

Table 4.1 compares the official growth rates published in the USSR and some alternative estimates for the national income (net material product) growth in 1922–85. It shows that official Soviet data are much higher than recomputed figures. If one assumes the recomputations to be more accurate,

Table 4.1 *The Soviet growth rates, 1922–85: alternative estimates (annual rate of change of net material product,* *in per cent)*

Years	Official figures	Western estimates	Alternative estimates
1922–40	15.3	5 to 6	8.5
1941–50	4.7	no reliable estimate	−0.6
1951–60	10.3	6.5 to 7.5	9.3
1961–70	7.0	5 to 6	4.2
1971–80	4.9	2.5 to 3	2.1
1981–85	3.6	2.0	0.6

* Net material product, or national income: this is the main aggregate in the Soviet national accounting system. Like the gross domestic (or national) product in the Western accounting system, it is a sum of values added, once the values of the inputs used in the production process have been deducted from the overall value of the production. But it does differ from the GDP or the GNP in three ways:

– it is net of the value of depreciation of the fixed assets;
– it is 'material' in the Marxist sense: the only items considered as material are the 'visible' goods, and services do not add to the national income except when they are attached to the supply of goods. For instance, freight transport generates a value added which is included in the national income, but not passenger transport. Such a distinction among 'productive' and 'non-productive' services has always been very difficult to apply. In addition it does not take into account a large number of services which are included in the Western definitions of GNP or GDP, such as education, health, administration, financial services, etc.;
– contrary to Western practice, it includes indirect taxes, as the latter are considered as the share of the net income accruing to the state, as distinct from the taxes paid out of the enterprise income. It might be called an aggregate at 'market prices', and not at 'factor cost'.

Sources: Columns 1 and 3: 'Stabilisation, Liberalisation and Reform', special issue of *European Economy*, no. 45, December 1990. For the alternative estimates, the quoted source refers to a Soviet source of 1990. Western estimates (column 2): compiled from various Western sources, including CIA estimates. The alternative figures are generally lower than the Western estimates, but only beginning from the end of Stalinism.

then the reliability of the official figures was greatest between 1951 and 1970, lowest during the Second World War, and again during the last years of the Brezhnev regime, which Gorbachev used to call the 'stagnation' (*zastoy*) years. Why such wide and fluctuating discrepancies?

'Wicked' figures

Were the Soviet statisticians (and emulating them, those from other socialist countries) cheating on purpose? Yes, without doubt, in many ways:

- Some data were never provided. Among the missing figures were those for everything related to defence, a number of demographic data (such as, for instance, the data on infant mortality or morbidity), social data (crime, accidents occurring in the workplace, natural or other disasters), economic data (there were no figures on the absolute magnitudes of prices and wages, except averages); financial data (many items, in addition to defence expenditures mentioned previously, were not reported), foreign trade data such as arms sales.
- The growth rates were exaggerated for various reasons. First, of course, the authorities wanted to show high growth rates. In Western practice as well, statistical offices may be induced by the authorities to display suitable figures; only this does not usually relate to growth. In France, for instance, the measurement of the price increases has often been a topic for disagreement between the unions and the government, because the increase in the price index triggered an increase in the minimum wage. In the same country and for political reasons, the level of unemployment was a matter of dispute between the government and the opposition in the beginning of the 1990s. Second, in socialist countries, enterprises were interested as well in over-reporting their output, as the overfulfilment of the plan triggered various bonuses. They were also interested in under-reporting the amount of their resources, so as to get more supplies or investment means, which would allow them to implement the output plan more easily. This kind of micro-economic cheating is not to be found in market economies, because the reporting enterprises have nothing to lose in reporting accurately, provided they are guaranteed that neither their competitors nor the tax officer will have access to the data. Third, and finally, the figures were biased because of wrong statistical methods. This has been amply discussed by Alec Nove (1987, 1992) and others. It was a particular case of the 'index numbers' problem. Over the period 1928–50 the growth rates were computed using as reference prices the 1926–7 prices. Statistically weighting an index with a remote base always shows higher growth rates than with recent reference prices; in addition, as the USSR was little industrialised in 1927, the new products which appeared later were

estimated at fictitious and high 1927 prices, exaggerating still more the growth rates.
- Agricultural figures were a special problem. Before 1953 all output data were grossly overestimated due to the fact that the harvest was recorded on a 'biological' basis, 'in the field'. Later the crop was recorded once harvested, but the numerous losses between the field and the consumer were never completely taken into account.

Were the Western figures better? Yes, because they gave lower and hence more credible estimates. But there were discrepancies among sources – not surprisingly, as the Western authors started from Soviet official figures on the physical output as their 'raw materials' (Nove, 1992, p. 430), and used various methods of aggregating and indexing, as well as different deflators. Western computations have already been criticised by the Soviet statisticians during the *perestroyka* period. The Soviet experts came to much lower estimates than the Western ones and especially than the CIA (Khanin and Selyunin, 1987, on the 'Wicked figures').

Is the full truth available now? In the West one often thought that statistical cheating was perfectly controlled and that the authorities had a kind of double accounting, with hidden files in some closed cabinet with the right and complete figures. Western experts gave credit to this feeling, especially as indeed, from time to time, some new data were disclosed, or some previous data corrected by the statistical offices. But the reality is much more worrying. When the transition began and when the statistical offices opened their books, along with calls for help to sort the data mess out, no hidden files were to be found. The system was lying to itself so as not to acknowledge its failures. Huge layers of economic history – to speak only of economics – remain unknown, and very little may be done to reconstruct what is missing.

Non-comparable data

It has always been near to impossible to compare Western and Eastern data on GNPs per capita. One had first to convert the main macro-economic aggregate used in the East, which was the net material product (NMP) (see Table 4.1), into a gross national (or domestic) product (GNP/GDP). To do so one had to estimate the value of the services to the people, which was not taken into account in the NMP. As many collective services in the East were provided for free, this added to the task. Then the aggregate in domestic prices had to be converted into a foreign currency (generally into dollars). This second step raised the problem of the suitable exchange rate. The currencies of the East were non-convertible and grossly overvalued according to the official rate. Other rates were computed and used, but in the same country there were multiple exchange rates according to product groups or according to the purpose for which they were used (commercial, and non-commercial rates). Finally, because of the autarky which isolated the socialist countries from the West, the structure of the relative prices was so distorted by comparison with the West that any aggregation was debatable.

The issue of relative prices deserves two further comments. First, price ratios would significantly differ in the East and in the West for the same goods. For instance, a car would cost much more in the USSR than in Western Europe in terms of oil, which meant either that cars were much more expensive in the USSR, or oil much less. This made the significance of a composite price index very questionable. Second, relative prices were very different, for the same pairs of goods, in consumer and in producer prices. In the West retail prices are roughly proportional to wholesale prices, and may be derived from the latter once one knows the VAT rate and the retailer's average profit margin. In the socialist countries, retail prices were decoupled from wholesale prices and were manipulated for policy reasons; thus there were hundreds of *ad hoc* rates of the turnover tax. As a result, any coherent calculation of an economically significant exchange rate was impossible.

This is why East–West GNP comparisons were so divergent according to the sources and methods. The World Bank itself never succeeded in reaching a widely accepted estimate, despite many years of efforts by a large team of experts (Marer, 1985). Table 4.2 provides an estimate for the year 1989. This table allows for a rough ranking of the socialist countries. There is not much significance in comparing Eastern European countries with middle-income market economies supposed to have a comparable GNP level (for example, South Africa and Hungary, or Romania and Panama). All problems have not been eliminated with transition. The vast divergence of the exchange

Table 4.2 *GNP levels: East–West comparisons (GNP per capita in dollars, 1989)*

		Formerly centrally planned economies				
Bulgaria	*Czechoslovakia*	*(GDR)*	*Hungary*	*Poland*	*Romania*	*USSR*
2,680	3,450	(5,000)	2,630	1,890	1,730	1,780

		Other middle-income economies				
Brazil	*Trinidad and Tobago*	*Portugal*	*South Africa*	*Mexico*	*Panama*	*Chile*
2,400	3,400	4,250	2,460	2,080	1,760	1,780

Sources: *World Bank Atlas 1991*; own estimates for the GDR.
For the USSR: *The Economy of the USSR, 1990*, joint report by the World Bank, IMF, OECD, and EBRD.

rates, deriving from the initial devaluations and rates constructed on the basis of purchasing power parity also leads to biased comparisons (see Chapter 7).

Much time has been spent on statistics. Maybe too much attention has been focused in the past on disputes over figures. Such disputes expressed the frustration of Western experts and of the lay audience facing the opacity of the communist regimes. Indeed, in the West statistical reports are not always transparent, nor open. But there is a democratic debate over these issues. No debate was allowed in the East. To question data meant questioning the regime, its aims and strategies.

The Aim and the Model

The Soviet textbooks of political economy phrased the 'basic economic law of socialism' in terms which did not change much over time: 'satisfying increasingly better the growing material and cultural needs of the people by means of the constant development and improvement of the socialist production, on the basis of a high technical level'. The wording was slightly altered, but the definition remained basically the same since its formulation in the official *Manual of Political Economy* which was drafted under Stalin's supervision and published in Russian in 1954. The final aim was to satisfy the needs of the people. These needs were estimated and defined by the plan, that is, by the party. To satisfy them one needed to increase output. Growth and qualitative improvement of the output required a voluntarist strategy, as distinct from the capitalist 'anarchy'.

The strategy applied in the USSR since the launching of the first Five-Year Plan in 1928 was based on a theory of reproduction, and on an industrialisation model.

The *theory of reproduction* was based upon a model developed by Marx in volume II of *Capital* to explain the crises of overproduction in the capitalist system. It was later reformulated by Lenin, then by Stalin. The theory shows that in a modern industrial economy the producer goods sector, which was called by Marx 'Department I', has to grow at a quicker pace than the consumer goods sector ('Department II'). This imbalance is due to the labour-saving character of technical progress, which increases the 'organic composition of capital' (the value of constant capital per worker, or capital–labour ratio; in Marxian terms constant capital means not just fixed capital, but also minimum working capital required for the needs of production). Productive potential exceeds the capacity of the market to absorb the product, which triggers crises.

This 'law of expanded reproduction' was significantly twisted by Marx's followers when applied to socialism. For Marx the law was independent from human volition, and had to lead to crises of over-producing; here lay the major contradiction of capitalism. For Stalin, under socialism such crises could not happen. In a socialist system demand does not set limits to growth, in contrast with capitalism where consumer demand has to be backed by the purchasing power of the wage-earners. The planning system has to respond to the needs of the people, which are increasing over time. Consequently the 'law of expanded reproduction' has to become a voluntarist rule. One has to invest more in Department I from the outset, so as to increase the productive potential in the long run. This will allow, in turn, an increase in production in Department II.

The rephrased theory thus implied that one generation (or more) would have to sacrifice itself so as to ensure the conditions of growth for its descendants. It was supplemented by an *industrialisation model*. In the initial phase of development a policy of *extensive growth* would be used, which would mean the following: increasing the numbers of industrial workers by forcibly displacing the agricultural labour force toward the industrial centres; building new plants, equipping them with new machinery; and developing untapped natural resources or new territories. Such a model was formulated by Stalin for domestic political purposes, to justify forced collectivisation that was meant to procure an agricultural surplus needed to finance the extensive development of the industrial sector. It was also used for international propaganda purposes, as it showed that a socialist country could be protected from crises, recession and unemployment, in the very years when the capitalist world was plagued by the Great Depression.

The growth strategy resulting from the model was based on several priorities: of investment upon consumption; of industry over all other branches; of heavy industry within industry; of the so-called productive (of material goods) sector, over non-productive activities (services). In addition, the 'capitalist encirclement' of the USSR and the requirements of war preparation led to the priority of a military–industrial complex. These priorities shaped the industrial structure in the USSR and later in Eastern Europe.

VARIANTS AND ALTERATIONS OF THE MODEL

All the socialist countries followed the Soviet model, including the developing ones for which it was still less adapted. We shall elaborate on the Eastern European trends at more length.

The Eastern European Variants

After the Second World War the USSR was in the position of imposing the Stalinist growth model on its satellites in Eastern Europe. It could claim that the strategy had been successful in allowing for the industrial take-off and for the victory in the war. The model was also an alternative to the economic policies for post-war reconstruction which were implemented in Western Europe, equally on a dirigist basis, often using planning methods and based on a rather extended public sector. Western Europe benefited from the Marshall Plan (since 1947), which had been offered to Eastern Europe, and actually accepted by Czechoslovakia, before the governments of these countries were urged by the Soviets to refuse it. The Soviet model thus appeared as a counter-fire to the Marshall Plan (Swain and Swain, 1993, pp. 57–8).

The implementation of the model

The industrialist strategy was applied without any differentiation to all the people's democracies, even to those already industrialised such as Czechoslovakia and the GDR. In 1967, during the Prague Spring, two Czech economists, Jiri Goldman and Karel Kouba, established that the model was a source of inefficiency and imbalances; later this kind of critique could not be voiced (Goldman and Kouba, 1967). The Soviet model made Eastern Europe strongly dependent on Soviet supplies of fuels and raw materials. According to the requirements of extensive growth it implied an increasing use of natural resources which were abundant only in the Soviet Union, with a few exceptions for specific commodities (e.g. Polish coal, Romanian oil, etc.). This model also led to a hypertrophic development of the heavy industry in all Eastern European countries. For most of the goods produced by this industry the Soviet union offered a guaranteed market, which was a second cause of dependence. The next chapter will show how this double dependence shaped the mutual relations of the Soviet Union and Eastern Europe.

The implementation of the model was not always imposed by the USSR. In one instance at least it was a choice made against the wish of the Soviet leaders. For nationalistic reasons Romania began to break away from the Soviet Union at the end of the 1960s. When Khrushchev decided in 1962 that the Comecon countries should specialise according to their comparative advantages and hence suggested that Romania should supply its partners with agricultural goods, Romania refused to comply and asked for a Soviet credit to build the giant Galati steel-mill. The request was rejected and the Romanians nevertheless built the complex with Western credits. This was the start of the large-scale steel industry in Romania, though the country lacked iron ore and energy resources (apart from oil). The West approved this defiant attitude of the Romanians (who often benefited from their opposition to the Soviets, especially in foreign policy matters; Romania was thus the first socialist country to be admitted to the IMF in 1972). The Soviets were right in stressing that it was irrational to develop a steel industry in Romania. This industry, disproportionate to the country's needs, allowed it to dump steel on Western markets before and mainly after the transition. One should add that large-scale steel investments were no less wasteful in other Eastern European countries. The main difference was that in Poland, Hungary, Czechoslovakia and Bulgaria they were supported by cheap (comparative to world prices) Soviet supplies of iron ore and energy.

The consequences of the strategy

The policies followed in Eastern Europe had fairly convergent results. *Investment* quickly took a large share in the national income, rising from rather low levels in 1950 in all the countries (see Table 4.3). The highest level was reached around 1975; in that year investment amounted to a share of between 25 and 35 per cent of the national income. Initially most of it was directed toward the productive sector. Despite the fact that investment was by the end of the 1970s reoriented toward the non-productive sector (i.e., consumer services, infrastructure for health care, education, recreation and leisure), in 1985 the service sector at large still employed less than one-fifth of the labour force (one-eighth in Romania). The socialist countries were in this respect far behind the developed market economies where the services sector accounted for about 50 to 60 per cent of the labour force in the 1980s.

Within the industrial sector *heavy industry* benefited most from the growth strategy. It employed large numbers of workers. The most favoured branches in terms of investment were mining, the steel industry, heavy-machine-building, and the chemical industry. The industrial policy thus strengthened the lobbies of the military–industrial complex, the leaders of which formed the most powerful stratum of the *nomenklatura*.

The wave of reforms initiated in the mid-1960s entailed a change in strategy. Extensive growth was becoming too costly as its sources were drying up. There was no more available labour force to move from the country areas or to put to work: agriculture was beginning to experience a shortage of workers, and the levels of employment of women were about the highest in the world. Additional material resources were lacking as well. Even in the USSR, natural resources, which had been exploited very wastefully, were becoming scarce. New investment capacities could less and less easily be put in operation due to the already very high rate of accumulation. The GDR was the first country to decide upon an *intensive* strategy of growth, soon endorsed by the other countries. Intensive growth meant only the need for an increased productivity of labour and capital. One way of achieving it would have been to find the means to increase the productivity of the already existing capital. Instead, the main stress was put on *modernisation*, which meant a shift toward new branches embodying technical progress, such as the electronics industry, automation, and the nuclear industry. This new policy could benefit from the *détente* in East–West relations and the subsequent dramatic increase in East–West trade,

Table 4.3 *Structure of production in the socialist economies by sector and by final use, and structure of employment, 1950–89*

	Bulgaria	Czecho-slovakia	GDR	Hungary	Poland	Romania	USSR
Distribution of NMP (national income) by sector (in per cent) Industry, Construction:							
1950	43.4	71.2	53.1	55.4	45.0	49.4	63.6
1975	60.9	75.6	66.4	53.1	70.8	65.5	54.8
1989	69.8	70.3	70.6	57.8	59.9	67.0	54.8
Agriculture:							
1950	42.1	16.2	28.4	24.9	40.1	27.3	21.8
1975	22.1	8.7	10.9	21.2	14.8	16.6	17.1
1989	12.8	9.6	11.0	14.5	14.7	15.8	22.8
Transport, communications, commerce							
1950	10.1	10.6	17.2	17.1	nd	17.4	10.1
1975	16.6	11.9	19.8	24.8	12.3	16.2	18.9
1989	17.3	19.5	14.7	24.6	22.3	14.6	22.4
Other sectors of material production							
1950	4.4	2.0	1.2	0.6	nd	5.7	merged
1975	0.4	1.0	2.9	0.9	2.1	1.7	with
1989	0.1	0.6	3.7	3.1	3.1	2.6	services
Distribution of NMP between consumption and investment (in per cent) 1950							
Consumption	80.0	83.0	91.0	77.0	79.0	nd	76.0
Accumulation[*] 1975	20.0	17.0	9.0	23.0	21.0	nd	24.0
Consumption	67.0	71.0	78.0	75.0	66.0	65.0	73.0
Accumulation[*] 1989	33.0	29.0	22.0	25.0	34.0	35.0	27.0
Consumption	82.0	83.0	78.0	78.0	60.0	75.0	77.0
Accumulation[*]	18.0	17.0	22.0	22.0	40.0	25.0	23.0
Distribution of employment by sectors in 1989 (in per cent)							
Agriculture	19.0	11.0	11.0	19.0	26.0	28.0	18.0
Industry and construction	46.0	48.0	49.0	30.0	37.0	43.0	40.0
Services	35.0	41.0	40.0	51.0	37.0	29.0	41.0

NMP = net material product (see Table 4.1 for definition);
nd = no data available.
[*] Accumulation includes net investment, changes in inventories and the building up of state strategic reserves.
Source: *Statistical Yearbook* of the CMEA, 1971 and 1990.

which occurred in 1970–5. Eastern European countries and the USSR obtained large credits to buy Western machinery, and expected to repay these credits back by exporting the goods produced in the turnkey plants acquired from the West. The rhetoric of industrial cooperation epitomised this process. The oil shock of 1973 and the following Western recession was a major blow to these expectations. However, the policy of modernisation was pursued, with growing difficulties.

The contradictions of intensification

The Western recession was a convenient excuse for the stalemate of the intensification policies. These new industrial policies failed mostly because of internal contradictions.

- Priority to new sectors never led to a scrapping of the traditional ones. The military–industrial lobbies successfully resisted any weakening of the standard heavy industry. This industry was very energy-intensive, and became more costly to sustain in Eastern Europe when oil prices were raised within the CMEA in 1975. This led to a search for a maximal energy self-sufficiency, which implied a greater reliance on coal and had a disastrous impact on environment.
- Despite the official modernisation rhetoric, the link between innovation and its industrial application were very weak. The reforms could never counteract the built-in risk-aversion and hence innovation-aversion of the socialist managers, who preferred routine production that made the plan easier to implement and brought them more bonuses (Berliner, 1976).
- Export-competitive goods on Western markets were provided by mass production of intermediary goods (such as chemicals, steel products, textiles), and consumer manufactured goods of low quality. Incidentally, all these goods, which are not high-technology-intensive, are still the main export assets of the countries in transition. Though claiming that they wanted to develop high-technology goods, the Eastern European countries were very much behind not only the developed West, but also the newly industrialising developing countries.
- In the West, multinationals promote modernisation through intra-firm and intra-product trade. Eastern Europe lacked this powerful instrument. Despite continuing industrial cooperation with the West the socialist firms could not enter the networks of the Western multinationals, which used them mainly as sub-contractors. Thus technology transfers remained limited. One could only partly attribute these weak technological links to the Western Cocom-monitored (see Chapter 5) embargo on high-technology exports to the East, which no doubt played a role, adding to the inefficiencies of the domestic policies,

and to an almost complete lack of cooperation among the socialist countries in this field.

'Intensive growth' thus remained a propaganda concept. This concept was convenient in establishing both a continuity with the Stalinist period and a shift from the Stalinist model. It could be argued that the model had been appropriate up to a given moment in history but that it had to be abandoned at some point, though remaining within the same ideological framework. The Soviet Union also claimed that it could no longer sustain the original model despite its endowments in natural resources. However, the country was able to avoid any substantial change in industrial policy, despite the commitments of the authorities to modernisation: between 1973 and 1985 the enormous oil rent earned by the USSR (see Chapter 5) left the party leadership free to continue the wasteful use of resources. Significantly, the shift in policy occurred at the beginning of *perestroyka* in 1986, along with the fall in world oil prices.

The Non-European Variants

Cuba and the Asian socialist countries also adopted the Soviet model. This turned out to be still more disastrous than in Eastern Europe. However, such an error of strategy is not limited to the socialist world. Theories of development in market economies have also led to the advocating of strategies of industrialisation, and the dilemmas of balanced versus unbalanced growth were much debated in the 1950s. At that time most of the new independent countries launched 'industrialising industrialisation' strategies (to use the wording inspired by François Perroux) coupled with strong state intervention. The orthodox socialist approach to industrialisation was not at odds with these currents of development economics, and in any case raised much fewer objections in the West than its forceful imposition on Eastern Europe.

In *Asia*, *North Korea* embarked under the leadership of Kim Il Sung upon an industrial programme based on the ideology of self-sufficiency (called *dzhuche*), helped however by raw materials and fuels imports from the USSR, which the country could pay for according to a clearing system of settlements. This system worked until 1990 and allowed North Korea to compensate its imports with its exports to the USSR; only the balance had to be paid for in hard currency, after a grace period. *Mongolia* had initiated a strategy of socialist industrialisation after the Second World War, concentrating on infrastructure, but was also developing light industry and the food industry. The country joined the CMEA in 1962 and in 1971 was given the status of a socialist developing country entitled to special assistance from the other CMEA members in the form of special credits and preferential prices. Consequently the country developed the areas in which its partners were most interested, mining and processing non-ferrous metals. In socialist *Vietnam*, industrial policy was subordinate to the needs of the war and heavily supported by the USSR. After the end of the war and reunification of the North with the South, Vietnam joined the CMEA in 1978 and diversified its strategy for development, in accordance with its CMEA partners' needs. Development of agriculture and food processing, with a special stress on tropical products to be sold to the European CMEA members, and of light industry, was added to the continuous expanding of mining and heavy industry (steel, cement industry). Withdrawal of the CMEA and of the Soviet aid by 1990–1 severely hampered economic growth.

China officially abandoned the Soviet model in the beginning of the 1960s, following the Sino-Soviet split and the end of the Soviet assistance. In fact the strategy had already been altered in 1958 with the 'Great Leap Forward'. According to this slogan, production had to grow at a quicker pace than in the take-off period, by 25 per cent annually instead of the 14 per cent achieved in 1953–8. The strategy was to be dualist. While big investments should be completed with modern techniques, new jobs should be created only in small enterprises located in the country, with a low capital intensity. At the same time collectivisation was to be launched on a large scale through 'people's communes'. The Great Leap ended in an economic disaster in 1959–61, and entailed human losses estimated in the West at 60 million people. The cultural revolution floated a new slogan in 1966: 'to take agriculture as the basis and industry as the dominant factor'. Shifts of population from the country to the cities were stopped so as to fix people in the country. After Mao-Zedong's death in 1976 a new course towards reforms was taken in 1978. Here, too, modernisation was stated to be a main aim for industrial policy; it was to be sustained by foreign investment.

Cuba had launched in 1959 a programme of agricultural diversification that was meant to end the monoculture of sugar, and of balanced industrialisation, without priority to heavy industry. The US embargo in 1960, together with domestic policy reasons, impaired the implementation of this programme. In 1963 the priority was given to the growth of the output of sugar, which would condition the development of other sectors such as the mining and processing of nickel and cobalt, citrus production, later tourism, and the nuclear industry. This strategy could be successful only if Cuba could export sugar, and required support from the USSR. The first sugar agreement was signed between Cuba and the USSR in 1964 and renewed until the end of the Soviet system; similar, but less advantageous agreements were signed with the other Eastern European countries. These agreements allowed Cuba to export its sugar to the socialist bloc at subsidised prices against oil, machinery, and consumer goods, while letting the country sell sugar for hard currencies on the world market as well. The ending of these arrangements and particularly of the low-priced oil supplies from the USSR plunged Cuba into a deep economic crisis.

Non-European socialist countries have followed the Stalinist model with two specific features. First, it was not imposed on them in the same way. Most of these countries endorsed the model for ideological reasons, because of the commitment of their own leaders to their conception of Marxism, and 'nationalised' it (as in China with the Great Leap Forward, or North Korea with the doctrine of 'Tzhullima', the racing mythological war-horse). Second, in the case of the CMEA members and partly of North Korea, the continuation, with some diversification, of the strategy was very much dependent on Soviet and Eastern European aid. The ending of this aid in 1960 may have been a blessing in disguise for China, which was then forced to alter the model, albeit in an initially disastrous way. Assistance provided in the form of trade preferences and direct aid collapsed much later for the other countries, which had been inefficiently applying a model not adapted to their needs and economic profile for much longer.

THE CRISIS AND THE QUAGMIRE

Two distinct questions have to be answered. What was the nature of the crisis which hit the socialist countries in the 1970s and the 1980s, and could it be named a crisis to begin with? Was it the main cause of the final collapse of the system? Our contention in this book is that the economic situation was not the main reason for the failure of the system, though it certainly contributed to the collapse. This section will deal mainly with the socialist countries of Eastern Europe, and the USSR. The non-European countries followed a different pattern: they experienced economic difficulties as well, in part as a consequence of the withdrawal of assistance by the 'developed' socialist countries, without abandoning the political and ideological system.

The Economic Crisis

Table 4.4 gives the rates of economic growth in the Soviet Union and Eastern Europe since 1950. A similar trend is to be observed for all countries. Growth steadily decelerated, bouncing up a little in 1966–70 due to the initial impact of the reforms. The shift toward 'intensification' did not slow the deceleration. On the contrary, the trend toward deceleration and even an absolute decline of the NMP increased in the years just preceding the fall of communism (Figure 4.1).

Was this trend due to the impact of the Western economic recession following the first oil shock in 1973? A large literature had developed on this topic by the end of the 1970s (Neuberger and Tyson, 1980). This explanation is certainly true, among others, for the countries of Eastern

The Past: Real Socialism

Table 4.4 *Growth rates in the Soviet Union and Eastern Europe, 1950–90 (annual change of NMP, in per cent)*

	Bulgaria	Czecho-slovakia	GDR	Hungary	Poland	Romania	USSR
1951–55	12.2	8.1	13.2	5.7	8.6	14.2	11.3
1956–60	9.6	7.0	7.4	6.0	6.6	6.6	9.2
1961–65	6.6	1.9	3.5	4.5	6.2	9.1	5.7
1966–70	8.7	6.9	5.0	6.7	5.9	7.7	7.1
1971–75	7.9	5.7	5.4	6.3	9.7	11.3	5.1
1976–80	6.1	3.7	4.1	2.8	1.2	7.2	3.7
1981–85	3.7	1.8	4.5	1.4	−0.8	4.4	3.2
1986–90	−0.5	1.0	−1.8	−0.5	−0.5	−3.5	1.3

Note: Official figures are used here. These figures exaggerate actual growth, as has been shown for the Soviet Union in the discussion over the measure of performance in the beginning of this chapter.

Source: *Statistical Yearbook of the CMEA*, editions of 1971 and 1986; ECE/UN, *Economic Survey of Europe in 1990–91*.

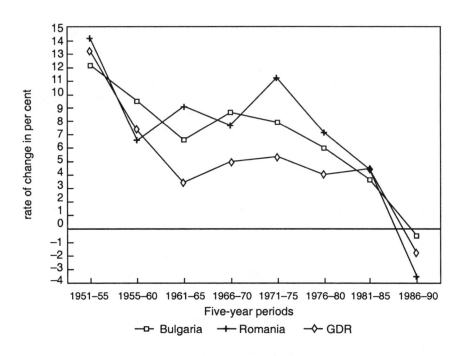

Figure 4.1(a) *NMP: annual rates of change: Bulgaria, Romania and GDR*

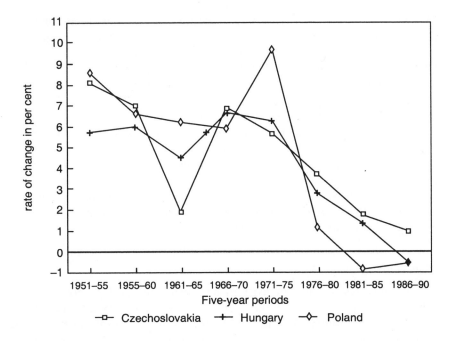

Figure 4.1(b) *NMP: annual rates of change: Czechoslovakia, Hungary and Poland*

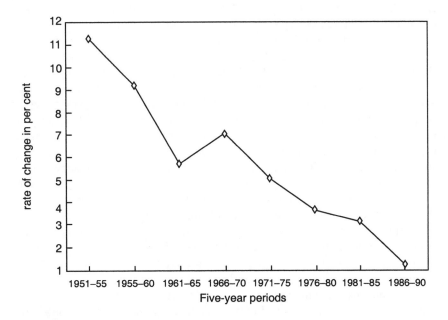

Figure 4.1(c) *NMP: annual rates of change: USSR*

Europe, which were hit through the deterioration of their terms of trade with the West, the increase of their trade deficits and the surge of their indebtedness in convertible currencies. As was already mentioned, the USSR benefited on the other hand from the increase in world oil prices, to which has to be added two indirect consequences: the increase in the incomes of the oil-exporting countries allowed the USSR to expand its arms sales to these countries, and the rise in the price of gold (also partly provoked by the Soviet invasion of Afghanistan in 1979) provided the Soviet Union with additional gains from gold sales.

Comparing the impact of the oil shock on capitalist and socialist economies, Western observers were mainly focusing their attention on quantitative indicators. Among the domestic indicators, the most significant were, in addition to the deceleration or decline in growth, the rate of unemployment and the rate of inflation.

Quantitative indicators

(1)   *Unemployment* did not exist in an open, measurable form. On the contrary, it was claimed in the East that these economies could face a shortage of manpower in the 1990s, due to unfavourable demographic trends. However, a large 'hidden' unemployment was to be found within the state enterprises, in the form of what Franklyn Holzman called 'over-full employment' (Holzman, 1976). Various reasons could explain why enterprises were induced to 'hoard' labour and to avoid lay-offs. Labour costs, though increased by taxes introduced in the course of the reforms, were not high enough to force enterprises to save labour. The main priority for socialist managers was to implement the output plan with least risk, and they knew that their enterprises would not disappear if their costs exceeded profits, because the bankruptcy laws were never applied even when they existed. All the hazards specific to central planning induced the managers to keep a reserve of manpower for various needs: to re-tool inadequate parts provided by the only supplier available according to the plan; to ensure repairs and maintenance, as there were no specialised services or subcontractors outside the enterprise; and to provide compulsory help to farms at harvest time. Very often a part of the manpower was just idle on the spot waiting for supplies to be delivered; when these finally arrived, all the workers were needed, working at full speed, to make up for the delay. It was often considered in the West that overmanning the enterprises was a deliberate policy to avoid unemployment. It was not – though full employment was indeed a goal. But the systemic features of central planning in fact had that effect, and the calls of the authorities for labour-saving practices by managers remained disregarded, even when the reforms were aiming at increasing productivity. A socialist manager was very much averse to job cuts, and this attitude survived after the transition.

(2)   *Inflation* as a process of continuously rising prices did not exist until the mid-1970s in the socialist countries. In the pre-war history of the USSR and immediately after the war in people's democracies as well, there had been outbursts of hyperinflation, which were mopped up by currency reforms. Apart from such cases of revolution-driven or war-induced inflation, the official price indices in the socialist countries displayed a remarkable stability. Was it an advantage of the system? Were the indices truthful? Did the absence of visible inflation prove the lack of inflationary pressures?

In '*classical*' Soviet-type economies prices were fixed by price offices. Thus they were expected to be at any level the authorities wanted them to be. The level of prices would change only when the methods of price-fixing were modified, or when for one reason or another the authorities decided that some categories of prices for some kinds of goods had to change: for instance, when in 1967 the Soviet authorities resolved to end the undervaluation of a range of producers' goods and increased therefore their wholesale prices. In such a system there could however be *hidden inflation* (Nuti, 1986). Official indices were not reliable. In fact, though enterprises reported stable prices, they often imposed higher prices on their clients, for two reasons. First, they were in a position to do that because of their monopolistic situation and the shortages of producers' goods. Secondly, they were interested in doing so whenever the output plan was expressed in gross value, because a price rise made the fulfilment of the plan easier to report. Retail price indices also failed to show actual inflation because they did not take fully into account the movement of free prices on the *kolkhoz* markets.

In addition to hidden inflation, there was *repressed inflation*, a much wider phenomenon still. Though incomes were steadily rising, the supply of *consumer goods* did not follow, and the adjustment could not be made through price increases as the prices were fixed and stable for all the goods sold in the state retail trade. Unwanted savings would then increase, and thus the level of the deposits in the savings banks could be considered as an indicator of repressed inflation. Once transition to the market had begun, the amount of money in saving deposits caused great concern, as it was thought that this 'monetary overhang' could create large disturbances – in fact, it was very quickly wiped off by the post-transition inflation. Repressed inflation could also occur in the *producers' goods* sector, for identical reasons. Here the gap between the steadily rising investment funds expressed in money, and the limited supply of investment goods, led to unwanted delays in implementing investment programmes. The programmes were initiated because they were planned on the basis of the financial means available; they were stopped because of the lack of corresponding material resources. They remained uncompleted for a long time; this was called in the official statistics 'unfinished investments' and could also be used to measure inflationary pressures. Finally one should take into account the hidden costs of undermaintenance and obsolescence.

In the *modified* or *reformed* economies *open inflation* began to show. Several countries decided to implement a policy of true prices reflecting the levels of production costs, by cutting subsidies to the consumer. In some of these countries this policy could not be sustained politically. In Poland the increase in retail prices was delayed several times after unsuccessful attempts (in 1970 and in 1976, each time because of protests and demonstrations already monitored by the dissident union Solidarity). It could be imposed only in 1982, after the Martial Law was put in force, and prices then rose by over 100 per cent. In Hungary, on the contrary, a continuing policy of controlled price increases on consumer goods led to an inflation rate of between 5 and 9 per cent annually during 1976–86, and allowed for a significant reduction of the shortages. Other countries applied sudden and episodic price increases (in Bulgaria, Romania, Czechoslovakia).

Finally *imported inflation* appeared on a limited scale after 1973, when in Eastern Europe some countries introduced a limited repercussion of external prices on domestic prices, so as to make the enterprises sensitive to the world price increases for fuels and raw materials, and to provoke a less wasteful use of these resources.

Qualitative indicators

Quantitative indicators were used to compare the situation in the West and in the East but remained misleading as they did not represent the same realities in both systems. In fact the rampant crisis of the system showed through qualitative indicators, such as the growing shortages, the low morale of the workers and the lack of incentives which would increase the propensity to work, the rising crime, and the development of the shadow economy.

Could all this be termed a crisis? No, if 'crisis' is defined as a sudden break with a previous state. Yes, if it means a continuous disaggregation and debasement which cannot be stopped by any reform. What were the prospects? The most probable according to Western experts was 'muddling through' during an indefinite period; alternatively, collapse was only one of the envisioned outcomes, together with a radicalisation of the reforms, or a movement back to some reactionary and totalitarian variant.

The Assessment

Is the socialist model of growth to be credited with some positive outcome? Obviously it has been very wasteful in human and material resources; it failed to achieve modernisation and left all the countries lagging behind the developed market economies. Could things have turned out differently? Though valuable and serious studies evidence, for instance, how Czechoslovakia and Austria were growing apart in terms of economic performance, it is impossible to prove how Czechoslovakia would have fared under a different regime; we would have to suppose all other things equal, while obviously they would not have been equal because of all the conditions involved.

Again, one has to revert to qualitative criteria. Why, to begin with, did socialism attract people in the developing countries? The answer is that the socialist policies were perceived as able to overcome extreme poverty and famine, which they actually did in China.

In the more developed socialist countries of Eastern Europe and in the USSR, socialism generated a specific consumption structure. Basic needs were satisfied, on a qualitatively low level: people could feed themselves, get housed (be it by sharing flats with other families), have access to health care, education, public transport at a low cost. Huge subsidies to this kind of consumption led to acute shortages, and to numerous parallel ways of overcoming these shortages as there were no market-clearing prices, and no real market to begin with. At the same time 'luxury' consumption was held back. The supply of consumption goods and services suffered from the low priority granted to these sectors in the growth strategy. Everything offered to the consumer was shabby, and the selection of goods was very poor. Neglected maintenance of housing and public services (hospitals, schools, etc.) led to an extraordinary depreciation of investment in the consumer sector. There was a pervasive rationing system, not so much through open administrative rationing, but rather through queues induced by the permanent shortages, or through bureaucratic regulation of the access to some goods such as cars or housing.

In principle these were egalitarian societies. Incomes were not very much differentiated. What really differentiated the levels of consumption and the standards of living was political weight or position, which gave access to better supplies or services; or the opportunities of participating in the parallel economy.

A high degree of security characterised the socialist societies, 'from cradle to grave'. Jobs were implicitly guaranteed, and the citizens of these countries just could not understand that in a capitalist country people wanting to work could not get a job. The wide range of free or quasi-free services was not perceived as an achievement of socialism, but rather as a set of mediocre and granted benefits. Looking at the capitalist world, large masses of people believed that if they were suddenly brought to that world they would be able to consume everything on display while retaining material security and reduced work standards proper to socialism.

There were no 'poor' in these societies, unless the whole population except the *nomenklatura* was to be ranged in this group. There were no wealthy either. Since transition began the privileges of the *nomenklatura* became better known. The residences for party members became hotels for foreign tourists; the living standards of the *nomenklatura* were complacently exposed in the media. According to Western European standards, their consumption opportunities did not exceed what is currently available in the West to medium-class households, though of course it was much over the ordinary people's standards in the East. Cases of pathological luxury such as the palaces of the Ceausescu family in Romania were exceptions. Any notoriously well-off style of living was suspected. *Nomenklaturists* and members of the mafia alike could never feel secure about their way of living, which had to be hidden and could end overnight by political or legal accident.

5 International Economic Relations

'Bloc' autarky is usually seen as the main feature of the foreign trade behaviour of the Soviet-type socialist economies. The framework for these mutual relations was the Council for Mutual Economic Assistance (CMEA, or Comecon, the better-known English acronym), which had been founded in 1949. Relations with other socialist countries accounted for 60 to 75 per cent of the overall foreign trade of each of the Eastern European countries by the end of the 1980s. The share was 62 per cent for the USSR, and 40 per cent for Yugoslavia though the latter was not a Comecon member. Except for China, Asian socialist countries also mainly traded with other socialist countries (with shares comprising between 70 and 90 per cent of total trade), and so did Cuba.

Trade with market economies always remained lower than trade within the socialist world. East–West trade took off and soared during the 1966–75 decade. It was stimulated by the international *détente* and by the modernisation policies carried on in Eastern Europe. After 1975 these policies were deterred by the impact of the two oil shocks, and by the escalation of a new cold war following the Soviet invasion of Afghanistan (1979) and Martial Law in Poland (1981). Trade with the Third World was in principle based on a political solidarity with countries following a 'socialist path of development'. It remained marginal, and increasingly subordinate to the economic interest of the East.

Autarky did not just mean that the socialist countries sought to achieve self-sufficiency, nor that mutual trade among them accounted for the greatest part of their total trade. Their systemic features entailed a 'functional autarky' which we shall analyse first, before turning to its consequences.

'FUNCTIONAL' AUTARKY

The phrase was coined by Franklyn Holzman (1974). It explains a paradox. While the USSR, a large country endowed with all kinds of natural resources, could indeed afford self-sufficiency, none of the smaller socialist countries could have survived without trading, not only with socialist partners, but also with the capitalist countries. Thus these countries never were utterly closed; moreover, they moved toward an increasing openness in the course of the reforms. However, despite their efforts, they could never become fully-fledged members of the international economic system, which their market economy partners expressed by labelling them state trading countries. In fact, state trading was just a part of this functional autarky.

State Monopoly of Foreign Trade

State monopoly was equivalent in the area of foreign trade to state ownership of the means of production. It had been established in Russia in April 1918 in the wake of the first nationalisations. In its traditional form to be found in all socialist countries up to the beginning of the 1980s, it meant that specialised state organisations were handling all trade relations with all trade partners (including partners belonging to other socialist countries). These FTOs (foreign trade organisations) were attached to the ministry of foreign trade and/or to industrial ministries. They acted like a screen between the foreign partner and the domestic enterprise. With the former, they dealt on the basis of international prices and in foreign currencies (either convertible or non-convertible depending on the trade zone). With the latter, they dealt in domestic prices and currency. They usually specialised in products and groups of products. Each country had forty to sixty such FTOs. The Soviet FTOs were very large and powerful. For instance, Soyuzneftexport which traded in oil was the single largest oil exporter in the world.

The traditional organisation

Western exporters usually complained about the constraints which were imposed on them by the FTOs. In fact this kind of organisation also entailed substantial advantages, which became better perceived once the system started to erode. The constraints were numerous. One could not deal with the final buyer; one did not know from the outset which FTO should deal with a given transaction. Once the right FTO was identified, the negotiations lasted weeks or months and were conducted in a bureaucratic style. These constraints as well as the large size of the FTOs actually prevented small and medium type enterprises of the West from getting access to this market. Advantages were however numerous as well. The rules of the game were fairly steady. The FTOs acted as monopsonies; there was no need to look for many potential buyers. Corruption did exist, but not on a large scale as compared with Third World practices. The FTOs' agents had rather modest requests and feared political control. These agents, though bureaucrats, had a technical level of competence which impressed their partners. They also knew very well how to foster competition among the capitalist sellers who wanted to win them over; for the exporters who lost at this game it was of course a disadvantage, but the firm that won the deal could often count on the loyalty of its partners, as the FTOs liked continuity in business. Once signed, the contracts were implemented and the payments made promptly. But once all deliveries were completed, there was again a black hole; Western firms were often frustrated by not being able to follow the operation of the equipments supplied.

The alteration of the monopoly

The domestic reforms that started in the 1960s also entailed changes in the state monopoly of foreign trade. In Hungary and Poland, just before the beginning of the transition to the market, a number of enterprises could trade on their own account. The FTOs themselves were turned into trade companies, which could export and import a variety of goods and were no longer confined to a narrow range of products. They also could have representations abroad, and engage in foreign investment. In the other countries, the FTOs became increasingly linked with domestic enterprises, or even integrated as trade divisions of the latter. In the USSR the reform occurred later, in 1986 and 1988, and was more limited in scope. In all cases, whatever the reforms, changes were not substantial. The domestic enterprises shied from engaging directly in trade, especially with capitalist partners. They were not used to having to search for new markets; when they had to import they preferred to rely on the skills of the FTOs. In relations among socialist countries, the reforming countries had to align with the traditional ones, and in particular with the USSR. A Soviet FTO would never agree to negotiate with a Hungarian or Polish enterprise instead of a FTO. Thus the most advanced countries could never totally control the pace of their reform; in the foreign trade sector they had to take their mutual dependence into account.

Foreign Trade Planning

Foreign trade was planned as any other economic activity. Let us look again at Table 1.1. In the standard material balance for a given good, imports were to be found on the resources side, and exports on the uses side. Foreign trade was a residual instrument for adjusting the balance. If planned domestic resources appeared to be insufficient, and if it was not possible to increase growth or to save on domestic uses, imports were required. Ways then had to be found of increasing some exports, looking at all the cases where domestic uses of planned production could be curtailed.

This approach has two aspects. First, foreign trade is treated as an activity secondary to domestic trade. Second, imports are given priority over exports: a country is supposed to export only or mainly to pay for imports.

Both features have not always been well understood, especially as the socialist rhetoric tried to obscure them. The advantages of international specialisation in the framework of the 'international socialist division of labour' within Comecon were upheld, especially following the adoption of the 'integration programme' of 1971. From the point of view of planning, this did not mean a departure from the 'residual' character of foreign trade; it simply meant that specialisation requirements had to be integrated into domestic planning, either as excess production over the country's own requirements for the goods it was supposed to specialise in, or as a deliberate discontinuing of production for goods to be imported from others. Specialisation was thus internalised, but never wholeheartedly as each country feared that its partners might well not comply with the commitments to buy, or, worse still, to supply. Khrushchev had been aware of this reluctance, and had rightly, according to the logic of the system, pleaded for some supranational planning to overcome this 'trade aversion' (Holzman, 1974).

The priority given to imports was obvious during the first modernisation phase, in the early 1970s, when one could speak of an 'import-led growth' (Hanson, 1982). It was apparently breached when Eastern Europe had to shift policies due to its rising indebtedness. By the end of the 1970s the catchphrase became 'export dynamism'. This new priority was not to be likened to the pressure put on Western firms to 'export or perish'. In the latter case the need for competitiveness spurs *firms* on to conquer foreign markets; the socialist countries were constrained by the lack of foreign currency, which meant that *countries* had to export first so as to be in a position to import later (Wolf, 1988).

Inconvertibility of the Socialist Currencies

The issue of inconvertibility in the socialist system has been very much discussed in the West, not always accurately. Some misconceptions have to be dispelled first. The consequences of inconvertibility will then be assessed, as well as the measures taken to alleviate them within the system.

Definitions and misconceptions

The currencies of the Eastern European countries and of the USSR were not convertible, in the sense that they could not be purchased or sold against other currencies at a single exchange rate without restrictions and for all purposes. The implied definition in this statement is a very extensive one. Sub-categories of convertibility may be distinguished, such as internal convertibility (for the residents of the country, including the joint ventures) or external convertibility (for the non-residents only); convertibility for current account transactions only, or for all transactions including capital account ones. There are few countries in the world in which currency is totally inconvertible. It would imply totally closed borders. Even in Albania, which may be termed the most closed socialist country in the past, foreign tourists were allowed, in organised groups; they could change their currency into Albanian leks to buy the few goods there were to purchase on the market. In other words, the minimum degree of convertibility is external convertibility for non-residents and exclusively for tourist transactions.

The usual definitions take it for granted that the domestic currency is always convertible into goods – that there is real, commodity convertibility. As we have seen, this kind of convertibility did not exist in socialist countries. In the production sector it was restricted through the administrative system of allocation in kind; money could be 'converted' into goods if the plan provided for it. In the consumption sector various kinds of rationing, as well as the extensive system of free or quasi-free goods allocated within social consumption schemes, also prevented money being able to buy what could be available to the consumer: money could not freely buy houses, cars, domestic holidays, educational or health services. Commodity convertibility, at high prices, existed fully on the free *kolkhoz*-type market, but on a limited scale due to the marginal size of this market. One has to add that the domestic currency was even not convertible into itself. As was mentioned (Chapter 1, p. 13), there was a dichotomy between 'consumers' money' (usually available only in cash as individuals were not allowed to use cheques, or scriptural money in general), and producers' money (available in principle only in scriptural form; enterprises could use cash only to pay wages, and these payments were strictly controlled). This dichotomy originated from different principles for fixing consumer and producer prices (see Chapter 4, p. 39).

The reforms in Eastern Europe moved closer toward commodity convertibility, which was however never achieved: it would have implied a free market, liberalisation of domestic trade and of prices, indeed the end of central planning.

The Western businessmen operating in the East did not grasp all that. One thing hindered them in their trade with their Eastern European and Soviet partners, and this was the demand for compensation or barter. Such demands intensified when the indebtedness of the socialist countries began to increase. To sell their goods, exporters had to buy back anything that was offered; often such goods were unexportable under normal conditions. Everybody then blamed inconvertibility: 'if these countries had a convertible currency they would not have to impose barter deals on us'.

The above argument is a macro-economic misconception. No country in the world is able to maintain a continuous trade deficit, except the United States of America whose currency is universally accepted as a world currency. All countries are very keen to restore their trade balance if it happens to be in deficit, and protectionist pressures result from this motivation. True, what is right at the macroeconomic level is not necessarily valid on the micro level. In a country with a convertible currency, imports and exports of a given firm do not have to balance as long as the overall trade balance is achieved. But in centrally planned economies the distinction between the micro and macro levels disappears or fades. Overall control is easier to achieve if each FTO is ordered to finance its assigned imports through equivalent exports by means of compensation.

The consequences of inconvertibility

Not only did inconvertibility hamper businessmen as exporters, or as partners in joint ventures willing to repatriate their profits or their capital in all cases when the joint venture did not generate convertible currency exports. It also reinforced the 'real' divide generated by central planning and FTOs between domestic and foreign activities. Inconvertibility went along with an official exchange rate which was a statistical unit of account used to convert foreign trade data expressed in various currencies, and a system of multiple exchange rates for various purposes. It had the following consequences:

- The planners had no means of selecting the best 'basket' of exports which would cover the required imports.
- There was no link between domestic and foreign prices. The latter could not influence the former in their overall trend, which was rather considered an advantage as it was a protection against imported inflation. They could not influence them in their structure either. The relative prices in the East were very different from the world relative prices. They were also significantly different among socialist countries. This is why, at the outset of the transition, convertibility was seen as a way of 'importing' a price structure close to the world prices. In the West as well, the price structures of the post-war European economies had been unified through liberalisation of trade and convertibility, and this example was often quoted.
- Though the domestic reforms should have created incentives for the enterprises to export on their own account, an overvalued domestic currency deterred them from seeking foreign outlets. This was partly remedied, through multiple exchange rates which aimed at stimulating the exports of selected products. But then a question remained unresolved: how to fix a proper exchange rate without freeing trade and lifting exchange restrictions?

Looking for a 'realistic' exchange rate

The reformers tried to find the 'right' exchange rate exactly as they had earlier tried to find the 'rational' price: they used sophisticated computations so as to provide proper signals to the enterprises and to the planners without introducing an actual market. Hungary and Poland set the pace (Liska and Marias, 1955; Trzeciakowski, 1978).

How does one find the right parity for the domestic currency? The different methods used amounted to estimating a purchasing power parity from a basket of exported goods. The value of a 'representative' basket where the exported goods were weighted according to their share in total exports was computed in domestic wholesale prices, and in foreign prices (the computation was made separately for the 'ruble' zone, and for the 'dollar' zone, i.e. for foreign trade conducted within Comecon in the unit of account of the organisation, and for trade in convertible currencies). The ratio of domestic to foreign prices yielded an exchange rate expressing the average amount of domestic costs required to earn one unit of foreign currency. A more refined computation was based on the marginal cost needed to acquire an additional unit of foreign currency.

Why was the calculated exchange rate not computed as a purchasing power parity for overall consumption, or GNP? First because the initial aim of such computations was to guide the export choices of the planners; second because the prices for many basic consumer goods were distorted by large subsidies differentiated according to the goods. Indeed, the exchange rate estimated from the general purchasing power parity (PPP) was substantially more favourable to the Eastern currencies than the exchange rate obtained from the specific 'export' PPP. Incidentally, this gap emerged in the early 1980s as a bone of contention between the World Bank and Hungary. The World Bank experts had estimated the GNP of Hungary using the general average PPP, which yielded a GNP per capita much over the upper limit of income allowing the country to benefit from World Bank loans as a developing country. The Hungarians contended that the specific PPP should be used, which put them under the critical benchmark. Their claim was accepted for political reasons, to demonstrate an international support for their reforms (King, 1991).

Though controversial, these computations were useful. They helped the planners in their choices; they provided incentives to the enterprises. But this was not convertibility. On the eve of the transition there were various rates to be found. In the USSR there was still an official, very much overvalued, exchange rate used only for statistical purposes. In the Eastern European countries the official rate geared to the Soviet ruble had been abolished in the 1980s, and replaced by a 'commercial' rate calculated as the average amount of domestic currency needed to earn a unit of foreign currency. Subsidies over this rate were used to promote exports, which amounted to using multiple exchange rates on a product-by-product basis. In the USSR, there were several thousands such multiple rates, called 'differentiated currency coefficients'. To this had to be added, in most countries, 'non-commercial rates' for transactions on services, and special tourist rates for foreign tourists. Hungary was undoubtedly the nearest to internal convertibility. Since 1976 it had abolished the official rate and introduced a single 'commercial' rate, which was unified in 1981 with the 'non-commercial' rate. Hungarian enterprises could buy foreign currency from the National Bank at the 'commercial' rate, provided they had enough domestic currency (forints); however, the Bank retained the monopoly for selling and buying foreign currency.

The quest for more accuracy in the field of foreign exchange was only directed to relations with the West. Intra-Comecon relations remained hardly affected, though they accounted for more than one-half of the overall foreign trade of the East. (See Figure 5.1; also Statistical Appendix, Table A.1.)

COMECON

International economic relations among socialist countries, and mainly within Comecon, not only accounted for most of their foreign trade, but also shaped the domestic economies by aligning the Eastern European countries on the Soviet model, and isolating them from the outside world.

How Comecon Worked

Originally the CMEA was a European organisation, created by Stalin as a response to the launching of the Marshall plan in 1947. The Communique on its creation (25 January 1949) was signed by the USSR, Bulgaria, Czechoslovakia, Hungary, Poland, Romania, and published in the party newspapers of these countries. Albania (1949) and the German Democratic Republic (1950) joined soon after. Albania unofficially left the organisation in 1961 when siding with China in the Sino-Soviet dispute. Legally, as the CMEA Charter did not have provisions allowing the expulsion of a member, Albania probably still could until 1990 have claimed its member-ship, surely a whimsical hypothesis . . . The organisation began to extend to non-European members in 1962 with the admission of Mongolia, a symbolic act designed to show that it was not confined to Europe and that it was meant to provide brotherly aid to underdeveloped socialist countries; Cuba was admitted in 1972 and Vietnam in 1978. No new member has been admitted since, and instead some applications were turned down, such as that of Mozambique in 1981 (Wiles, 1982).

Western journalists liked to call Comecon the 'common market of the East'. The Comecon was never a market, still less 'common'. Trade among its members was always negotiated and conducted bilaterally. Initially, the similarities in domestic structures of foreign trade planning and organisa-tion imparted a substantial homogeneity to this trade, which began to alter only in the 1980s when reform trends started to diverge.

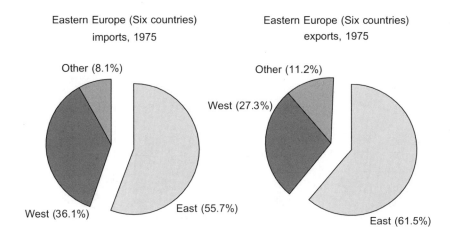

Eastern Europe (Six countries)
imports, 1975

Other (8.1%)

West (27.3%)

West (36.1%)

East (55.7%)

Eastern Europe (Six countries)
exports, 1975

Other (11.2%)

East (61.5%)

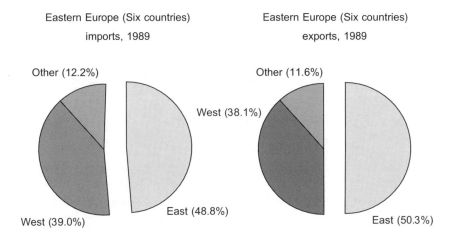

Eastern Europe (Six countries)
imports, 1989

Other (12.2%)

West (38.1%)

West (39.0%)

East (48.8%)

Eastern Europe (Six countries)
exports, 1989

Other (11.6%)

East (50.3%)

Figure 5.1   *Eastern Europe and the USSR: exports and imports by direction, 1975 and 1989, in percentage of overall trade*

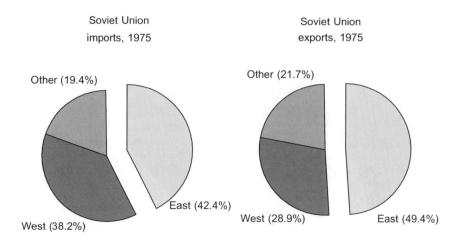

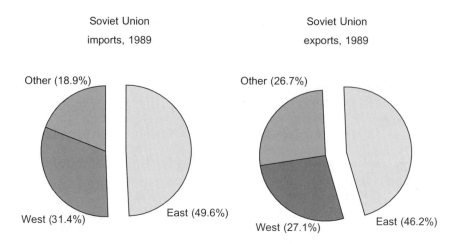

Figure 5.1 (cont.)
Note: 'East' refers to East European countries, members of the CMEA and the
Soviet Union.
'West' refers to Western European countries, North America and Japan.

Source: See Appendix Table A1.

Trade

The operation of Comecon was confined to a few rules that were absurd but necessary, because in any trading system one needs to have *prices* for mutual trade, and a *currency* in which transactions are expressed and settled. In principle, according to the rules defined in 1958, but which became operational in 1964–5 only, intra-CMEA *prices* were supposed to be based on the world market prices calculated as an average of the five previous years, and fixed for a duration of five years. The intra-CMEA pricing rule resulted in terms of trade following the long-term trends on world markets, which since the end of the Korean War were disadvantageous to primary goods exporters and importers of manufactures. Thus the Soviet terms of trade with Eastern Europe had declined by about 20 per cent in 1958–70 (Hewett, 1974).

Following the first oil shock on the world market in 1973, it was decided in 1975 to revise the intra-CMEA prices every year, but to go on fixing them as the average of world market prices of the five previous years. Actually the rule applied mainly to primary goods, for which a 'world' price could be identified. Thus the increase in world oil prices was passed on intra-CMEA prices with a lag. Price-setting for manufactured goods resulted basically from bilateral bargaining.

Settlements were made in a unit of account called the 'transferable ruble', whose official rate of conversion into Western currencies was close to the official rate of the Soviet ruble. There were no actual payments between the member countries. The International Bank for Economic Cooperation (IBEC), which was set up in 1963 when this so-called system of multilateral settlements was agreed upon, kept the books for each country; the amounts of its trade transactions were reported as assets or liabilities, and in principle it should not have mattered whether a given country's trade was bilaterally balanced or not as long at it was balanced overall. In fact each country tried to avoid maintaining a surplus in any bilateral relation; as trade was planned in each country, and organised on a bilateral intergovernmental basis, there were no 'free' goods available to be sold or bought outside the system of trade agreements. Thus, a debtor position resulted in fact in an automatic credit from the IBEC; a creditor position could not be used for buying, and could not be converted into another currency, as the transferable ruble was neither convertible, nor, despite its name, transferable from one partner to another.

International specialisation

Comecon was thus a fake market. It was supposed mainly to ensure *coordination of the national plans*, but it never managed to achieve that task either. The conflict of interests between the USSR and its partners may be considered as the main reason why plan coordination never began, and indeed Khrushchev, and later Brezhnev, failed to involve the partner countries in any supranational scheme, though only Romania balked openly. In addition, technically it would have been impossible to achieve it. There was no concept of a coordinated plan, no methodology of constructing one. There were very few multilateral specialisation agreements, short of some branches such as car manufacturing, nuclear industry, or computers (Sobell, 1984). Each country was reluctant to give up self-sufficiency because it mistrusted its partners.

The pattern which eventually emerged in the 1970s and 1980s is said to serve the Soviet interests while being disadvantageous to Eastern Europe. Is it really so? Yes, if by that we mean that the USSR could get large supplies of some finished goods (Hungarian Ikarus buses, Bulgarian forklift equipment, GDR railway wagons, Polish ships, Czechoslovak nuclear equipment) or parts (for instance for the Lada car, these parts being manufactured in each of the Eastern European countries in return for finished cars). But these goods were of a poor quality by Western standards, and the Soviet Union repeatedly complained about this. The Eastern European countries complained as well, arguing that goods manufactured to accommodate the Soviet needs were unexportable to the West. Should the Soviet Union be held responsible for the fact that it allowed its partners to dump on its market large quantities of otherwise unsaleable goods? This is a very common argument nowadays, on the grounds that the inefficient production structure of Eastern Europe originating from the Soviet pressure in the 1950s, which had imposed the Stalin-type 'extensive' growth model, actually made the East dependent on the Soviet supplies of raw materials and on the Soviet market for sales of goods processed with these materials. But then, who won?

How the East was Won

In the previous section we have seen that Comecon was just non-existent as an economic body: it was neither a market, nor a supranational instrument of planning. Had it any reality whatsoever?

Once more, we have to go back to the foundations of the system. Behind Comecon the communist party's monopoly was to be found, along with the dominant role of the Soviet party. The Warsaw pact (signed in 1955, to counteract NATO) expressed the same monopoly in the area of international security politics, and had indeed supranational military powers. While in the economic sphere Comecon itself was powerless, it was supplemented by summit informal 'conferences' of the heads of the communist parties, which always met just before crucial decisions to be taken by Comecon on its structure, charter, or orientations. In addition, Brezhnev used to hold successive bilateral meetings with his counterparts during vacation time, in a Crimean resort, to discuss economic as well as political issues.

Did that mean that political domination served the economic interests of the USSR? Whatever the intentions of the Soviet Union, the answer is no. This issue has been one of the most debated in the sovietological literature. Already in the early 1960s, in a several-year-long debate with Horst Mendershausen, Franklyn Holzman had proved that the USSR was not systematically discriminating against its CMEA partners through the prices which it charged them (by comparison with selling prices to the West) or the prices it paid them (by comparison with the prices paid to the West) (see Holzman, 1962 and 1965; Mendershausen, 1959 and 1960). The debate re-emerged in the 1970s, and after 1973 and despite the changes in the price mechanism made in 1975 the Soviet price for oil appeared to be much lower in CMEA trade than in trade with the West. The comprehensive econometric study by Marrese and Vanous (1983) showed that the particular pattern of Soviet export *and import* prices with the CMEA led to substantial losses for the Soviet Union in terms of forgone gains from trade with the West. Also, the study sought to evidence that such losses were a permanent feature of Soviet trade with the CMEA, and that they had only been exacerbated after the rise in world oil prices in 1973. What was significant here was not that the Soviet price for oil was lower than the world price (and remained so until 1985), but that the relative price of Soviet oil in terms of Eastern machinery was structurally much lower than the world oil price relative to Western machinery, once an adjustment was made for the low quality of Eastern goods. Table 5.1 summarises the issues of the 'subsidy debate'.

The authors felt that they had to explain such findings, especially because the amount of the Soviet 'subsidy' or 'indirect transfer' was so large, and because it did not fit with the traditional picture of the Soviet Union as the political leader of the bloc. The answer was then that the USSR was granting subsidies for 'unconventional gains' such as political and ideological allegiance and military security.

Eastern European authors have never agreed upon the existence of such transfers. The few of them who entered the debate argued that the level of prices was not a substantial issue. One had to look, they said, at the substance of the CMEA mechanism, which was in the long run detrimental to all partners because it perpetuated an obsolete production structure and isolated the CMEA countries from the world economy (Köves, 1983).

Thus Comecon was a negative-sum game: everybody had been losing. It no longer makes sense in elaborating on the various projects aiming at improving its mechanisms. The last project was launched in 1988, not just by coincidence at the same time as the drafting of the Single Market within the EEC. It provided for a 'unified socialist market'. But then it was already too late to save the Comecon, or too early to envision a new kind of union

Table 5.1   *The issues of the 'subsidy debate'*

Years	Price of Soviet oil sold to CMEA[1]	Terms of trade of the Soviet Union in trade with CMEA[2]	Balance of trade of the Soviet Union with the CMEA countries[3]	Variations of oil supplies to the CMEA countries	Overall impact (apparent subsidy)[4]
1960–73	>	−	+	increasing	+
1974	<	−	−	increasing	+
1975–85	<	+	+	increasing	+
1986–7	>	+	−	increasing	=
1988–9	>	+	−	increasing slightly	−
1990	>	−	−	decreasing	−
1991	=	+	− (deficit decreasing)	falling	−

1.   > = over world price (at the official exchange rate transferable ruble/dollar);
    < = under world price;
    = on the level of world prices.

2.   + = increasing terms of trade (prices of Soviet exports to CMEA grow faster than prices of Soviet imports from the CMEA);
    − = decreasing terms of trade (prices of Soviet exports to CMEA grow slower than prices of Soviet imports from the CMEA).

3.   + = surplus of the Soviet Union;
    − = deficit of the Soviet Union.

4.   'Apparent' means that dynamic losses of Eastern Europe (for instance, a distorted structure of economic activities, or the isolation from Western markets) are not taken into account.
    + = positive 'subsidy' from the Soviet Union to the CMEA countries;
    − = negative 'subsidy';
    = overall impact impossible to ascertain.
    (In all cases, with the 'official' exchange rate of the transferable ruble to the dollar.)

Sources: The literature on the 'subsidy debate' and in particular Marrese and Vanous (1983); Köves (1983); Holzman (1985); Desai (1986); Brada (1988 and 1991).

among Eastern European market economies. The blueprint of the 'unified market' thus not only failed to be implemented, it was totally discarded. The 45th session of the CMEA in January 1990 decided upon a quasi immediate shift to 'world prices' and settlements in hard currencies. The 46th session (June 1991) formally put an end to the organisation, whose legacy however would endure much longer.

TRADE AND COOPERATION WITH THE CAPITALIST WORLD

The world as seen by the socialist countries was divided up on an ideological basis. Socialism was pitted against capitalism. Capitalism in itself was not a homogeneous whole. Developing countries were meant to have priority, and among them the 'socialist-oriented' countries, initially called 'the countries following a socialist path of development', until too many of them had turned back on that path, such as Ghana, Indonesia, Egypt, Somalia and others. Finally, by political order of closeness, came the capitalist developed countries, which however were economically most significant to the East.

The South: A Costly Partnership

Were the socialist countries exploiting the South, or helping it? The commonly accepted view in the West is that East–South relations were just a variety of the North–South relations. Both displayed the same commodity pattern. The socialist countries were purchasing primary products at conditions which were not more favourable to the South in terms of prices or guaranteed outlets. They were selling manufactured goods, mainly equipment which could not have been sold to the West and was not adapted to the needs of the South. Nobody has forgotten the notorious case of the Soviet snow-ploughs sold to Guinea, back in the 1960s (Lavigne, 1988, p. 102).

Trade, not aid

Let us elaborate a moment on these snow-ploughs. They exemplify the routines of central planning and their impact on trade. In this case, snow-ploughs were part of a shipment of locomotives. In the USSR locomotives are always supplied with snow-ploughs in front. The Soviet plant had got an order to deliver the locomotives, from the FTO which was dealing with Guinea. It fulfilled the order, without any contact with the ultimate buyer, and was paid in rubles as if the goods were sold to a domestic buyer. It was not the least interested in what happened next: if the snow-ploughs were of no use, just take them away, no need to fuss!

In quantitative terms, East–South trade remained marginal. It never accounted for more than 1 per cent of world trade. It was concentrated on a small number of countries in the South. The ten top partners accounted for 65 to 80 per cent of total trade, the most consistent ones over time being Egypt, India, Iraq, Iran, and Libya. Imports were driven by the Eastern needs for raw materials, oil, food products, including grain in the case of the USSR. Prices paid were in line with world prices in all cases where they could be computed. Often Eastern imports from the South were used to repay trade and cooperation credits extended in kind, allowing Third World countries to buy Eastern machinery, and to realise big projects such as dams and power stations, steel mills, oil refineries, cement plants, developing of the mining industry. The big puzzle here was the amount of Soviet arms sales. There was a 'residual' between the amount of the overall Soviet exports to the Third World and the identified exports, in the range of 50 to 60 per cent of the Soviet sales to the South. This 'residual' was supposed to hide arms exports; the issue absorbed considerable effort from many Western experts, and was never completely clarified.

Initially the settlements between the East and the South were made mostly in clearing; by the end of the 1970s trade agreements had moved toward hard currency settlements except for Third World socialist countries and a few other exceptions, and trade with the South became thus a non-negligible source of hard currency for the East.

The major contention of the socialist countries was that trade in itself should be considered as an assistance, in particular because it was linked with cooperation that helped the South to industrialise and hence to develop.

A controverted assistance

Was this type of assistance really adapted to the South's requirements? Western experts denied it. The following points have been stressed:

- Aid was small as a percentage of the GNP. The most favourable figures computed in the West yielded shares of between 0.1 and 0.25 per cent, lower than the average share of the Western ODA (official development assistance) in Western countries' GNP, which was 0.35 per cent in the 1980s.
- Aid was small when compared to the Western ODA; it amounted to 10 per cent of it in 1985.
- Aid was extended on harder terms than Western ODA and contained very few grants. Eastern countries acknowledged that but contended that grants were a way for the West to get rid of its surpluses, and did not really help the South to start helping itself (the famous motto 'don't give thy poor neighbour a fish, teach him how to fish' was quoted *ad nauseam*).
- Aid was economically tied because it was in most cases granted in kind on credit, in the form of supplies of equipment and technical assistance by Eastern experts; the recipients could not choose and had to use low quality and inappropriate equipment.
- Aid was politically tied as it benefited above all the developing socialist countries: Cuba, Vietnam, Mongolia and Cambodia absorbed 70 per cent of total aid in the 1980s. When the socialist-oriented countries (Afghanistan, Ethiopia, Angola, Mozambique, South Yemen) were

added the share was 85 per cent. The political bond was enhanced by the fact that the USSR was by far the largest donor, extending over 85 per cent of the total.
- This aid was directed mainly toward the building of heavy industry, and induced the recipient countries to follow the socialist strategy of development, which turned out to be a wrong choice. Third World countries were also persuaded to increase their state sector and adopt a planning system if they wanted to get socialist aid.

This critical assessment was largely justified, though the USSR tried to fight the arguments put forward. In 1982, a large political offensive was launched in the UN, when the Soviet delegation claimed that its assistance amounted to 1 per cent of its GNP, without any serious evidence for it. Whatever the figures and the claims, the USSR, and ranking second the GDR, assisted such countries which without their help would have got no assistance at all. This was the case of the socialist Third World countries; following the collapse of the USSR and of the GDR, Cuba, Vietnam, Mongolia and some other 'client' countries were to experience great difficulties.

In addition, the USSR probably helped the Third World more than it wished. Data disclosed in 1990 have shown that the indebtedness of the developing countries toward the USSR, recomputed in dollars, amounted overall to over $66 billion, to which one had to add the transferable ruble debt of the developing *socialist* countries, of over 58 billion in dollar equivalent (*Izvestia*, 1 March 1990; comment in Lavigne, 1991, p.371). These figures may be inflated; in any case, most of it will not be recovered, though some agreements were later concluded with individual debtors such as India.

Which party was really less developed?

Should the East have helped the South at all? It was implicitly assumed that the Eastern European countries and the USSR were, if not 'rich' countries (a categorisation they indignantly discarded, particularly during the debate on the New International Economic Order in the 1970s), at least more developed than the Third World countries. In the USSR, at the end of the Gorbachev period public opinion had already begun to balk at the budgetary expenditures for assistance to the Third World: 'rather Baku than Kuba', the saying went.

The communist ideology required that the East should help the South; assistance was necessary so as to prove that there was an alternative to capitalism. The collapse of communism reversed the situation. Now, together with the South and in competition with it, the East is asking for assistance and getting it.

Such an inversion of roles prompts a question: What is under-development? Eastern Europe is poorer than the oil-exporting countries following the oil shock, and less technologically advanced not only than the newly industrialising countries of South East Asia but also than Malaysia, India or Brazil. Russia has natural resources and has achieved high-tech buildup in the military sphere but lags behind in civilian technology probably even more than Eastern Europe. The GDR, the 'jewel' of socialist Eastern Europe in terms of industrial development, turned out to be in need of an overall scrapping of its industrial capacities. Human capital is the only asset which seems to remain: the level of education and training of the population is the distinctive feature in comparison with the Third World, and even in this matter, South East Asia or Latin America offer the same advantages.

Eastern European countries in transition are not prepared to accept identification with the Third World. Communist propaganda unfailingly supported the demands made by the Third World to capitalist countries and sided with them in international fora. It consistently upheld anti-racist attitudes, while the general attitude of the public was rather hostile to Third World nationals. The people in the East had very little experience of living with racial minorities due to the small number of immigrants, if one excepts foreign students mainly from Africa, or occasional parties of workers as temporary migrants, mainly from Cuba and Vietnam. The collapse of communism engulfed anti-racist values as well. The countries in transition emerged as the new bastions of racism: ethnic tolerance is one more casualty of this story.

East–West Relations: War or Peace?

Has *détente* favoured East–West trade? The usual understanding is 'yes'. East–West trade soared with the emergence of détente, of which the first political sign was the trip to Moscow by General de Gaulle in 1966, and the most significant the German–Soviet treaty of 1970. It declined in the 1980s along with the new tensions with the USSR on Afghanistan and Poland. Actually this is an over-simplifying view. East–West economic relations always were what they are now, after the transition: an economic necessity for the East, a political asset to the West with few economic advantages and some very serious economic drawbacks.

Trade and détente

The East–West rhetoric obscured the fact that East–West trade has strictly followed the economic trends; it has prospered in periods of sustained growth, it has declined in periods of recession. The rhetoric culminated with the first Conference on Security and Cooperation in Europe (CSCE) which ended in 1975. Thirty-four European countries from East and West endorsed a Final Act signed in Helsinki. The economic 'basket' of the CSCE fostered trade and cooperation 'among countries with different economic and social systems', and hence the spirit of Helsinki became mentioned in all toasts and celebrations following the signing of trade agreements and contracts. East–West trade was also used politically in the West. Through 'linkage' or 'leverage' policies the West, and especially the United States, attempted to influence the USSR so that it would authorise emigration of the Soviet Jews, leave Afghanistan, allow the democratic process to unfold in Poland.

In fact East–West trade strictly adjusted to the economic interests of both parties. Trade flourished when these interests coincided. This happened at the turn of the 1970s when the Eastern countries decided to step up modernisation, and when the Western firms found a thriving market for the sale of turn-key plants. Even following the first oil shock, trade was still booming for some time, because Eastern countries' borrowing allowed the Western banks to recycle petro-dollars, and because the Western partners were confident that the USSR would never let its 'brother countries' down: this was the famous 'umbrella theory', which definitively faded out when Poland in 1981, then Romania in 1982, asked for rescheduling of their official debt to the governments.

The USSR, though it was the country most responsible for the political tensions that had developed in the end of the 1970s and the beginning of the 1980s, successfully expanded its Western trade. Here again the economic interests of the USSR and the West coincided. The USSR needed equipment to develop its energy resources and thus go on benefiting from the high price of energy carriers. It was the last large-scale buyer of equipment in the world when there was no longer a market due to the recession. Western Europe needed the Soviet oil and especially natural gas. The USA administration tried in 1981 and 1982 to block both the Western European sales of pipes and equipment for the Urengoy gas pipeline linking Western Siberia with Western Europe, and the purchase of gas by the major EC countries, and lost on both counts. At the same time, President Reagan in April 1981 recalled the grain embargo imposed on the USSR in January 1980 by his predecessor President Carter as a sanction against the Soviet invasion of Afghanistan, because the interests of the US farmers as grain exporters were in line with the Soviet interests as buyers. Soviet–West trade dramatically collapsed only in 1986, when the political climate had improved following Gorbachev's accession to power, while world oil prices had plummeted, which deprived the USSR of a large share of its hard currency gains.

All these developments show that political events, however dramatic, did not affect East–West trade as much as economic trends did. Could East–West trade have developed much more in the absence of any systemic barrier? Probably not. Lasting non-systemic constraints hindered this trade, and still do.

The limits to East–West trade

Western businessmen complained about *systemic* constraints such as inconvertibility, the monopoly of foreign trade, state ownership, central planning, red tape and political-bureaucratic interference, and restrictions in setting up joint ventures. All these were serious obstacles, along with the impact of the 'bloc' autarky which implied that the Comecon members were supposed to seek suppliers within the bloc first. Even for large Western enterprises the approach of the Soviet and Eastern European markets was not easy, and always remained rather 'exotic'. The systemic barriers acted as protectionist tools. The socialist countries either had no tariffs or did not use them except as bargaining instruments when they began to be admitted to the GATT. A tariff can work, i.e. prevent a domestic buyer from purchasing an imported good, only on two conditions: (i) if the importing firm has genuine autonomy in deciding what to buy and from whom; (ii) if the domestic prices of imported goods are linked with the external prices. Neither of these conditions existed, or existed only partly, as we have seen above in discussing state monopoly of foreign trade and inconvertibility.

The pervasive impact of these systemic barriers led to the conclusion that if and when they were lifted, trade with the West would expand. This was indeed the case, especially as intra-Comecon trade collapsed much quicker than expected, and was partly reoriented to the West (see Chapter 9). But the *structural* limits remained as they were. Here one has to differentiate the USSR from Eastern Europe. The USSR was a huge market for equipment and machinery; it sold commodities needed by the West, of which few (such as non-ferrous metals and aluminium exports, for instance) could hurt Western producers. For the West, Eastern European countries were not as attractive as the USSR. They were smaller markets; as suppliers they could only offer 'sensitive' intermediate goods, such as steel, textiles, chemicals, and food products, because most of their manufactured goods were not adapted to the Western demand and of too low quality (Table 5.2 and Figure 5.2). Their exports to the West were often contained by anti-dumping procedures; they were accused of selling at prices inferior to the 'normal value' of the goods in the GATT's wording, and they could not argue on the basis of their actual domestic prices because they were treated as state trading countries, with artificial costs and non-convertible currency. As will be seen later (Chapter 9) not much of this changed even after the transition.

Could the socialist countries have enhanced their competitiveness? They claimed it would have happened, had not the West erected a *strategic embargo* against them, depriving them of access to high technology. Embargo surely existed in the form of the unofficial CoCom (Coordinating

Table 5.2   *Eastern Europe and the USSR: commodity composition of trade with the West in 1990 (in per cent of total trade)*

Commodity groups	Exports to the West		Imports from the West	
	Eastern Europe	Soviet Union	Eastern Europe	Soviet Union
Primary products	28.5	23.1	15.1	23.6
of which:				
Food	16.9	2.4	10.0	20.2
Raw materials (excluding fuels)	5.1	8.9	4.3	1.9
Mineral fuels	10.7	56.5	3.2	0.7
of which:				
Oil	5.6	40.6	2.1	0.7
Gas	0.1	11.7	no imp.	no imp.
Manufactures	60.0	14.4	79.9	74.1
Semi-manufactures	21.4	9.5	22.2	22.9
of which:				
Iron and steel	7.2	2.6	2.8	6.3
Chemicals	9.3	4.4	14.4	11.9
Machinery and transport equipment	13.6	3.4	41.3	42.5
of which:				
Road vehicles	1.6	1.6	4.0	1.5
Transport equipment	6.8	1.0	11.2	10.9
Specialised machinery	4.8	0.7	21.5	24.1
Industrial consumer goods	25.0	1.5	16.5	8.7
of which:				
Textiles	3.4	0.4	6.4	1.9
Clothing	9.8	0.0	1.9	1.1
Total	100.0	100.0	100.0	100.0

Note: As seen from the table, the share of sensitive goods (food products, iron and steel, chemicals, textiles and clothing) amounted to 46.6 per cent of Eastern European exports on the eve of the transition.

Source: Computed from the data given in *ECE/UN, Economic Bulletin for Europe*, vol. 44, December 1992, p. 67.

Committee), established under the aegis of the United States and located in Paris in an annex of the US Embassy. The list of the commodities subject to embargo has been widened or scaled down according to the intensity of the Cold War. It reached its highest extension in the 1950s, then was reduced in stages until the late seventies and was again expanded in the early 1980s. Since 1949 CoCom had monitored Western exports of high technology to the East. But CoCom was rather more an excuse for the East failing to

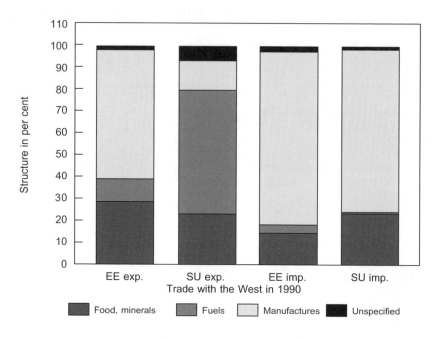

Figure 5.2(a)   *Eastern Europe and the USSR: commodity composition of trade*

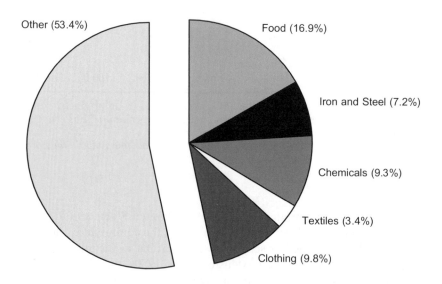

Figure 5.2(b)   *Eastern Europe: exports to the West, 1990: share of sensitive products*

control technical progress. The system itself blocked modernisation and innovation. For the West, the strategic embargo was a guarantee that everything had been done to prevent the USSR and its satellites from expanding militarily or economically, or, later on, to sanction them for their international misbehaviour. CoCom indeed survived the transition for a few years, and was only in 1995 turned into a new organisation no longer directed primarily against the former Soviet bloc. The new body, called the Wassenaar Arrangement after the name of a suburb of The Hague, includes Russia and the Central European countries among its members. It is meant to provide *a posteriori* exchange of information on sales of conventional arms and dual-use technology to certain developing countries such as Iraq, Libya, Iran, North Korea, and other countries engaged in conflict such as Yugoslavia or some countries of South-East Asia. The beginnings of this new forum were quite difficult because some of its members, namely Russia and the Czech Republic, still derive substantial amounts of export revenues from arms sales to these countries.

II

The Present: Transition in the Making

6   The End of the System

Why did the system collapse? Why did it collapse so quickly following the first jolt? In the 1980s it had become commonplace to predict that the system could not go on like this and was doomed. However, everybody was taken by surprise, even those who anticipated the ultimate outcome. I remember listening in 1990 to a lecture by Janos Kis, the Hungarian former dissident philosopher involved in political action after the beginning of the transition: 'Anyone who'd tell me to-day that a year ago he predicted what would happen is a liar. Anyone who'd tell me to-day that he knows where we are going to stand one year from now is a charlatan.'

Everybody now proffers his or her interpretation of the collapse. One may explain it as a combination of accident and necessity; of domestic and external causes; of economic and political determinants; as influenced by the West or as due to developments within the socialist system; as mainly attributable to Soviet policies or as imputable to Eastern European actions. Is it relevant to ponder on the causes, once everybody has agreed that the process is irreversible? Yes, and not just to please academics' longing for rationale. Understanding the causes may help to discern the directions of the transition process and its difficulties, and also to explain why non-European countries show a different pattern.

I believe that politics unlatched the process. The socialist economic system as it existed had been failing for a long time but might have gone on 'muddling through' indefinitely. Politics also explains why violence and war sometimes erupted, while elsewhere the process was softer. In any case a political event marked the beginning, whether we consider it the breach of the Berlin Wall on 9 November 1989 or the Polish elections bringing to power the first non-communist majority on 4 June 1989 – which was also the day of the shooting on Tiananmen Square that ended the students' Beijing Spring.

THE CAUSES OF THE COLLAPSE

What collapsed was the 'really existing socialism' whose foundations were analysed in Chapter 1. Only three years after the October Revolution, in 1920, Ludwig von Mises, the Austrian neo-classical economist, had predicted that the system could not work. Yet the Stalinist model strengthened and was imposed upon Eastern Europe after the war. With some changes it lasted for over four decades more. Then it crumbled with incredible speed. Why?

The Roots

If one looks at the way the actually existing socialism operated, once the political terror was lifted following Stalin's death there were plenty of reasons explaining why the system should collapse; but it didn't; so the question is, what made the system last?

Inherent economic flaws

For more than thirty years the communist leaders have been warning that the system was working inefficiently and that reforms were needed, with the well-known phrases about 'improving planning and management', 'increasing productivity', 'shifting to an intensive growth policy'. Western experts agreed on the inefficiency symptoms; they disagreed on the feasibility of a reform.

The following symptoms, or imperfections as they were usually called in the Eastern official parlance, were usually mentioned:

– growth was declining;
– productivity of labour and capital was low; output per worker was decelerating over time, and output per unit of fixed assets dramatically declined, especially after the mid-1970s;
– technical progress was implemented slowly, even when available, and the lag with the West was growing;
– the military buildup was absorbing a large part of the GNP, especially in the USSR where the CIA estimates put it in the range of 16 per cent in the 1980s;
– in the USSR, the agricultural sector remained backward despite gigantic investments, and could not provide food self-sufficiency;
– the standards of living and consumption were mediocre.

Such a state of affairs was explained by policy errors, and also by the external environment, of which the components were: the oil shocks (in the case of Eastern Europe this had entailed foreign trade deficits and a growing indebtedness: in the case of the USSR it had, on the contrary, created a bonanza that had dispensed with serious reforms); the Western recession that had made access to Western markets more difficult. The external political environment of the post-*détente* era was quoted as well. The Eastern analysts underlined the stiffening of high technology export controls; the Western experts stressed the military buildup in the USSR which increased the share of military expenditures in the budget and the GNP and prevented any improvement in the consumption level.

By 1985, just before the accession of Gorbachev to power, the Western experts offered several scenarios, referring to the trends that were then observed (cf. Chapter 3):

- continuing inadequate reforms as in the USSR, leading to stagnation or to an open crisis;
- the strengthening of conservative trends in the GDR and Czechoslovakia, with only cosmetic reforms leaving the central planning system intact; the system seemed more viable here due to a better standard of living than anywhere else in the East, and to better conditions for modernization sustained by powerful industrialist lobbies;
- market-oriented reforms in Hungary, Poland and to a lesser degree in Bulgaria, stopping short of actually introducing the market and discarding the plan and the bureaucracy;
- the status quo, for atypical cases such as the 'communism in one family' in Romania, where the populace was, amazingly to Western eyes, enduring the hardships imposed on it by the regime. Albania could be ranked among the last remnants of the Stalinist regime as well;
- finally, uncertainty in the case of Yugoslavia, a fake market economy, just enough committed to reforms to benefit from IMF packages, politically controlled by a very authoritarian party whose power was challenged by national–ethnic disputes; an expert aptly named it 'feudalised socialist mercantilism' (Rusinow, 1989, p. 59).

The global outlook, or most probable baseline scenario, has been summed up by the late Ed Hewett, exactly as most of his colleagues would have viewed it (Hewett, 1989, p.4): 'some reforms, and some changes in policy, both of which have a positive effect on performance; but nothing bold or terribly decisive. It amounts to "muddling through" with sufficient flexibility to avoid the most treacherous pitfalls, but with sufficient conservatism so that the more dramatic possibilities for improving the situation remain unexplored.'

Obviously there are many good reasons for explaining *post factum* why the system could only collapse. Among many others, a synthetic exposition may be found in Easterly and Fisher (1994). Both authors deride the very 'mistaken' assessment expressed in *The Soviet Economy: Toward the Year 2000* (Bergson and Levine, 1983), according to which there was scope for reform and resumption of growth in the USSR. They contend that the clue to the Soviet collapse must be found in the systemic inability to substitute capital for labour: thus, while capital was growing, labour force per unit of capital was not declining, and hence the rate of return to new investment had to decline to a level of near zero by the mid-1970s. Apart from the fact that this looks like a rather trivial explanation (besides, the point had been made earlier, and the authors pay tribute to Martin Weitzman for it; they claim that recently available data make it the more convincing), we still remain with the question: why did the collapse occur *so late?*

Political and social causes

The economic situation in itself could not explain why the whole system collapsed at a given point. Are, then, specific social and political reasons to be found?

It is not enough to say that the society had lost any trust in the regime. This had happened long ago. Communism did not represent moral values any more. The corrupted ruling class was despised; people saved their forces and efforts for themselves, and any attempt to 'mobilise' them for the socialist sector could only misfire.

Western influences are sometimes put forward to explain the collapse of communism. The masses began to have an idea of a 'civil society' and aspired to it. Again, this was not new. They had developed an idealised image of Western society through travelling to the West and from Western tourists, TV, and radio broadcasts. All these channels were not so easy to get to, but all the more effective. What spark set the fire ablaze?

The Start

The socialist economic system rested upon the monopoly of the party. Hence a breach in this monopoly triggered the collapse. It had to happen in the USSR. Whatever their disputes, the communist parties were linked by their solidarity for survival. When the legitimacy of the Soviet communist party was allowed to be questioned in the USSR, and when the Soviet party renounced support of that legitimacy in the 'brother' countries, any spark could set the fire. That happened soon after Gorbachev came to power.

Perestroyka

Though the last stage of the Soviet reform, called *perestroyka* or restructuring, raised immense hopes, it is not very relevant now. The economic programme launched by Gorbachev was remarkable for its weaknesses.

(1)   Two blunders were made at the start in 1985–6. First, the proclaimed anti-alcoholic campaign was fighting just one sign of public loss of morale; it incensed the people, generated crime, made speculators richer and the state poorer. Second, the catchphrase of 'stepping up growth' was strongly reminiscent of Stalinist parlance. Of course the external and internal situation had deteriorated: the people felt that it was only too easy to invoke at the same time the bad harvest of 1985, the Chernobyl catastrophe of 1986 and the fall in world oil prices, to demand an exceptional effort.

(2)   *Perestroyka* was announced in 1985, really launched in 1987, and stopped short of any radical change. In 1987 the enterprises got more rights

but remained under central command through the so-called 'state orders' which were central planning in disguise. Private ownership was not legally acknowledged. So-called 'individual activities' were supposed to be a substitute for private enterprise; their scope was very limited. The new law on cooperatives (1988) offered greater opportunities to entrepreneurship but these were mainly used in the services sector to launder mafia money. The leasing contract (*arenda*) in agriculture did not motivate the small minority of would-be farmers on their own, who dreaded a reversal in policy and the hostility of the other peasants. Endless administrative restructuring that was meant to simplify bureaucracy in fact created additional red tape.

(3)   Ineffectual as it was, *perestroyka* however managed to destabilise the Soviet economy and to create an open crisis situation in 1989. While prices remained fixed, inflationary pressures mounted, and the word 'overhang' became largely used to denote the gap between effective demand and available supply at fixed prices. The budget deficit was increasing, and rationing was being introduced in the big cities. At the end of 1989 the first stabilisation and reform blueprint was made public. This programme drafted by the minister in charge of reform, the economist and academician Leonid Abalkin, was to be followed by many others (see next chapter, Box 7.1).

(4)   *Perestroyka* did not imply abandoning either socialism as an ideology, or the party monopoly, though Gorbachev undertook to massively replace the party cadres. Western economists strongly criticised the concept of 'regulated market socialism' which expressed that stance.

Glasnost

Glasnost is a political concept that is hard to render in one word. Usually it is translated in English as 'openness' (Nove, 1992, p. 395) or 'public disclosure' (Lapidus, 1991, p. 141), with authors however feeling that it should be explicated. Thus it is described as 'a freeing up of access to information, the gradual erosion of censorship, and the progressive elimination of taboos on subjects that had previously been impossible to discuss in the mass media' (Dallin and Lapidus, 1991, p. 3), or 'encouragement of more open expression in public communication in order to mobilise support for the reform programme' (Remington, 1991, p. 97), or 'freedom of criticism, discussion and publication' (Nove, 1992, p. 396). In the field of economics *glasnost* had an immediate impact on the overall performance of Soviet workers. Their already low productivity went on decreasing as they were increasingly immersed in reading the papers and watching the television during working hours. Political pluralism was introduced in 1990 and the party's monopoly on power was ended explicitly in February 1990. However its implicit ideological monopoly was ended only in 1991, following the failed 19 August *coup* against Gorbachev. It is not so easy to date the moment when Gorbachev decided that the Soviet party would no longer interfere with the political changes in the brother countries' parties. In any case the process began with a double abstention. The Soviet party did not condemn the so-called 'Round Table' negotiations, which opened in February 1989, between the Polish leadership and the opposition represented by Lech Walesa, the president of Solidarity. It did not block the progress toward multipartism in Hungary which had begun in the first months of 1989. The transition could start.

Is this analysis exaggerating the 'Gorbachev factor'? One may also turn things differently. The Soviet communist party was no longer interested in its economic domination in Eastern Europe because the situation in the USSR had become economically and politically critical. The communist power then collapsed in Eastern Europe because it derived its legitimacy from the USSR, beginning with the countries – Poland and Hungary – where this power was already most eroded.

THE FIRST STEPS OF THE TRANSITION: CENTRAL EUROPE

Table 6.1 shows the stages of the political revolution in Eastern and Central Europe, which preceded economic transition. While in Part I we have merged all these countries in the phrase 'Eastern Europe', from now onwards we are going to differentiate among groups. One country will shortly go out of our focus. This is the GDR, which has been absorbed into the Federal Republic of Germany. The first circle of the transition comprises three countries of Central Europe: Poland and Hungary, soon joined by Czechoslovakia following the 'velvet' Revolution in November 1989. The second circle includes the Eastern European countries proper, a designation which we prefer to that of 'Balkans': Romania, Bulgaria, Albania, parts of the former Yugoslavia, to be joined in 1993 by Slovakia. (See Table 6.2 for the new geopolitical picture of the former communist Eastern Europe.) The case of the USSR will be discussed in the next section devoted to the final collapse of the socialist system.

The GDR: A Merger

The GDR was a symbol of maximum communist rigidity, and also of what could be called a 'success story' within the communist camp. It lost its political and economic identity in less than one year following the breach of the Berlin Wall (9 November 1989), first when the economic and currency union was implemented on 1 July 1990, then when the political union was decreed on 3 October 1990. The GDR became the five new provinces, 'Neue Länder', of united Germany. The area faced the same stabilisation and restructuring problems as the other countries. The German government swiftly moved on the stabilisation front (in fact the currency union was the most radical instrument of macroeconomic policy) and on privatisation. The latter was tackled by an *ad hoc* institution, the *Treuhandanstalt*, a state-owned holding company whose task was to restructure and sell East German assets or else to close the enterprises down, a process to be completed by end-1994. The Western part of the country devoted more effort to this task and many more funds than the total assistance made available to the remaining countries in transition. Apart from the financial burden, the material losses were huge: a large share of the productive capacities were simply dismantled as obsolete and harmful to the environment. Human costs were to be large as well: while the GDR population had one of the highest activity rates in the world (the share of working population to total population of working age was over 80 per cent in 1989), the rate of unemployment had already reached 10 per cent of the labour force in 1991. The developments within the New Länder are not going to be elaborated upon hereafter. The GDR is no longer a state, and it is no longer part of the East. Its transition has been a unique experience. Two lessons may be derived from this experience for the other countries in transition. First, even with favourable conditions such as extensive access to finance and expertise, the transition was painful for the East Germans: many lost their jobs and suffered a decline in their standard of living. Second, the transition process bypassed them: they did not take the decisions, and a very small part of the assets in their region could be recovered by them in the short run. The East Germans thus shifted from the paternalistic rule of the communist state to the paternalistic control of the capitalist state-and-business establishment.

The PHARE Countries

In July 1989, during the Summit of the G-7 (the group of the 7 most industrialised countries in the world), it was decided to empower the Commission of the European Communities with the coordination of assistance to Poland and Hungary. At a time when the transition was not yet perceived as irreversible, the purpose was to strengthen the commitment of both countries to building democracy and a market economy. The Commission then launched a programme called PHARE. (PHARE is originally a French acronym meaning: Pologne, Hongrie, Assistance à la Restructuration Economique. It may easily be transposed into English: Poland, Hungary, Assistance to the Restructuring of the Economy.) Both countries were clearly designated as the most advanced in their progress toward these aims. In 1990 other countries were added to the PHARE list: Czechoslovakia, Bulgaria, Yugoslavia, later Romania. The first two recipients of the PHARE aid kept their lead, at least in terms of total assistance received. Czechoslovakia claimed to be part of the leading group

Table 6.1 *The stages of the political revolution in Central and Eastern Europe, 1989–91*

Countries:	Bulgaria	Czechoslovakia	GDR	Hungary	Poland	Romania
Stages of the political revolution:	January 90: the leading role of the CP is abolished	November 89: the students and the people demonstrate against the regime (the 'velvet' revolution)	9 November 89: breaching of the Berlin Wall	October 89: multipartism is accepted by the party	September 89: first non-communist government	December 89: overthrow of the Ceaucescu rule; a national salvation government is formed
	June 90: free parliamentary elections		April 90: first non-communist government headed by L. de Maizière	March-April 90: the non-communist opposition wins the elections	December 90: election of Lech Walesa as Head of State (the only case of a direct election by the people in the countries in transition)	May 90: the National Salvation Front wins the parliamentary elections and Ion Iliescu is elected president of the Republic
	August 90: election of a non-communist president as head of state Zh. Zhelev	June 90: the non-communist parties win the parliamentary elections	July 90: economic monetary union with the FRG October 90: political union with the FRG	August 90: a non-communist head of state, Arpad Göncz, is elected	October 91: first free parliamentary elections	
	October 91: the non-communist opposition wins the elections to Parliament		December 90: first legislative elections in unified Germany			

Official launching of the economic reform:	February 1991: price liberalisation devaluation of the lev	September 90: adoption of a 'scenario of economic reform'	Beginning in July 90: economic and monetary integration within Germany	1989–90: continuation of the reforms already under way	January 90: launching of the first 'shock therapy big bang' (macroeconomic stabilisation, liberalisation of prices and trade, small-scale privatisation)	April 1991: the first reform programme, prepared as an IMF-agreed package, is launched (price liberalisation, stabilisation)
	October 1991: beginning of small privatisation	January 91: launching of a 'big bang' type stabilisation programme; beginning of small privatisation through auctions		February 91: stabilisation programme agreed with the IMF; continuing reform not embodied in a programme document		August 91: law on privatisation

Table 6.2   *The countries of Central and Eastern Europe: official names, population and territory*

Official name of the country	Area (thousand sq. km)	Population (in millions, 1990)
Republic of Albania	28.7	3.2
Republic of Bulgaria	110.9	8.9
Czech and Slovak Federal Republic	127.9	15.7
divided since 1 January 1993 into:		
the Czech Republic	78.9	10.3
the Slovak Republic	49.0	5.3
Republic of Hungary	93.0	10.5
Republic of Poland	312.5	38.0
Republic of Romania	237.5	23.2
Socialist Federal Republic of		
Yugoslavia	255.8	23.8
since 1991–2 divided into:		
Federal Republic of Yugoslavia	88.4 (S)	9.9 (S)
(Serbia[1] + Montenegro)	13.8 (M)	0.8 (M)
Republic of Croatia	56.5	4.8
Republic of Slovenia	20.3	2.0
Bosnia and Herzegovina[2]	51.1	4.5
FYROM[3]	25.7	2.0

[1] Including its two autonomous provinces, Vojvodina and Kosovo.
[2] Following the Dayton Agreements (December 1995) the country has been divided into two separate entities, the Federation of Bosnia and Herzegovina (FBH) which is ethnically Muslim-Croat, and the Republika Srpska (RS) which is ethnically Serb.
[3] The Former Yugoslav Republic of Macedonia. This is the internationally recognised name of the state, which calls itself the Republic of Macedonia, a designation that is not accepted by the international community due to the opposition of Greece.

in 1990, and indeed each of the three countries signed the so-called 'Europe' agreements on the same day, 16 December 1991, becoming thus 'associated' with the EC. They did not carry on transition with the same methods, at the same speed, with the same outcomes. What united them was their geographic position in Central Europe, their resolve to return 'back to Europe' as soon as possible, in line with their complete break with their communist past.

   (1)   The first steps on the way to the market had been made by *Hungary*, still under the communist rule. A bankruptcy law was enacted in 1986, though hardly implemented in the following years. A two-tier banking system had been introduced in 1987. The National Bank of Hungary (NBH) retained the right to issue money and perform the regulatory functions of a central bank. Several big commercial banks emanating from the dismantling of the NBH lending directorates and regional departments were extending

credit to the economy, along with new, smaller commercial banks which were set up by enterprises, local governments, and cooperatives, some them including the participation of Western capital. In 1988 the Company Law provided for creating joint stock companies, and in 1989 the Transformation Law allowed state enterprises to convert themselves into such companies. By 1988, all forms of ownership were legally on the same footing: state, cooperative including non-agricultural activities, private (with an upper limit of 30 persons employed in private enterprise since January 1988), and foreign (with 100 per cent foreign ownership permitted since 1 January 1989). In 1985–7 the economy was suffering from slow growth, low productivity, a growing rate of inflation and a large current account imbalance coupled with a rising debt service. In January 1988 Hungary introduced an austerity programme with the approval of the IMF. The programme was meant to curb domestic demand, to restore the budget balance and to generate a hard currency surplus in trade. At the same time a restructuring programme had been launched with the support of the World Bank, which was to provide funding for the implementation of a tax reform and for modernisation projects in agriculture and food processing. All the ingredients of a stabilisation-cum-transformation programme were already in place, under the aegis of a weakening and divided (among conservatives and a reform-minded majority) party.

(2)   In *Poland* the situation was catastrophic in 1989. Unlike Hungary, the political situation had been clarified following the Round Table agreements concluded on 7 April between Solidarity and the communist government. On the economic front, the programme outlined in the agreements provided for institutional transformation, along with a reallocation of investment toward the consumer goods sector, and of budgetary expenditures toward social sectors such as housing. At a time when price control co-existed with inflation, no detailed macro-economic policy had been devised. However, inflation was swiftly moving toward hyper-inflation, for four reasons: a large budgetary deficit (due to growing subsidies on the one hand and tax laxity on the other, with state enterprises negotiating tax exemptions with the authorities); a huge external debt; a current account deficit; increases in incomes not matched by increases in supply. The minister of Finance of the new government formed in September, Leszek Balcerowicz, an economist and academic, launched on 1 January 1990 a stabilisation plan which was to become the symbol of the 'shock therapy'. The plan was drafted by a team of Polish experts with the help of Western advisers including the Harvard University economist Jeffrey Sachs. This plan capitalised on the popular support gained by Lech Walesa, the leader of Solidarity which had won the elections of September 1989, and on the unconditional commitment to the free market by the government.

(3)   *Czechoslovakia* had not moved far on the road to transformation. The economy was still a standard centrally planned, state-owned and party-

controlled economy. But the current economic situation was good. External accounts were balanced, the economy was growing slowly but there were no dramatic shortages and the level of consumption and living was perhaps still higher than in the GDR. Prices were stable through price control, and there seemed to be no major inflationary pressures. The movement which had achieved the Velvet Revolution under the political and moral leadership of Vaclav Havel, the Civic Forum, seemed to have some margin of manoeuvre in launching a wide-scale, step-by-step restructuring programme rather than introducing drastic stabilisation measures. The economy was not over-heating and its main problems seemed to be how to modernise obsolescent industries and to free decision-making of enterprises once the tutelage of the party on the economy had ended. Nevertheless the 'shock therapy' model was chosen for reasons that will be detailed in the next chapter.

The *Eastern European* countries, *Romania, Bulgaria and Albania*, where reform started later and more hesitantly, share two features. They were less developed than the Central European ones. They remained for a longer time ruled by leaders close to the former political regime. Stabilisation programmes and transformation measures were launched later, in 1991–2, and hampered by lack of political consensus. Is there a link between a lower development level and the difficulties in breaking unequivocally with communism? The question may also be asked for Yugoslavia, where transition developed in the context of the civil war.

TRANSITION THROUGH BREAKING UP

Once freed from communism, the countries in transition sought to emancipate themselves from the links that kept them together in the past, and were only cemented by the communist party's monopoly. This happened both within the hard core of the communist bloc and within multinational states.

The Collapse of Comecon

Comecon and the Warsaw Pact organisation were dissolved almost at the same time in the middle of 1991. In both cases it was necessary to settle the legacies of the past, and decide whether something had to replace the former organisation.

The Warsaw Pact, created in 1955, was a military and political organisation. It deserves mention here only for the sake of comparison with what happened in the economic field. The main sequel of the Warsaw Pact was the need to repatriate the Soviet troops stationed on the territory of member countries. The repatriation schedule and the settling of the costs incurred were harder to negotiate than expected. Only in the case of the troops stationed in East Germany was the burden for both sides (the Soviet Union and the ex-GDR) supported by one stakeholder, i.e. Western Germany. In all other cases, Central and Eastern European countries (except Romania, which did not have Soviet troops on its soil) had to restore the land and the buildings occupied by the armed forces at higher costs than expected. The Soviet Union, later Russia, had to provide for jobs and housing for the military back from Eastern Europe, while the country itself was in crisis. No new system of collective security replaced the Warsaw Pact. In fact Eastern and, yet more, Central European countries would have liked to become part of Nato or associated with it, exactly as they wanted to be economically reintegrated within Western Europe. To this claim a very oblique satisfaction was given, when in 1991 the secretariat of the CSCE was moved to Prague with symbolic functions.

Comecon had to be liquidated as well. The Western world almost unanimously hailed the phasing out of the organisation, until the drawbacks of the vacuum thus created became obvious, much later.

The legacies: debts and assets

Once the decision to dissolve Comecon had been taken in 1990, all that operated within the organisation or in parallel with it was dismantled. Bilateral and multilateral agreements and programmes became void. The fate of the CMEA *institutions* was however not the main problem. Compared with Western similar international organisations, the CMEA had not developed an overwhelmingly large bureaucracy. Of course, dismantling its committees, standing commissions and institutes has created redundancies, but the impact of these lay-offs is small compared with the impact of the domestic reforms. *Financial* matters were more difficult to settle.

In the beginning of 1990, there was within Comecon a net debtor, the USSR, and a net creditor, the GDR, *vis-à-vis* all the other members of the organisation. The USSR used to be a structural creditor until 1986. Over the years 1974–86 the USSR had accumulated a surplus of about 18 billion transferable rubles (TR) in its trade in goods with its partners, which was a benefit to them as it amounted to a credit with a zero rate of interest, the TR being inconvertible and non transferable, as was explained in Chapter 5. This surplus had apparently vanished by 1988. To begin with, it might have been much smaller (according to their statistics, the partner countries recorded a cumulated overall deficit of 11 billion TRs for the same period). In addition the USSR was in deficit (for a non-published amount) in trade in services. Finally a part of the surplus had been rescheduled (as was the case in relations with Poland). In any case in 1988–9 the USSR had already accumulated a debt of 6.5 billion TRs, and was again to be in deficit in 1990.

The settlement of the Soviet balances was reached through bilateral agreements with the partner countries. The first to be concluded was between the USSR and Hungary in 1990. It was an interesting exercise in cross-rates. The most favourable arrangement for the USSR's partners would have been to have their TR surplus converted at the official IBEC rate, over-valuing the ruble, which would have enabled them to get a large amount in dollars; that was what they claimed, though in the past they had implicitly discarded this rate when fixing their own commercial rates. For the USSR it would have been most advantageous to benefit from the cross-rate between the dollar and the ruble that derived from the Hungarian exchange rate for these currencies, and that strongly devalued the ruble, something the Soviets had criticised in the past. The negotiators settled for an average rate just in between both claims (see Table 6.3). Similar agreements were to be concluded with the other countries in the second part of 1990. In fact, these agreements were all stalled in 1991. The Soviet Union and its partners disagreed on the outstanding amount of the debt, which had increased in the second half of 1990 and even in 1991. They also disagreed on the schedule of reimbursement, and on the interest rates. In addition, new claims on the USSR emerged in 1991 in relation to the Soviet military pull-out of Hungary, Czechoslovakia and Poland, as it was evidenced by the Eastern European countries that the damage caused by the Soviet troops to the environment, in addition to the other costs of the pull-out, was much

Table 6.3   *The collapse of Comecon: ruble/dollar cross-rates, end-1989*

Bulgaria	Czech.	Hungary	Poland	Romania	USSR	IBEC
1.9	2.3	2.6	3.6	1.6	0.6	0.67

Note: The cross-rates express the value of one dollar in transferable rubles (according to the commercial exchange rates of the various CMEA countries). In the Soviet–Hungarian case, the most favourable arrangement for Hungary would have been to have its 800 million transferable ruble surplus converted into dollars at the official IBEC (the Comecon Moscow-based International Bank for Economic Cooperation) rate, close to the official Soviet rate, overvaluing the ruble (it would have got 1.2 billion dollars at the end-1989 IBEC rate). For the USSR it would have been advantageous to benefit from the Hungarian ruble/dollar cross-rate, which would have yielded a 310 million dollars debt. The perverse aspect of the game was that each negotiator would have gained if applying the rules set by the other one (of course for other purposes). The negotiators settled for an average rate of 1.09 ruble for one dollar, which provided Hungary with 734 million dollars (this sum was meant to offset future deficits with the USSR).

Source: Press reports.

greater than expected initially. As these new claims cannot be assessed quickly this issue is bound to add lasting uncertainty to the settlement of Soviet–East European claims. After the collapse of the Soviet Union itself at end-1991, the Soviet liabilities were to be transferred to Russia. Most of them were not yet settled by 1994. Arrangements were reached beginning in 1995 with Poland and Hungary.

The other country to have surpluses on all its partners was the GDR. Here the difficulties of a settlement were compounded by the effect of the currency union between the FRG and the GDR, and by the peculiarities of the East German trade accounting. The outstanding East German claims, to be claimed by unified Germany in hard currency, amounted to 10 billion transferable rubles at the beginning of 1991, i.e. to about 23 billion DM, of which 15 were against the USSR, 2 against Poland, 1.7 due by Czechoslovakia, 1.3 by Hungary, 1.2 by Bulgaria and Romania each (ECE/UN 1991, p. 76).

The new rules of the game

As we saw in Chapter 5, it was decided in 1990 to shift immediately to world prices and hard currencies in mutual trade. The emerging pattern of intra-CMEA prices, as anticipated at the beginning of 1990, was supposed to be much closer to the *relative* world prices, with an increase in the price of primary goods in terms of manufactures. A reversal was therefore anticipated in the Soviet balance with the East: instead of the deficits observed in 1988–9 and expected for 1990, it was thought the USSR would obtain a surplus in convertible currencies, which experts had put for 1991 in the range of 10–11 billion dollars. These assumptions were made prior to the increase of oil prices following the Iraqi crisis in August 1990, which significantly increased the expected Soviet surplus even in the event of a reduction in the quantities supplied.

The assumptions for what was going to happen in 1991 were based upon two hypotheses. The first one was that the new system of prices and settlements would actually work. The second was that apart from this basic change in the rules of the game, all other things would remain equal and in particular the commodity composition of trade. Eastern Europe would still be dependent on Soviet supplies of energy, and the Soviet enterprises would still ask for Eastern European machinery and consumer goods.

The *first assumption* proved wrong. The shift to world prices did not play a significant role in the regional trade after January 1991. Prices were not relevant in the past because arrangements in kind mattered more than prices, for systemic reasons embodied in domestic mechanisms as well as in the international one. What happened once this international trade mechanism was dismantled? Trade in primary commodities proved to be largely inelastic to prices. The Eastern European countries would have bought more of Soviet oil had the Soviet Union supplied them, even at higher prices than before – though their demand for energy decreased due to the domestic recession in these countries. There is no evidence that the Soviet Union has reduced its supply for price considerations. The cuts, which reached one-third of the 1990 level according to the Economic Commission for Europe (ECE/UN 1992, p. 88), have primarily been the effect of domestic difficulties in the energy sector. They also result from the general chaos in the country and the disruption of the former command links, with sovereignty over natural resources being claimed by the Republics and even by the direct producers.

Trade in manufactures appeared to be much more sensitive to non-price determinants such as quality and performance than to price movements (meaning that even very large cuts in Eastern European prices for machinery would not necessarily dissuade Soviet buyers from seeking Western suppliers). But even more, manufactured goods exports from Eastern Europe to the USSR emerged as the major casualty of the new system of settlements.

The *shift to settlements in convertible currencies* was a crucial component of the new rules (Csaba, 1991). It was probably an illusion to believe that it could be immediately implemented. The legacies of the past suggested that transitory arrangements amounting to bilateral clearing in hard currency might be sought. The situation as it developed in the second half of 1990 and in the beginning of 1991 actually appeared very confused. Several bilateral trade agreements were concluded between the Soviet Union and its partners, providing for a transition period during which part of bilateral trade would be conducted on the basis of 'barter packages' of goods specified in 'indicative lists' (ECE/UN, 1991, pp. 79–80). But, pressed by its economic crisis, the Soviet Union had to secure hard currency from all its exports, and allegedly 'was unable to pay' for its imports. Hence the collapse in imports of manufactured goods from the East, which was indeed the major feature of Soviet–East European trade in 1991, and reached 50 to 70 per cent (according to goods) of the already depressed level of 1990.

The second assumption about what was to happen in 1991 was thus equally wrong: not only was the shift to the new rules not realised, 'things did not remain equal' as far as trade flows in volume and composition were concerned. Trade collapsed overall, and still more for the Soviet imports from Eastern Europe (manufactured goods) than for the Soviet exports (raw materials).

The most obvious solution was to look for bilateral arrangements with the Soviet Union and with the Soviet republics, particularly with Russia, Ukraine, Bielorussia and the Baltic states. By the end of 1991, there was a whole network of bilateral agreements and *ad hoc* arrangements involving, on the one hand, Soviet and republican agencies, and on the other, Eastern

European governments, banks, and business associations. An increasing number of deals were negotiated directly on the enterprise level though it was very difficult to trace them. To go further supposed an orderly disintegration of the former USSR.

The Disintegration of the Multinational States

Before its collapse the communist system counted three federal states: the USSR, Yugoslavia and Czechoslovakia. None of these three structures, though very different, resisted transition.

The Yugoslav case

Yugoslavia is a puzzling case. From 1985 it was classified by the United Nations as a 'developing market economy'. It had no longer any of the standard features of a planned economy, except the most crucial one: the monopoly of power of the communist party. Though the political life was far from democratic, the aura of the self-management ideology and the reality of decentralisation gave Yugoslavia credibility in international public opinion. The Yugoslavs themselves hardly understood how their compli-cated self-managed system worked. An opaque terminology described it, such as the 'self-management communities of interest', which were supposed to manage the social services, and the 'basic organisations of associated labour', which were linked in 'work organisations' (enterprises) through 'self-management agreements'. In fact the whole system was operating through networks of localist interests. The six Republics (see Table 6.2) and the two autonomous provinces of the Republic of Serbia (Vojvodina and Kosovo) benefited from the dismantling of the federal powers in the 1960s and 1970s, and this was again wrongly perceived in the West as an example of decentralisation, identified with greater democracy. It looked at the end of the 1980s as if Yugoslavia did not need a 'transition' proper, but rather a structural adjustment programme. Indeed a long-term stabilisation pro-gramme had been adopted in 1983 with the support of the IMF but was not implemented. In 1988 a new stabilisation programme was drafted, but in 1989 the rate of inflation was over 1200 per cent and social unrest in the form of strikes and political demonstrations was rising. The 'rich' Republics of the North (Slovenia and Croatia) no longer wanted to contribute to the development of the poorer ones. The Federal government and the party itself had lost popular support as facts about corruption and even huge financial scandals were revealed, such as the bankruptcy of the Bosnian food processing enterprise Agrokomerc in 1987 which shook the political and party establishment and evidenced the links between the enterprises, the banks, the local governments and the power.

The new Federal government which came to power in January 1989 launched in December a stabilisation programme which might be seen as an advanced version of the Polish shock therapy model, with the following measures: a restrictive monetary policy, wage control, the freeing of prices, cuts in budgetary spending, and convertibility of the dinar which was pegged to the DM. The party monopoly of power was abolished in January 1990 and the supremacy of self-managed social ownership was ended by a law on social capital in August 1990.

The programme failed due to the lack of political consensus among the Republics. Slovenia and Croatia began to move out of Federal, that is Serbian, domination throughout 1989 and 1990. Both Republics declared themselves independent in June 1991. At that time war had already begun. The disaggregation of the state was endorsed by the European Community which in 1992 recognised the independence of both states. The following story is one of ethnic war among, and within, the parts of the former Socialist Federative Yugoslavia, with an increasing involvement of the international community in words rather than in deeds. A 'normal' transition to the market could be pursued from 1992 onwards only by one of these parts, independent Slovenia.

The dismantling of the USSR

Western policy-makers and international organisations were taken aback by the disaggregation of the USSR, though many experts had long been warning about the looming burst of the Empire (Carrère d'Encausse, 1979). Gorbachev's international public image obscured the nationalistic and ethnic pressures, which first erupted in October 1987 into an open uprising in the High Karabakh, a little-known enclave inhabited by Armenians within the Republic of Azerbaijan. Centrifugal tendencies prevailed in efforts to rebuild a united community of nations.

Centrifugal tendencies. Very soon all the Republics and within them the ethnic minorities, whether or not endowed with a special regime during the Soviet period, began to claim various statuses (see Table 6.4) ranging from recognition, autonomy or sovereignty to independence. In 1989–91 all the former Soviet Republics declared themselves sovereign and/or independent, as well as the autonomous Republics in Georgia and Russia. The ethnic minorities began to claim some rights as well. According to the last census, in 1989 there were in the USSR 128 national minorities, and excluding those with less than 100,000 people they still amounted to fifty-six!

The West was not very happy with these centrifugal developments. As in the case of Yugoslavia, in the beginning Western governments and international organisations wanted to preserve some union. The Baltic countries were a special case as they had lost independence much later than

Table 6.4   *The former USSR and its successor states*

Name of the state	Area (thousand square km²)	Population (1990, in millions)
Former USSR	22,403.0	288.6
Estonia[1]	45.1	1.6
Latvia	64.5	2.7
Lithuania	65.2	3.7
Russia (Russian Federation)[2]	17,075.4	148.0
Ukraine	603.7	52.0
Belarus	207.6	10.3
Moldova	33.7	4.4
Armenia	29.8	3.3
Georgia	69.7	5.5
Azerbaijan	86.6	7.1
Kazakhstan	2,717.3	16.7
Uzbekistan	447.4	20.3
Kyrgyzstan	198.5	4.4
Turkmenistan	488.1	3.6
Tajikistan	143.1	5.3

[1]   Lithuania, Estonia, and Latvia were all recognised by the international community following the coup of August 1991 against Gorbachev.
[2]   The Baltic Republics, which were incorporated into the Soviet Union following the 1939 Molotov–Ribbentrop (Soviet-German) pact, were the first to declare independence, in March 1990 (Lithuania) and August 1991 (Estonia and Latvia). Eleven of the twelve remaining republics signed the CIS agreement on 21 December 1991 (see text). The remaining republic, Georgia, joined the CIS at end-1993.
Source: *World Bank Atlas.*

the rest of the Empire, and even in this instance it was felt that they should come to some understanding with the USSR, later with Russia.

In 1991 the Soviet economy was in deadlock. No federal economic programme was acceptable any more in the context of the conflict which opposed the president of the USSR Mikhail Gorbachev and the new president of Russia Boris Yeltsin, elected in June 1991. The anti-Gorbachev coup was at least partly triggered by the opposition of the old guard of the party against the union Treaty among the Republics which was ready to be signed on August 19, the day of the coup. The Republics were no longer paying their taxes to the federal budget. Some of them started to introduce their own currency. Inter-republican trade collapsed due to the general disorganisation of the economy and to autarkic tendencies which emerged in the form of custom duties, quantitative restrictions and embargoes resorted to by the Republics and even by smaller national units, down to individual cities. Privatisation could not be started as each Republic was claiming sovereignty on the assets located on its territory or even outside its boundaries.

The first recomposition attempts. The Russian president Boris Yeltsin attempted to rebuild a Commonwealth of nations, first between the 'Slavic' states (Russia, Ukraine, and Belarus, which was the new name for Belorussia), then between all the new Independent States when eight other Republics decided to join the new grouping. The CIS (Commonwealth of Independent States) was officially formed on 21 December 1991 between all the former Republics except the Baltic States and Georgia (which was to join later, in October 1993), and the USSR was officially dissolved nine days later. The CIS is neither a state, nor a federation, confederation or even a commonwealth (despite its name). It is a club of rather unwilling heads of state, engaged in conflicting relations (of which the most ominous opposes Russia and Ukraine over questions of nuclear security), and in variable coalitions.

Neither politically nor economically is the CIS heir to the USSR. The genuine heir is Russia, and this has been acknowledged diplomatically, as Russia has moved into the former Soviet embassies and in the Soviet seats in international organisations. How Russia would be able to conduct its own transition while compromising with its partners within the CIS appeared in the beginning of 1992 as the major challenge of the economic transformation in the former USSR.

The 'velvet divorce' in Czechoslovakia

This last case of a split within a state was a surprise. Nationalistic claims were considered in the West as non-existent in the Czech Republic and rather restrained in Slovakia. Federalism was indeed a Soviet creation following the normalisation process after 1968. But pre-war Czechoslovakia was an example of the few democracies in Central Europe, since the creation of the Republic in 1918, and until the partition of the state in 1939 forced by Germany. Was the split inevitable, beyond the devolution that had already occurred in 1990–2? The division between the Czechs and the Slovaks is rooted in historical, religious, ethnic and linguistic specifics, that are comparable to those which may be found in Western democracies, and that indeed sometimes lead to splits, especially when they are combined with inequalities in development and personal conflicts among politicians.

The Czech–Slovak break-up is thus rather atypical of the other cases of disintegration in the transition period. In these latter cases a common logic is to be found. The system had a centre which in the case of the USSR was Moscow and the Soviet communist party. The centre regulated inter-republican and inter-state relations through political influence. The autocephalous centre in Belgrade performed the same functions in communist Yugoslavia.

THE RESISTANCE TO TRANSITION IN NON-EUROPEAN SOCIALIST COUNTRIES

The non-European socialist countries managed their transition to the market in a very different way from the European ones, and also differed among themselves. Here are their particulars briefly summed up:

(1) The party remained in power; only in Mongolia were other parties admitted to participate in the elections held in 1990 and 1992. Except for that country, the communist party remains dominated by historic figures (Fidel Castro in Cuba), by family dynasties (in North Korea Kim Jong Il was the heir-designate to his father Kim Il Sung, and indeed moved into power when the latter died in July 1994), or by traditional oligarchies (in China and Vietnam).

(2) Except China, all these countries were linked with the USSR, either as members of Comecon (Mongolia, Cuba, Vietnam) or as recipients of assistance (all of the above plus North Korea and Laos). The severing of these links strongly disorganised these economies.

(3) In Vietnam, China and Mongolia the transition to the market has begun under the guidance of the party. Mongolia followed the Gorbachev model, then the Yeltsin model and shifted from a kind of *perestroyka* to stabilisation-cum-privatisation. In Vietnam and China, the reforms began at the end of the 1970s along similar lines in agriculture, on the basis of the so-called 'household responsibility system' in China and the leasing contracts in Vietnam, both allowing for large decision-making power extended to the family within a collective framework. It has dramatically improved the supply of food products. The private sector in industry and trade had been allowed to expand since 1979 in China, 1986 in Vietnam. The large state enterprises remain in public ownership and were still subject to central planning and bureaucratic control at the beginning of the 1990s.

(4) The opening of the socialist non-European economies to trade with non-socialist countries and foreign direct investment was both a boost to growth and an incentive to reform. In Cuba it was almost the only element of a reform.

The Soviet communist party has tried to impose the concept of a 'world socialist system'. This concept has collapsed as well. As was said in China in

1989, the year when the student uprising was crushed on Tiananmen Square, 'the centre of socialism has shifted to the East'. Is this specific socialism doomed as well? This may well be in the long run. In the meantime it is resisting substantial political changes. Tiananmen has been castigated in the West, but Western investors proved to be more confident in this system than in the uncertainties of any transition to a European style of government.

7 Macroeconomic Stabilisation

The transformation of the former centrally planned economies began in Poland and Hungary. These two countries were the first in the transition to democracy, and also the first to benefit from the international community's involvement in the process of transition through assistance and advice provided by the 'PHARE' programme.

As seen in the previous chapter, Poland was the first test case. The new policy-makers committed to the free market and their advisers rejoined in the feeling that a 'shock therapy' was needed immediately to stop hyperinflation, to cure the budget deficit, and to initiate structural reforms. This was the Polish 'Big Bang' launched on 1 January 1990 (see Gomulka, 1992). Similar packages were later devised for the other countries in transition, whatever their initial situation and their distinctive features. These packages basically applied the methods already experimented with in developing countries, with an enthusiastic or half-hearted endorsement by the policy-makers depending on the domestic political setting.

It was expected that the stabilisation programmes would restore external and internal balances in the countries, and also bring about a recession, which would bottom out in the one or two years following the inception of the programme. Then, it was anticipated, the structural transformation could really develop.

What happened did not meet these expectations. Even in the most favourable cases, i.e. in Central Europe (Poland, the Czech and the Slovak republics, Hungary, Slovenia), though stabilisation achieved some successes, they were below the initial hopes of experts and policy-makers. The supply response either did not follow or was greatly delayed. Output fell more than anticipated. Structural changes have lagged everywhere. In Eastern Europe (Bulgaria, Romania, and the three Baltic countries) as well as in the former USSR, though commitments to the same packages have been expressed, the outcomes have been much worse than in Central Europe. True, in these less favourable cases the stabilisation therapy has not been fully applied, or has been managed amidst political struggles and internal disruption.

How are these results to be explained? Should one blame the proposed cure, or its implementation, or was it just the price to pay for getting out of decades of communism?

THE STABILISATION POLICIES

Stabilisation policy implies a package of measures, which are linked with the beginning of a structural reform. The agenda of the reformers has everywhere been based on a similar menu. But decisions had to be made as to the sequence and the speed of the chosen measures.

The Package

The stabilisation packages usually consisted of the following measures:

(a) *price liberalisation*, through the reduction of subsidies to consumer and producer prices (with exceptions to be found everywhere for housing, utilities, and energy prices, that were to be freed several years later), and the deregulation of price fixing, going along with the *liberalisation of domestic trade*;

(b) *balancing the government budget* through increases in taxes; in particular, taxes on excess nominal wages have been introduced or raised, so as to fight inflation at the same time, see point (d), better tax collection, and cuts in government spending (beyond reducing of price subsidies);

(c) *a restrictive monetary policy* through an increase in the Central Bank interest rate so as to restore a positive real interest rate (in Poland new rates were even applied to old loans); a direct regulation of bank lending was also applied in most cases;

(d) in the beginning of stabilisation, *an incomes policy* aiming at stopping the inflation spiral (in Poland this was done through a weak indexation of the nominal wage during the first months of the stabilisation, and a tax on wage increases in the state sector; in Czechoslovakia an agreement among the government, the employers and the unions determined both the desirable level of decrease in real wages and the permitted rate of increase in nominal wages; in Hungary increases in nominal wages were controlled through a tax on the wage bill, coupled with alleviations if the enterprise succeeded in cutting jobs by the same ratio as the increase in the average nominal wage);

(e) *foreign trade liberalisation* through the lifting of export and import licences and quantitative restrictions, and the permission given to all enterprises to engage into foreign trade on their own, while state foreign trade organisations were dismantled; tariffs, which were meaningless in the previous system of administered trade, at the same time became 'active' instruments of trade policy, and were lowered so as to express commitment to trade liberalisation; *current account internal convertibility* of the domestic currency (meaning that domestic enterprises and up to certain limits households were allowed to freely buy and sell foreign currency for current purposes); *devaluation of the domestic currency* bringing it down to the (black) market rate, with differences among the countries as to the subsequent exchange rate regime, a fixed nominal exchange rate being usually preferred in the beginning.

Such packages were 'heterodox' stabilisation programmes that combined standard monetary and fiscal restrictions with several 'anchors' (Bruno, 1992, p. 752; ECE/UN, 1992, p. 43), which may bring to mind programmes applied in Israel or in Mexico. Typically stabilisation was anchored to nominal variables such as the rate of exchange and money wages, and to real variables (real money supply and/or real interest rate). Some authors distinguish stabilisation programmes between primarily money-based (I) and primarily exchange-rate based (II); each variant maybe associated either to an orthodox approach (A) or to an unorthodox approach (B), which would lead to a classification into four main groups (in IA one would find IMF-based programmes for Russia, Ukraine and Kazakhstan; initial programmes for Bulgaria, Romania and Slovenia would be ranged in IB; other Central and East European countries, including the Baltics, would come under IIB) (Bofinger *et al.*, 1997, p. 6)

Structural measures aiming at creating a private market economy were simultaneously put on the agendas, including:

(f) launching privatisation, and the dismantling of the former state monopolies; introducing free competition rules, free entry on the market for business creation, and a free, flexible labour market;
(g) setting up a market environment through the reform of the banking and financial sector and tax reform;
(h) developing a social safety net meant to replace the former all-embracing protection system 'from cradle to grave', and also to cushion the impact of the austerity measures and of the structural transformation;
(i) initiating an industrial policy so as to identify the 'winners' and 'losers' in the industrial activities to be restructured; defining the activities in need of support and devising appropriate policies such as subsidies, protective tariffs, etc.; taking care of the environment, at least so as to stop the damages caused during the former regime.

Among the measures aimed at structural transformation, those under headings (f) and (g) had to be immediately launched or at least announced so as to add credibility to the stabilisation packages. The two last groups of measures were looked at as much less urgent in the first stages of the transition. The need for a social safety net began to be reckoned with when the countries were faced with unsustainable fiscal deficits and it was necessary to find a way of financing social benefits, especially pensions, in the future. Environmental concerns were taken seriously inasmuch as they affected the interests or the safety of Western countries, and such countries as Ukraine or Bulgaria learned how to capitalise on these concerns for getting additional aid.

Tactical Choices

Once the strategy was defined, tactical choices had to be made. These choices raised hot debates in the beginning of the transition, which now seem rather irrelevant. The lack of experience of the policy-makers, coupled with the feeling that there was an optimal recipe to apply so as to move toward a market economy, may explain why the issues of sequencing, or of the choice between gradualism and shock therapy, were so extensively discussed.

The sequencing

Was there an optimal sequence to follow in the implementation of the stabilisation package? Considering the scope of the policies to be implemented, it seemed that the proposed measures should be introduced in some order, even if policy-makers were determined to move fast. A general consensus was reached on the point that stabilisation, coupled with liberalisation, should precede structural transformation. However the problem of credibility was seen as essential, so that even at an early stage announcements of systemic measures, such as a quick move toward privatisation and demonopolisation, were highly recommended by experts (see Nuti, 1991, and the survey by Jeffries, 1993, p. 336 ff.). In fact three issues have dominated the sequencing debate. They were related to the freeing of prices, to the liberalising of foreign trade, and to the financial sector reforms.

(1) The first issue in the sequencing debate was the *liberalising of prices*. There was a widespread concern about a surge in inflation, beyond the expected initial jump once controls and subsidies were lifted. Because most of the producers and retailers were large state enterprises, it was feared that they would behave as 'monopolies' and tend to increase prices to the maximum profit level allowed by the market, at the same time increasing wages and thus fuelling an inflationary spiral (hence the taxation on excess wage increases). In addition, common knowledge on the socialist economies suggested that there was a very high 'monetary overhang' in the household sector due to repressed inflation and shortages, and that all this excess demand would pour in as soon as the prices were freed. Thus there was some argument over the issue of demonopolising first, before freeing the prices,

and eliminating the overhang first as well. Both debates soon faded away. It became obvious that demonopolising could only go hand in hand with privatising and hence take time. Besides, as we have seen in Chapter 3, large state-owned enterprises could not be likened to market-type monopolies. Their initial micro-economic adjustments in the transition context were survival-ensuring rather than profit-maximising. On the other hand, the monetary overhang was everywhere eliminated much more quickly than anticipated through the price hikes, which wiped out households' savings.

(2) The second issue in the sequencing debate was *foreign trade liberalisation*. The standard package implied the opening up of the domestic market along with a strong devaluation of the domestic currency, and a current account convertibility. This had at least four advantages. Firstly, price liberalisation would be automatically coupled with competition from abroad, which would prevent the domestic monopolies from too sharp increases in their prices. Secondly, the distorted price structure inherited from the past would be corrected by an 'imported' price structure reflecting relative word prices. Thirdly, as an outcome of the devaluation, and provided a fixed or pegged exchange rate regime was selected, the exchange rate would provide a firm nominal 'anchor' for the stabilisation programme. Finally, a depressed exchange rate would deter imports, so that there would be no need for high tariffs at a time when more openness was required, if only to win the favours of the European Community (this fourth argument however contradicts the first: the higher the protection from devaluation, the less there is competition from abroad).

Despite these good reasons, the simultaneity of trade and price liberalisation has been questioned. It has been argued that excessive devaluation and excessive opening up of the economy exaggerated the initial price shock (Nuti and Portes, 1993), and that too early an exposure to external competition could devastate the domestic economy (McKinnon, 1992).

(3) The third debated issue relates to the *banking and financial reforms*. Though such reforms belong to the phase of structural transformation, the standard instruments of monetary and fiscal stabilisation require a two-tier banking system, which would allow the Central Bank to influence the monetary creation by the commercial banks through an interest rate policy. They also require a well-functioning, modern tax system. If the budget deficit is to be reduced, not only expenditures are to be cut, but tax collection must be improved, preferably with a new, sophisticated range of taxes combining direct and indirect taxation (Calvo and Frenkel, 1991). But if this is indeed a precondition to successful stabilisation, the lack of a full banking and tax reform will impair a successful monetary and fiscal stabilisation.

In the course of the reforms, the debate over the sequencing gradually subsided to the essential principle of credibility. Rather than the sequencing itself, the determination of the policy-makers to proceed with the announced measures was found critical, i.e. one moved from the issue of sequencing to that of *political credibility*. Thus the policies conducted in the Central European countries were opposed to those announced, but not systematically implemented, in Eastern Europe and in Russia.

The speed of the transition: 'big bang' versus gradualism

This issue, which was hotly debated in the first year of the transition and opposed the Polish and the Hungarian cases, has lost much of its interest, as soon as it was recognised that stabilisation should be conducted swiftly, and that structural reforms can only be implemented over a number of years, because of the change in institutions and behaviour that such reforms require.

The origins of the debate stem from the difference between the initial situations of the two first countries following the path of transformation, Poland and Hungary (see previous chapter). Stabilisation was obviously required in Poland, which in 1989 was plagued by hyperinflation coupled with shortages, by a large budget deficit and an unserviceable external debt (see Statistical Appendix, Table A.2). Hungary was also in need of stabilisation, but not with the same urgency. It had suffered from a high double-digit inflation since 1988, and the government budget had been in deficit since 1985, though the ratio of the budget balance to the GDP was improving. The foreign debt, which had been stabilised in 1982–3 due (already) to a stabilisation programme negotiated with the IMF, had again increased since 1985 and had become the highest in Eastern Europe in per capita terms, but Hungary went on servicing it and did not ask for rescheduling.

The issue was very soon influenced by Czechoslovakia stepping into the circle of the countries in transition, and selecting the shock therapy model under the guidance of Vaclav Klaus, appointed minister of finance in 1990. The implementation of the model started on 1 January 1991, less out of necessity as the macro-economic indicators were good (low inflation, low budget deficit, and very low foreign indebtedness), than as the expression of the political victory of the conservatives.

In fact similar packages were adopted in the three countries which initiated the transition. The same aims were set (to achieve external and internal balance) with the same instruments (a stringent monetary and fiscal policy). Though very close to standard IMF packages these measures were actually imposed by the governments which came democratically to power and which claimed full responsibility for their action, though acknowledging the role of Western advisers who had worked with the domestic economists (see Bruno, 1992, p. 743; Balcerowicz, 1995; Drábek, 1995).

Why then oppose 'big bang' and gradualism? The answer is political. 'Big bang' or 'cold turkey' programmes express an intellectual and political commitment to a monetarist, neo-classical vision, along with a willingness to radically break away from the past. The big bang is a kind of insurance against any temptation to look for a 'third way' (any version of 'market socialism'). The launching of the 'shock therapy' used shock phrases such as the famous 'one cannot jump over a chasm in two leaps', a very inappropriate wording indeed as what was in question was more like climbing a steep mountain than crossing a chasm. The choice of the shock therapy meant that the new government excluded any move back to the past, and capitalised on the political and social consensus so as to impose drastic measures which would immediately lower the standard of living, with the promise of a quick recovery, instead of a muddling through. The governments of Poland and Czechoslovakia had precisely this profile. However, in the case of Czechoslovakia and later the Czech Republic, 'important elements of a gradual approach can be found' (Hoen, 1996, p. 17) in the way the government tolerated the survival of loss-making enterprises so as to prevent a surge in unemployment.

Conversely, in Hungary, the communist power had already collapsed even before 1990 through internal divisions and was totally discredited, so that there was no need to exorcise it. On the other hand, the new coalition which came to power in 1990 was itself very divided and could not agree on a clear-cut programme; it was constrained by its electoral promises and by the firmly anchored feeling of the population that Hungary had already been on the road to a market economy for many years and need not suffer the sacrifices endured by other countries. That the whole issue is mainly a credibility problem may be evidenced from the fact that no transition government ever proclaimed itself gradualist. Hungary definitely applied a gradualist policy in the beginning of transition, with an undisputable continuity with the past reform trends, but its government never claimed to do that, and instead repeatedly declared itself committed to a quick transition to the market (on the policies implemented, and the ensuing conflicts with the IMF, see Csaba, 1995). Actually, in Hungary, a real 'shock therapy' programme was announced and implemented only in 1995, by the 'post-communist' government that replaced the right-wing coalition in 1994.

There was never a consistent theory of gradualism. While shock therapy concepts were widely advocated for policy-making (see, for instance, Sachs and Lipton, 1991; Winiecki, 1993a), there has been no specific plea for gradualism, only recommendations to the effect of softening the initial shocks whenever there had been an 'overshooting'. It would be a sheer misconception to confuse gradualism with the evolutionary approach, which is nonetheless often done (see Chapter 10). This approach is a complex set of theses dealing with institutional and micro-economic developments, not with macro-economic policies. Evolutionists do not object to 'big bang' type stabilisation *per se*; they object to the assumption that the market is supposed to exist already when it does not (Murrell, 1992).

Finally one has to mention the cases when there was neither shock therapy (as in Poland, Czechoslovakia, Estonia, Latvia or, in 1991–2, in Bulgaria) nor implicit 'gradualism' (as in Hungary until 1995, Slovenia, Romania and Lithuania), but rather 'a shock without the therapy' (Ellman, 1992) as in Russia. The various successive programmes announced and partly launched in Russia in 1992–3 were based on a shock therapy concept (if only to please the IMF and Russia's creditors), but were altered due to political conflicts between parliament and government, or between the government, on the one hand, and the Central Bank, various lobbies linked with the previous *nomenklatura*, and the regional forces and lobbies, on the other. As a result the measures outlined were never fully implemented: prices were not fully freed, credit was not really tightened, nominal wages were allowed to outgrow inflation, and the convertibility of the currency was fully implemented only in 1996.

The 'gradualistic' argument tends to support an alternative policy opposed to the shock therapy concept. The obvious case is Hungary, which explains why the 'gradualists' are frequently Hungarian authors (Köves, 1992; Ábel and Bonin, 1992; Szamuely, 1993). Gradualistic views have been expressed in 'big bang' countries by authors who did not share their government's views (Vintrová, 1993, for the Czech Republic), or who cautioned against over-optimism (Minassian, 1994, for Bulgaria).

The gradualistic line of thought usually stresses two arguments. The first one is obviously that shock therapy cannot apply to structural reforms: one cannot privatise overnight, even in the most radical give-away schemes; one cannot reform the banking system overnight. The second is that the beneficial outcomes attributed to shock therapy might have been obtained at a lesser social cost. Both arguments are rejected by the 'shock therapists'. Structural transformation does require time, they admit, but its efficiency is enhanced by a quickly conducted stabilisation. Nobody can tell whether the social costs of transformation would have been lower under an alternative policy, and in any case these costs may be alleviated by proper compensation schemes. The stabilisation packages experienced until now have all been very similar. The only significant difference among them has been the political resolve of their implementation, up to extreme cases such as Ukraine where the reform packages never really took off the ground.

THE OUTCOME OF THE STABILISATION MEASURES

We review the distinctive features and macro-economic outcomes of these programmes, and discuss the reasons why output fell to a much greater extent than expected.

The Main Features of the Stabilisation Programmes

The building blocks of the stabilisation programmes actually implemented are shown in Table 7.1. These are a combination of initial packages, changes due to domestic political events (new elections, change of government) or to external shocks (such as war in former Yugoslavia, the split of the Czech and Slovak Federal Republic), and alterations following agreements with the IMF. The former USSR is a special case. While the Baltic countries have embarked on stabilisation policies similar in design to those of Central Europe, most of the former Soviet space is struggling with problems resulting from the split-up of the country, the heavy legacies of the Communist past, and an erratic implementation of the reform packages. Most of the Western attention concentrates on Russia within the former Soviet space. Indeed what happens in Russia is bound to influence the whole area (see Chapter 9). Box 7.1 illustrates the vacillation of the Russian programmes.

Various forecasts have been made at the inception of the stabilisation programmes, by international organisations, or Western experts. Domestic governments have set targets in their programmes, with instruments to meet the targets, which are recalled in Table 7.2. The expected outcomes were the following: that inflation would decrease after a once-for-all sharp rise in prices following the ending of subsidies; that the budget deficit would be reduced; that the balance of payments situation would improve. Along with these positive effects a deterioration in real indicators was anticipated, with a drop in output, consumption and investment, but this was supposed to be a rather limited and short-lived phenomenon, with a quick recovery following the implementation of market-type policies.

Though actual outcomes differed, the general trend was in all cases a much bleaker picture than anticipated. Even when stabilisation was more or less achieved it remained fragile. Output declined much more than expected, and the start of recovery occurred later, even in Central Europe which offered the best prospects.

The Achievements in the Monetary–Financial Field

The aims of the stabilisation programmes were to curb inflation, restore the fiscal balance and improve the external balance. One can describe the actual outcomes as follows:

- an outburst of *inflation* followed by a stabilisation of the inflation rate, at moderate to high levels. Even in the most successful countries the inflation rate is still well above the Western European average;

Table 7.1   The initial building blocks of the stabilisation-cum-transformation
programmes in Central and Eastern Europe, 1989–94

Blocks of the transition	Hungary	Poland	Czechoslovakia (until 31 Dec. 1992)
POLITICAL REFORM: see Table 6.1			
PREVIOUS ECONOMIC REFORMS			
Type*	'New Economic Mechanism'	Reformed Soviet model	'Prague Spring' repressed, 1968
Dates	(1968; revised in the 1980s)	1966, 1973, 1982	Reformed Soviet model 1980–1
CONCEPT OF THE TRANSITION	'Gradualism'	'Shock therapy'	'Shock therapy'
MACRO-ECONOMIC STABILISATION	Restrictive monetary, budgetary and income policy launched by steps, 1990	Launched 1.1.1990; restrictive economic policy since then	Launched 1.1.1991; restrictive economic policy since then
PRICE LIBERALISATION	Gradual since 1975	January 1990	January 1991
DEMONOPOLISATION ('anti-trust' laws)	Anti-monopoly law in force as of January 1, 1991	Anti-monopoly office created in 1991	Law on the protection of competition (February 1991); Commercial Code (Jan. 92)
PRIVATISATION Restitution to former owners	Partial compensation	Very limited compensation	Yes (laws October 1990, February 1991)
Private ownership of land	Yes (June 1991)	Yes, since 1956	Yes (June 1991)
Small privatisation	Began in 1990	Began in 1989	Began in 1991 (law in Oct. 1990)
Large-scale privatisation	Began in Sept. 1990	Began in 1990	Law in February 1991
Main privatising institutions	State Property Agency (created in 1990); Hungarian State Holding Company (1992)	Ministry of Ownership Transformation (1990) usually called Ministry of Privatisation	Privatisation Ministries (Czech and Slovak) set up in 1990

Czech Republic (since 1 January 1993)	Slovakia (since 1 January 1993)	Bulgaria	Romania	Slovenia
See Czechoslovakia	See Czechoslovakia	Reformed Soviet model closely following Soviet changes (1965, 1979, 1987)	Specific centralised model (1967, 1979) deceptively called 'self-management'	Self-management Yugoslav style
Ultraradical reform continued	Previous policies with demagogy	'Shock therapy' concept; stalled implementation	'Gradualism'	Erratic combination of 'gradualism' and radical reform
Restrictive monetary and fiscal policy	Restrictive monetary policy, budget balancing relaxed	Stringent monetary policy, not enough consistent fiscal policy	Lax credit policies, ineffective fiscal policy	Cautious and effective fiscal policy, tight monetary policy
Price controls covering about 5 per cent of GDP in 1993–4	Some prices (energy, rents) still controlled in 1993–4	February 1991; energy prices and rents still controlled in 1993–4	3 stages (Nov. 1990, April and July 1991). Controls reinstated in 1993	Gradual liberalisation since 1991
1991 law amended in line with EU regulations (1993)	1991 law amended in line with EU regulations (1993)	Law on the protection of competition (May 1991)	Law on unfair competition	Law on the protection of competition (1993)
See Czechoslovakia	See Czechoslovakia Law on restitution to churches (1993)	Yes (1991 – land, 1992 – other assets)	Limited (laws of 1991 and 1994)	Yes
See Czechoslovakia	See Czechoslovakia	Yes (1991 and 1992)	Yes (1991)	Yes
Completed in 1992	Completed in 1993	Slow start in 1992	Slow start in 1993	Starts in 1993
Second round in 1994	Process stalled in 1993–4	Law in 1992; voucher scheme in 1994	Begins in 1994	Property Transformation Act (1992)
Czech Ministry of Privatisation, Fund of National Property	Slovak Ministry of Privatisation, National Property Fund	Privatisation Agency, State Fund for Reconstruction and Development	National Agency for Privatisation (laws of 1990 and 1991), State Ownership Fund, Restructuring Agency (1994)	Agency of Privatisation, Development Fund

Table continued overleaf

Table 7.1 continued

Blocks of the transition	Hungary	Poland	Czechoslovakia (until 31 Dec 1992)
BANKING REFORM (creation of a double tier banking system)	Since 1987; banking laws end 1991	Since 1987–8	Since 1990; banking law, 1991
SETTING UP OF CAPITAL MARKETS (opening of a stock exchange)	Budapest Stock Exchange opened June 1990	Warsaw Stock Exchange opened April 1991	Prague and Bratislava Stock Exchanges opened in April 1993
SOCIAL PROTECTION SYSTEM			
Unemployment benefits (in per cent of average wages)	Yes (70% first year, 50% following year) reduced to 12 months in 1993	Yes (in % of the minimum wage)	Yes (65% of the wage during the 6 first months, 60% the following months)
Minimum wage	Yes	Yes (periodically revised)	Yes
Indexation of wages (on the price index)	Yes, in the state sector; since 1990 tripartite negotiation on a national level	Yes (coefficient 0,6 since May 1990) until end-1992	Yes (indexation of the real wage)
OPENING UP THE ECONOMY			
Liberalisation of foreign trade (ending the state monopoly)	Complete in 1991	Complete in 1990	Complete in 1991
Single exchange rate	Since 1981	Since 1990	Since 1991
Internal convertibility	Since 1990 (de facto)	Since 1990	Since 1.1.1991
New laws on foreign investment	1989 amended in 1990	1988 amended in 1991	1988 law, amended 1992 Commercial code
Relations with international organisations:			
EEC (EU)	Association agr. (1991)	Association agr. (1991)	Association agr. (1991)
IMF	Membership in 1982	Membership in 1986	Membership in 1990
GATT	Membership in 1973	Membership in 1967	Founding member (1948)
External debt situation	Medium risk rating, no default	50% of official debt forgiven by the Paris Club with the London Club (1994)	Good rating

* Soviet model = reform based on some autonomy granted to state enterprises and on some market-type incentives, in the framework of a centralised planning system.

Czech Republic (since 1 January 1993)	Slovakia (since 1 January 1993)	Bulgaria	Romania	Slovenia
Czech National Bank + 25 commercial banks (not counting foreign banks)	Slovak National Bank + 17 commercial banks (1993)	Since 1987–90; banking laws 1991–2	Banking reform Dec. 1990, Banking laws April 1991	Central Bank independence October 1991, banking law Jan. 1993
Prague Stock Exchange (Apr. 93) RM Electronic trading system (periodic privatisation auctions)	Bratislava Stock Exchange (Apr. 93) RM-Slovakia trading system (periodic privatisation auctions)	Sofia Stock Exchange (Jan. 1992)	Bucharest Stock Exchange (1995)	Ljubljana Borza (1991)
Yes (reduced in 1993; max. duration 6 months)	Yes (reduced in 1993; max. duration 6 months)	Yes (for 12 months; about 60 per cent of average wage in 1992)	Yes (for 9 months)	Yes (max. duration 2 years)
Yes	Yes	Yes	Yes	Yes
Partial	Yes, partly	Yes, partly	Yes, partly	Partial
Yes	Yes	Yes (1991)	Yes	Yes (1991)
Yes	Yes	Yes	in 1992	Yes (8 Oct. 1991)
Yes	Briefly suspended in 1993	Controlled	No	Yes
No	No	In 1991 (liberalised in 1992)	In 1990	Law of Oct. 1988 liberalised in 1993–4
Association agr. (Oct. 1993) Yes	Association agr. (Oct. 1993) Yes	Association agr. (March 1992) Yes (1990)	Association agr. (March 1992) Yes (1972)	Trade and coop. agre. (Nov. 1992) Yes (Jan. 1993)
Yes	Yes	No (observer status)	Yes (1971)	No
Good rating	Medium-risk country	High-risk country Agreement with London Club (1994)	High-risk country	Good rating

Sources: General information on the reforms; the principle of the table and partly its construction are based on tables published in the *Economic Survey of Europe* in 1990–91 and in the following vols for 1991–92 and 1992–93 (Economic Commission for Europe, New York).

Box 7.1 *The reform plans devised for the USSR/Russia*

A. The Soviet period (1987-91)

June 1987:	Blueprint of *perestroyka* (radical restructuring of economic management) adopted by the Communist Party.
November 1989:	Programme for transition to a mixed planned market economy (Academician and deputy prime minister Abalkin's programme).
May 1990:	Government programme to a regulated market economy (prime minister Ryzhkov's programme).
August–September 1990:	Programme for a transition to a market economy (500-days programme), presented by a team working under the direction of Academician S. Shatalin.
April 1991:	Anti-crisis programme approved by the Supreme Soviet and presented by prime minister V. Pavlov.
June 1991:	Yavlinsky–Allison plan for transition to be implemented in five and a half years (G. Yavlinsky was one of the members of the Shatalin team; Graham Allison, a professor at Harvard University. Their plan was the basis of M. Gorbachev's discussions with the G-7 at the July 1991 Summit).

B. The Russian reforms (1992–8)

The Gaidar-Yeltsin reform (January-February 1992 and later adjustments)

(a) *Building blocks* (Stabilisation Programme of 2 January 1992 and February 1992 Memorandum of Economic Policy, prepared to win the approval of the IMF, actually granted in April 1992):

   – Liberalising of prices as of 2 January 1992 (for 90 per cent of consumers' prices and 80 per cent of producers' prices). Prices of basic food items, medicines and rents remain controlled for the consumers, and energy prices for the producers.
   – Liberalisation of domestic trade.
   – Stringent monetary policy announced, based on high interest rates.
   – Budget expenditures cuts (defence spending, subsidies).
   – Minimum wage and pensions regulation; no incomes policy.
   – VAT introduced first at a rate of 28 per cent, then lowered to 15 per cent.
   – Privatisation programme to be started (decree of 29 December 1991).
   – Single fixed exchange rate to be introduced for the ruble by April 1992.
   – Liberalising of foreign trade, except for energy carriers, the exports of which are to be regulated by quotas.
   – Principle of close and liberalised economic relations between Russia and the former republics of the USSR.

(b) *Implementation in 1992–3*

- Implementation conducted first by a Gaidar-inspired government (Gaidar himself appointed prime minister in June 1992), then by the Chernomyrdin government, supported by the lobby of the 'industrialists', since December 1992.
- Political resistance to the complete freeing of prices and social pressure for wages increases (including minimum wages).
- Liberalisation of small-scale trade (street vending) completed though marred by racketeering and crime; large-scale retail trade and wholesale trade still monopolised.
- Lax monetary policy of the Central Russian Bank since mid-1992; negative real interest rates until end-1993.
- Budgetary targets not met; deficit rising from 1.5 per cent of GDP in first quarter to over 20 per cent by the end of 1992; substantial tax evasion.
- A unified rate is introduced in July 1992 but the enterprises still have to surrender part of their currency earnings at a special, less advantageous, rate; the single exchange rate is floating and grossly undervalued (average monthly wage expressed in US dollars is 8.9 in 1992).
- Limited trade liberalisation; discretionary licence system remains.
- Small privatisation conducted at a quick pace; large-scale privatisation beginning in October 1992 with a 'voucher' scheme. Land privatisation halted due to lack of a law on private property of land (the law is adopted only in October 1993).
- Monetary disintegration of the CIS area, and disruption of trade flows.

(c) *New reform attempts and patching up of programmes (end-1993 to 1994)*

- October 1993: Gaidar team back in power after Yeltsin's storming of the Parliament building; the building blocks of the 1992 programme are reassessed and tough monetary and budgetary policies are applied.
- December 1993: following the parliamentary elections and the defeat of the reformers, Gaidar and his team are pushed out of office; Chernomyrdin however continues the line of previous Gaidar monetary and budgetary policies.
- Monetary policy overshot, real interest rate reaches 8 per cent a month in April 1994.
- Budgetary policy fails target; ratio deficit/GNP exceeds 10 per cent during first quarter.
- July 1994: second phase (cash-based) of privatisation beginning.
- Some attempts at reintegration within the CIS.
- October 1994: the ruble depreciates by 27 per cent against the dollar.
- December 1994: the war against the Chechen Republic is declared.

(d) *Slow and uneven progress in transformation* (1995-8)

- Two economic programmes for reform, restructuring and growth (1995–7 and 1997–2000) confirm the previous trends.
- Inflation is brought down to 11 per cent (end-year annual rate); the ratio budget deficit/GDP remains high at 8 per cent in 1997.

- Fall in output comes to a stop in 1997 with 0.4 per cent growth of GDP.
- Yeltsin re-elected July 1996; Chechen war ends in August 1996.
- Foreign debt owed to governments rescheduled by the Paris Club of official creditors in 1996; debt owed to foreign banks rescheduled by the London Club in October 1997.
- Structural transformation is slow; large-scale privatisation is marred by scandals and government inability to control monopolies; recurrent strikes react to the non-payment of wages; the tax code is not yet adopted as of beginning 1998.
- March 1998: prime minister (since 1992) Chernomyrdin is fired and replaced in April by a young technocrat, Sergey Kiriyenko.
- February–March 1998: exchange rate of ruble falls; large capital outflows due to political and economic uncertainties.
- April–May 1998: outburst of financial crisis, fought by increased interest rates and tight monetary and fiscal policy.
- 17 August 1998: the ruble is devalued by 34 per cent, falling from about 6.3 rubles to the dollar to 9.5 rubles. A restructuring of the domestic debt is announced and part of the foreign debt is frozen for 90 days. In the following days the currency slips to 14 rubles to a dollar and the stock exchange index plunges 25 per cent. The Central Bank of Russia stops keeping the exchange rate of the ruble within the limits of the sliding currency corridor (6.0–9.5).
- 23 August 1998: President Yeltsin dismisses the government and appoints Viktor Chernomyrdin acting Prime Minister.
- 11 September 1998: After having twice refused to endorse the appointment of Chernomyrdin, the Duma votes for the minister of Foreign Affairs Evgeni Primakov as Prime Minister. This is seen as a victory of the Communist Party and announces a change from market-oriented policies towards more dirigist ones. Ruble falls to R20 for 1USD. Monthly inflation is 38 per cent in September and is expected to reach 80–100 per cent for the year 1998 due to money printing. GDP declines by 9.9 per cent compared with September 1997.

Source: 'Stabilization, Liberalization and Devolution: Assessment of the Economic Situation and Reform Process in the Soviet Union', *European Economy*, no 45, December 1990; for the Russian reform, press reports and OECD (1997b).

- great difficulties in maintaining the budgetary *deficit* at 'acceptable' (as defined in IMF packages) levels, with some exceptions (such as the Czech Republic, Slovakia, Slovenia);
- successful *exchange rate stabilisation*; deterioration of foreign trade and current account balances; emerging problems with short-term capital inflows.

Inflation

In most of the countries *inflation* remains high. Tax measures such as the introduction of VAT led to a rebound of inflation in all the countries that resorted to this measure (see Table 7.2). Despite the fact that overall *managed "low" inflation* inflation has been coming down, this did not allow for a relaxation of the austerity programmes. Even in the countries which obtained the best results in fighting inflation, and managed to bring the annual rate under the 10 per cent mark, such as the Czech Republic, Slovakia and Slovenia, inflation rates in 1997 were still at least three times higher than the Western European average for the same year (which was slightly under 2 per cent). All the other countries in transition display much higher rates, although only Bulgaria and to a lesser degree Romania were still struggling with hyperinflation in 1997 (see Appendix Table A.2 and Figure 7.1).

Two phases may be identified (with some approximation as not all the countries displayed similar trends): an initial, and expected, sudden surge in prices; a stabilisation phase marked by the decrease in inflation rates, which nevertheless still remain high. One may then ask why there has been an initial surge in prices, up to hyperinflation levels, and why it is so difficult to bring down inflation once the initial price hikes have been reduced.

(1) *An initial surge in prices* had indeed to be expected due to the low level of administered prices. The sign of *effective market-clearing prices* has been the end of the shortages. Even when shortages still remained as in Southern Eastern European countries and in the former CIS countries, the standard queues so representative of Soviet-type economies soon disappeared. Street vendors appeared everywhere, and so did Western-imported consumer goods, be it at prices not affordable to the common citizen.

Actual prices resulted from various influences. First of all, they became much more differentiated across each country than they used to be in the past, which expresses the emergence of fragmented local markets (except in cases where the former distribution channels were still in place and imposed unified prices, or where these channels had been taken over by foreign retail chains). Secondly, the black (or free) market prices existing prior to the transition influenced price-fixing in the beginning, before demand began to collapse after the wiping out of the monetary overhang in the household sector. Thirdly, due to the opening up of the economies the prices (absolute and relative) for foreign goods were fixed on the basis of the foreign prices, often with some 'overshooting', meaning that these goods became soon more expensive (in foreign currency terms) in the East than in the West. Foreign prices also influenced the levels and structure of the prices for tradable (exportable) goods. Finally, the price-makers (large industrial or retail enterprises) mostly set their own prices exactly as they were doing when they were preparing their price proposals before approval by the planning or policy-making authorities in the past. Namely, they marked up their costs, adding to their current expenditures a percentage of profit more or less at random, up to what the market would bear (Menshikov, 1994). Typically, they did not adjust by trying to lower their costs, except for the few most successful enterprises. The monopolistic behaviour of the

Table 7.2 *The main instruments of the stabilisation programmes, 1990–7*

Instruments	Hungary	Poland	CSFR (since 93: Czech Republic)
Start of stabilisation programme	Various emergency programmes in 1990–1. Genuine shock therapy introduced in 1995.	1 January 1990.	1 January 1991.
Degree of price liberalisation	84 per cent of consumer prices free in 1997. Energy prices still controlled, to be freed in 1998.	90 per cent of prices freed on 1.1.90; in 1997, energy prices, rents and medicine prices still controlled.	Most prices deregulated by end-1991, except for rents and energy prices, which were increased substantially in 1997.
Exchange rate regime	Adjustable rate through periodical devaluations up to 1995; since then crawling peg with devaluations at a pre-announced rate within a fluctuation band of ±2–2.5 per cent around a central rate.	Fixed, then crawling peg since October 1991. Since May 1995 introduction of a fluctuation band of ±7 per cent around a central rate that is adjusted at a pre-announced rate.	Fixed and stable since 1991 up to 1996; fluctuation band of ±7.5 per cent Feb. 1996; floating rate since May 1997.
Tax regime[*] VAT	Introduced January 1988. In 1997: 12 and 25 p.c.	Since July 1993. Rates: 0; 7; 22 p.c.	Since January 1991. Maximum rate 23 per cent, reduced since 1995.
Individual income tax	Progressive taxation top rate 42 p.c. in 1997.	1997: three rates, 20, 32 and 40 per cent.	15 to 40 per cent in 1997.
Corporate income tax	18 per cent since 1995, plus tax on dividends of 20 p.c.	In 1997: 38 per cent.	Since 1996, 39 per cent, to be reduced to 35 per cent.
Interest rate (real)	Positive since 1993.	Positive since 1995.	Positive in 1991–2 and since 1994.
Income policy	Wage bill tax on wage increases over a given rate, abandonded in 1993; tripartite negotiations on nominal wage level.	1990–4: wage bill punitive, progressive tax on excess wages in the state sector; replaced since 1995 by tripartite negotiations on the level of base wages.	Wage bill tax on excess wage increases in 1991–3; tripartite negotiations on nominal wage levels; controls reinstated in 1996 due to very strong nominal wage growth.
Anchors of the stabilisation programme	Real: M.	Nominal: W, f. Real: M, i.	Nominal: W, f. Real: M, i.

[*] Rates in per cent

M = money supply; W = wages; f = exchange rate; i = interest rate

Sources: ECE/UN (1993), (1994b); Bruno (1992); OECD country economic surveys; EBRD (1997).

Slovakia (since 1993)	*Bulgaria*	*Romania*	*Slovenia*
see CSFR.	1 February 1991, later stopped. Genuine shock therapy introduced in 1997.	1 November 1990, stalled later; new programme launched 1997.	1992
see CSFR. Energy prices still regulated.	Full liberalisation by 1997.	Almost full liberalisation in 1995 but for energy prices, freed in 1997.	Almost full liberalisation in 1994 but for energy prices, raised in 1997.
Pegged rate to a basket of currencies with fluctuation band of ±7 per cent since 1996.	Managed float regime until 1997; since July 97 currency board pegged to the DM at at a rate of 1DM = 1000 Bleva.	De facto regulation until 1997. Since Feb. 1997 floating rate.	Floating rate (de facto based on DM).
Since January 1993. Rates: 7; 23 p.c. to be increased.	Since April 1994. 18 per cent in 1994; 22 per cent since July 1996.	Since July 1993. Rates: 9; 18 p.c.	Introduced in 1998.
Max. rate 42 p.c.	Max. rate 40 per cent.	Max. rate 60 per cent.	Max. rate 50 per cent.
Since 1994 40 per cent.	40 per cent.	38 per cent.	25 p.c. on dividends.
Positive since 1994.	Positive since 1994.	Positive since 1994.	Positive since 1993.
Collective bargaining since 1993. Some controls reinstated in 1997.	Wage bill tax on wage increases over a given rate until 1993, reinstated later; tripartite negotiations on nominal wage levels.	Wage bill tax on excessive wage increases; collective bargaining over wage levels.	Collective agreements in some sectors. Law on minimum wage since 1997.
See CSFR.	Nominal: W, i. Implicitly nominal f.	Implicitly real W.	Real: i.

Table continued overleaf

Table 7.2 continued

Instruments	Estonia	Latvia	Lithuania
Start of stabilisation programme	1992	1992	1992
Degree of price liberalisation	Almost full liberalisation in 1992 but for energy prices.	Almost full liberalisation. Some controls on energy prices.	Largely liberalised prices; controls on energy and basic utilities.
Exchange rate regime	Currency board pegged to the DM since 1992 (1DM = 8 kroon)	Fixed rate pegged to the SDR basket since 1994.	Currency board pegged to the USD (1 USD = 4 litai) since 1994.
Tax regime* VAT	VAT + indirect taxes generate 50 per cent revenues (VAT = 18p.c.).	VAT rate: 18 per cent.	VAT rate: 18 per cent.
Individual income tax	Flat rate 26 per cent.	Flat rate 25 per cent.	Maximum rate: 33 per cent.
Corporate income tax			
Interest rate (real)	Positive since 1996.	Positive since 1994.	Positive since 1996.
Income policy	No regulation except for civil servants.	No regulation except for a minimum wage.	No regulation since 1993. Minimum wage statutory.
Anchors of the stabilisation programme	Nominal: f.	Nominal: f.	Nominal: f.

state-owned enterprises certainly pushed prices up, not as a result of a market-type profit maximisation behaviour, but rather because these enterprises sought to maintain employment and to keep the movement of nominal wages as close as possible to the movement of prices. The inflationary risks of such behaviour were alleviated, first, by incomes policies where they existed; second, as was the case in Russia, by the recourse to part-time work and delays in the payment of wages.

Price increases were not evenly distributed. When prices were freed, typically the food prices were the first to increase, due to the immediate curtailing of the large food subsidies. This precipitated a sudden increase of the share of food in the consumers' budgets, and a decline in overall demand which soon restored the market equilibrium. Next the prices for services increased, later and more gradually than food prices, because some public services were not deregulated immediately (e.g. rents, heating, public transport, etc.) (Szpringer, 1993). These delays in price liberalisation are mentioned by some analysts as one of the main causes of a possible rebound of inflation in the future (World Bank, 1996, pp. 38–9) One has to remember that small privatisation began and expanded in the services sector, in areas where domestic prices had previously been totally preserved from foreign influence (such as personal services, catering). As prices were dramatically low in these areas, compared to world prices, there was a large margin for increase, which was successfully used by the 'new small entrepreneurs'. It was also, as Winiecki (1993b, p. 9) points out, very difficult to find equilibrium prices in this sector as the whole sector had been under-developed for so long, and as the suppliers had no experience of a market (short of what they might have learned in moonlighting, an activity very popular for many personal services). Thus sectoral inflation originating in the services sector may be long-lasting, first because of the relative (to other sectors) growth of services, and second because of the initial indetermina-tion of equilibrium prices in the field.

(2) Why is it so difficult *to bring inflation down below a given level?* Apart from the structural reason already given, i.e. the delays in lifting the ceilings on energy and utilities prices, there is the commonsense argument that bringing inflation down from high levels may be easy in the beginning, but increasingly difficult for small levels. Other reasons have to be discussed. The dominant explanation for continuing inflation is the *excessive money supply*. In addition, *demand* and *supply*-side explanations have been suggested.

In the view of the reformers and of their foreign advisers, because *excessive money supply* was the first cause of inflation, most of the countries declared themselves committed to a policy of positive real interest rates, which in several stabilisation packages constituted a major anchor of the stabilisation policy (as in Poland and Czechoslovakia), along with a money supply target (Table 7.2). Interest rate policy has usually been combined

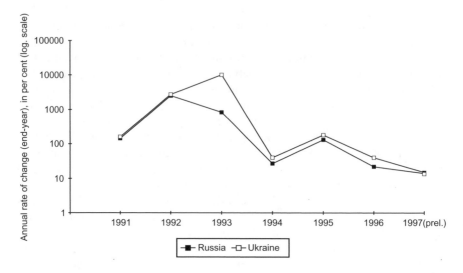

Figure 7.1(a)   *Consumer prices, 1991–7: Russia, Ukraine*
Source: EBRD (1998).

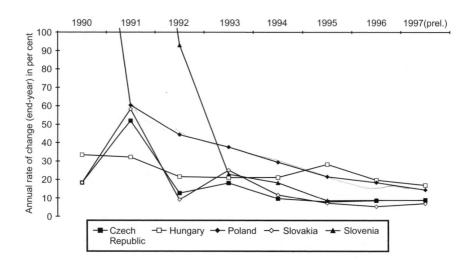

Figure 7.1(b)   *Consumer prices, 1990–7: Central European countries*
Source: EBRD (1998).

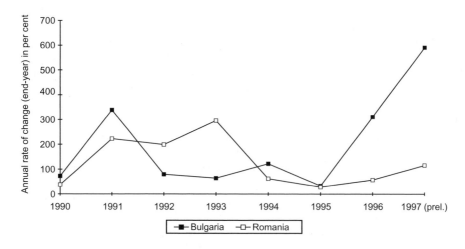

Figure 7.1(c) *Consumer prices, 1990–7: East-South European countries*
Source: EBRD (1998).

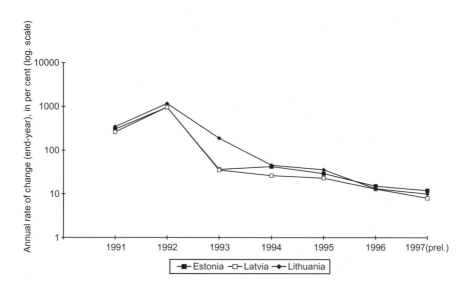

Figure 7.1(d) *Consumer prices, 1991–7: Baltic countries*
Source: EBRD (1998).

with direct control of the money supply (through high obligatory reserve requirements ratios, and credit limits). Positive interest rates were indeed a major component of the targets negotiated by the countries in transition with the IMF. However one has questioned the impact of high interest rates on inflation. Calvo (1991) thus shows that high interest rates may generate generalised bankruptcy which in turn brings back inflation. Also, high interest rates induce the main borrowers (the state-owned enterprises) to seek non-bank money, i.e. to increase inter-enterprise debts. When the latter reach a very high level the government is induced to inject money in the enterprise sector, and inflation soars again, which is what happened in Russia. But are inter-enterprise arrears an inevitable outcome of stabilisation policies? The World Bank study on transition strongly denies this point: 'Cross-country experience shows that *credible* [emphasis mine, ML.] stabilisation, including a consistent refusal to inject new credit, is the best way to combat increases in arrears' (World Bank, 1996, pp. 39–40).

What was the impact of *real factors* in the continuation of inflation? On the *demand* side, inflationary pressure did not originate from the household sector, not just because monetary overhang was very soon wiped out following the liberalising of prices. There was no wage–price spiral in most of the transition countries. Increases in nominal wages did not match price increases in the beginning of transition, due to income policies which were meant to sustain the monetary policy. It was expected, which proved right, that the under-development of the monetary system, and in particular the weak influence of monetary signals on state-owned enterprises, would require an additional 'anchor' in terms of nominal wages control. Such a control was ensured with the help of various instruments, such as a weak indexation of wages on price increases, taxes on excess wages, and contractual negotiation procedures among the government, the enterprises and the representatives of the workers (see Tables 7.1 and 7.2). Indexation of nominal wages, be it weak, and the existence of contractual procedures certainly fuel inflationary anticipations. But some alleviation of the hardships of transition had to be promised to the masses. It may well be argued that instead of using the nominal wage level as an anchor, one should have used the lowest *real* wage compatible with the macro-economic adjustment, and index the initial value of this wage at the new prices, with a higher rate of purchasing power protection (Nuti, 1991, p. 163). Using the nominal wage anchor even with a weak indexation may create self-sustaining inflation; if the rate of inflation is greater than expected when fixing the nominal target, it may lead (as was the case in Poland in 1990) to a drastic, unwanted drop in real incomes.

After an initial fall, real wages have been increasing in most of Central and Eastern Europe since 1994–5 (Appendix Table A.2). Their contribution to continuing inflation was felt rather on the *supply-side* factors, which on the whole explain the relatively high levels of inflation even in countries which have been the most successful at containing it. Increases in *real product wages* (nominal wages deflated by the change in the producer price index) have an inflationary impact when they are not compensated by an increase in productivity or by a reduction in the profit margins of the enterprises (see Table 7.3 below). Increases in *material costs*, in particular of energy, occurred due to the loss of cheap energy supplies after the collapse of the CMEA and of the USSR, followed by the selling of energy – Russian oil and gas – at world market prices; it was also due to the liberalising, be it belated, of domestic energy prices. Other material costs increased as well, especially for imported inputs following the devaluations of the national currencies. To the impact of material costs as factors of cost-push inflation one should add financial costs, namely high interest rates.

Budgetary balance

A tight fiscal policy has been the second most important component of stabilisation packages. It is linked with monetary policy, as the main source of financing budget deficits is money creation (see Figure 7.2).

Mixed results have been obtained in the field of *budget deficits*. In general, fiscal imbalances tended to increase, for various reasons that reinforced themselves:

- The drop in output reduced budget revenues while increasing the need for social expenditures.
- Once the subsidies and the investment programmes were cut it was difficult to find additional ways of reducing expenditures; in the countries most plagued by deficits and in particular in the former CIS countries, one little commendable way was to momentarily stop paying civil servants.
- Tax evasion, which already plagued the former system, grew and was increasingly difficult to track due to the inadequacy of the tax structure and instruments (this is the main reason why VAT was introduced in many countries – a measure that also fuelled inflation, in the form of one-time monthly outbursts).

Fine-tuning was very difficult to achieve. Most of the clashes between countries in transition and the IMF occurred over budget deficit issues. For instance, in Poland and Hungary the share of the deficit in the GNP exceeded in 1992 the ceiling target agreed with the IMF, for various reasons. One of the them was the necessity of maintaining or developing social security financing, under the pressure of public opinion. The other important reason lay in the deterioration of enterprise performance and the tax evasion behaviour of the enterprises. As a result, both countries were unable to meet the conditionality requirements of the IMF. The subsequent

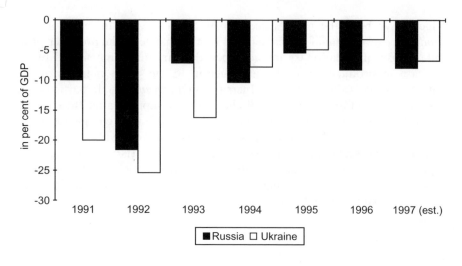

Figure 7.2(a)   *Budget deficit, 1991–7: Russia, Ukraine*
Source: EBRD (1998).

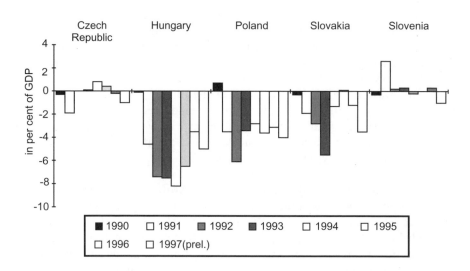

Figure 7.2(b)   *Budget deficit, 1990–7: Central European countries*
Source: EBRD (1998).

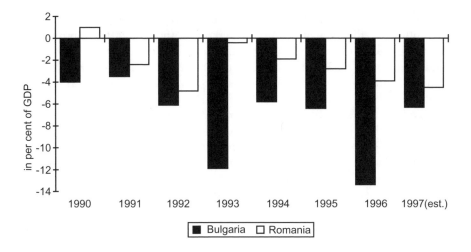

Figure 7.2(c) *Budget deficit, 1990–7: Bulgaria, Romania*
Source: EBRD (1998).

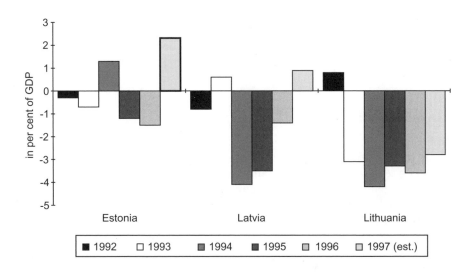

Figure 7.2(d) *Budget deficit, 1992–7: Baltic countries*
Source: EBRD (1998).

agreements reached in 1993 with the IMF for both of these countries exemplify the dilemma of the policy-makers. Either the latter comply with the ceiling admitted by the IMF for the deficit/GDP ratio and are able to secure not only IMF financing but other credits from the international financial markets – in which case, however, the policy-makers are confronted with an opposition which demands more public expenditures, especially in the social field. Or the policy-makers bow to the opposition, especially when elections are near, and lose international financing and credibility. The same dilemmas were faced in 1994 by Romania and Bulgaria. Tax issues explained the delays in the implementation of stand-by agreements between the IMF and Russia in 1996–8 (see Chapter 9).

The way fiscal deficits were financed contributed to sustaining inflation. External finance was out of the question in most cases in the first years of the transition, because of the existing indebtedness and the lack of credibility of the countries. Non-monetary financing (i.e., borrowing on domestic financial markets, by issuing government securities) was also often impossible due to the lack of development of the financial markets. In the countries which were able to do so, this had as a side-effect the reduction of credits available to the enterprises, because government bonds were preferred as less risky and more liquid than credits to the economy. Thus the main method of covering the budget deficit was borrowing from the Central Banks, which mechanically increased the money supply.

As Figure 7.2 shows, most of the Central and Eastern European countries have achieved fiscal stabilisation, which allows some of them to state that they would successfully comply with the Maastricht convergence criteria on this account (see Chapter 9). Such an achievement is however fragile and highly volatile, because it is largely dependent on the restructuring of the banking and financial systems, as the Bulgarian crisis (1996–7) has shown (Box 7.2).

External stabilisation

In Eastern and Central Europe and in Russia, the *external balance* situation improved significantly in the first years (1990–2) of the transition. In all countries, exports to the West (and especially to Western Europe) steadily increased. This expressed both a reorientation of exports formerly directed to the CMEA region and particularly to the former Soviet Union, which collapsed in 1990–2, and the effect of the strong devaluation of the domestic currencies. But since 1993 an opposite trend is showing in the trade balances as well as the current account balances of most countries, as may be seen from Appendix Table A.2.

To understand these trends, one has to look at the exchange rate regime, at the reorientation of exports, and at the level of the international indebtedness.

Box 7.2   *The Bulgarian crisis of 1996–7*

Until 1996 the Bulgarian economy displayed the trends observed in transition economies that had followed the path of 'shock therapy': a period of depression followed by a gradual recovery in output (see below, Figure 7.4c), disinflation (Figure 7.1c) and trimming of the fiscal deficit (Figure 7.2c). In 1996, there occurred a 10 per cent drop in GDP, inflation exceeded 300 per cent and the budget deficit soared to 13 per cent of the GDP.

Why did instruments that had proved efficient elsewhere fail in this case ? Several answers may be suggested. Taken together, they point to the following conclusion: Bulgaria has suffered from a combination of all the liabilities that have plagued other countries to a lesser extent, while lacking most of the assets of these countries.

A. Bulgaria has suffered from the collapse of Comecon more than any other member

The share of the USSR in Bulgaria's overall trade was higher than in any other Comecon member (see Appendix Table A.1), and consequently the country lost most of its markets in 1990–1. In this respect, Bulgaria was much more in the situation of the former USSR republics after the break-up of the USSR than in the standard situation of Eastern European countries.

B. It had a huge foreign debt burden

While the former Soviet Republics could start their transition almost debt-free as Russia took over their foreign debt, Bulgaria had a high level of foreign indebtedness amounting to 140 per cent of GDP in 1991. The arrangement with the London Club creditor banks in 1994 (see Table 7.1) was a mixed blessing because following the arrangement Bulgaria had to start servicing its debt again. In addition, Bulgaria benefited from very little foreign assistance until 1994.

C. The legacies from the past were particularly devastating

Bulgaria had a large state-owned sector, which was unviable, as many state-owned enterprises were geared to the Soviet market and should have been closed down. Bankruptcies started only in 1996, most of the state enterprises being the main employers in their region and hence protected from closures by the authorities. Privatisation did not really start before 1997. The state-owned enterprises were bailed out through soft loans from the banks (also state-owned). The banks, burdened by bad loans, could only retain some liquidity from household deposits.

D. The macro-economic policy was not consistent

The main anchor of the stabilisation policy was the base interest rate of the Central Bank. When high interest rates became unsustainable, because they triggered an increase in the domestic debt, the Central Bank had then to finance the fiscal deficit, which it did through monetisation, provoking an increase in inflation in 1996. This in turn eroded the confidence of the public, which began to withdraw its deposits from the commercial banks. At the same time the Central Bank had to stop defending the domestic currency because its foreign exchange reserves were depleted. A run on the lev followed along with an outflow of capital.

E. **The economic crisis provoked a political turnaround which allowed the introduction of stringent measures under international pressure**
The banking and currency crises culminated in January–February 1997, with hyperinflation (the monthly rate was 250 per cent in February 1997), depreciation of the currency, and the collapse of several banks. A new government came to power in April 1997 with a programme of radical changes and the support of the IMF. It could thus win enough credibility to introduce a very radical measure, which was the establishment of a currency board on 1 July 1997. The Bulgarian lev was pegged to the DM at a rate of BGL 1000 = DM 1 (a 90 per cent devaluation over its previous rate). Inflation fell to a monthly rate of 1.8 per cent by the end of 1997, and the budget deficit ratio to the GDP was cut by 2 in 1997, along with a continuing fall in output and in real wages (see indicators for Bulgaria, Appendix Table A2.). But the structural issues of transformation (bank reform, privatisation) remained largely unaddressed.

Source: ECE/UN (1997a), (1998).

(1) The results of 1990–2 have been achieved through an *over-devaluation of the domestic currencies*. The promotion of exports required a continuing devaluation of the currency. This is why only a few countries have opted for a *fixed rate regime* (Poland between January 1990 and October 1991; Czechoslovakia until 1997). A fixed exchange rate provides a nominal 'anchor' to the stabilisation programme and hence helps to curb inflation. It is essential that the stability of the new exchange rate be credible. Otherwise people will expect repeated devaluations and this will provoke inflationary expectations as well. Thus the initial devaluation must be large enough to be credible, and subsequent inflation must remain contained so as to avoid an over-appreciation of the currency which would require a new devaluation. But then the initial devaluation may deter necessary imports, and induce wasteful exports. Calculations (see Table 7.3) show that in Central Europe and Russia devaluations put the rate of exchange (expressed in units of domestic currency required to buy a unit of foreign currency) much below the purchasing power parity. This is also exemplified by the comparison of dollar wages in the countries in transition and in some developing countries. In 1990, the average dollar wage in Hungary and Poland was well below the average dollar wage in Paraguay or Thailand (Asselain, 1994, p. 837).

If inflation is nevertheless high, the currency soon becomes overvalued, which happened in Poland in 1991. The fixed exchange rate is no longer sustainable as the country suffers losses in competitiveness. *Floating rates* allow the balancing of demand and supply of the domestic/foreign currencies but induce sharp fluctuations of the nominal rate and feed inflationary expectations. They deter foreign investments, as prospective investors fear instability, unless a very predictable monetary and fiscal policy is conducted. However this regime has been used in Russia (since

1996 Russia has applied a sliding currency corridor regime; see Chapter 9, Table 9.2), Bulgaria (until 1997), Romania (managed float until 1997), and Slovenia. The middle way is the *crawling-peg regime* with a pre-announced (daily or monthly) rate of devaluation. It has been introduced in Poland in October 1991, while Hungary moved in 1995 from an adjustable rate regime to a crawling-peg system. In both countries there is a fluctuation band around the central rate, of plus or minus 2–2.25 per cent in Hungary and plus or minus 7 per cent (10 per cent since February 1998) in Poland. Both countries established a pre-announced monthly rate of devaluation, of 0.9 per cent (Hungary) and 1 per cent (Poland, lowered to 0.6 per cent mid-1998) against the basket of currencies to which the domestic currency is pegged. The Czech Republic had to introduce in February 1996 a fluctuation band around the central parity of its currency, of plus or minus 7.5 per cent, to deal with the real appreciation of the koruna resulting from large capital inflows. In May 1997, after several months of a banking and currency crisis, the fixed peg was abandoned for a floating rate regime.

Bulgaria, too, experienced a crisis in 1996–7 (Box 7.2), which ended with the establishing of a *currency board* system taking effect on 1 July 1997. The currency board is tantamount to the most extreme loss of sovereignty. Under this system, money supply is tied to the level of foreign exchange reserves, as the Central Bank must back all issuances of money by its existing reserves.The government could thus no longer cover the budget deficit, bail out loss-making enterprises or rescue troubled banks through money printing. Before Bulgaria, other countries have experienced the system, though in a less troubled context. The first case in a country in transition was Estonia, which established a currency board when it created its own national currency, the kroon, which since 1992 has been pegged to the DM at a rate of DM1 = Ekr8. Lithuania established a currency board system in 1994 and pegged the litas to the USD at a rate of 4 litai for one dollar, as an instrument of the stabilisation policy. A currency board regime was advocated in 1998 for Russia as well in the wake of its financial crisis.

What is the best exchange rate regime? The IMF, although in principle in favour of flexible exchange rates, has not objected to a fixed nominal rate in the case of Poland, and has later approved the currency board experiences in Estonia, on the basis of a pragmatic, case-by-case approach (Citrin *et al.*, 1995). The Bulgarian currency board was also approved and supported by the IMF. Some authors argue that sound fiscal and monetary policies matter most, i.e. 'orthodox' stabilisation without a nominal exchange rate anchor, and that success has been obtained whatever the exchange rate regime, 'by both floaters and peggers', when looking at the experiences of 15 countries in transition up to 1996 (Budina and van Wijnbergen, 1997, p. 53). Nuti (1996a, p. 155) considers 'exchange rate floating within a crawling band . . . as a seemingly efficient compromise between floating and fixed regimes' – indeed, following Poland, Hungary and the Czech Republic have resorted to it. Rosati (1996, p. 178) sees as optimal the sequence going from the initial devaluation-cum-convertibility, followed by a period of fixed exchange rate regime, then a period of an adjustable crawling-peg regime, to a flexible rate within a predetermined band. From this we may infer that there is no optimal exchange regime for the time being. Unlike the CIS countries, the countries that have applied for EU membership will see their range of choices restricted when they prepare for EMU membership (see Chapter 9).

Are the currencies of the countries in transition overvalued or under-valued? All of them have been initially undervalued; most have appreciated in real terms, especially the Russian ruble (Table 7.3 and Figure 7.3a). Obviously it is very difficult to determine the equilibrium exchange rate here, not only because convertibility is not complete. Even if we had full convertibility, including that for capital transactions, the underdevelopment of the capital market itself would lead to wrong signals. The standard models explaining how long-term rates of exchange are determined by the fundamentals are already unsatisfactory in the case of developed economies with sophisticated capital and monetary markets and a long experience in openness. We would suggest that in the conditions of the transition, a gradual narrowing of the gap between the current exchange rates and the purchasing power parities of the domestic currencies – without losses in competitiveness – would be a sign of a successful stabilisation-cum-transformation (Asselain, 1994; Figure 7.3b).

(2) In the first years of the transition, the improvements in current account balances achieved along with a *reorientation of trade* toward the West have been due to 'distress exports' of any commodity available, and facilitated by the agreements with the EC which liberalised trade for a large range of commodities. The commodity composition of trade has changed very slowly since the beginning of the transition. *On the export side*, agricultural goods and semi-products such as textiles, steel products and chemicals still retain a large share. The problem is not only that most of these goods are 'sensitive' in trade with the European Union members, and hence affected by restrictions (agricultural goods) or prone to suffer from anti-dumping measures or safeguard clauses (steel products, chemicals). The main obstacle here lies in the lack of competitiveness of the Central and Eastern European countries for high value-added manufactured exports, which is itself due to the delays in industrial restructuring. The main competitiveness factor is the low cost of labour, which is gradually eroded by the increases in wages and the appreciation of local currencies (see Table 7.3 and Figures 7.3a and c). The situation is different for Russia, whose large natural-resources endowments allowed the country to rely even more on oil and gas exports than during Communist times, and hence to maintain trade surpluses. The downward trend in oil prices since end-1997 entailed a

shrinking of these surpluses which may be wiped out in 1998. *On the import side*, there has been everywhere a surge in import demand for machinery and still more for consumer goods from the West, especially as industrial activities sharply declined and as retail channels were soon largely

Table 7.3 *Exchange rates, purchasing power parities and real product wages in selected countries in transition, 1991–7*

	1991	1992	1993	1994	1995	1996	1997 (prel)
Poland							
Real ER (CPI-based), zl/$US, 1990 = 100	69.8	88.7	97.2	94.1	104.2	93.1	105.5
Ratio of nominal ER to PPP	2.01	1.99	2.09	2.09	1.76	1.69	1.83
Average monthly wage in $US	166	213	215	231	285	324	351
Real product wages in industry, 1990 = 100	116.4	126.8	131.7	140.6	145.2	162.3	173.9
Hungary							
Real ER (CPI-based) ft/$US, 1990 = 100	87.6	75.2	71.4	68.6	63.6	61.7	63.8
Ratio of nominal ER to PPP	1.75	1.61	1.6	1.56	1.5	1.55	1.65
Average monthly wage in $US	240	282	295	317	310	307	316
Real product wages in industry, 1990 = 100	100.6	111.4	121.9	131.8	124.1	123.5	124.4
Czech Republic							
Real ER (CPI-based) kc/$US, 1990 = 100	101.6	87.6	74.7	67.1	56.7	48.0	51.7
Ratio of nominal ER to PPP	3.54	3.08	2.79	2.54	2.14	2.04	2.24
Average monthly wage in $US	129	164	200	240	308	356	347
Real product wages in industry, 1990 = 100	68.4	74.7	83.8	92.9	102.0	114.4	122.4
Russia							
Real ER (CPI-based), R/$US 1992 = 100		100	49.4	28.7	19.9	15.2	14.9
Ratio of nominal ER to PPP		11.5	4.48	2.46	1.82	1.42	1.43
Average monthly wage in $US		24	62	107	116	154	163
Real product wages in industry, 1992 = 100		100	91	74.5	51.1	55.7	63.4

Notes: ER = exchange rate; PPP = purchasing power parity; CPI = consumer price index; real product wages: nominal wages deflated by producer price index.
Sources: ECE/UN (1998); Podkaminer *et al* (1998).

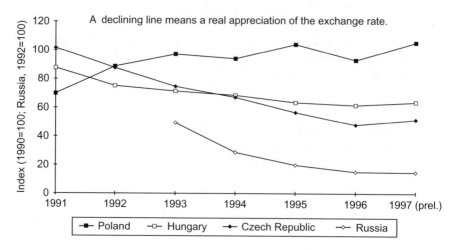

Figure 7.3(a) *Real exchange rate index, CPI-based, in national currencies per USD, 1991–7*

Source: Table 7.3.

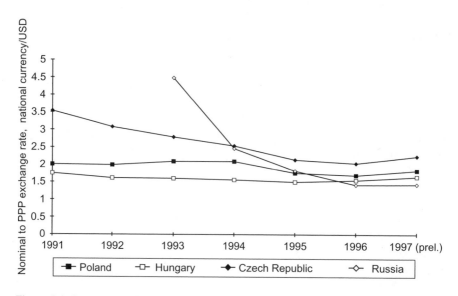

Figure 7.3(b) *Ratio of nominal to PPP-based exchange rate, in national currencies per USD, 1991–7*

Source: Table 7.3.

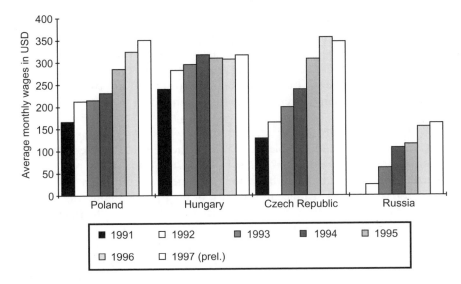

Figure 7.3(c)   *Average monthly wages in USD, at nominal exchange rate, 1991–7*
Source: Table 7.3.

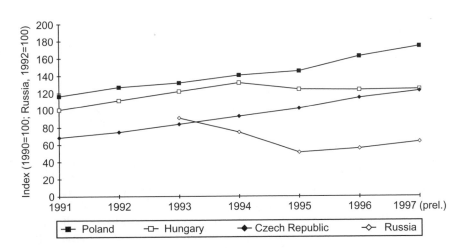

Figure 7.3(d)   *Real product wage index, PPI-based, 1991–7*
Source: Table 7.3.

controlled by Western distribution chains eager to crowd out local consumer goods. In the beginning this import drive was successfully contained, despite the lifting of trade restrictions, by the strong devaluation of the currencies. Very soon (starting from 1992, see Appendix Table A.2) the trade balances began to deteriorate in Central and Eastern Europe, and this is certainly a main concern for the European Union in view of the future membership of these countries.

(3) In most countries, the level of the *foreign debt* remains a serious constraint (see Appendix Table A.2). Why is the debt status so essential for macro-economic stabilisation? This is because of the IMF role in the process. Macro-economic stabilisation packages were all agreed with the IMF. International assistance in the form of debt rescheduling was granted by banks or governments only following the seal of approval by the IMF on domestic programmes, as was the case for Poland (see Table 7.1 p. 124) and Russia (see Box 7.1 p. 128). While these programmes were always quite stringent when drafted, their fiscal commitments were often reversed in budgetary votes by the legislative assemblies, leading to higher deficits than had been decided by the governments, mainly so as to increase social expenditures. The approval of the IMF was then withdrawn – and along with it prospects for debt agreements – until a new budget could be hammered out.

However the most indebted countries in the beginning of the transition, Poland and Hungary, managed to reduce their debts, through arrangements with creditors or by good management. Debt service/exports ratios decreased and the level of currency reserves increased overall in the Central and East European countries. In addition, capital inflows into these countries radically changed in nature. In the past, centrally planned economies borrowed to finance their machinery imports, with officially supported commercial credits from the Western banks, or to finance the servicing of their debts. Later, in the first years of the transition, credit was linked with assistance from international financial institutions or Western governments. Since 1993, large private capital inflows in the form of portfolio investments or medium-term credits became available, in line with the increasing involvement of the countries in transition in the international financial markets, and the improvement in their creditworthiness. (See Chapter 9.)

What was the impact of these inflows on macro-economic stabilisation? In principle, attracting capital inflows is positively linked with fighting inflation: high interest rates attract foreign capital, and help to contain inflation. But such inflows have negative effects as well: first, high interest rates crowd domestic borrowers out and impair growth; second, capital inflows help accelerating inflation, as they translate into an increase in the domestic money supply which in turn has to be fought by high interest rates that fuel continued currency inflows. This kind of vicious circle is not specific to countries in transition. It is counter-attacked by sterilisation policies, in the form of open market operations (the Central Bank sells public securities to commercial banks so as to absorb excess money supply), or of tighter requirements for commercial banks, which are requested to hold increased minimum reserves or to keep an increased amount of deposits in the Central Bank. Open market policies are costly in terms of interest paid to holders of state securities. Such policies are never totally effective, especially when the authorities do not want to resort to capital movements controls (which would be contrary to a commitment to achieving foreign exchange liberalisation and full convertibility). The continuation of capital inflows accelerates the real exchange rate appreciation though it is not the only (perhaps not the main) cause of this appreciation (ECE/UN, 1997b, p. 138), with adverse effects on imports and exports. Imports increase, which might be positive if there is an increase of machinery imports and hence investment. Increased consumer goods imports may be fought by various methods such as a temporary import surcharge or compulsory deposits of a certain amount of money representing a share of the import value, but these techniques, used for instance by the Czech government in 1997, are contrary to the trade liberalisation policy and must be temporary.

In the long run, capital inflows are damageable when they turn into a normal way of financing current accounts. If these inflows are mainly short-term, even in the case of medium-term portfolio investment in domestic bonds, there is a risk of volatility, and of a run on the domestic currency. This happened in the Czech Republic in 1997, when domestic and Western investors withdrew their funds from the Czech banks, which forced the Central Bank into devoting a large share of its reserves to maintain the currency peg and this ultimately led to a departure from the fixed peg. The financial markets in Central and Eastern Europe are still thin and underdeveloped. These features protect them against a huge contagion effect from global crises such as the East Asian crisis of 1997–8 or the Russian crisis of 1998. At the same time, they are vulnerable to rather small shifts in investors' strategies. Thus in August–September 1998 the Russian crisis provoked erratic movements on the Central European exchanges and weakened the domestic currencies, because operators specialised in emerging markets sold their holdings in Central Europe in order to compensate for losses in Russia.

Let us now turn to the real indicators. While the monetary and financial trends have been disappointing, though some successes have been achieved, real indicators have displayed a much gloomier picture. The deflationary policies conducted had the expected result of bringing about a recession, that was, however, unexpected in its magnitude.

The Achievements in the Real Field: The Fall in Output

Still in 1997, only Poland had regained its GDP level of 1989. The decline in GNP for the countries reviewed in Appendix Table A.2 is of about 20 per cent for the years 1990–2 in the best cases. Figures also show a dramatic fall in investment. The downtrend in consumption was brought about by the decrease in real wages. Recovery began in Central and Eastern Europe only in 1993–4. Though growth rates were quite high in 1994–5, they began to slow down in 1996–7. The situation remained much worse in the former Soviet Union countries, where recovery had hardly begun as of 1997 (Figure 7.4; Appendix Table A.2).

The human impact

Parallel with the drop in output, there was an overall deterioration in the '*human development*' situation as measured by the set of criteria used by the UNDP (see Appendix Table A.3). The HD index improved only in Poland.

Unemployment displayed some paradoxical features. It was not extremely high in the beginning of transition by Western standards, taking into account the slump in production (see Figure 7.5). This is not a positive trend; it shows that the enterprises did not adjust to recession by cutting their work force, but rather by maintaining some activity be it at a reduced pace and with a low productivity. It also shows that despite the bankruptcy legislation in force, the governments were reluctant to provoke a large wave of bankruptcies, for political reasons. In a situation when a satisfactory social safety net cannot be put in place because of budgetary constraints, the easiest way for the governments to cushion the effects of the austerity policy is to refrain from closing large state enterprises and to implicitly endorse their social protection functions, inherited from the old regime. (For a general discussion of unemployment in transition, see Boeri, 1994; OECD, 1993 and 1994.)

Unemployment is, since 1996–7, stabilised at levels varying from 10 to 18 per cent in Eastern Europe, and at 6 per cent in the Baltic countries. In the CIS countries, registered unemployment is very low, in the range of 1–4 per cent, but true unemployment is supposed to be much higher, between 6 and 14 per cent (ECE/UN, 1998, p. 45). While in the former Soviet Union the low level of unemployment may be explained by the legacies of the past and the uncompletedness of the restructuring process, the worrying question for Eastern Europe is: why, despite the resumption of growth, is the level of unemployment still so high? Several answers may be offered. First, the increase in productivity has been greater than the increase in output, and hence the firms had no need to hire additional workers. Second, the enterprises still retain some legacies from the past, even in the countries that recovered most successfully, and they go on hoarding labour (Blanchard, 1997, p. 6).

Why did output decline so strongly?

A wide discussion developed in the first years of transition on the reasons for the initial large drop in output. Later, the debate shifted to another issue: how to achieve a sustainable growth in the countries in transformation, and in this context, what are the links between liberalisation and growth, on the one hand, and between inflation and growth, on the other?

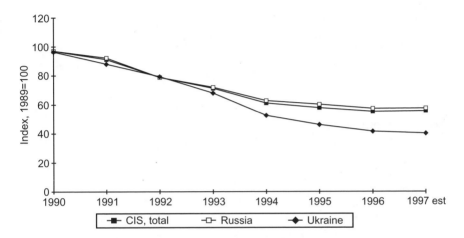

Figure 7.4(a) *GDP index, 1989–97: CIS (overall), Russia, Ukraine*

Source: Appendix Table A.2.

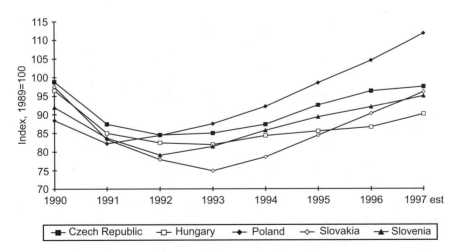

Figure 7.4(b) *GDP index, 1989–97: Central European countries*

Source: Appendix Table A.2.

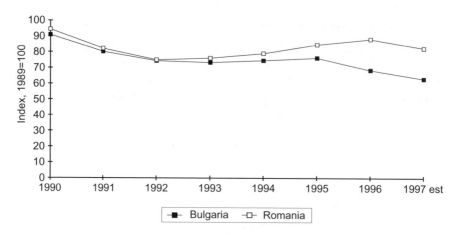

Figure 7.4(c)   *GDP index, 1989–97: East-South European countries*
Source: Appendix Table A.2.

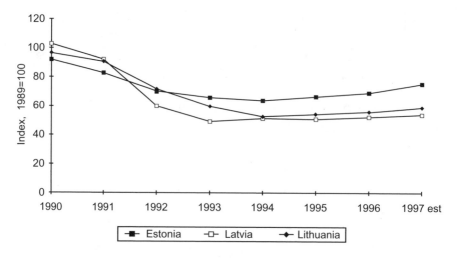

Figure 7.4(d)   *GDP index, 1989–97: Baltic countries*
Source: Appendix Table A.2.

Did something go wrong? Most experts and policy-makers acknowledged that they were baffled by the sharp decline in output. Soon, a large debate erupted (see Bruno, 1992; Girard, 1992; Kolodko, 1993; Köves, 1992; Nuti, 1993; Portes, 1992; Williamson, 1992b, among others). We borrow from Nuti (1993) a classification of the reactions into three groups: incredulity, complacency, 'gradualism'. As output recovered, new contributions reverted to the issue.

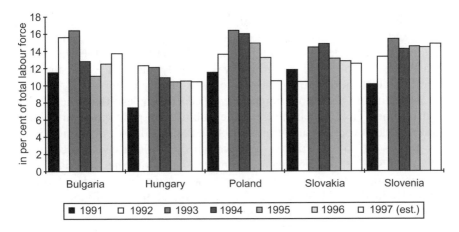

Figure 7.5(a) *Unemployment as per cent of labour force, 1991–7: countries with high unemployment rates (over 10 per cent in 1997)*

Source: ECE/UN (1998).

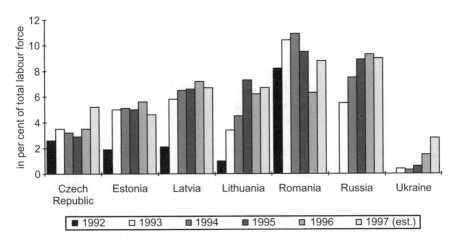

Figure 7.5(b) *Unemployment as per cent of labour force, 1992–7: countries with medium to low unemployment rates (under 10 per cent in 1997)*

Source: ECE/UN (1998).

Nothing went wrong

The 'incredulity' reaction is the following: true, the situation appeared bad, but this is only an illusion. The recession mainly meant that a large share of production was formerly produced without any demand just to meet the requirements of the plan, according to Kornai's scheme of a resource-constrained economy (Kornai, 1980). Not only was this decline explainable, but in addition it was useful because such activities in fact generated a negative value-added (see McKinnon, 1991b; Hughes and Hare, 1991). Moreover, as statistical recording was initially inaccurate for the new private sector, the output of this sector was grossly undervalued, and the actual reduction in output might have been much less than the official figures show. Thus, the architect of the stabilisation programme in Poland, Leszek Balcerowicz, argued that in 1990-1 Polish GDP declined not by 18 per cent as official statistics have shown but by 5–10 per cent (Balcerowicz, 1994). This is a double-edged argument. True, on the one hand, the contribution of the private sector may well have been under-recorded, especially in the field of services for which the statistical offices had very little experience. On the other hand, 'negative value-added' production is still manufactured in many state-owned enterprises, with a still lower productivity than in the past. Logically, if it is argued that the removal of negative value-added production means an addition to the GNP, then one should admit that its continuation means that the recorded GNP is above its actual level. Unfortunately neither of the two sides of the argument can be proved with the statistical tools available.

The same incredulity reaction also relates to other real indicators. For instance, the fall in real wages as an outcome of deflationary policies has been questioned. It has been said that the computing of an index of real wages as the nominal wage index deflated by the consumer price index did not yield an accurate picture, as it did not take into account the variety of consumption patterns. Secondly and more important, a statistical real wage index does not take into account qualitative factors such as the reduction of the time spent in queues, which amounts to an increase in welfare (ECE/UN, 1994b, p. 140; for Russia, Koen and Phillips, 1993). Finally, to compare real wages before and after the stabilisation shock is faulty, the same line of argument runs, because real wages were artificially high due to an artificially low consumer price index deflator (because prices were administered and because inflation was hidden).

Some of these considerations have to be retained, but certainly not to the point of denying the reality of the decline in real wages. Those authors who call up housewives in support of their argument should remember that while it is certainly frustrating to stand in queues, it is frustrating as well not to be able to go out shopping because your purse is empty. In the first stage of the transition real wages did fall as a result of stringent stabilisation policies. When such policies were implemented at a later stage as in Hungary in 1995, this had an immediate impact on real wages (see Appendix Table A.2). In the countries that did not succeed in stabilising their economy and resuming growth, real wages went on deteriorating. In the countries which were bottoming out, real wages stopped declining or started rising (see Appendix Table A.2 and Figures 7.6a to 7.6d). Is this because wage earners more successfully resist wage cuts when the economy looks healthier, or because the growth in output, itself the result of productivity gains, allows for some wage increases? Both reasons may apply jointly.

Output had to fall, if not that deeply

The 'complacency' attitude means agreeing that the initial situation was bad, but should have been so. This is by far the most common attitude: not surprisingly, since most of the actors have a vested interest in arguing that

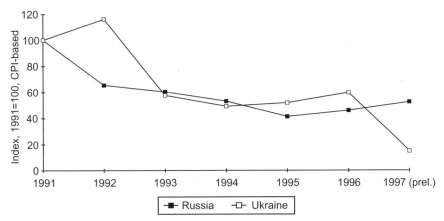

Figure 7.6(a)   *Real wage index, Russia and Ukraine, 1991–7*

Source: Appendix Table A.2.

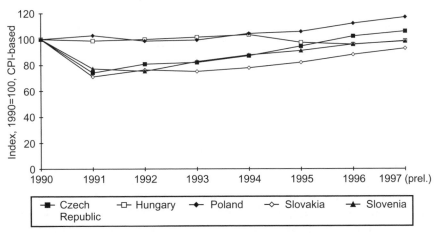

Figure 7.6(b)   *Real wage index, Central European countries, 1990–7*

Source: Appendix Table A.2.

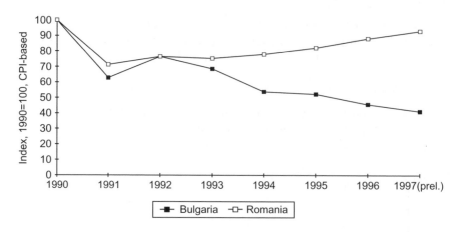

Figure 7.6(c)   *Real wage index, East-South European countries, 1990–7*
Source: Appendix Table A.2.

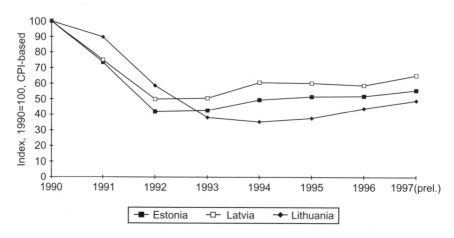

Figure 7.6(d)   *Real wage index, Baltic countries, 1990–7*
Source: Appendix Table A.2.

things are normal. This is the case of the policy-makers, but also of the advisers and experts.

The *policy-makers* are prone to use external shocks as scapegoats. In 1991 the 'external shock' argument was predominantly quoted. The aftermath of the Gulf war which temporarily increased the price of oil, the collapse of trade with the USSR linked with the fall of Comecon, and the disintegration of the USSR itself, were supposed to be largely responsible for the recession. However the price of oil did not remain high for long; and most of the enterprises (especially in heavy industry) which traded predominantly with the USSR were not closed – or we would have witnessed many more bankruptcies. Most of the experts also supported this argument however. It was only in 1993 that some of them began to question it (see Bofinger, 1993, challenging the conclusions of Bruno, 1992, and Rodrik, 1992). In 1992, a new external shock hit the Balkan countries, which were affected by the Western embargo on the FR of Yugoslavia: Bulgaria, Romania, Slovenia and Macedonia could rightly claim that it contributed to the output decline (though black-marketeers and smugglers undoubtedly benefited from it).

Western economists have usually stressed that stabilisation policies should have a deflationary effect on *domestic absorption* 'even in well-functioning market economies' (IMF, 1992, p. 67). Then the problem is mainly not to implement an excessively deflationary policy (Williamson, 1992b; Brada and King, 1992). The two most debated issues in this respect, already discussed above along with the instruments of stabilisation, have been the initial extent of the *devaluation* (Asselain, 1994), and the '*credit crunch*' (Calvo and Coricelli, 1992, and 1994 on the second topic). Initial *overdevaluations* brought real wages down to an excessively low level, and fuelled imported inflation which had then to be fought with still more restrictive policies. The *credit crunch* achieved through high interest rates did not hit so much the state-owned enterprises that could resort to inter-enterprise indebtedness, as it did the nascent private sector and the small enterprises, as well as the agricultural sector, hampering their development.

When the *supply side* is considered, we have the 'J-curve effect': as in the case of a devaluation, the introduction of a stabilisation programme brings about a reduction in supply not just as an effect of the demand shock, but because of rigidities in the supply response. This is linked by Gomulka (1991) with a Schumpeterian-like process of 'creative destruction': resources allocated to unproductive uses in the past are no longer used, and thus become available for future, more productive uses, once the economy fully responds to the market signals: then there will be an upward movement along the right side of the 'J'. Unfortunately what we have observed was, rather, an L-curve, with a protracted though decelerating recession. We are then back to a theory based on the excesses of stabilisation which decrease demand (Brada and King, 1992), or to stressing the rigidities in the supply, which are inherited from the past (Linotte, 1992) or due to the slowness of structural reforms (Bofinger, 1993). Rigidities can also be explained by the obstacles, in the form of red tape, discriminatory taxation, or credit restrictions from state-owned banks, faced by the emerging private sector (Mundell, 1995). Once the countries in transition began to recover, the GDP index exhibited another letter-shaped curve, in U-form (Blanchard, 1997, p. 1), as may be seen in Figure 7.4(b).

Blanchard's explanation for the fall in output is systemic: the main reason is what he calls 'disorganisation', that is the disruption of former links among centrally-planned entities, which were not immediately replaced by market operation, in addition to the impact of price liberalisation and the elimination of subsidies. The state firms were used to dealing with a single supplier for each input. Once liberalisation occurs, the situation does not change overnight as to the number of suppliers, but the difference is that in market conditions the suppliers have other, private market opportunities, which the buyer does not know about. Hence there are numerous bargaining failures, and the production originating from the state sector collapses (Blanchard, 1997, pp. 17 and 31). The systemic argument was indeed invoked earlier in a slightly different form (Roland and Verdier, 1997).

It is remarkable that in the early analyses, the return to a growth path is not discussed. Of course a Keynesian-type of macro-economic policy is out of the question, as it would contradict the essence of the deflationist packages applied. As summed up by Stanislaw Gomulka (1994, p. 100): according to these theses, 'the [post-transition] recessions are created on the demand side, but must be solved on the supply side'. This dominant view has been criticised by Alec Nove as a 'gap' in transition models. The standard model assumes that investment will generate growth as soon as the free market forces are able to operate fully in a stabilised context. But 'investment in what, financed how, by whom?' (Nove, 1994, p. 865).How should the state be involved? Several years elapsed before the analysts really dealt with such questions.

There were alternatives

The third reaction to the slump in output amounted to blaming shock therapy: there were alternatives. This is a counterfactual argument. Policy-makers or their advisers may consider alternative policies, especially to distinguish themselves from predecessors or competitors, but when one looks back at what actually happened there cannot be alternatives, and there is little point in discussing, for example, what would have happened had Russia followed China's path. It is not pointless however to ask why the chosen path has been so similar, whatever the differences in outcomes, in the European countries in transition, Russia included. One obvious answer is the role of international organisations, particularly the Bretton Woods institutions (the IMF and the World Bank) and the European Union. We shall revert to this role in Chapter 9.

In any case, stabilisation had become an almost obsolete debate by the end of the 1980s. The discussion has shifted to the definition of the best conditions for a sustained growth.

How to achieve a sustainable growth

As the two main directions of macro-economic stabilisation have been liberalisation and curbing of inflation, it is not surprising that the relation between growth and these two components of reform has been investigated. The standard model that has inspired the transition process is the IMF–World Bank structural adjustment package (dubbed the 'Washington consensus' because of the location of the two Bretton Woods institutions: see Williamson, 1994) that has been experienced first in developing (especially Latin American) countries in the 1980s. The model has been redesigned in the mid-1990s so as to make more room for structural long-term transformation and measures aiming at a sustained growth (Box 7.3). Hence the need to show a positive relation between growth, on the one hand, and liberalisation-cum-stabilisation, on the other.

The relation between liberalisation and growth has been suggested in a paper that was first presented at an OECD conference in 1996 and inspired the World Bank report *From Plan to Market* (de Melo and Gelb, 1997; World Bank, 1996). The bottom line is that liberalisation is an essential engine of growth because it provokes the expansion of formerly repressed activities such as domestic trade, finance and business services, and exports to market economies, while it entails the contraction of 'overbuilt' sectors such as industry and in some cases agriculture. 'On average . . . the expansion of repressed sectors begins to offset the contraction of overbuilt sectors after about three years of reform' (de Melo and Gelb, 1997, p. 76). The process is quicker in the 'advanced reformers' (Group 1, a group of five countries comprising Poland, Hungary, the Czech and the Slovak Republics, and Slovenia). Group 2 is made up of 'high-intermediate reformers' (Albania, Bulgaria, Romania and the three Baltic countries); and Group 3 of 'low-intermediate reformers' (Russia, Moldova, Kazakhstan and Kyrgyzstan). Group 4, of slow reformers, includes Belarus, Ukraine, Turkmenistan and Uzbekistan. Countries plagued by civil war or conflicts are not included. The degree of reforming is measured by a 'Cumulative Liberalisation Index' (CLI) with three weighted components: liberalisation of internal markets; liberalisation of external markets including a free foreign trade regime, elimination of all trade controls but 'low-to-moderate import duties', and current account convertibility; and liberalisation of private sector entry. Group 1 countries have a CLI of almost 7. Slow reformers display an index of 2 on average.

The link between inflation and growth, also mentioned in this study, was elaborated upon in another article by the First Deputy Director of the IMF, Stanley Fisher, and two other economists from the Fund (Fisher, Sahay and Végh, 1996). Is there an inflation 'red line beyond which growth will not be sustained' (Fisher *et al.*, p. 46), the limit being an annual rate of 40 per cent following what has been evidenced from developing countries (Bruno and Easterly, 1995)? Or should one take into account the fact that countries in transition are not yet standard market economies and that before structural transformation is completed it is impossible to reduce the rate of inflation much below that limit (for instance, to aim at a one-digit inflation rate)

***Box 7.3**   The 'Washington Consensus'*

1. Fiscal discipline
The overall budget deficit (including, in addition to the central government's deficit, also those of the provincial governments, of the state enterprises, and of the central bank), should be small enough to be financed without recourse to the inflation tax. The operational deficit should be no more than about 2 per cent of the GDP.

2. Public expenditure priorities
Expenditure should be redirected from politically sensitive areas – such as administration, defence, subsidies to 'white elephants' and indiscriminate subsidies – to such neglected fields as health, education, and infrastructure.

3. Tax reform
Tax reform involves: broadening the tax base, and improving tax administration.

4. Financial liberalisation
The goal is to achieve a moderately positive interest rate.

5. Exchange rates
The exchange rate must be unified (at least for trade transactions) and set at a level sufficiently competitive to induce a rapid growth in non-traditional exports.

6. Trade liberalisation
Quantitative restrictions should be replaced by tariffs, and these should be gradually reduced until a uniform low tariff (in the range of 10 per cent) is achieved.

7. Foreign direct investment
Barriers impeding the entry of foreign firms should be abolished. Foreign firms should be able to compete with domestic firms on equal terms.

8. Privatisation of state-owned enterprises

9. Deregulation of economic activity
Regulations should be maintained only to ensure safety, environmental protection, and prudential supervision of financial institutions.

10. Property rights
These should be secured without excessive costs, and made available to the informal sector.

The Declaration on cooperation aiming at sustained growth of the world economy (first discussed at the Madrid 1994 meeting of the IMF's 24-member Interim Committee and restated in October 1996 in Washington) may be seen as a modified version of the Washington consensus. Among the 11 points of the Declaration, most relevant to the situation of the countries in transition are point 1 (monetary, fiscal and structural policies are complementary and reinforce each other), point 3 (there is a need to create a favourable environment for private savings), 7 (budgetary policies have to aim at medium-term balance and at the reduction in public debt), 9 (structural reforms must be sustained, with a special attention to the labour markets), as well as points 10 and 11 (cautioning against corruption in the public sector and money laundering in the banking sector) (*IMF Survey*, 21 October 1996).

Source: Adapted from Williamson (ed.) (1994), pp. 26–8.

without adversely affecting growth? The answer, supported by a detailed econometric study, is that decline in inflation and return of positive growth go together, and that 'for growth to begin, annual inflation should be less than 50 per cent' (Fisher *et al.*, p. 63). This hypothesis is also supported in an IMF working paper (Christoffersen and Doyle, 1998) which stresses the importance of the inflation-output threshold while putting the threshold significantly lower than in the Fisher *et al.* (1996) study, in the range of 13 per cent. Above that range disinflation should promote growth, but other variables are important, and the authors underline the importance of export growth for stimulating output growth.

Yet another hypothesis would suggest that structural reforms associated with stabilisation are critical to growth. It is very difficult to model the full impact of structural reforms, and the studies based on the Washington consensus usually only retain the liberalisation component of the reform, as in the study by de Melo and Gelb (1997) quoted above. Issues such as the financial sector reform or the government's role in building a market environment are not discussed in this line of thought. In the aftermath of the East Asian financial crisis the Washington consensus is however increasingly under attack, including from within the Bretton Woods institutions. Thus the chief economist of the World Bank, Joseph Stiglitz, criticised the IMF bailout conditions in East Asia that imposed stringent stabilisation measures inducing a severe recession, and called for a 'post-Washington consensus' (Stiglitz, 1998). Perhaps unfortunately for the countries in transition, the East Asian crisis and along with it the reconsideration of standard stabilisation policies came too late to offer an alternative policy mix.

8 Privatisation and Structural Reforms

Structural transformation was supposed to begin at the same time as the 'stabilisation-cum-liberalisation' programmes. Its main building block was privatisation, which meant creating a greenfield private sector, and changing formerly state-owned enterprises into privately owned ones. Privatisation may also mean making existing state enterprises, either earmarked for further privatisation or remaining in state property, work as market-oriented firms, a process called marketisation or commercialisation in Central and East European countries. Reforms of the banking and tax systems, and creation of capital markets, were also among the first priorities of the policy-makers and advisers. Though most of the advisers also advocated the creation of a social safety net, which was meant to replace the former state 'paternalism', this is often seen as a 'luxury' in the East, as well as the safeguard of the environment. Labour-market reforms have been hard to conceive, as the old system was never confronted with an unemployment problem. Developing an industrial policy so as to organise an orderly dismantling of obsolete branches while providing for the growth of new sectors is still very low on the scale of priorities as it is generally identified with nostalgia for the old system.

This chapter will deal first with the privatisation policies, then with the other areas of the structural transformation, moving from first-priority targets to less obvious areas. This survey will thus include the banking and financial sectors reform, the tax reform, labour-market reforms, the building of a social safety net, and the specific tasks of transformation in agriculture.

PRIVATISATION

The concepts and practice of privatisation turned out to be much more complex than was thought in the beginning of transition. We shall look at the definitions of privatisation, its aims, its mechanisms, the main difficulties that were encountered, and finally the outcomes in the early stages of the transformation. Table 8.1 summarises these issues.

Definitions

In a narrow sense privatisation may be defined as a legal transfer of property rights from the state to private agents. State property includes what belonged to the state itself, and also to the socialist cooperatives. Does it include 'social ownership' as well, in the sense used in self-management, Yugoslav style? This is indeed a difficult question, and before the break-up of Yugoslavia the 1989 Law on the Circulation and Disposal of Social Capital amounted to an implicit nationalisation prior to divestiture (Uvalic, 1992, p. 184). Private owners may be individuals as well as legal entities, including foreigners.

A broader definition includes all measures contributing to the de-statisation of economic activity. In this sense privatisation may be consistent with a large state-owned sector, provided state enterprises are managed according to market rules and exposed to competition. Accordingly most of the present state sector in developed economies, with the possible exception of public utilities, would qualify as already 'privatised'. Similarly, the transformation of standard socialist cooperatives into market-type genuine cooperatives would also mean a shift toward privatisation.

Private property does not necessarily mean full ownership; transfers in the form of long-term leases, for instance (provided they genuinely transferred property rights, which was not the case with the Soviet *arenda* Gorbachev-style), may also qualify.

Finally, privatisation should also include creating entirely new enterprises. In this sense privatisation is tantamount to liberalisation; it means that anybody might engage in any kind of legal activity provided he/she complies with a minimum of rules.

In what follows we concentrate on the de-statisation of state-owned assets, which is the main problem in all the transition countries.

The Aims of Privatisation

In transition economies, privatisation understood in a broad sense may pursue different aims (Bornstein, 1992; Jackson, 1992a). *Politically* it means taking away property from the state and creating a new class of capitalists and entrepreneurs. *Equity considerations* suggest returning property to those who have been forcibly deprived of it during the nationalisation process, or giving priority to employees for buying shares in their enterprises; or even giving away state assets to the citizens. Privatisation may be pursued for *efficiency* reasons. If the latter are dominant, privatisation is no longer an aim *per se*. Better management of existing state enterprises, on the basis of a hard budgetary constraint following their marketisation, may increase productive static efficiency, if these enterprises are subject to competitive pressure. Allocative efficiency will be increased through privatisation only if there is a market environment with many buyers and sellers, the least possible barriers to entry and exit of the market, and a low degree of external protection. As in market economies entering into a privatisation process, the aims may be *financial*. If conducted through capital markets privatisation generates revenues to the state. Finally the governments may want to use privatisation as an additional *instrument of stabilisation*, and offer state assets for sale so as to eliminate the 'monetary overhang' whenever the savings of the population are large at the beginning of transition.

Whatever the initial illusions, the last two aims soon receded. Inflation wiped out the monetary overhang wherever it existed, and weakened the propensity to save. Hungary was the only country to have entertained some illusions as to the *fiscal potential* of privatisation, and this is why the government initially decided upon not giving away, but selling off state property. Experience has shown that far from bringing revenues to the state, privatisation is costly even when assets are sold rather than given away. The most striking example is that of the German *Treuhandanstalt* which wound up activities (end-1994) with accumulated debts of DM 270 billion, to be met by the federal budget of Germany, while receipts from sales amounted only to DM 53 billion. In the privatising countries, the costs incurred consist of various items: fees to the foreign accounting and consulting companies for estimating the value of the assets sold; expenditures of the privatisation agencies; recapitalising or debt consolidation. In Hungary, for instance, as Peter Mihályi (1997, pp. 91–3) shows, up to 1996 the privatisation-related expenses amounted to 28.4 per cent of the revenues from sales of state-owned assets. Costs are minimised, but far from nullified, when the assets are given away; but in that case receipts are nil (or close to nil); Sutela (1997) argues that voucher privatisation may indirectly increase fiscal revenues, namely through the development of secondary markets for shares, but such revenues are difficult to trace and in any case presumably low. Sell-off procures revenues, but at the expense of greater costs in restructuring.

In Poland *equity* considerations have been dominant in allowing the most extensive workers' preferential share in the assets of privatising companies. The tripartite 'enterprise pact' signed in February 1993 by the government with trade unions and employers allowed workers to decide on the form of privatisation for their enterprise, and to be represented in top management (with one-third of the seats). The workers were also granted 10 per cent of the shares of their enterprises at privatisation. However the implementation of this programme started only in 1995. Beginning from 1997, according to the August 1996 Law on commercialisation and privatisation of state-owned enterprises, the consent of the management and employees was no longer necessary.

In Czechoslovakia *political* goals have turned the privatisation process into an aim *per se*. The government wanted to take state property away from its former Communist management, which had largely survived the change in the political regime. Hence the speed of privatisation was crucial, and it was impossible to resort to sell-offs. Thus Czechoslovakia was the first country to launch a 'voucher-type' programme which allowed citizens to obtain shares of state companies at a symbolic nominal price. For the same reason, Czechoslovakia has been the only country providing for physical restitution of industrial assets in addition to land and housing nationalised after February 1948. After the Czech–Slovak split, in 1993 the Slovak Republic adopted a restitution law providing for financial compensation to those whose claims had not been met in kind.

The privatisation in Russia may also be explained by *social and political motives* above all, though efficiency was mentioned as an important aim in the privatisation programme. In the recurring conflict between the government and the parliament a quick transfer of property rights to millions of voters was meant to generate political support for the government and the presidency.

The Mechanisms of Privatisation

As has been noted, privatisation *in a broad sense* is tantamount to liberalisation. As soon as it was allowed to engage in retail trade and other small business activities, private enterprise emerged spontaneously. It generally began with 'street sales', which were a striking feature of the post-'big bang' Poland in January 1990. Then all kinds of service activities developed, especially those for which the main input was human capital: consulting, private teaching, engineering and computer services. Very often such activities had already long been conducted in the framework of the 'parallel economy' under the communist system. Later on this type of entrepreneurship was supported by laws on 'small privatisation', meant to transfer small state assets to private persons, mainly in trade and services, truck transport, construction, through sales of assets, by direct trade sales, by auctions officially not open to foreigners, and through leasing arrangements.

Large-scale privatisation of big enterprises has been, on the contrary, slow everywhere. Time was needed for setting up the institutions of privatisation, adopting the legal framework, finding buyers for the state-owned assets, monitoring the sequencing of the privatisation process, and selecting the enterprises which would not be privatised or would be so later. Even when the quickest method has been selected, and assets were given away to the population, as in Czechoslovakia and later in Russia, at least eighteen months were needed for completing each 'wave' of the process. More important still, privatisation cannot be seen as achieved once the ownership of the state enterprises has been transferred into non-state hands. The former state enterprises are still burdened by old debts, have obsolete equipment, an inadequately trained management, and very often the wrong industrial specialisation. The new property rights are not yet clearly defined. Restructuring and governance problems have thus to be solved before one can speak of a 'standard' private market economy.

In a very simplified view, the main methods of privatising big state-owned enterprises amount to three variants: sale to foreign investors, sale to domestic capital, and give-away schemes. Sometimes restitution is mentioned as a privatisation method. We do not share this view. Restitution was rather a way to 'clear the slate', out of political considerations. It did not end up in a physical turning back of the property to former owners, except in the Czech case, and in other countries for a limited range of assets. In many cases it was not decided upon immediately, and lengthy political debates on the issue took place. Thus we shall briefly recall the main features of restitution as a preamble to the implementation of the three main methods, or as an accompanying device to the last two methods, which have also been associated, officially or unofficially, with arrangements granting former managers and/or employees a preferential access to ownership. These main methods have always been combined in the privatisation process. The most usual sequence has been the following: selecting enterprises to privatise; trying to sell them either to foreigners or to domestic buyers; in view of the length of the process, introducing at some point (exceptionally from the very beginning, as in Czechoslovakia) a mass privatisation programme; going back to sales of state property so as to complete privatisation. In all cases, the difficulty of involving outsiders has been a strong inducement to insiders' privatisation, sometimes called 'spontaneous' when it occurred informally. Before going through these variants, we shall briefly describe the institutional framework of the process.

The institutional framework

In all countries, even the most committed to 'laissez-faire', the state or a parastatal agency had to organise and monitor the process. The governments of the countries in transition were usually reluctant to involve themselves deeply into the privatisation process. Hence the institutional framework has been kept to the minimum in most countries. The powerful *Treuhandanstalt*, the agency which has conducted the East German privatisation with extensive financial and legal means including ownership and control functions, has not been a model. Instead, the privatisation process has been dispersed among various bodies, according to the issues to be addressed (Table 8.1).

(1) The *government* as a whole supervises the process. Decisions involving very big enterprises are taken at the Council of Ministers level. Current supervision is ensured by privatisation ministries, committees or special agencies. These agencies have launched the privatisation, monitored it, and when provided for in the law endorsed the plans proposed by the enterprises themselves. In some cases local governments have been entitled to similar functions; these authorities were generally in charge of conducting small privatisation.

Table 8.1 *The main issues of the privatisation process in the countries in transition*

A. Main ways of creating a private sector

Greenfield privatisation (the setting up of new enterprises).	Transfer of state enterprises into the hands of new owners or lease of state property.	Corporatisation along with state ownership of assets and market-type management.

B. Privatisation institutions

Ministry of privatisation (Cz, Slk, Pld, Baltic states, Ukraine) or Minister without portfolio (H) or special department within a Ministry of Economic Reform (Rom).	State Property Agency (H); (National) Privatisation Agency (B, Rom, Sln) State Committee for the Management of State Property (Russia, Uzbekistan).	State Assets Management Co (H; merged with State Property Agency in 1995); State (or National) Ownership (Property) Fund (B, Cz, Slk, Rom, Ukraine, Russia); Treasury ministry (Pol, 1995) Development Fund (Sln).
Applies the general policy of privatisation under the government's control; selects the objects to privatise; examines the privatisation projects submitted by the enterprises; participates in setting up legal rules for privatisation.	Supplements the ministry of privatisation or acts as the main agency of privatisation. Protects state property during the process, oversees privatisation programs, implementation of process; assists in negotiations with foreign investors; evaluates the outcomes.	Management of state assets, either not yet privatised or due to remain in state property; restructuring of state-owned enterprises.

C. 'Small-scale' privatisation (small enterprises, mainly in the services sector and in construction; housing; land)

Restitution to former owners: – in kind or with attribution of an equivalent asset : Cz, Slk, B; (for land: Rom, Est); – in form of a compensation in cash: when otherwise impossible (Cz, Slk, B, Lat, Lit); – in privatisation vouchers: B, H (for land), Sln. No restitution in CIS countries. Restitution does not apply to non-residents as a rule.	Divestment of state assets: – closing down of enterprises; – sale by parts and redeployment of physical assets (in Pol, procedure of 'liquidation'); – sale by auctions (in most countries); – leasing, also by auctions; – buy-out by employees or by management (H, Pol, Russia), sometimes financed with vouchers for 'large' privatisation; – give-away schemes (for land (B, Rom), and housing).	Financing of privatisation – domestic capital; – foreign capital (in principle not allowed, or allowed under restrictive conditions; in fact largely resorted to, through straw-men).

→

D. 'Large-scale' privatisation (large industrial or service enterprises, banks)

Methods not implying revenues for the state.	Methods based on domestic capital.	Methods based on foreign capital.
Give-away schemes (so-called 'mass privatisation'). Main method applied in Cz; in Slk before partition of Czechoslovakia; in Lit, Romania (since 1995) Russia, Sln. Supplementing other methods in B, Lat, Pol.	'Spontaneous privatisation': usually not recognised as a privatisation method; is in fact the indirect outcome of give-away schemes, and the direct outcome of 'liquidation' procedures (Pol), of direct sales to the public, or of management buy-out schemes (Russia). Case-by-case sales on the capital market: has been practised when possible everywhere, and mainly in H.	Direct sale to foreign investors which retain the majority of the capital. Desired method everywhere; practised on a large scale in H.

Abbreviations: B = Bulgaria; Cz = Czech Republic; E = Estonia; H = Hungary; Lat = Latvia; Lit = Lithuania; Pol = Poland; Rom = Romania; Slk = Slovakia; Sln = Slovenia.

Sources: Various reports and sources on privatisation (see text); EBRD (1997).

(2) The question of the *ownership* of the state enterprises has raised many difficulties. In the past, under the principle of 'socialist ownership of the means of production', the state was the owner of these means. Was it the individual owner of each state enterprise? This was never clarified, and actually did not need to be, as what mattered was party control and administrative direction, the latter being done by the branch ministries. As both the party and the branch ministerial framework were suppressed after the collapse of communism, one had to decide about the ownership of the enterprises during the privatisation process. Ownership rights were given either to the same agencies as the ones conducting the privatisation process, or to special agencies or funds. Prior to privatisation, in most cases the state enterprises were *transformed into joint-stock* companies, a process called 'marketisation' ('commercialisation', corporatisation) with the state remaining the sole shareholder, under various schemes depending on the agencies which exercised the ownership rights. The different words used to name the process are not clearly distinguished. Usually it is assumed that commercialisation refers to the formal process of giving a legal identity to the firm, while corporatisation suggests that a management structure is established (with clear rules for selecting managers and board members) and that the

firm is supposed to operate according to a profit-maximising behaviour in a competitive environment (see Estrin, 1994, especially chapters 1 and 2). The same agencies also had to manage the state-owned enterprises which had been singled out as strategic and were due to remain in public ownership or to be privatised at a later stage. Such enterprises usually included infrastructure enterprises (railways, ports) and utilities (electricity and gas distribution, telecommunications).

Let us now turn to the three main privatisation methods mentioned earlier. But first we shall discuss the restitution issue, and last, having outlined the basic methods, we shall point to their most frequent outcome – insiders' privatisation.

Restitution

Equity considerations point to the need, prior to privatisation, to restitute what has been taken away by the communist power from the former owners, or at least to compensate the latter (or their heirs) for the loss of property. Once the principle is admitted (which has been the case in Central and Eastern Europe and in the Baltic States), the implementation is difficult. One has to identify the former owners, many of whom are deceased or have emigrated abroad. Even when only resident and still-alive former owners are entitled to claim their property back, their identification may raise problems especially if the same asset is claimed by several persons. It is necessary to establish the date of the nationalisations that are to be compensated. In most cases only communist nationalisations were taken into consideration, which excluded earlier cases of confiscation by post-war non-communist governments. This provision turned out to discriminate against Germans (Nazis and non-Nazis alike) and against Jews, as mentioned in Chapter 2 (Slovakia in 1993 decided to compensate the Jews expropriated between 1945 and 1990; in Poland, a law of March 1997 provides for the restitution of churches, schools and churchyards owned by the Jewish churches before 1 September 1939). A decision also has to be made about whether the restitution will be made in kind or in terms of a compensation (through cash payments, privatisation vouchers or securities), and in the latter case whether it will amount to a hundred per cent compensation or whether there will be some discount. Compensation in turn raises the problem of the proper evaluation of the asset, in countries where there was no land cadastre, and where the book value of industrial assets was fictitious. Finally it must be determined who is entitled to restitution: all former owners or their heirs, only residents, and in the case of land all claimants or only farmers? For instance Hungary admitted reprivatisation of land only, and even in this case only to the benefit of recipients committing themselves to farm it for at least five years (law of 1991); in all other cases the claimants were entitled to tradable compensation vouchers. Institutions are usually not allowed to claim restitution; churches are an exception in some countries, and this has been hotly debated in particular in Czechoslovakia.

Table 8.1 sums up the issues and the solutions retained. In all cases, whatever the solutions, restitution proved a very politicised issue not only domestically but also in bilateral relations (such as in the case of the Czech–German discussions on the compensation for the ethnic Germans of the *Sudetenland*). Restitution also alienated many people and groups (among them peasants) in the countries in transition. It delayed small and large privatisation. Even once the claims were formally settled, the solutions were not satisfactory. Compensation in cash has usually been a small fraction of the real value of the asset. Compensation in form of securities or privatisation vouchers has left claimants with assets difficult to use or trade at good conditions.

Privatisation with the help of foreign capital

In the beginning of the transition there were hopes of a large involvement of foreign capital into privatisation. Under the communist regime, a legal framework for foreign investment had been created in all countries: in the 1960s in Yugoslavia (1967), in the 1970s in Hungary, Romania (beginning in 1972) and Poland (1976), in the 1980s in Bulgaria (1980), Russia (1987), and Czechoslovakia (1989). Once the transition had begun, ambiguous attitudes developed about foreign direct investment. On the one hand, the new governments hoped very much to attract foreign investors, and the legislation was accordingly made much more favourable than it was before. On the other hand, the authorities had to take care of nationalistic feelings and dispel the idea that foreigners would select the best choices so as to make big profits. The sensitiveness of public opinion is particularly high when ownership of land is concerned. Even in Hungary, the country which may be seen as the most open to foreign capital, the land law passed in April 1994 severely limited foreign investment in agriculture by banning new purchases of land by foreigners (*Financial Times*, 7 April 1994), and the referendum on this issue which was scheduled for the end of 1997 was declared unconstitutional by the Constitutional Court (*ibid.*, 15 October 1997).

Foreign investment is certainly not a solution for achieving overall privatisation. True, in Hungary foreign investment accounted for around 75 per cent of the proceeds received from privatisation between 1990 and 1992, and after a decline of this share in 1993 and 1994, it soared again to 80–90 per cent in 1995–6 (Matolcsy, 1997, p. 166). In 1994, foreign capital accounted for 31 per cent of the nominal capital of the companies, which compares with the share of foreign assets in Austria, amounting to 25–30 per cent (Hunya, 1997, p. 289). It seems doubtful that in any of the other countries in transition foreign capital might account for more than 10–15 per cent of the total assets. By the mid-1990s, the figure was 7 per cent for the Czech Republic and for Poland, the two countries that had attracted the largest share of foreign investment into Central Europe after Hungary (Hunya, 1997, p. 290).

As an instrument of privatisation, foreign direct investment has definite qualitative advantages. It solves the restructuring problems by passing them on to foreign firms – however, as foreign capital selects the best enterprises these are also the least in need of restructuring (as compared with other candidates for privatisation). Without establishing a firm correlation, it may be stressed that the countries which experienced the strongest recovery in investment since 1993–4 (Hungary, the Czech Republic, Slovenia, Estonia and Poland) have also attracted significant inflows of FDI per capita (with the exception of Slovenia). Foreign investment is thus a powerful engine of modernisation. But as well as being difficult to lure into a country, it is also difficult to control by national governments in Central and Eastern Europe, as the big multinationals are much more powerful than small countries with no business experience.

There is however another way of looking at foreign direct investment: as a means of integrating the countries in transition into the global economy. This will be discussed in Chapter 9.

Sale of assets to domestic capital

In some cases this method is tantamount to the former one. Even though small-scale privatisation was officially not open to foreign capital, in fact in many cases (especially in Czechoslovakia and Hungary) foreign funds were extensively used, through family or other informal connections, to privatise hotels, restaurants, and other personal services.

The lack of domestic capital soon emerged as the major stumbling block of overall privatisation. Most of the available domestic savings were quickly absorbed by the small privatisation. Poland and especially Hungary tried to sell big state enterprises through public offerings, tenders, or individual sales. In both countries only a few hundred companies could be sold that way. Each transaction took a long time, delays being caused by the need for financial and management restructuring, and emerged as quite costly in terms of assets evaluation (involving foreign accounting companies and consultants charging high fees). The experiences were even less conclusive in other Eastern European countries. Ultimately most of the countries evolved toward the 'free distribution' model which was devised in Czechoslovakia as the main privatisation method.

The story does not end here. First, domestic savings had to be channelled into privatised firms to finance new investment. Second, with the exception of the Czech Republic, most of the countries succeeded in privatising only a part of state-owned assets through mass privatisation schemes. Once these schemes have been completed, the assets that have not been sold (or are not saleable) to foreign investors, or are not to remain in the hands of the state wholly or partly, have to be disposed of via sales, be it with sizeable rebates – the last hypothesis is connected with 'insider' privatisation. The issue of domestic savings is thus crucial. This is one of the less-known areas in the economies in transition, as is stated in the EBRD *Transition Report 1996* in its Part III on 'Promoting savings' (EBRD, 1996). Beyond the obvious statement that the savings and investment rates in per cent of GDP sharply declined since the beginning of transition, there are few reliable measures for household and enterprise savings. Hungary, which provided the most detailed data, displayed an overall savings rate of 13 per cent to the GDP in 1994, down from a ratio of 27 per cent in 1990 (EBRD, 1996, p. 82). The availability of savings is not the only problem. How to mobilise these savings for productive uses? This raises the question of financial intermediation. In many countries, investment funds, usually set up as instruments of voucher privatisation, have collected vouchers from the population and become major shareholders of privatised enterprises; they have also provided additional finance for privatisation, especially as in many cases the most powerful of these funds were partly or wholly owned by banks. The banks themselves have been among the last state-owned economic agents to be privatised. This means that in countries where financial intermediation through the banking system is still dominant, privatisation through sales to domestic investors amounts to transferring state assets from state institutions or agencies to state-owned banks or other financial intermediaries. Banking reforms and restructuring thus emerge as a crucial and very complex issue.

Does the recent emergence of booming capital markets in Eastern Europe (see below pp. 186–92 on banking and financial sectors reform) change the picture? The new stock markets are very narrow and volatile, the public offerings procedures lack transparency, and finally the households lack financial experience and see stock deals rather as a form of gambling than as a form of investment. Actually capital markets did not contribute much to privatisation. For the few companies quoted, they appeared as a useful valuation instrument.

Expert advice offered to the countries in transition has emphasised the potential role of pension funds, which might at the same time broaden the range of securities offered on the stock exchanges, mobilise domestic capital and contribute to the reform of the social security net. The issue will be discussed below in conjunction with the social security reform. In any case, from the sketchy evidence available, contractual savings (in form of life insurance schemes or pension funds) are still a tiny fraction of GDP (less than 1 per cent in the most favourable cases; see EBRD, 1996, pp. 89–90).

Mass privatisation schemes

Free transfers of shares to the citizens may involve two main variants: (i) distribution of vouchers, or coupons, to be converted into shares in operating companies; (ii) distribution of shares in investment funds or holding companies that in turn have shares in companies. A combination of both occurs when the citizens are permitted to ask an investment fund to manage their vouchers for them.

Czechoslovakia opted for variant (i) as the main method for privatising large enterprises. The process was launched in the beginning of 1992, involving about 2000 enterprises of which almost 1500 were auctioned (PlanEcon, 1993a). After the partition of the country, while Slovakia was waiting before launching the second wave, the Czech Republic decided in 1993 to go ahead for nearly 1000 companies; this second wave began in April 1994. (For a detailed account of voucher privatisation in the Czech Republic, see Leeds, 1993; Svejnar and Singer, 1994; for comparisons with other countries' schemes, see Bornstein, 1997.) The process was declared as completed by 1 March 1995.

Poland chose, within its 'Mass Privatisation Programme' to experiment with method (ii) for a significant number of state enterprises (400, then 512). The programme was announced in June 1991 and prepared during the year 1992, with great delays due to difficulties in setting up investment funds. The final version of the programme was ultimately approved by the Polish parliament in April 1993, following a government/parliament conflict which expressed frustrations as to the many uncertainties surrounding the programme. Actual sell-offs began at the end of 1995; a new privatisation law was adopted in 1996. Overall, out of the 8441 state-owned enterprises existing in 1990, slightly over 6000 had initiated the privatisation process by end-1966 by the various methods applied by the Polish government, but only 1719 had completed this process (Blaszczyk *et al.*, 1997). Poland is thus a case for very gradual privatisation, which did not hamper either its economic recovery or its progress in transition.

In 1993 the *Hungarian* government first contemplated a shift toward a mass privatisation plan, due to the delays in implementing privatisation by sell-offs. The new plan, decided upon in April 1994, included a higher contribution from the citizens than in Poland and Czechoslovakia, which was to be financed through cheap credit. It was also less 'massive' as only 70 companies had been included in the first round, to begin end-1994. The plan was approved in view of the approaching general elections (held in May 1994); as the elections were lost by the government, this scheme was stalled.

Other countries have launched mass privatisation schemes, with mixed results. *Slovakia*, once separated from the Czech Republic, decided to temporarily stop the programme. A second wave of voucher privatisation was launched in 1994 but was cancelled in 1995. The voucher holders (65 per cent of the population) have received bonds maturing at the end of the year 2000 in exchange for their vouchers. Before maturity, they could use their bonds to buy shares in the National Property Fund, pay for health insurance, or for housing, and privatisation has slowly continued in the form of direct sales (EBRD, 1997, p. 198). *Romania* officially launched its mass privatisation programme in 1992 by distributing privatisation vouchers to about 17 million citizens so as to let them acquire 30 per cent of the capital of the 6300 companies to be privatised, but nothing followed. A new programme was decided upon in July 1994, probably to comply with the government's commitment to the IMF, according to which half of the industrial enterprises should have been privatised by 1994. The new voucher programme was approved in 1995, and the distribution of vouchers ended in October 1996. By the end of 1996 only 45 per cent of the enterprises due to be privatised were in private hands; only 13 per cent of the large enterprises had been transferred away from the state. A new privatisation law was passed in early 1998, but its implementation was delayed because of the political crisis that developed in 1998. *Bulgaria* amended its 1992 law on privatisation in June 1994 to pave the way for mass privatisation. All Bulgarian citizens could acquire investment coupons, paying a symbolic fee; these bonds were not tradable but could be used to buy shares in enterprises or in investment funds. The voucher scheme applied to 1000 enterprises and 20 per cent of state-owned assets between October 1996 and June 1997 (EBRD, 1997, p. 159). The case of *Slovenia* is very interesting. The country remained attached to the idea of 'social ownership' and engaged into privatisation later than the central European countries, especially as the self-managed enterprises, Yugoslav style, were generally better managed than state-owned enterprises elsewhere. Privatisation began effectively in 1995. It has essentially been based on the voucher method, with preference given to the employees in the distribution and acquisition of shares. In addition ownership certificates have been issued to all Slovene citizens, with a nominal value depending on the age of the citizen – a feature quite specific to Slovenia. These shares could be exchanged against shares either in enterprises or in investment funds. Table 8.2 summarises the different variants.

The Baltic countries and the former CIS countries have also launched or at least decreed privatisation programmes. In the Baltics, the country most committed to the voucher method has been *Lithuania*. From late 1991 until mid-1995 the voucher method was used, but failed to produce significant results; the vouchers were mainly used to acquire the state-owned housing stock. The second phase, beginning in July 1995, relied on direct sales (EBRD, 1997, p. 184). The *Russian* scheme is based on the privatisation law of 1991 amended in 1992. *All* Russian citizens each received 10,000 rubles' worth of privatisation vouchers, beginning in October 1992, immediately tradable in cash or exchangeable against shares in enterprises selected for

Table 8.2 *Mass privatisation schemes*

Methods	Advantages	Drawbacks
Issue of vouchers that are used to buy enterprise shares or may be entrusted to investment funds (Cz; Slk before partition; B since 1994).	Moral compensation for Communist past injustice, which deprived the people of what belonged to them in principle.	No revenues for the state Inflationary when vouchers are freely transferable.
Distribution of shares on subsidised credit (H).	Swiftness of the procedure; the valuation problem is suppressed; no need for restructuring.	Risk of speculation from investment funds (Cz, Russia).
Issue of certificates of investment funds set up by the state, which have a stake in the companies to be privatised (Pol, Rom, Sln).	No need for capital. Political support.	Time-consuming procedure when investment funds are involved from the outset (Pol).
Issue of vouchers which may be exchanged against shares or certificates of investment, freely traded on the market, or used for employee buy-back schemes (Russia).		Actual use of the procedure to foster employee ownership, openly (Russia) or unintendedly (in most countries).
		The procedure leaves open corporate governance problems.

Abbreviations: B = Bulgaria; Cz = Czech Republic; H = Hungary; Pol = Poland; Rom = Romania; Sln = Slovenia; Slk = Slovakia.

privatisation. Enterprises, after being transformed into joint-stock companies at the initiative of their management or of employees, and being selected for participation in the programme, were auctioned at direct public auctions opened to nationals and foreigners. Three variants could be selected by the staff of the enterprises to be auctioned. Variant 1 provided for free allocation of 25 per cent of the charter capital to all employees, in non-voting shares. Variant 2 allocated 51 per cent of the shares to the employees at 1.7 times their book value on 1st January 1992 (a gift, in a situation of high inflation) and with voting rights, plus an option of a further percentage of voting shares. Variant 3 allowed a group of employees to get 20 per cent of the voting shares at book value under the commitment to restructure the enterprise within a year, plus a further 20 per cent if the restructuring was successful. The rest of the shares was auctioned in all three variants. Bidders could pay in cash, or in vouchers. Of the large state enterprises 70 per cent were thus privatised by end-June 1994; past that deadline the vouchers were no longer valid. A second wave followed, to auction the rest of the enterprises to be privatised, on commercial conditions, and proceeded much more slowly. A new privatisation law was approved in 1997 by the Russian Duma. It was meant to give a legal basis and more transparency to valuation and privatisation procedures, after several notorious deals had evidenced the dominant role of insiders.

It seems thus obvious that whatever the initially preferred methods, all countries have been trying mass privatisation schemes, generally combined with other forms of divestiture, for three main reasons: (i) it was quicker than any other (but still could take time if technical constraints and political obstacles interfered, as in the Polish case); (ii) it was politically appealing as it amounted to a massive gift to the electoral constituency; (iii) it appeared as an irreversible commitment to capitalism (Nuti, 1994). The first reason has been dominant, either at the outset of the process as in the Czech case, or to accelerate protracted privatisation by standard methods. In the mass privatisation variant applied in Czechoslovakia, the giving away of the enterprises to be privatised and their valuation were realised in the same process, through the auctioning of the shares in several rounds: a time-saving and money-saving procedure, but which was very close to a lottery-like scheme as the prospective shareholders had very little information on the performances and the market potential of the enterprises. 'Instant' models of privatisation were favoured in the early literature (Blanchard *et al.*, 1991, ch 2). Later, most Western economists and experts have grown cautious, and even those in favour of quick privatisation recognised that there was a risk of going too fast in a voluntarist approach (Aghion and Blanchard, 1993; and Aghion, 1993).

Spontaneous, or insiders', privatisation

Spontaneous privatisation is not a specific method of privatisation, but a way for insiders to appropriate formerly state-owned property. It is often defined as the way for members of the former communist *nomenklatura* to become owners of the companies they managed before (or of the best parts of these companies), in a more or less legal manner. This happened first in Poland and Hungary, in fact under a legal cover. In both countries, still under the communist regime, state enterprises were first granted more rights, with enterprise or workers' councils getting involved in the management and even (in Hungary) into the selection of the enterprises' directors. Then state enterprises were transformed into joint-stock companies. The managers used the new legal framework to split up state companies, and transform the best sections into limited liability companies or joint ventures, securing jobs for themselves and the most skilled of their employees, and leaving in state ownership only the non-profitable parts of the previous state enterprise (Marrese, 1992). In Czechoslovakia the process was prevented by the fact that there was no adequate legal framework in the beginning of the new regime, and also because of a greater social and political intolerance toward the former *nomenklatura.*

Since 1990 such deals have no longer been possible legally. In Poland, however, the very widely applied procedure of so-called 'liquidation', that was the sale of some viable parts of an enterprise to a new private company usually set up by the former managers and employees, was in fact a legalisation of 'spontaneous' privatisation. In other countries spontaneous privatisation has developed as well, though generally denied, or else acknowledged as a deformation of the legal process.

In principle, this kind of privatisation should not be confused with privatisation initiated by the state companies themselves. This takes place when the companies are allowed or encouraged to present 'privatisation plans' submitted to the state authority in charge. However, one cannot exclude that 'insider information' leads, in this case as well, to some kind of 'spontaneous privatisation'. In the Russian schemes, spontaneous privatisation thus appears as semi-legal because the employees had to prepare a privatisation plan (to be approved by either the State Committee for Management of State Assets, or by local authorities), and because the preferred scheme among the three variants outlined above has been 'variant 2' transferring 51 per cent of the shares to 'insiders'.

It is very difficult to reach a sober assessment on this issue. Eastern governments and Western experts alike are very much against this form of privatisation. It looks too much like Western insider trading and legacies of communist *nomenklatura*'s privileges combined. The uncomfortable reality of dominant insiders' ownership is reluctantly acknowledged. There are a few exceptions to such an attitude. Thus the Hungarian economist Péter Mihályi boldly equates ' "Large" privatisation = Spontaneous privatisation', and cautions against an ideological condemnation of the phenomenon (Mihályi, 1993, p. 34). In the Hungarian case, this has led to a complex corporate structure linked by cross-ownership; 'this shift,' Mihályi argues, 'from a relatively monolithical structure of state ownership toward the cross-ownership model is a spontaneous evolution fed by the energy of the Hungarian managerial class and made possible by the benign neglect of the country's political masters' (Mihályi, 1993, p. 38).

Is the process bad *per se*? The question is hardly relevant as there is no real choice on a large scale. The countries in transition each need thousands of managers. While it was relatively easy to find a few dozen experts among former dissidents or quasi-dissidents to take jobs in the new state administration, it is impossible to find enough good managers to replace the previous managerial class. This class may be trained. The former communist managers are able to act with a view to maximising their own economic interests, which they did in the past, and which is after all the quintessence of capitalism. As the majority of them (if not all) never really believed in communism but just pretended to, there is no risk that they would help to bring the old regime back. And if not them, who else? If they are excluded on political grounds, then the alternative would be political appointees of the opposite side, lacking experience and probably less apt as the few apt people are already in business.

As the privatisation process is winding up, the Western critics of insiders' privatisation have shifted from privatisation methods proper to the issue of corporate governance in the privatised companies. It is argued that insider-owned firms are less prone to conducting deep restructuring and less efficient than outsider-owned firms, though case studies do not always point in this direction (see Aghion and Carlin, 1997, p. 259). Blanchard (1997) considers that 'outside ownership is typically needed for full restructuring to take place' (p. 87) but that insider ownership may be dominant for political reasons. However if and when insider privatisation does not lead to restructuring, resale of the workers' shares may lead to outsider ownership which would then permit restructuring. How to replace insiders' by outsiders' ownership? The difficulties signalled in this section (limitations to foreign ownership, lack of domestic capital, lack of developed capital markets) prevent a massive resale of insider-owned firms, and it is rather naive to presume that in such a process, 'good managers should survive an ownership transfer from insiders to outsiders' (Aghion and Carlin, 1997, p. 258), or that collusion in resale may be easily avoided.

When is privatisation over? Some countries have decided upon this question. In Hungary, privatisation is to be over in 1998. The APV (the institution which merged in 1995 the State Property Agency and the State Holding Company) will then retain shares in 109 companies overall, with 50 companies remaining in 100 per cent state ownership. In the Czech Republic, voucher privatisation was decreed completed in March 1995, but the crucial bank privatisation was not yet over in 1998. Most of the countries in transition have not set firm deadlines. The other solution is to resort to benchmark ratios. According to the EBRD measure of progress in transition, large-scale privatisation is supposed to be over with 'more than 75 per cent of enterprise assets in private ownership with effective corporate governance' (EBRD, 1997, p. 15; see Table 8.3 at the end of this chapter). None of the countries in transition has yet obtained the mark '4+' sanctioning this state, though three countries had reached in 1997 the ratio of 75 per cent of private sector contribution to the GDP (the Czech Republic, Hungary, and Slovakia). Anyhow the measures of privatisation are delusive. The data lump all private property rights together, adding the production (or employment) in grassroots enterprises and in privatised enterprises (industrial firms, farms, banks, etc.). The extent of privatisation is not always specified (does one include only 100 per cent private enterprises, or 50 per cent, or less ?). Hence comparisons are difficult (Anderson *et al.*, 1997, p. 137). The main problem is corporate governance. When is it going to be 'effective' and comparable to industrial market economies' standards? The statement is bound to remain subjective and biased by political considerations. Categorical judgements should be avoided. The wave of privatisations which spread in the developed world in the 1980s and 1990s should caution against premature assessments for the former communist countries – after all, privatisation could not yet be considered as 'over' in France in 1998. Rather than arguing about benchmarks and thresholds, one should concentrate on what remains to be done.

Post-Privatisation: Restructuring and Governance

There has been some delusion in the beginning of transition about the possibility of restructuring the state-owned enterprises *before* privatising them. This was the main idea behind the first Polish mass privatisation scheme: the National Investment Funds were supposed to restructure and if needed wind up the enterprises they were in charge of. Because of the delays in implementing this programme, restructuring was in most cases skipped. In nearly all the countries restructuring occurred *after* privatisation, as opposed to the 'restructuring first' model of the *Treuhandanstalt* in East Germany (Carlin and Mayer, 1992). Thus case studies on restructuring increasingly focused on an approach assessing at the same time the quality of governance and the efficiency of restructuring.

Restructuring

Restructuring policies implied closing firms judged unprofitable, or sections of firms, and laying off workers (Aghion and Blanchard, 1993); reorganising the production process as a whole; recapitalising the enterprises; pursuing an anti-monopoly policy and splitting up the enterprises (see Charap and Zemplinerova, 1993, and Carlin and Mayer, 1992, for a clear statement of the issues). *Organisational restructuring* was a by-product of the privatisation process, as enterprises to be privatised had everywhere to submit plans which defined their future internal structure, which often implied a splitting-up of the enterprise into several parts and more or less extended lay-offs, and outlined the industrial strategy for the future. *Financial restructuring* could not be ignored as soon as the bankruptcy legislation was introduced and implemented. All these forms of restructuring apply not only to privatised companies but also to state-owned enterprises, either to remain in state ownership or to be privatised much later.

We are not going to discuss here all the aspects of restructuring. We focus on two issues. First, is there a clear anti-monopoly policy in the countries in transition? Second, when firms are debt-ridden and unprofitable, is there an effective bankruptcy legislation?

Competition on the domestic market means *demonopolisation*, a very complex issue. On the one hand, clearly the huge state monopolies of the past must be dismantled, and in some countries (Hungary and Poland) the process had begun, rather unsuccessfully, even before the transition. On the other hand, the Western developed world is one of big companies. What has been witnessed in countries in transition is a development of small and medium enterprises (SMEs) essentially in the services sector, based upon restitution policies and on *de novo* creation of small businesses. SMEs did not emerge from the splitting-up of state monopolies. In all countries anti-monopoly laws have been enacted, sometimes with anti-monopoly committees to implement them, but in the vast majority of cases the laws were not applied. Few anti-mergers decisions have been taken. When action has been engaged, it has usually resulted in fines, rarely collected entirely, against monopolistic practices, mainly in wholesale trade. A significant case is that of Russia, where the anti-monopoly law of 1991 has been amended 30 times, but where the anti-monopoly regulations do not seem to apply to the biggest groups in the country, the financial industrial groups (see below in this section). The much-publicised actions taken in 1997 against the biggest Russian monopolies, Gazprom and the Unified Energy System, were directed more against the lack of transparency of the governance and the ownership structure, than against the monopolistic principle of gas and electricity distribution itself. The partly privatised long-distance telecommunications company Svjazinvest is also to keep its dominant position on the telecom market.

Overall, in the sectors controlled by foreign investment, investors have often been motivated exactly by the prospect of gaining a monopoly position in the country. The countries that prepare their accession to the EU are introducing laws on 'restrictive practices' on the model of the EU legislation; Hungary was the first with a law entering in force by 1 January 1997. It is to be expected that, like in incumbent EU members, the attitude towards large firms with a dominant position will be a compromise between national support to industrial 'champions' and the EU commission's stance on fair competition. The largest Central and East European firms are in any case not yet to be listed among the European giants – only four such firms were on the list of the first top 500 European companies (*Financial Times*, 22 January 1998): the Czech SPT Telecom, the Hungarian oil company MOL, and two pharmaceutical companies, the foreign-owned Hungarian Richter Gedeon, and the Croatian Pliva.

Bankruptcy laws have not played a large role in restructuring. Among the potential micro-economic agents that might have an incentive to provoke the winding-down of a company, there are the creditors of the company: the suppliers (for the amount of their invoices), the wage-earners (for their wages), the banks and other institutional or individual creditors (for their loans) and the state along with parastatal organisations (for taxes and contributions to social security). None of these agents is likely to behave in the same way as in a standard market economy. Suppliers are themselves indebted and are used to settling part of their debts through various arrangements such as barter or inter-enterprise credit. Wage-earners prefer to forgo part of their wages or to receive some compensation in kind, instead of losing their job if the company is liquidated. Banks are often so burdened by bad loans that they avoid bankruptcy procedures which, if successful, would deprive them of most of their assets, and prefer keeping non-performing loans on their balance sheet to jeopardising their own existence. The state authorities are used to tax avoidance and bad collection, and social considerations may also favour a status quo. This explains why the actual number of bankruptcies has remained very small, though the relevant legislation has everywhere been adopted or revived. Even in the countries where the authorities have shown the greatest resolve, the lack of experience and capacity of courts has been a limiting factor, as in Hungary and Poland.

Instead of bankruptcies, the governments have favoured special actions to clean up loss-making enterprises, often under the pressure of international financial organisations. The first experiment was made in Hungary in 1992 when the government selected fourteen 'strategic' state-owned enterprises accounting for a quarter of the country's exports, cleared state debts and provided new funds and ultimately closed five of them (EBRD, 1997, p. 73). An interesting experiment was conducted in Poland, under the 1993 Enterprise and Bank Restructuring Programme (EBRP). A 'conciliation' procedure was introduced for bank-led workouts of problem firms. The outcome of two years of operation and about 400 agreements between nine banks and 139 state-owned enterprises is mixed. The programme did not spur privatisation. It did not result in strong restructuring. It was useful in slowing down layoffs, reducing debt service and thus giving firms some breathing space (Gray and Holle, 1996). Bulgaria launched in 1996 an ambitious programme of financial 'isolation' and liquidation of 64 loss-making enterprises accounting for 29 per cent of the losses in the economy, with the support of a special funding by the World Bank for lay-off compensations to the workers (OECD, *Bulgaria*, 1997a). It seems that the implementation of the programme, and the disbursement of World Bank funds, have been delayed. Under the pressure of the IMF, the Romanian government decided in August 1997 to close seventeen loss-making companies while promising a 12-month wage severance pay to the laid-off workers; the release of a tranche of an IMF stand-by loan followed next month (*Financial Times*, 12 August 1997; and OECD, *Romania*, 1998).

The mixed results in restructuring and closing loss-making entities may be related to the quality of governance, insofar as the management of both private and non-private companies becomes the main issue. Here one has to distinguish between small-scale assets and large-scale units. While small-scale privatisation most often leads to family businesses, the corporate governance of the privatised large-scale state-owned enterprises is not easy to clarify.

Corporate governance

In all transition countries, the former state-owned enterprises may now be divided into three groups. The first is made up of the enterprises already privatised. Within this group, the only sub-group more or less easy to identify from the point of view of management and control comprises the companies under foreign control, but these are the minority, and only in Hungary account for a significant share in industrial output. The bulk of the privatised companies consists of commercialised (corporatised) large firms. The second group is made up of state firms preparing themselves for privatisation and submitting projects to that effect to the institutions in charge. Finally the third group is made up of state-owned enterprises either to be privatised in the future or to remain in the state sector. There is no clear policy as to what kind of enterprises should remain in the state sector, short of a small number of utilities. (In Romania there has been a definition of the scope of the state sector to remain; it would comprise energy distribution, mines, railways, the postal service, with a French-type status of 'regies autonomes'. But even those are to be privatised partly or totally according to new legislation of 1997: EBRD, 1997, p. 192.) Most of the enterprises in this group are, or are being, transformed into stock companies. As will be shown, all the three groups (with exception of the 100 per cent foreign-owned firms) are evolving toward the same kind of corporate governance.

Some pioneering studies have explored the behaviour of the firms under transition conditions (Brada *et al.*, 1994, for Hungary; Pinto *et al.*, 1993, for Poland; Sereghyova, 1993, for Czechoslovakia; Carlin *et al.*, 1995, for Central Europe and Russia; Estrin *et al.*, 1995, for Central Europe). The number of studies soon expanded as the micro-economic data on enterprise management became available and as numerous organisations financed such studies conducted in cooperation with Central and East European researchers. Numerous symposia and conferences were devoted to it. Here we can only offer a guide for further reading, and suggest some conclusions (see the very extensive survey by Carlin and Landesmann, 1997; special issues of journals such as *Moct-Most*, 1997, *Economics of Transition*, 1997; Part II of OECD, 1997d; World Bank, 1996).

What comes out of these studies is that there is no 'ownership frontier' as far as performance is considered – successful and unsuccessful firms are to be found on each side. What the successful firms have in common is a quick adjustment to market conditions, 'survival strategies' to secure markets and finance in the beginning, moving toward more long-term strategies with time. 'Perhaps the most surprising finding in the surveys of enterprise restructuring and performance in the transition economies is the relative absence of clear-cut differences between privatised and state-owned firms; they both shed labour and close inefficient units, but they seldom engage in new strategic investments or "deep restructuring"' (CEPR and IEWS, 1996a, p. 19). Complexity and ambiguity are the main features to be observed, which makes the conclusions 'tentative and heuristic', and 'subject to caveats' (Carlin *et al.*, 1995). The only clear-cut difference is between majority foreign-owned firms and all others.

Theoretical studies on corporate governance of firms in transition usually discuss the issue in terms of the principal/agent approach (see Frydman *et al.*, 1993b, 1994 and 1996, vol. 2). How are the managers to be controlled? We know that in the past the system functioned on the basis of a political hierarchy without property rights. In present conditions, who is to control the managers? In capitalist firms, external control is exerted by the owners (shareholders), by the creditors, or by the market (competition leading to bankruptcy if the firm performs poorly; threat of take-over). In labour-managed firms, there is an insider control by employees. What kind of control is emerging now?

Privatisation in the West had to deal with the problem as well. One of the major concerns of the privatising authorities was how to prevent, in the conditions of an open, largely deregulated market, an excessive concentration of capital in the hands of a small number of big shareholders, who could easily buy out the shares from thousands of small, not so well informed new capitalists. This was achieved through the policy of 'hard core' stable shareholders, which in France were selected outside the market by a specific procedure conducted through the ministry in charge of the privatisations. Thus is can be said that in the French case, and more generally in developed market economies undertaking privatisation, the problem has not been just where to find capital but *what* kind of capital to use. Letting the market do the job can lead to concentration of capital in politically unwanted hands. Establishing 'hard core' shareholders can raise harsh political disputes if it is shown that the government in charge of the privatisations favoured its friends. In France, the 'hard core' (*noyau dur*) policy evolved in the second privatisation programme starting in 1993 toward a system of intricate cross-shareholdings between industry, banks and insurance companies under the control of the state (Lavigne, 1995).

In Eastern Europe, it was an illusion to think that under any privatisation scheme one might witness on a large-scale a class of small capitalist-minded shareowners emerging spontaneously and ready for controlling the management of its assets. In mass privatisation schemes, in most cases the population was mainly interested in cashing in the distributed shares. People tried to sell their shares even when no trading in the shares was allowed for some time, a provision to be found in all cases except in Russia (and in

Hungary concerning the compensation vouchers allocated to claimants in the 'restitution' issue). What gradually emerges in the privatised companies is a complex ownership structure involving banks, investment funds, other enterprises, state asset management agencies, and local governments, with a network of cross-ownership. The actual managers are the former ones in many cases, due to the difficulties of finding thousands of able managers willing to do the job. There is little the new governments are able (and even willing) to do to control the whole process.

This brings us to a crucial, and embarrassing, question: Who are insiders and who are outsiders? Standard theory is unambiguous. Insiders are managers and employees retaining shares. Outsiders are all others, including banks, investment funds, other financial intermediaries such as insurance companies, other corporations, and of course foreign investors (CEPR and IEWS, 1996a, pp. 17–18). But how do we qualify situations with cross-ownership involving the major micro-economic agents? Analysts have to acknowledge that there is a 'blurred distinction between insiders and outsiders under transitional conditions' (Carlin and Landesmann, 1997, p. 91). Whenever there are instances of active managerial behaviour, these 'are not obviously compatible with a competitive market economy. These ambiguous cases include the exploitation of market power but also, the setting up of holding and internal companies. They pose a challenge for theorists and policy-makers, as it is unclear from a normative point of view whether they should be discouraged or encouraged' (Carlin *et al.*, 1995, p. 450). For instance, Czech voucher-privatised firms are considered as undisputable cases of outsider-ownership, and hence governance (Aghion and Carlin, 1997, p. 259). However, in the specific conditions of Czech post-privatisation, ownership was transferred to state-controlled banks and to investment funds which in their majority were managed by these banks. If one could be sure that these 'outsider owners' used their rights to fire the former managers of the privatised firms and to replace them with new ones, then one could define this type of governance as governance by outsiders. But in most cases the reconcentration of ownership following the mass privatisation in the Czech republic led to a revival of old networks linking the enterprises, the banks and the former nomenklatura. In such a situation it becomes much more difficult to speak of 'outsiders' governance'. Actually it has now been decided that the Czech investment funds will be forced to sell their holdings and allow initial investors – holders of vouchers – to withdraw their capital, so as to provide companies with new shareholders and to improve the structure of ownership (*Financial Times*, 20 April 1998).

This evolution means that all forms of privatisation ultimately lead to an unwanted spontaneous privatisation model, with enterprise governance by the insiders, and complicated cross-ownership links. The case of Russia is extreme. After the completion in mid-1994 of the voucher-based privatisation programme, the cash-based second phase of privatisation proceeded very slowly until 1997, and in conditions of increasing opacity. In 1995, the major large Moscow banks offered to help finance the government budget deficit through loans collateralised by state shares in certain firms (twelve enterprises were selected, among them major oil companies and Norilsk, the major nickel combinate in the world). The Presidential decree of 31 August 1995 regulating these loans provided that each loan package would be bid against packages of state shares in open auctions, that would however exclude foreign investors; shares would become the property of the bidders if the loans were not repaid on time. All the auctions were surrounded with controversy and scandal. The most notorious deals were in 1997 the acquisition of the controlling minority of Norilsk by the strongest financial group, Oneximbank, which later bought, in suspicious conditions, 25 per cent of Svyazinvest, a large telecommunications company. The new law on privatisation of June 1997 aimed at clarifying procedures for privatisation auctions. Actually all regulations are without impact on the growing integration between big companies, banks and government central or local organs. This trend is embodied in the growing power of 'FIGs', financial-industrial groups, whose legal status goes back to a decree of 1993 and a law of 1995. The most influential FIGs are grouped in an association of 40 members. The so-called 'oligarchs' who head these FIGs hold the real power in Russia and are opposed to any reforms that would introduce more transparency in the operation of the economy.

The natural monopolies do not fall under the jurisdiction of the Anti-Monopoly Committee, such as the electricity grid (UES, of which less than 10 per cent of equity is privatised), and Gazprom, the largest gas company in the world. Gazprom is in fact uncontrolled by any outside entity. The Russian Federation still owned 40 per cent of it in 1988. The various attempts of the government to introduce more clarity in its operation, by appointing a board of state representatives to manage the share of the state, by opening it to foreign investors at up to 9 per cent of equity, and by having it audited by an international company, Price Waterhouse, have been unfruitful. The OECD Survey on Russia rightly describes Gazprom as a 'quasi-fiscal institution', mentioning that while Gazprom does not pay its tax debts to the state in due time, it is also a creditor of major Russian cities and regions that do not pay for their gas supplies, and hence is implicitly supporting federal subsidies to energy prices, which makes it the more invulnerable (see OECD, *Russian Federation*, 1997b).

To improve corporate governance, what is often suggested is a system of strong independent financial intermediaries (Frydman *et al.*, 1993a, and 1996, vol. 1; Jackson, 1992b). This leads us to the other areas of structural transformation, which is critical to the privatisation process.

OTHER AREAS OF STRUCTURAL TRANSFORMATION

Structural transformation means building a broad market environment. Liberalising prices and trade has been part of the stabilisation programmes. Creating a market environment first means having a modern financial and tax system. It also calls for cushioning the impact both of stabilisation and of structural transformation through building a new social security network. Growing attention has been paid to the functioning of the labour markets: it has been acknowledged that the good functioning of a labour market does not automatically result from liberalising the supply and demand of labour and setting wages free. Finally, we shall look at a largely neglected sectoral issue of transformation, structural changes in agriculture.

The Banking and Financial Sectors Reform

Banking reform and the setting-up of *capital markets* are generally seen as most urgent and related problems, and part of the building blocks of stabilisation-cum-transformation (see Table 7.1).

The beginnings of the new banking system

In the socialist countries there was a system based on a 'monobank' endowed with all the banking functions: it was issuing money, acting as the Treasury of the state, and as the sole source of credit for the economy. The first task was thus to create a two-tier banking system, with a Central Bank and independent commercial banks. In Hungary and Poland such a two-tier system had already been established before transition began, and was emerging in the Soviet Union under the *perestroyka*. In Czechoslovakia a banking law was introduced just after the 'velvet revolution' of 1989; in Romania and Bulgaria, as well, two-tier banking emerged after the beginning of the transition. In all cases the process began with separating the Central Bank activities from those of the newly created commercial banks, and endowing the latter with the bulk of the former State Bank resources. Competition was introduced in this sector by allowing enterprises, local administration, individuals, and foreigners to set up new banks, under various provisions.

Several roles were conceivable for this new banking system: to support the stabilisation programme; to provide finance to the economy (the era of consumers' credit is yet to come); and to facilitate privatisation and enterprise control.

(1) The banking system was supposed to manage the monetary side of the stabilisation programme. High interest rates were set. The Central Bank was to control commercial lending through the usual array of methods available

in Western practice. In fact, its policy amounted in the beginning to sheer quantitative credit tightening. Standard open market policies were not possible due to the lack of a financial market. Re-financing procedures work well when they are based upon a variety of high-quality corporate bills or government securities. All of this was missing. Hence the policy of the Central Bank has been to restrict credit, and at the same time, in selected cases, to allow commercial banks to rescue big state companies on the verge of bankruptcy. However, this emergency credit by no means met the needs of the enterprises. As a result, as we have seen in the previous chapter, a huge inter-enterprise indebtedness emerged everywhere, together with large payment and tax arrears. Such a situation was very damaging on three counts. First, it deprived stabilisation policy of one of its main instruments; even with high interest rates, there was no adjustment on the enterprise side; enterprises could survive and pay wages (be it partly and in kind) even when they were poorly performing, and inflation could not be reduced. Second, the banks were not in a position to exert pressure on the management of the enterprises, since they abstained from taking action against bad debtors as they were reluctant to reveal a large percentage of non-performing loans (Begg and Portes, 1992). Third, while there were some (state and private) well-performing enterprises which deserved to get credit by all standard criteria, there has been an adverse selection effect; these enterprises had to pay higher rates, as the banks had to raise their provisions because of bad loans, and thus to seek higher profits through higher spreads (between their lending rates and the cost of their borrowing from the Central Bank). This has actually led the best Hungarian companies, and later firms from other Central European countries, to borrow from foreign rather than from domestic banks.

(2) The substitution (at least in part) of inter-enterprise indebtedness for banking credit in turn severely constrained the privatisation process. The choice was between privatising without financial restructuring, as in the case of mass privatisation, which gives citizens shares in debts as well as in assets, and attempting a financial restructuring (including recapitalisation of the enterprises) before privatisation. In fact financial restructuring, even when preferred in principle (as in Hungary and Poland), was hardly affordable on a large scale (see Hunya, 1993). Most of the enterprises were indebted both to banks and to other enterprises. This deterred foreign investors, prompted shareholders in the case of mass privatisation to get rid of their shares by selling them to investment funds or on a black (grey) market, and ultimately strengthened insiders' control.

Recapitalising of banks has been resorted to. It has been strongly recommended in the early Western literature (see Begg and Portes, 1992), and first implemented in the Czech Republic (in 1991, through the establishment of a special institution, the *Konsolidacni Banka)*, and in Hungary, where the bad loans have been purchased against government bonds by a state agency, the State Development and Investment Company. In both cases there was very little capital injection and thus it was rather a transfer of bad loans to the state, which amounted to sharing of the debt burden between generations (Csáki, 1993, p. 19). In 1993 the process had to be repeated in Hungary, involving bank and enterprise debt consolidation as well (ECE/UN, 1994b, ch. 5). Western banks and international institutions such as the World Bank and the EBRD have been involved in technical assistance in this field.

Apart from the bad debts, which according to an estimate from the EBRD amounted to 60 per cent of the balance sheets of the eastern banks in the beginning of the transition (Robinson and Denton, 1993), the banking business is plagued by fraud, bribery and negligence which has emerged during financial scandals. Such scandals have been endemic in Russia where the new banking sector of slightly less than 2000 banks is plagued by overdraft with the Central Bank, fraud and money-laundering linked with Mafia control, and by open crime.

(3) The reform blueprints did not explicitly assign to the banking system the function of controlling the privatised enterprises. The banks were expected to assist the cleaning-up of the enterprise sector through bankruptcy procedures, but it was soon acknowledged that they would avoid triggering bankruptcies so as not to expose their bad loans. They were not expected to become major stakeholders in the enterprises. Out of the two basic Western models, the reformers in the countries in transition by and large preferred the US–UK model, where banks perform savings and lending activities but are not involved in corporate activities, to the 'German–Japanese' model where banks have close equity links with enterprises (see Corbett and Mayer, 1991; Steinherr and Gilibert, 1994; Steinherr, 1997). The first model is associated with a developed securities market and with networks of financial intermediaries such as investment and pension funds. The second model involves much closer links between banks and the management of corporations. It has also led to an expansion of financial intermediation by the banks themselves, increasingly in association with the insurance sector. It may entail a high concentration of the financial system, 'with all financial services provided by a small number of universal banks' (Steinherr, 1997, p. 113). But basically, despite the 'banking snobbery' to be found in Central and Eastern Europe, with a drive to have at once a whole array of financial intermediaries as in the West, what the countries in transition need is 'a reasonably efficient, ordinary banking system that collects short-term deposits, handles transfers of funds, furnishes working capital to small and medium-sized businesses, and is sufficiently well capitalized to cover ordinary banking risks . . . At a low level of development at least, the bank versus markets misses the point. These are not alternatives: banking needs to precede markets' (Steinherr, 1997, p. 112). This is perfectly sensible, but . . . modest. As one Eastern

banker half-resentfully half-sarcastically told me when I was airing similar ideas: 'We are no children. We are now grown-ups, and we want to have all that grown-ups have.'

What emerged in fact was the worst of both worlds. Banks became major shareholders in privatised companies, either directly or through the investment funds they had set up. They also remained major stakeholders in state-owned companies, either through the debts owed to them or through personal links inherited from the past. At the same time, capital markets developed in a volatile way. Non-controlled financial intermediaries expanded as well, and often turned out to be very fragile financially.

The main directions of bank reforms

Bank reforms have been discussed in special issues of journals (for instance, *JCE* 1997, vol. 25, no. 1, or *Moct-Most*, 1997, vol. 7, no. 3), in special surveys (OECD Proceedings, 1997e; CEPR and IEWS, 1996a), and in numerous articles. The bulk of these publications emerged in the mid-1990s, following the wave of debates on privatisation, as it was becoming obvious that the transformation process at large was hindered by the bad operation of the banking system. Two issues were mainly discussed: the banking crises; and the privatisation of the banks, which is seen as an instrument for recapitalising and restructuring the banking sector as well as forcing it to comply with prudential rules.

Banking crises have been numerous and have affected not only the less experienced countries in market economies, such as Latvia and Lithuania in 1995, or the less advanced in transition, such as Bulgaria and Romania in 1996–7, but also the country which was considered as the most liberalised and market-oriented, as was the Czech Republic in 1996–7. Each of these crises has its own story (Keuschnigg, 1997, pp. 18–19). The components of such crises typically are: a legacy of non-performing loans (especially short-term) to state-owned enterprises; too quick a financial liberalisation allowing too many new banks on the market; inadequate macro-economic policies (high inflation prompts firms to seek credits that are to be serviced easily; conversely, however, with tight monetary policies followed by a decrease in inflation, firms are left with bank debts to service at a higher cost). Finally, the combination of inexperience of bank management, insufficient prudential regulation, and large opportunities and incentives for fraud led to dramatic bank failures and deposit withdrawals (Steinherr, 1997, p. 123; Keuschnigg, 1997, p. 21).

The remedy for such crises was sought in *privatisation*, although very often private banks have first displayed major insolvencies (Steinherr, 1997, p. 123). In a few countries there has been a decoupling of bank restructuring from bank privatising (as in Poland and Hungary in the beginnings of transition). Bulgaria, after having tried to bail its state-owned banks out of bankruptcy through the issuing of government bonds, with high costs to the government due to the high interest rate carried by these 'ZUNK' (the Bulgarian acronym) bonds, pledged itself to privatise all the state-owned banks except the Savings Banks by the end of 1998. In the Czech Republic, the remaining state-owned banks are to be privatised in 1999; in March 1998 the Investiční and Poštovní Banka was privatised by the sale of the state's 36 per cent stake to the Japanese Nomura Bank, a radical departure from the nationalistic tradition of this country (*Financial Times*, 18 March 1998). Hungary started the privatisation of the big state-owned banks in 1995 with the help of the EBRD. In Poland, five of the nine banks hived off from the National Bank of Poland had been privatised by end-1997, also with the help of the EBRD, and the sell-offs were to accelerate in 1998 following the coming to power of a new government in November 1997.

The banking picture is more dramatic in Russia. The number of banks decreased from 2600 in 1966 to 1740 by October 1997. Fourteen banks account for 67 per cent of the banking system leaving aside the state-owned Sberbank (Savingsbank), the largest bank in Russia followed by the foreign trade bank Vneshtorgbank which are the only majority state-owned banks in Russia. They are all involved in financial-industrial groups, all have privileged political relations with the central and local governments, and all have now developed international connections and alliances which makes them players on the global financial markets (see *Le Courrier Financier de Moscou*, French Embassy in Russia, issues 258–263, 1997). Though the Russian banking sector is overall considered as under-capitalised, oversized and illiquid (EBRD 1996, p. 170), such a statement does not apply to the big banks, but rather to the smaller ones, unable to respond to the credit requests of small and medium enterprises, or to attract the deposits of the population in a situation where at least 50 per cent of savings are kept in dollars and in cash. The Russian financial crisis of 1998 illustrated the fragility of the banking system. The devaluation of the ruble in August 1998 was a heavy blow as the banks had accumulated large liabilities in dollars while keeping most of their assets in rubles. The subsequent rescheduling of the domestic debt repayments has dried up foreign credits to the banks, while preventing them to cash in their treasury bills holdings. In turn, many banks became unable to pay the depositors wanting to retrieve their money in rubles or in dollars. By end-August, five of Russia's largest banks decided to merge in two bigger groups (*Financial Times*, 26 August 1998). By end-1998, most of the smaller banks (about 720) were expected to go bankrupt.

Central and Eastern European banks have to comply with EU prudential regulations in all the countries that have applied to membership in the EU, including the Cooke ratio (a minimum capital adequacy ratio of 8 per cent), and a maximum exposure to a single client amounting to 25 per cent of the own capital of the bank. In addition, they have to introduce deposit insurance schemes to protect their depositors. In Russia, too, a ratio of capital to risk-weighted assets was introduced in 1996, but at a level of 6 per cent, while it is generally reckoned that in countries with a risky environment the Cooke ratio should be increased.

The emerging capital market

The need for *capital markets* has often been quoted as a precondition for privatisation. The lack of capital markets, even in the countries which have introduced a stock exchange, is indeed obvious, and prevents large-scale privatisation through public offerings, which is the dominant method used in the West. One should nevertheless remark that even in the Western economies it took many decades to turn the national stock exchanges into a sophisticated global network, and that a stock exchange can hardly operate without capital, which is the case now in the East.

The countries in transition have begun with symbols rather than with realities. In most countries a stock exchange has been set up, or revived (see Table 7.1). Such institutions are certainly useful in helping people to become familiar with the notion of a capital market, but they play a very small role and do not assist the privatisation process in the way capital markets do in the West. Some countries have more than one exchange. The Czech Republic has in addition to the Prague Stock Exchange, an over-the-counter electronic RM-system that trades the shares of the privatised-by-vouchers companies, and organises auctions of these shares. The Slovak Republic duplicated the format with the Bratislava Stock Exchange and the RM-system in 1993. Romania revived its Bursa de Valori in 1995 and established in 1996 an over-the-counter market, the Rasdaq. These emerging stock markets are small – a few dozen stocks are quoted at best, and on the bond market government securities dominate – and very volatile. In all countries securities commissions have been established on the Western model; the latest case, in January 1998, was the setting up of a securities and exchange commission in Prague, following the fall of the conservative government that had never agreed to set up an institution limiting the free movements of the market.

The emerging markets in the countries in transition are vulnerable to financial scandals, which are likely to occur often due to the lack of experience of the operators, and the control established by the new mafias on these activities. The MMM scandal in Russia, where a finance house collapsed after having issued, with a dramatic advertisement campaign, bogus shares whose value had risen eight times in three months, epitomises the gullibility of the public (*Financial Times*, 1 August 1994). So did a similar case in Romania, where in 22 months a pyramid scheme called

Caritas managed to attract deposits from four million Romanians for a total amount of $ 1 billion! (*Financial Times*, 22 February 1994), and in Albania, where the collapse of financial pyramids in 1997 resulted in a major political and economic crisis.

The Russian capital market is a special case. There are a dozen active exchanges in the country, which trade the stocks of a few major companies but mainly government securities such as the GKOs (treasury bills), the OFZ (federal loans bonds) and the MinFins (hard-currency bonds). The most liquid stocks are traded on the RTS (Russian Trading System or *Rossiyskaya Torgovaya Sistema*) which links the regional exchanges. Half of the transactions are made outside the RTS and the exchanges, and are directly negotiated by banks or companies, mostly on foreign markets. An increasing number of Russian companies have issued ADR (American Depositary Receipts), beginning with the major oil companies. The main attraction of the Russian stocks – and this is still more valid for Ukrainian stocks – is the cheapness of the companies. The main deterrent, with the volatility of the market, is the opacity of the market and the lack of adequate protection of shareholders' rights.

The GKOs (short-term treasury bills), which had become a major instrument of financing the Russian budget deficit, were a critical component of the 1998 crisis. According to economic orthodoxy it is sounder to finance a budget deficit by emitting government securities (purchased by domestic agents, mainly banks, or foreign investors) than by printing money. But it increases the domestic debt burden, especially if interest rates have to be high so as to attract buyers. The interest rate on GKOs oscillated in the first seven months of 1998 between 25 and 100 per cent. When in end-August 1998 the Russian government announced a restructuring of its domestic debt, it was estimated that foreign investors held about 17 bn dollars worth of GKOs out of a total 40 billion dollars. The proposals for restructuring involved a swap of part of the GKOs either into eight-year securities denominated in dollars with a rate of interest of 5 per cent, or into ruble-denominated bonds maturing in between three and five years, with interest rates from 30 to 20 per cent (*Financial Times*, 27 August 1998). Any solution will entail large losses and impair the credibility of the Russian securities for a long time. However one should not forget that the foreign investors (banks, investment funds) that bought into the Russian emerging capital market were attracted by high yields and should have been aware of the risks. It was a form of gambling, spurred by the remarkable performance of the Russian stock exchange in 1996 and most of 1997. Still in February 1998 there were net inflows from abroad into the GKO market. But by end-August the value of the stock index had fallen by two-thirds since the beginning of 1998. Investors just underestimated the Russian risk, confident that the ruble would not be devalued and counting on the bail-out of the international financial institutions if something went wrong.

Future prospects for enlarging the emerging capital markets

There is a great deal of confusion and misunderstanding as to the role of the new investment funds created in the wake of privatisation. In mass privatisation schemes, they facilitate the distribution of vouchers and the auctioning off because beneficiaries prefer to entrust their vouchers to these funds. In Poland, the Mass Privatisation Programme went further; the national investment funds instituted by the law of 1993 were supposed to manage, restructure and increase the value of the assets of the state-owned companies to be privatised; 33 per cent of the shares of each such company had to be attributed to one of the twenty funds to be set up (their number was later scaled down to fifteen), and 27 per cent of its shares had to be distributed among the other funds in approximately equal parts (Bossak, 1994). The setting up of the funds was delayed because of political disputes and started only in 1996. Each of the fifteen funds will own a bulk of the shares of about thirty companies of the 512 (initially, 400) participating in the scheme. The citizens have received tradable certificates against a nominal payment; these certificates could be exchanged for shares in the NIFs once the latter were listed on the Warsaw Stock exchange, which happened in May 1997 (Blaszczyk *et al.*, 1997). The purpose was to create strong financial intermediaries. Who is to manage the funds ? The initial idea was to have foreign experts (preferably of Polish descent). But it turned out to be very difficult to get good professionals to come to Poland, even for a high salary (however inferior to Western standards). As soon as the funds began to operate, legal disputes emerged between foreign managers (usually belonging to consulting companies) and Polish appointed managers (*Wall Street Journal*, 26–27 April 1996). In Poland and elsewhere, the investment funds are likely to be managed by three categories of people: imaginative individuals with a more or less clean (politically and ethically) background, who soon master the rules of the financial game and develop speculation on their account (the notorious Harvard Capital fund in the Czech Republic, and its chairman, now settled in the Bahamas, are a case in point); bank or state-owned firms' managers, who will strengthen 'spontaneous' privatisation; and political appointees. A combination of two or three of these options is no less possible.

Other institutions of the type that operates on developed financial markets are yet to expand. This is the case in particular of insurance companies. In Central and Eastern Europe, the former state-owned monopolistic insurance companies are still dominant, even when partly privatised, with the exception of Hungary where the state insurance companies have been privatised early with the involvement of foreign companies. But the potential role of insurance as a vehicle for raising finance is far from understood yet (see special section on life insurance in EBRD, *Transition Report 1996*, chapter 7).

A related issue is the constitution of pension funds, especially as the social security system is to be reformed. Three countries had adopted a law on pension funds by the end of 1997: Hungary (1993), the Czech Republic (1994) and the Slovak Republic (1996). In 1997 Poland introduced a new Investment Fund Act authorising the establishment of a wider range of investment funds than existing before. It may spur the development of pension funds as the parliament passed a bill in the same month providing for the setting up of individual pension accounts by private financial institutions (EBRD, 1997, p. 191). The contributions to the funds are still low and the impact on the capital markets negligible (Impavido, 1997).

The Tax Reform

Reforming the tax system is a part of the structural transformation but is also crucial to the stabilisation programme. The new tax system should provide resources to the budget, be transparent, as simple as possible, and not too heavy on enterprises and individuals so as to avoid stifling entrepreneurship. Most of all, the levying of the taxes by the governments should be perceived not as an arbitrary charge imposed on taxpayers, but a just contribution to collective expenses. In the past, enterprises used to bargain about the taxes they paid and negotiate them with the state authorities, an attitude which was replaced by sheer evasion and avoidance in the beginning of the transition.

During the transition, the state sector has been initially discriminated against in the field of taxation. For instance, in Poland state enterprises have been subjected to high taxation in the form of a 'dividend' on profits unrelated to actual profits, exactly as in the former system. At the same time, 'hidden subsidies' allowed the state enterprises to survive though unprofitable. The implicit subsidisation is embodied in the reluctant implementation of the bankruptcy regulations, as we have seen.

Tax reforms are being implemented as a part of the structural transformation process, while taxes are used in the stabilisation programme, with mixed results because of tax evasion (see Table 7.2). The basic format includes a personal income tax generally progressive, a proportional tax on corporate profits, a value-added tax, and various indirect taxes (on gasoline, alcohol, tobacco, etc.). The evasion factor, which affects the revenues from direct personal or corporate taxation, may explain why many countries moved toward the introduction of a value-added tax, not only because this is part of the approximation of their tax regulations with those of the European Community. VAT is less painful for the public than income tax, and less easy to evade. The rates are higher than in Western Europe, averaging 22–25 per cent for most items. But VAT is not easy to monitor, and in market economies it took several years to master it (Newbery, 1997,

p. 440). For instance in France it was formally introduced in 1958, and generalised only in 1966.

A new system of personal income taxes and corporate profit taxes is gradually introduced. Specific taxes on excess wage payments have been levied as a part of the incomes control policy but have been suppressed in most countries.

The tax reforms are however very slow to implement. The tax administration is not sufficiently trained to manage a complex tax system. The accounting rules do not allow for a precise monitoring of the corporate profit tax. Finally as the foreign investments have large tax benefits the domestic taxpayers feel that the burden of the tax payments falls on them (see Kodrzycki, 1993). The adoption of a tax code in Russia has been delayed several times until 1998, though the government managed to pass some tax-raising measures by decree in July 1998.

The failure in implementing large-scale tax reforms has of course an impact on the expenditures to be financed by the budget. The lack of resources is the main obstacle to building an efficient social safety net.

Building a New Social Safety Network

The need for a *new social safety net* is widely recognised by governments and Western experts, both to cushion the impact of the stabilisation and structural transformation, and to shape new attitudes, away from the former overall protection system provided by the Communist state. Social expenditures are mainly financed from the budget, and through contributions from the enterprises (and the employees, in most countries) in proportion to wages. Local governments are also involved in covering social expenditures, with still fewer resources. The pressing requests for a balanced budget urged by the IMF have often clashed with the political needs for maintaining the level of social expenditure (such was the case in 1993 for Poland and in 1996 for Hungary – in the last case, Hungary abstained from drawing on a stand-by loan while its government was being urged by the IMF to cut welfare expenditures).

Contrary to a widely held assumption in the West, the main problem is not unemployment. Growing unemployment is still a recent phenomenon, and still manageable insofar as it first hits women or young people who have some support in their family. Unemployment benefits have been introduced; they are generally rather low and allocated for a short period. The social transfers in nature (i.e. free health services) are still provided but are of very low quality and with low wages for the medical personnel, while paying for health care is developing more or less legally and is unaffordable for most people. In Central and Eastern Europe, health care expenditures account for 6 per cent at most of the GDP (they account for 8 per cent in Western

Europe), while morbidity is increasing. The hospitals lack equipment and drugs. Health care reform plans generally include the shift to private insurance schemes, which do not seem quite realistic. These schemes would require a developed general insurance market which does not exist (and could also provide much needed financial intermediaries, see section on capital markets above). They would impose a heavy load on the enterprises which would have to finance the major share of it for their employees. Alternatively, they would have to be financed by increased personal income taxes, a very unpopular measure to propose to any parliament.

But the main problem is that of the pension system. Retirement age is generally low (the usual limit being 55 years for women and 60 years for men), the population is ageing, and retired people form the bulk of the 'new poor' as inflation has eroded their very low pensions. The situation is probably the worst in the former Soviet Union countries, where in addition to the deterioration of the level of the pensions the latter are often not paid. Most of the countries in transition are engaged in pension reforms. The main approach to such reforms is derived from World Bank guidelines issued in 1994. The state-run system is scaled down and would in the future provide for a minimum amount of pension benefits, to be paid to less beneficiaries as pension age is to be increased and to become uniform for men and women. A mandatory system of private pension funds would pay additional pension benefits, and be financed by payroll taxes. In addition, there would be voluntary private funds for those willing, and able, to guarantee themselves a higher pension. This is roughly the system envisaged in Poland in 1997, and implemented in Hungary from July 1998. The Czech Republic, the Baltics, and Russia are considering similar schemes (*Financial Times*, 30 January 1998).

Labour Market Policies

Should one have a section on such a topic in a chapter on structural transformation? The free-market-oriented vision is that liberalisation and flexibility are the master words here. In centrally planned economies labour movements were no longer constrained, or were so only indirectly (by the regulation and the subsidisation of housing, which made it very difficult to move from one place to another). There was however only a quasi-market for labour, as wages and the level of employment were regulated for the enterprises, and as the various social security benefits were distributed at the level of the firm, and managed by branch trade unions, to which affiliation was compulsory. Hence it would seem that once all the regulations were lifted, one would have automatically a flexible labour market on which quantities and prices would be freely determined among the labour suppliers – the workers – and the enterprises.

In fact, post-transition inertia did not bring about flexibility immediately. Enterprises had to be forced to shed redundant workers, through the hardening of the budget constraint, and also prevented from bowing to the workers' pressure and increasing wages, which was achieved through excess wages taxes. Once the market was operating, one would have to take care of the unemployed through appropriate benefits and active retraining programmes.

What is certainly surprising is that the tasks of taking care of unemployed and pursuing active labour-market policies were so successfully managed in Central and Eastern Europe, with so little previous experience, considering how unsuccessfully Western developed market economies tackled the same problems in the 1990s. Certainly the legacies of the past helped to bear the burden of unemployment. Enterprises sometimes kept employees at a lower salary to allow them to benefit from what was left of the social advantages offered by the firm. Bankruptcies were delayed. At the same time, unemployment increased in most countries (except the Czech and Slovak Republics, and former Soviet Union states) to levels higher than in Western Europe. After 1992 unemployment benefits were strongly curtailed; the maximum duration was reduced and the coverage rate as well. Nevertheless the unemployed did not demonstrate against these changes – was it a legacy of the past when it was felt that only lazy, unwilling-to-work people were unemployed? Actually, there was indeed a wide-scale implementation of active labour-market policy programmes which had positive results (Boeri, 1997a and b).

Agriculture in Transition

Structural transformation is usually discussed with industrial problems in mind. Transition to the market in agriculture however raises specific problems. Even in market economies agriculture is usually protected, and the market for agricultural goods and inputs has its own regulations. For the countries of Central and Eastern Europe that are to join the European Union, integration means that the agricultural sector will have to adapt to the rules of the Common Agricultural Policy (CAP). Legacies from the communist past are also specific in this sector as the peasants' class was treated differently from the workers' class. For all these reasons the role of agriculture in the transition to the market must be discussed.

Privatisation in agriculture is a special case combining the problems of restitution and those of giving workers special rights. Only in Poland and in Yugoslavia were agricultural cooperatives dissolved during the communist regime (in the 1950s) and the land returned to the farmers. In other countries the process of collectivisation had generally followed a land reform which expropriated large landowners and distributed property among the peasants. Wherever the principle of land restitution has been retained after the collapse of communism (in Bulgaria, Hungary, Romania, Albania, and the Baltic States), it was coupled with redistribution to the farmers in kind (but generally not in full property of all the land confiscated) or in farming rights. In Czechoslovakia, the issue was highly complicated by the fact that the land had never formally been taken away from the peasants, and by the beginning of the transition about half of the land was actually owned by non-rural dwellers. In Russia, ownership rights have been granted to the farmers on their privately cultivated plots, but the question of buying and selling larger tracts of agricultural land was a matter of strong disagreement between the government and the parliament, the latter blocking the actual implementation of the law on land private ownership. The situation was only settled legally at the end of 1993, by means of a presidential decree allowing for a free land market (not open to foreigners, though), and entitling each member of a state or collective farm to a part of the farm property. But because of political reluctance on the farms and lack of precise rules for the implementation of the decree, no land market emerged. A new presidential decree in May 1996 restated the principle of private land ownership, and several versions of the Land Code were discussed in 1996 and 1997, the Russian Duma being opposed to foreign ownership of land.

The privatisation in agriculture also exemplifies an ethical and political conflict between the principle that the land should be returned to those who have been dispossessed by the communists, and the principle that the land should belong to whoever farms it. In most of the countries in transition, and even in those most committed to the free market, property rights in agriculture remain unclear. Despite the distribution of land to private owners, and the dissolving of the cooperatives which had in most countries to turn into joint stock companies or voluntary associations and re-register as such, little has changed. The private farmers have guaranteed rights on what was in the past their personal plot and may expand it legally, but have no access to credit, and no training as managers. They have to deal with suppliers and wholesale distribution companies which are largely mono-polised. The former cooperatives have on the whole better management skills, and provide some social security benefits. Capitalist farming on a large scale is so far impossible, and the forcible elimination of cooperatives would be very counterproductive. In actual fact, the legally revamped cooperatives have proven the segment of the former communist ownership structure the most unyielding to change. However, it should not be looked upon just as a case of political resistance to transition.

The legacies of the past are very ambiguous. Western literature has repeatedly stressed the higher performance of small private farming as opposed to collective farming, by quoting statistics showing that with a very small percentage of total cultivated land the private plots provided for a very high share of agricultural produce. We have stated earlier (Chapter 3) that this was a distorted view; the higher productivity of the private plots could be attributed to the fact that the latter 'lived on' the cooperative through diverting its human and material inputs. Nevertheless the myth of an intrinsic superiority of small private farming over large cooperative farming is still very much established, though it should not be clear why in market conditions small farming should be productive in the East while it is in great difficulty in the West (see Maurel, 1991; and ECE/UN and FAO, 1997). The vitality of the cooperatives might suggest a potential revival of the agricultural sector, which has been badly affected by transition. In most countries, agricultural output collapsed in the years following transition, and did not recover fully later. Peasants have had to pay for more of their inputs, largely imported and hence affected by the devaluations of the national currencies. Exports to the West were impaired by the protectionism of the European Union. National consumption of food products has massively shifted to Western products; food imports from the European Union were facilitated by the subsidisation mechanisms of the CAP.

Agricultural policy is thus a very complex issue. Early liberalisation has left the agricultural sector in a very difficult position. This sector did not benefit from the end of price subsidies on food as the profits from higher prices were appropriated by the retail distribution chains. It endured the full impact of increased interest rates, which stifled investment. It also had to pay higher taxes than in the past. The farm constituencies began to ask for support, especially as since the opening up of the economy, food imports had increased, in particular from the European Union. Since 1992 there was in Eastern Europe increased pressure for import protection and subsidies, using a CAP-like format. Several countries (Poland, Hungary, and the Czech Republic in particular) have set up agencies for regulating the market, but the lack of resources has limited the impact of these agencies. The agriculture sector in Eastern Europe looks with hope at the prospects of higher benefits from the CAP once the countries are admitted to the EU, and this issue is bound to become one of the most difficult in the enlargement process, as we shall see in the next chapter.

To conclude this chapter on structural transformation, we attach the EBRD scoreboard whereby this institution assesses since 1994 the 'progress in transition' through an array of criteria covering most of the areas discussed above (Table 8.3).This is not to say that we fully agree with the selection of criteria or the ratings. But the EBRD assessment deserves a mention since it has become a benchmark for researchers and policy-makers, and also for other international institutions.

Table 8.3　Progress in structural transformation: the EBRD indicators

	Priv/ GDP (%)	Lspriv	Sspriv	Enter restr.	Price lib.	Forex lib.	Comp. pol.	Bank. Reform	Capital markets
CzR	75	4	4+	3	3	4+	3	3	3
Hun	75	4	4+	3	3+	4+	3	4	3+
Pol	65	3+	4+	3	3	4+	3	3	3+
Est	70	4	4+	3	3	4	3	3+	3
Slovn	50	3+	4+	3−	3	4+	2	3	3
Slovk	75	4	4+	3−	3	4	3	3−	2+
Rom	60	3−	3	2	3	4	2	3−	2
Bulg	50	3	3	2+	3	4	2	3−	2
Latv	60	3	4	3−	3	4	3−	3	2+
Lit	70	3	4	3−	3	4	2+	3	2+
Albania	75	2	4	2	3	4	2	2	2−
Russia	70	3+	4	2	3	4	2+	2+	3
Belarus	20	1	2	1	3	1	2	1	2
Ukraine	50	2+	3+	2	3	3	2	2	2
Moldova	45	3	3	2	3	4	2	2	2
Kazakhst.	55	3	3+	2	3	4	2	2+	2
Kyrgyz.	60	3	4	2	3	4	2	3−	2
Turkmen.	25	2	2	2−	2	1	1	1	1
Uzbek.	45	3−	3	2	3−	2−	2	2−	2

Status: August 1997.

Countries: CzR = Czech Republic; Hun = Hungary; Pol = Poland; Slovk = Slovakia; Slovn = Slovenia; Rom = Romania; Bulg = Bulgaria; Est = Estonia; Latv = Latvia; Lit = Lithuania.

Priv/GDP: officially declared share of the private sector in the creation of GDP

Lspriv (Large-scale privatisation)
4　　Standards typical of advanced industrial economies, though the state of corporate governance may be unclear; 70 to 75 per cent of state assets privatised.
3+　More than 50 per cent of state assets privatised; still substantial insider ownership, though corporate governance improves.
3　　More than 25 per cent of state assets privatised; substantial insider ownership, corporate governance improves little.
2　　Beginning of implementation of comprehensive privatisation schemes.
1　　Little private ownership

Sspriv (Small-scale privatisation)
4+　Standards typical of advanced industrial economies; no state ownership of small-scale enterprises; effective tradability of land.

4   Complete privatisation of small companies with tradable ownership rights.

3   Nearly comprehensive proramme of small privatisation implemented.

2   Substantial share privatised.

Enter. restr. (Enterprise restructuring):

3   Significant and sustained actions to harden budget constraints and to enforce bankruptcy legislation.

2   Moderately tight credit, weak enforcement of bankruptcy legislation; de-monopolisation is slow.

1   Soft budget constraint (lax tax and credit policies); few efforts to promote corporate governance.

Price lib. (Price liberalisation):

3   Substantial progress on price liberalisation ; energy prices, utilities not completely freed.

2   Substantial remaining price controls and state procurement.

Forex lib. (Foreign exchange liberalisation)

4+   Completed, with only some restrictions for capital movements.

4   Quasi convertibility of the domestic currency for current operations.

3   Remaining exchange controls.

2   Some liberalisation of import and export controls; almost full current account convertibility but the forex regime is not transparent and may have multiple rates.

1   Widespread export/import and foreign exchange controls.

Comp. pol. (Competition policy)

3   Some efforts to promote a competitive environment; reduction of entry restrictions; difficulties in breaking up of large monopolies.

2   Competition policies and institutions beginning to be set up.

1   No competitive legislation or policy.

Bank. reform (Banking system reforms)

3   Fully established two-tier system; framework for prudential regulation; significant presence of private or foreign banks though the banking sector remains state-owned in its majority; beginning of a lending policy though banks remain risk-adverse and lack experience in assessing the solvency of the enterprises, thus restraining credit and contributing to generate interenterprise arrears.

2   Liberalisation of interest rates and credit allocation; limited use of directed credit or interest rate ceilings.

1   Two-tier system; no further reform.

Capital markets:

3   Creation of investment vehicles (investment funds, insurance or pension funds); opening of stock exchanges; issuance of securities by private enterprises and by the government.

2   Legislation for the setting up of stock exchanges; some trading in government bonds.

1   Little progress in reforms.

Overall rating: One could get an overall rating through an unweighted summing up of ratings obtained in Columns 2 to 9, which would support the choice of the European Commission in selecting the first group of countries to begin negotiations for EU accession (confirmed by the December 1997 Summit of the EU, see Chapter 9). Estonia is doing best among the Baltic States and Slovenia among the South-East European countries. As to the 'exclusion' of Slovakia, it has been motivated mainly by political reasons (the lack of respect for the rights of minorities, the lack of compliance with the rule of law, and what is felt in the West as the lasting influence of former Party and police cadres).

Source: Adapted from EBRD (1997).

9 Reintegrating the World Economy

Following the collapse of communism, the countries in transition wished to be reintegrated in the world economy as market economies, after decades of 'bloc autarky' within the Council for Mutual Economic Assistance (CMEA). This has readily been accepted in principle in the West. It was expected that these countries would take action to abandon their past behaviour as 'state-trading' countries and become 'normal' partners.

Misunderstanding developed as to these claims and acknowledgements, with mounting disillusion and acrimony on both sides. The European countries in transition, including the former USSR, expected a preferential reintegration: as parts of Europe, to which they profess to belong, due to long-lasting historical links and to geographical connections. The Central and Eastern European countries demanded firm commitments as to future membership in the European Community (European Union since November 1993), and the ex-Soviet states, first of all Russia, asked to be treated as partners if not associates in the first stage. Outrage was felt when the Western countries recommended that, notwithstanding these claims, some steps should be taken to restore mutual links and trade within Eastern Europe and between this region and the former USSR. Frustration was expressed when it became obvious that the new 'Europe Agreements' did not open the European markets for a whole range of sensitive products. Since 1993, when the European Union accepted the principle of an enlargement to the East, the conditions to be met have been felt as discriminatory, by comparison with the former enlargements, and the procedures imposed upon the applicants have been resented as tedious and dragging.

The Western world has promised to extend assistance in various forms. Here, too, disappointment gathered, on both sides. The donors felt that their commitments were high, while the beneficiaries claimed that assistance was small in size and scope, and inefficiently managed. Controls exerted by the donors, and first of all by the international financial institutions, were often felt as interfering with national sovereignty. As the transition process went on, private capital relayed official grants and lending, and the countries in transition are now becoming integrated in the global financial economy, with some of the risks involved with this development.

HOW TO RECONSTRUCT REGIONAL ARRANGEMENTS IN THE EAST

In this section we are going to discuss two related though substantially different issues. The first is the rationale for trade and payments arrangements in Eastern Europe. The second is the way of stopping the disintegration of the former Soviet space. What unites these issues is the historical reference to the experience of post-war Europe. In the West both questions were hotly debated just after the beginning of transition, for two reasons. The first was that the double disintegration of the CMEA and of the Soviet Union caused a shock which was held responsible for the large collapse in output in the countries in transition. The second reason was political. With regard to Central and Eastern Europe, as there was a mounting claim in the region for quick accession into the European Community, to suggest a revival of severed links was seen as a way of postponing the accession demands. Regarding the uncertainties stemming from the breaking up of the USSR, it was felt that Russia was the only great power capable of maintaining some order in the region, and perhaps of assisting the recovery of its former partners in lieu of the West, of course with some help that would be redistributed by Russia to its smaller partners. All these concerns and expectations soon disappeared. Growth resumed in Central and Eastern Europe, and the European Union had to accept the enlargement as an inevitable, though protracted, process. With very few exceptions, the post-Soviet countries were not ready to accept the economic interference of Russia even when they still claimed some benefits inherited from the past such as low energy prices.

The collapse of foreign trade among the countries in transition, which was already obvious in the very beginning of the transition (see Chapter 6), persisted in the following years. 'Eastern' trade, i.e. trade among Eastern European countries as well as between them and the successor states to the USSR, fell on average by 60 per cent in three years, the share of this trade in the total trade of the region with the world reaching an average of 30 per cent. Trade among the successor states to the USSR, once the USSR was dissolved, fell still more steeply. Table 9.1 sums up these developments.

One has to look differently at the two areas, Central and Eastern Europe on the one hand, and the former USSR on the other. The reorientation of the Central and Eastern European countries toward the West is irreversible. The CMEA was not really an economic union, or a supranational organisation. Trade flows among its members were geared to the needs and interests of the Soviet Union. Despite significant trade interdependencies between the Central and Eastern European countries on the one hand, and the USSR on the other, the national economies were not deeply connected, and all endeavours to increase intra-branch and intra-product industrial cooperation in the area have failed. This specific weakness of the

Table 9.1 *Patterns of foreign trade in the countries in transition: initial changes in direction (1991–3), and shares in 1990, 1993 and 1997*

Developed market economies	1991	1992	1993	1990	1993	1997 (prel.)
	Growth rates, in per cent			Structure by direction		
Eastern Europe						
Exports to:						
World	−6.9	−4.0	−0.1	100	100	100
Transition economies	−24.6	−20.6	−7.3	41.1	30.5	26.2
Former Soviet Union	−25.1	−31.7	−14.2	22.3	9.2	10.3
Eastern Europe	−20.1	−8.7	−9.7	12.7	16.7	13.2
Developed market economies	6.6	0.8	1.2	49.5	58.0	66.5
Developing countries	−11.8	11.7	5.6	9.4	11.5	7.3
Imports from:						
World	−4.1	3.3	10.4	100	100	100
Transition economies	−19.8	−0.6	4.0	36.8	30.1	23.7
Former Soviet Union	−9.3	−3.4	7.9	18.3	16.1	11.5
Eastern Europe*	−25.8	−3.3	-2.3	12.5	11.9	9.7
Developed market economies	7.8	10.8	12.9	53.3	61.6	67.4
Developing countries	−9.2	−17.6	8.6	9.9	8.3	8.9
Former Soviet Union/Russia*						
Exports to:						
World	−24.6	−16.8	4.5	100	100	100
Transition economies	−35.0	−14.5	−10.6	25.9	26.3	26.8
Eastern Europe	−40.8	−30.6	−5.1	18.8	17.0	14.4
Developed market economies	−16.2	−14.6	7.6	49.5	59.7	58.1
Developing countries	−29.0	−30.6	11.2	24.6	14.0	15.1
Imports from:						
World	−35.9	−16.8	−27.5	100	100	100
Transition economies	−43.4	−37.4	−32.3	29.4	22.1	18.3
Eastern Europe	−5.6	−51.0	−51.1	23.2	10.7	9.3
Developed market economies	−31.0	−10.8	−29.6	52.9	60.6	67.4
Developing countries	−35.8	11.9	−10.3	17.7	17.3	14.3

* Trade of the Baltic states not included.
** Russia only after 1991.
Source: ECE/UN, 1994a, 1996a, 1998.

CMEA scheme greatly helped Central and Eastern European countries to sever their mutual links, despite the blow caused in the fall in trade.

The collapse of intra-CIS (Commonwealth of Independent States) trade is of a different nature. It has been provoked by the economic collapse of the USSR, by political conflicts, and by the inability of Russia to solve the monetary problems of the area with its partners. The USSR was a single state under the cover of a Federation. Its industries were interdependent, not in the Western, market sense of intra-industry links, but out of political decisions which had created intricate networks of administrative links. If these relations are not replaced with a new, normalised foreign trade, the recovery of the CIS economies may take much more time than expected.

Is There a Rationale for a Central and Eastern European Regional Grouping?

History, economic theory and politics all provide ambiguous answers. The reality check has shown that there was, after all, some ground for a viable regional link, once the issue became dispassionate.

History

Economic links among Central European countries are recent history. They have always until 1989 been forcibly imposed. Before the Second World War, Nazi-ruled Germany had politically and economically tied most of these countries through a whole set of arrangements, including a system of settlements in clearing aimed not just at facilitating trade but at exploiting Germany's partners and isolating them from Western democracies. After the Second World War these countries, whatever their stand during the war, were forced into the Soviet bloc. A study published by the Institute for International Economics in Washington (Collins and Rodrik, 1991), taking the year 1928 as the last pre-war 'normal' year for investigating trade patterns, concluded that 'although suggestive, the 1928 composition of trade is far from being a reliable guide for future trade patterns' (p. 41), especially because of the shifting role of individual Western countries in world trade. Accounting for that, the authors propose a model which provides a projection of pre-war trends assuming that East Central European countries would not have become 'socialist', and would have behaved in line with several 'comparator' countries in Europe. This exercise leads to several conclusions: (i) there should be a very strong reorientation of trade to the West and especially toward EC countries; (ii) trade with the Soviet Union should decline dramatically; and (iii) trade among the Eastern countries might stabilise and even increase (in proportion to total trade). The authors acknowledge that the model has not fully taken into account some variables and hypotheses, such as the impact of past specialisation in the region, the consequences of EC trade policies, or the event of a recovery of the Soviet market, the latter not being considered as plausible.

Was the post-war Western cooperation, in the framework of the Marshall Plan, relevant to the post-transition situation? An extensive literature has been published on the subject. The Marshall Plan was proposed in June 1947 by the US Secretary of State, offering US help for the economic reconstruction of war-devastated Europe. In July 1947 the European Committee for Economic Cooperation was set up; this was the precursor of the OEEC (Organisation for European Economic Cooperation) which itself evolved into the OECD. The European countries developed their cooperation under the direct pressure of the United States. The Marshall Plan supported the creation of the EPU (European Payments Union) along with the commitment to liberalise trade in Europe. The EPU was set up in 1950 so as to facilitate a gradual and coordinated transition to convertibility of the European currencies. In 1951 the Marshall Plan transfers came to an end. In the same year the ECSC (the European Coal and Steel Community) was created. In 1957 the Rome Treaty instituting the Common Market was signed. In 1958 the EPU had achieved its task, as all the European currencies were convertible, and was dissolved.

This story was used both by supporters of an Eastern EPU or trade union (van Brabant, 1993; Bakos, 1993) and by its critics. The difficulty lies in establishing a link between the Plan and the post-war economic events. Within a ten-year period, the European countries reconstructed their infrastructures, resumed growth, successfully fought inflation, balanced their budgets, liberalised their trade, made their currencies convertible, and launched a common market, at the same time healing political wounds among nations which had fought each other during the war. How can one separate the impact of the Marshall Plan, of the political game between the United States and the European countries, of the national policies, of the drive toward European cooperation? Was the Marshall Plan 'the most successful structural adjustment programme in history' as claimed in de Long and Eichengreen (1992), or the catalyst of economic cooperation, as former French Prime Minister Raymond Barre, who worked in the European Cooperation Administration, sees it (Barre *et al.*, 1992b)? There are strong analogies in the initial situation in 1947 and in 1989: countries devastated by war or by decades of communist economic management; strong enmities among the nations, due to war or to history; readiness of a rich partner to help against some conditionality, in his own interests. However the differences are considerable. In 1947 the European economies were developed market economies, which normal way of operating had been suspended for a few years only. Before the war these countries already dominated the world scene and already conducted about 40 per cent of their foreign trade among themselves.

Economic theory

In international economic theory various approaches may be selected to support one view or the other. Gravity models suggest that neighbours are prone to trade together, though economists generally distrust them. The Heckscher–Ohlin model and the derived theories would support the rationale for Russia – East Europe trade relations as these are based on complementary factor endowments, but would not so much advocate an expansion of intra-East European trade, as the economic structures and endowments of Central and East European countries are very similar.

However countries with similar industries may well develop intra-branch trade, or trade similar goods in an imperfect competition approach.

Anyhow, applied international economics are devised for market economies. Thus one may well assert that countries in transition should first turn into market economies. Trade among them will develop according to a market rationale only if this initial condition is fulfilled; no artificial grouping can be a substitute for the market.

One may also question any model aiming at establishing what should be the 'normal' level of trade among the former CMEA countries. Using a gravity model, Dariusz Rosati (1993) shows that 'normal' trade among the countries of Central and Eastern Europe and with the USSR would be rather below the (already depressed) levels of 1989–90. Two French scholars, using the standard gravity model and a refined version including the differences in transport costs among the Central and East European countries in comparison with their average transport costs, reach the same conclusion (Cheikbossian and Maurel, 1996). Harriet Matejka (1994) challenges any such approach. First the statistical distortions are such, before and after the collapse of the CMEA, that it is virtually impossible to claim robust results. Second, to assume that a 'normal' state would be the intensity of trade among countries displaying comparable economic characteristics, is to ignore that the transition economies are not only moving to a market system but are, at the same time, undergoing a formidable upheaval which is changing all economic relationships. Thus, to apply to them parameters calculated for established market economies, or for them at an earlier stage, is simply meaningless.

Politics

The political arguments have been the most compelling. Once transition to the market and to democracy was under way, East European countries did not want any arrangement reminiscent of the former CMEA. They were still more opposed to any conditionality linking assistance with the commitment to regional cooperation. However CEFTA (Central European Free Trade Area) was reluctantly created.

The CEFTA

Central European countries form what the West is still calling 'the Visegrád group', a phrase not very popular among them. The Visegrád agreement was indeed signed in February 1991 between Poland, Hungary and the CSFR (Czech and Slovak Federal Republic). The Final Declaration recommended 'free movement of capital and labour', to be promoted by 'the development of market-based *economic cooperation*', cooperation in infrastructure development, and in the ecological sphere. But no explicit mechanism or regulations were to ensure that the goal be met (Visegrád,

1991). Following the signing of the first 'Europe agreements' in December 1991, which established a free trade area between each Central European country and the EC, the 'Visegrád group' also established a *free trade area* (CEFTA) by an agreement in December 1992. Since January 1993 this group has had four members, following the split between the Czech and Slovak Republics. Though the CEFTA was hailed in the West as creating a market of 64 million, the main outcome of the new agreement was to level the playing-field. Mutual concessions have been devised so as to ensure that mutual trade would not be discriminated against by comparison with trade with the EC. In September 1995 it was decided among the existing members that CEFTA could be enlarged to admit new members from Eastern Europe who were members of the World Trade Organisation (WTO) and had signed an Association Agreement with the EU. Slovenia was admitted in 1996, Romania in 1997, Bulgaria in 1998, and the Baltic states have expressed an interest though they are not yet members of the WTO. Tariffs for industrial goods had all been eliminated by 1 January 1997, with a few exceptions (such as imported cars in Poland). Agricultural trade has been freed to a lesser extent. As in the Europe Agreements, each member may impose some measures such as import surcharges in case of balance of payment difficulties.

Eastern economists who are most in favour of the development of intra-regional trade, or rather the less opposed to it, would advocate liberalising mutual trade (beyond what is provided for in the agreement), dismantling the existing barriers to the regional flows of investment, and eliminating the unnecessary costs of mutual trade and in particular the use of Western intermediaries (Inotai and Sass, 1994). Poland suggested the liberalisation of labour force migrations, and also the establishment of a CEFTA bank on the EBRD (European Bank for Reconstruction and Development) model to finance regional investment projects. Slovakia has pleaded for permanent headquarters. These suggestions were never accepted (Richter, 1997). CEFTA seems thus to be confined to a minor role, and while the share of trade within CEFTA has slightly increased after 1993, it remains very small as compared with the share of its members' trade with the West (Hrnčíř, 1997, p. 97). In 1997, the share of intra-regional trade in total trade of the CEFTA members had dropped back to its 1994 level, at 14 and 10.5 per cent for exports and imports, respectively (ECE/UN, 1997b, p. 52). Few people thus recommend a strengthening of CEFTA in view of a revival of mutual trade, and those who do favour a customs union among the CEFTA members argue that such a move may reduce the delays in the process of accession to the EU (ECE/UN. 1996b, chapter 4).

While CEFTA might in the future include the Baltic states, cooperation among the latter began with a free trade zone agreement signed in September 1993. The agreement covers industrial and agricultural trade but not trade in services. It does not provide for establishment freedom, labour movements, or removal of non-tariff barriers. It is not surprising that it seems to have little impact on intra-Baltic trade, which is stable at about 10 per cent of total trade (Sorsa, 1997, pp. 169–70), despite some acceleration in 1996. A customs union might be established in 1998. In addition the three Baltic countries became members of the Council of Baltic Sea States created in March 1993 which regroups the members of the Nordic Council (since 1952, Finland, Sweden, Norway, Denmark and Iceland) and the other countries bordering the Baltic sea, i.e. the three Baltic states, Germany, Poland and Russia. The Baltic Council is a rather loose structure which aims to foster cooperation in the fields of economy, environment, transport and communications.

What is going to happen to CEFTA and to the Baltic free trade area following the accession of some of their members to the EU? (see below, The Accession Process, p. 228). The division of the applicants in two groups decided by the EU will cut both regional groupimgs into two parts, because the first round of negotiations is conducted with five countries only (the Czech Republic, Hungary, Poland, Slovenia and Estonia), the five other applicants presumably joining later. For Slovakia, the EU membership of the Czech Republic will put an end to the customs union between the two countries. The new EU members will have to denounce the CEFTA arrangement (Estonia will have to denounce the Baltic free trade area arrangement) as incompatible with EU regulations. Their relations with their former partners will be regulated by the EAs concluded between the EU and each of the applicants (Matejka, 1998). Some restrictions to imports from the non-EU members will follow, especially for agricultural goods and for industrial sensitive goods. It is thus ironical that the European Commission sought to promote regional arrangements in the early 1990s only to destroy them through the enlargement process itself.

Trade and Payments Arrangements in the CIS Space

The Commonwealth of Independent States which links Russia and, according to the Russian-coined word, its 'near-abroad', is neither a customs union, nor a payments union. The disintegration of the Soviet Union compelled the successor states to look for an arrangement whereby some of the links uniting them in the past could be maintained. However regional integration progressed very slowly, and has no bright prospects (Clement, 1997).

The attempts to form an economic union

The CIS was established in December 1991 as a loose arrangement between the former Republics of the USSR, except the Baltic states and Georgia (the latter decided to join the organisation in October 1993 to prevent its own internal disintegration). Since 1992 numerous attempts to strengthen the organisation have been made, in various directions: liberalising mutual trade (February 1992), setting up an Interstate Bank to manage settlements within a single currency zone (October 1992), adopting a Charter that provided for cooperation in the establishment of a common economic space with free movement of goods, capital, labour, and services, and in the promotion of mutual trade (January 1993), setting up an economic union (September 1993), preparing a customs union, and deciding to create an Interstate Economic Commission (1994). These arrangements have been purely declarative, and largely repetitive. In April 1998, a CIS Summit held in Moscow failed to adopt proposals on a free trade area and a single economic space. Meanwhile, intra-CIS trade remained largely centred on Russia which accounted for about half of the mutual trade flows, and kept falling (with all reservations due to the inconsistencies of the different partners' trade statistics, and to the importance of non-recorded barter trade).

Russia keeps trying to revive the customs union and the idea of a single economic space. The customs union is since 1996 effective among Russia, Belarus (in 1996 both countries signed a Treaty establishing a 'Commonwealth of Sovereign States'), Kazakhstan and Kyrgyzstan. In April 1998 Tajikistan was admitted to the union. The actual impact of the union does not seem clear, especially as the political willingness of the partners may be questioned. The biggest trading partners within the CIS area, Russia and Ukraine, signed a 'Treaty of Economic Cooperation for 1998–2007' in February 1998 providing for unified tax and tariff policies and a coordination of exchange rate policies.

Sub-regional arrangements are also developing. A summit of the *Central Asian states* was held in Tashkent in January 1993 so as to discuss the possibility of a Central Asian Common market. On 1 February 1994, an agreement went into effect between Kazakhstan, Uzbekistan, and Kyrgyzstan on the creation of a less ambitious 'common economic space'. Free circulation of capital, goods, and labour will be allowed, and common policies on credit, prices, taxes, customs, and currency should be set. As a first move, customs posts were removed on the common borders of the three states. However, it is difficult to see how the three states will be able to coordinate their economic policies, as Uzbekistan is far less advanced in reform than its two partners, and only in February 1994 did it regulate private property (Brown, 1994). Actually mutual trade fell in value and in real terms in the years following the agreement (EC/UN, 1997a, p. 206).

In addition, the Central Asian countries all became members of the *Economic Cooperation Organisation* (ECO), with the last country, Tajikistan, to join in February 1993. ECO was established in 1985 by Iran, Pakistan and Turkey, and joined in 1992 by Azerbaijan and Afghanistan. In July 1993 the heads of state of ECO agreed to establish a trade and investment bank, a reinsurance firm and a shipping company. These institutions have yet to be implemented. At the 1995 Summit of the organisation, an ECO Transit Trade Agreement was signed to promote regional trade (Pomfret, 1997b).

The *Black Sea Economic Cooperation* (BSEC) was established in June 1992 between 6 CIS members (Armenia, Azerbaijan, Georgia, Moldova, Russia, Ukraine), Turkey, Bulgaria, Romania, Greece and Albania. This Turkish initiative was meant to develop economic cooperation in various areas (transportation, communications, tourism, statistics, agriculture, energy, environment, health care, and R & D). The organisation lacks the institutional structure needed to enforce its directives, and is affected by the military and political tensions in the Black Sea region. The BSEC has a symbolic potential in offering cooperation between CIS states, South Eastern Europe, and two Western states. It has yet to establish itself politically, institutionally, and economically (Connelly, 1994).

What is the explanation for the disappointing outcomes of the attempts to restore economic links among the successor states to the USSR? Is this due to political reasons, or to economic logic?

Intra-CIS trade issues

The reality of the collapse in intra-CIS trade is undisputable though impossible to assess precisely because of discrepancies in statistics from the different countries, the importance of barter trade, and the uncertainties about the prices applied in mutual trade. Trade fell by about 15–20 per cent in 1991 and 25–40 per cent in 1992 (EBRD, 1993). Since 1992 intra-CIS trade kept falling, except for a small rebound in 1996. While in 1990 almost three-quarters of the exports of the Soviet Republics, now members of the CIS, were intra-regional, in 1997 the share of intra-CIS exports was about a quarter of the overall CIS exports (ECE/UN, 1998, p. 145). In this trade Russia has a large surplus which it tries to reduce by increasing its imports, decreasing its exports still further, and raising its export prices. Why did trade fall in such proportions?

Explanation 1. Trade has fallen as a result of the decline in *overall production*. Thus the key to a resumption in trade would be a resumption of growth. This does not seem to be the right explanation as non-CIS trade has increased.

Explanation 2. Trade has fallen as the result of the *disaggregation* of the Soviet Union. According to the general view, there was in the past a single economic space with a high degree of integration and specialisation, that has suddenly been broken up. This is a misrepresentation. The Soviet Union was held together by a highly integrated political and administrative structure. Economically it was far from integrated. True, huge federal firms were supplying customers all over the Union, at high transportation costs; such links bear no rationality and should be severed. The planned distribution-system (*Gossnab*, see Chapter 1, p. 6) linked suppliers and buyers in such a way that often two producers located in the same area – let us say, a processing plant and a machinery firm manufacturing equipment of the kind used by the processing plant – had both to trade with a supplier or a customer located thousands of kilometres away, instead of trading with each other. The idea of a high degree of specialisation must also be reconsidered. Specialisation existed mostly on paper. The deadlocks of the administrative supply system were such that the big communist firms tried to manufacture themselves all that was needed for their operation in terms of spare parts and components instead of relying on specialised deliveries. Thus, at the same time, trade links within the Soviet Union were above *and* below what economic rationality would have commanded.

Explanation 3. Trade has fallen due to specific *restrictions in bilateral trade*. Some of these restrictions and quotas have been lifted since 1992, but many remain especially for countries that are not linked by a free trade or customs union agreement, and new barriers in the form of duties and special levies have been introduced. For the most important segment of intra-CIS trade, which consists of imports of energy and raw materials especially from Russia, bilateral arrangements still prevail.

Explanation 4. The main problems are those due to *energy trade*. In 1992 the Russian oil and gas prices charged to the Newly Independent States (NIS) were lower than world prices by 50 to 30 per cent, and in addition payments were often delayed. Overall the Russian trade subsidy to the NIS was said to amount to an equivalent of 17 billion dollars (*ITAR-TASS*, 13 July 1993) for the year 1992. The subsidy declined over time but still in 1997 Russian prices for sales of crude oil to CIS countries were under the world level, although prices for other raw materials converged towards the world level and occasionally exceeded it. This situation has led to large Russian trade surpluses with its CIS buyers, to high payments arrears, and to repeated cuts in oil, gas and electricity deliveries (ECE/UN, 1997a, p. 147). Russia has also proposed to some of its debtors debt-for-equity swaps in form of the acquisition of pipelines or oil fields.

Energy trade flows should decline in the long run. Production in the Soviet Union used to be very energy-intensive, both because of the importance of the heavy industry, and because of the low cost of energy which induced all users to waste it. It is only desirable that the related trade flows be strongly reduced, and that such outdated and obsolete (compared with world standards of energy consumption) interdependencies be suppressed.

Explanation 5. The issue of energy raises the more general question of the *costs and benefits in inter-republic trade*, in the past and in the future, and it may be contended that trade collapsed because Russia cannot afford and does not want to go on supporting the 'near abroad'. A study based on the analysis of past inter-republic links using Soviet input–output tables (Senik-Leygonie and Hughes, 1992) argues that Russia has in the past 'subsidised' the other republics – its 'satellites' – in two ways. First, Russia supplied them with underpriced raw materials and energy and at the same time allowed them to maintain a large internal 'deficit' with it, within the framework of inter-republican trade. Secondly, Russia financed the trade deficits of the other republics with the rest of the world. It may indeed be argued that, as Russia accounted for a larger share in the USSR's exports to the rest of the world than in its imports, the republic also financed the aggregate external balance of the Union as a whole. The mechanism is compared by the authors of the mentioned study (Senik-Leygonie and Hughes, 1992, p. 372) to that of intra-Comecon subsidies in the past, as interpreted by Marrese and Vanous (1983): a bargain between economic gains and political advantages, as if Russia was 'buying' the right to exercise central power through subsidising its partners.

Thus the break-up of the Soviet Union is freeing Russia from the burden of subsidising both 'deficits' of the other Republics, in trade with the rest of the world and in inter-republic trade. Russia is also in the best position to trade on its own with the rest of the world due to its size and resources. It still relies on its present comparative advantages and mainly exports raw materials, energy and intermediate goods.

To sum up, there are many reasons explaining the collapse in mutual trade among the states of the former Soviet Union. This brings us to a conclusion: there is no point in 'reviving' trade links. New trade flows are emerging and will develop in the course of market transformation. Thus the latter should be accelerated, but this cannot be done forcibly, especially when political disputes add to the picture. This is not to say that facilitating measures and initiatives are useless. Also, the transportation system is acting as a bottleneck and should be improved, with project-based international aid, for example for rebuilding pipelines, modernising railways and highways. An even stronger conclusion is supported by the World Bank, which believes that a regional arrangement would complicate the process of the CIS countries' joining the WTO, but would moreover distort trade flows (quoted by ECE/UN, 1997b, footnote 141).

Should a new payment system be devised to help trade flows? The answer is certainly yes if one believes that trade is impaired due to the lack of payment instruments. It should be no if one believes that it is rooted in the legacies of the past.

The problem of the ruble zone

Once the break-up of the USSR was consummated, the question of the currency to be used in the former Soviet space arose. Initially the international community (independent experts and international organisations as well) favoured the variant of a ruble zone under Russia's control. Several circumstances led to a change of mind. These were the growing monetary crisis in Russia itself, and the moves of several states toward establishing their own currency (see Table 9.2). The ruble zone then appeared as non-feasible, and various forms of a payments agreement, or payments union, were put forward. The IMF itself changed its mind. After having supported in 1992 the ruble zone concept, it shifted in 1993 to a preference for the payments union: only the states with a separate currency could get IMF credits.

The payments union has never been set up, but an extraordinary amount of literature flourished on the topic. We guess that this was due to the excitement of international monetary economics theorists and experts. The issue of the optimum currency area is one of the most interesting fields of modern monetary theory. A live experiment, with policy-making opportunities, is very seldom at hand. What Western economists could not guess, as they were used to rational economic modelling and to consistent policies, was that the former Soviet Union states would constantly vacillate from one solution to the other and ultimately chose the worst of both.

There has been a large theoretical literature on the monetary integration of the former USSR (to quote a very small selection, see CEPR, 1993; Bofinger and Gros, 1992; Eichengreen, 1993; Eichengreen and Uzan, 1992; Williamson, 1992a; Wolf *et al.*, 1994). The discussion focused on different issues. In the international monetary theory literature the usual departure point is the following: why should sovereign countries with a national currency abandon their currency independence and chose to form a currency area (hence the discussion of the optimal currency area deriving from the works of Mundell and McKinnon; see Bofinger *et al.*, 1993) or a payments union?

The solution of a ruble zone, or area, was soon dismissed when it became obvious that Russia as the dominant partner had neither the willingness nor the capacity to accept the financial burden of sustaining a ruble area scheme in exchange for economic and political influence. Was a monetary arrangement of some kind more workable, either as a European Payments Union type or as a multilateral arrangement based on a fixed exchange rate like the initial Bretton Woods system? Such an arrangement could only work if there were some cooperation among the members in conducting the same stabilisation policies, if the bilateral deficits were not too big, and if external financing was available. As none of these conditions were met, a third solution was the only viable one: that each country pursues its own stabilisation policy with a separate currency to be ultimately made convertible. Table 9.2 shows the status of the national currencies in the successor states of the USSR.

Table 9.2 The status of the currencies in the successor states of the USSR

State	National currency	Exchange rate regime	Monetary operation
Russia	Ruble	Floating rate until July 1996. Since then sliding currency corridor exchange rate regime with initial limits of 5,000–6,100 rubles for 1 dollar. Since January 1998 following currency reform limits fixed at 5.27–7.13 rubles for 1 dollar. Band extended to 6.0–9.5 rubles on 17 August 1998; ruble in fact floating following this devaluation.	Exclusive use of the ruble as the domestic currency (as from 1 Jan. 1994). New denomination as of January 1998 (1 new ruble = 1,000 old rubles).
Estonia	Kroon (June 1992)	Currency board regime. The kroon is pegged to the DM at a fixed rate of 1DM = 8 kroon. Full capital and c.a. convertibility.	
Latvia	Lat (March 1993)	Fixed peg since February 1994. De facto pegged to the SDR** basket. Full capital and c.a. convertibility.	Latvian ruble was used until 1993.
Lithuania	Litas (June 1993)	Currency board regime introduced in April 1994 (1$ = 4 litai). Full capital and c.a. convertibility.	Talonas (coupons) used until 1993.
Ukraine	Hryvnia (Sep. 1996)	Fixed rate (1$ = 1.76 hryvnia), then (April 1997) currency corridor (1.70–1.90 hr. for 1$; 2.50–3.50 since Sept. 1998). Full c.a. convertibility.	Kupon in 1991; karbovanets in November 1992. The karbovanets has been exchanged for hryvny at a rate of 1 hr = 100,000 krb.
Azerbaijan	Manat (March 1992)	Since 1994 rate based on a basket of currencies. Double exchange rate until March 1995. Limited convertibility.	Azeri ruble used for non-cash transactions until Jan. 1994.
Armenia	Dram (November 1991)	Floating rate introduced in 1994.	Full c.a. convertibility.

Georgia	Lari (Sept. 1995)	Managed float. Full c.a. convertibility.	Ruble coupons since April 1993. De facto linked to the Russian ruble until introduction of lari.
Kyrgyzstan	Som (May 1993)	Exchange rate fixed on the basis of currency auctions. Full c.a. convertibility.	
Kazakhstan	Tenge (Nov. 1993)	Managed float. Full c.a. convertibility.	
Tajikistan	Tajik ruble (May 1995)	Exchange rate fixed on the basis of currency auctions. Numerous exchange restrictions.	Soviet ruble until Dec. 1993, then Russian ruble until May 1995.
Uzbekistan	Sum (1995)	Multiple exchange rate regime (official rate, auction rate, special commercial rate). Numerous exchange restrictions.	Sum-coupons introduced Nov. 1993.
Turkmenistan	Manat (Nov. 1993)	Multiple exchange rates. Official rate set at auctions. Numerous exchange restrictions.	Ruble until Nov. 1993.
Belarus	Belarus ruble (1994)	Dual exchange rate. Official rate fixed within a dollar band. Numerous exchange restrictions on foreign currency and Russian ruble.	Russian ruble until Aug. 1993, then coupon zaichik (bunny).
Moldova	Leu (Nov. 1993)	Floating rate. Full c.a. convertibility.	

* c.a. = current account
** SDR : Special Drawing Rights.

Since the collapse of the Soviet Union, there have been numerous payment arrangements ad hoc with Russia. The mutual debts between Russia and the former Soviet Republics are not yet settled.
Source: EBRD (1997); various press reports.

The IMF explicitly supported the implementation of the separate currency policy. It helped it to better monitor and control the structural adjustment programmes, as in the case of Estonia and Lithuania, and of Kyrgyzstan.

This section has shown how difficult it is to achieve a restructuring of the former trade areas to which the centrally planned economies belonged. Turning to the West not only expresses hopes for an improved market access. It was also a way of escaping the almost impossible task of rebuilding mutual relations out of the present chaos.

Table 9.3 shows membership of Central and East European countries and of the CIS in regional and international economic organisations.

THE REORIENTATION TO THE WEST

As seen from Table 9.1, the countries in transition quickly reoriented their trade to the West after 1990. The most significant block of these East–West relations is trade between the EU and the ten countries of Central and Eastern Europe that are applicants for admission into the EU. It amounts to about 5 per cent of EU countries' trade, around 55–60 per cent of CEEC's trade, and around 55 per cent of exports and 65 per cent of imports of the countries in transition in their overall Western trade. The future members of the EU are all engaged since 1996 in the 'pre-accession' process, and five of them actually started accession negotiations in April 1998.

Countries outside this process are nevertheless strongly influenced by it. They include, first, the countries of the southern tier: Albania, and successor states of Yugoslavia with the exception of Slovenia which belongs to the applicants' group. These countries are potentially to be reintegrated into Europe sometime – when internal chaos, in the case of Albania, and sequels of the war and ethnic conflicts, for Yugoslavia, Macedonia, Croatia, and Bosnia and Hercegovina, are wiped out. Among the CIS countries, Russia, though not an applicant, nevertheless claims to be a privileged partner of the EU. Ukraine, Moldova, Belarus, also 'partner countries' to the EU, have not relinquished hopes of being one day EU members, a stance supported by geography and geopolitics.

Reorientation to the West may also mean movements of people who under the communist regime were deprived of the political right to emigrate or to move freely outside the borders of their countries. The citizens of the countries in transition have discovered that trade liberalisation does not go hand in hand with population movements liberalisation.

The First Stage of Reintegration: The Europe Agreements

The so-called 'Europe Agreements' (or association treaties), were first signed by the EC with the Central European countries (Poland, Hungary,

Table 9.3 *Membership of Central and East European countries and of the former Soviet Union countries in regional and international economic organisations (as of beginning 1998)*

	CEFTA	CBSS	BFTA	CSS	CUA	CACS	ECO	BSEC	OECD	IMF	WTO	EU1	EU2
Poland	x	x							x	x	x	x	
Czech Rep.	x								x	x	x	x	
Slovak Rep.	x								c	x	x		x
Hungary	x								x	x	x	x	
Slovenia	x									x	x	x	
Romania	x									x	x		x
Bulgaria	x									x	x		x
Albania										x	a		
Estonia	i	x	x							x	a	x	
Latvia	i	x	x							x	a		x
Lithuania	i	x	x							x	a		x
Russia		x		x	x			x	c	x	a		
Belarus				x	x					x	a		
Ukraine	i							x		x	a		
Moldova								x		x	a		
Armenia								x		x	a		
Azerbaijan							x	x		x			
Georgia								x		x	a		
Kazakhstan					x	x	x			x	a		
Uzbekistan						x	x			x	a		
Kyrgyzstan					x	x	x			x	a		
Tajikistan							x			x			
Turkmenistan							x			x			

x = member; a = applicant ; i = expressed an interest in membership; c = cooperation.

CEFTA = Central European Free Trade Area; CBSS = Council of Baltic Sea States; BFTA = Baltic Free Trade Area; CSS = Council of Sovereign States; CUA = CIS customs union agreement; CACS = Central Asian Common Space; ECO = Economic Cooperation Organisation; BSEC = Black Sea Economic Cooperation; OECD: Organisation for Economic Cooperation and Development; IMF = International Monetary Fund; WTO = World Trade Organisation; EU1 = first round of countries admitted to start accession negotiations with EU in 1998; EU2 = second round of countries (no deadline for beginning of negotiations).
Source: Adapted from Clement (1997).

and the CSFR) on 16 December 1991. They have been renegotiated with the Czech and the Slovak Republics after the splitting of Czechoslovakia and new agreements were signed with both countries in October 1993. They extended in March 1993 to Bulgaria and Romania, in June 1995 to the Baltic States and in June 1996 to Slovenia. Whereas the Europe Agreements did not explicitly contain a provision committing the EC members to take steps towards membership of the Central and East European countries in the EC, it was implicitly assumed that sooner or later it would be impossible to resist these countries' explicit wish. Indeed the Europe Agreements mentioned that 'the final objective of [the given country] is to become a member of the Community, and that this association, in the view of the Parties, will help to achieve this objective': a very cautious statement indeed, which did not commit the Community, and which was agreed upon after lengthy discussions. But the process proved to be irreversible: in April 1994, following the entry in force of the fully ratified Europe Agreements, Hungary and Poland officially applied for membership in the European Union, and later all the other 'associates' followed suit.

These agreements are not obsolete. They remain in force until the applicant countries are admitted into the EU, which may take at least five years following the beginning of the negotiations with the first applicants in 1998. In the field of trade, the Europe Agreements (EAs) provided for asymmetrical and gradual trade concessions, and foresaw the establishment of a free trade area between each Central European country and the EC within ten years of the entry in force of each agreement. *For the goods regulated by the agreements*, i.e. industrial goods, and among them only those not regulated otherwise, the main commitments of the EC in the agreements signed in 1991 were the following:

- *Quantitative restrictions* were to be removed for all industrial goods within one year of the entry in force of each EA.
- *Tariffs* were removed immediately for most of the goods. For 'semi-sensitive' or 'sensitive' goods tariffs were to be reduced gradually within quota-levels, with an increase in the quota-level, over a period not exceeding five years. 'Sensitive' goods include textile products other than those regulated by the Multi-Fibre Arrangement, iron and steel other than the ECSC (European Coal and Steel Community) products, chemicals, footwear, glassware, motor vehicles, furniture.

The reciprocal commitments for the Central European countries were spread over a longer period: seven years for Poland, and nine years for Hungary and the CSFR. In addition, these countries were allowed to resort to new restrictions or tariffs, while the standstill clause applied to the EC countries. These facilities were granted in the case of nascent industries, or activities undergoing structural transformation.

These provisions seem very generous indeed. However this basic framework did not apply to a range of products for which special protocols had been negotiated. These were:

- *agricultural goods*, ruled by the Common Agricultural Policy. For these goods the EC mainly confirmed provisions already included in the Generalised System of Preferences (GSP), which was granted as of January 1990 (Poland and Hungary) or 1991 (the CSFR). A few additional concessions have been made in 1993. But trade in agricultural goods was in principle excluded from the envisaged free trade area.
- *textile goods regulated by the MFA* (Multi-Fibre Arrangement). A special annex to the Europe Agreements provided for a complicated schedule, because the MFA itself was to be dismantled by the completion of the Uruguay Round. Actually tariffs on textile goods covered by the MFA were eliminated by January 1998, ahead of the dates set in the Uruguay Round accord.
- *coal and steel* products regulated by the ECSC. Here the schedule was basically the same as for industrial sensitive products, however with additional provisions as to competition rules, and as to the transparency of public subsidies.

To sum up, the market access provided for in the Europe Agreements (EAs) is not so generous as it may seem:

(a) The most extensive concessions were already granted earlier, either in the GSP, or in the trade and economic cooperation agreements concluded in 1988 with each of the Central European countries. They were then unilateral. According to the EAs they imply a reciprocity, albeit asymmetrical.

(b) The tariff facility for nascent or restructuring industries looks very generous. One must not forget, however, that in the first stages of transition trade liberalisation was very abrupt. While they were preparing the EAs the Central European countries literally dismantled their tariffs, whose average level fell to 5 per cent in the SFR, 8 per cent in Poland, 15 per cent in Hungary beginning 1991. Though trade liberalisation is usually part of the standard reform and stabilisation package, several Western experts had already suggested at that time that some temporary tariff protection would be useful (see McKinnon, 1991b, and the debate with Williamson, 1991b, p. 38). Such proposals became more pressing later, especially as the initial protection offered by the over-devaluation of the Central European currencies was wearing out (Nuti and Portes, 1993). Other pressures were less high-principled. Multinationals established in the East, especially in the car industry, strongly lobbied in favour of increased tariffs: in particular, Volkswagen in the Czech Republic, or Fiat in Poland (Bobinski, 1992). This in turn angered the United States which felt discriminated against, and provoked reservations from the GATT (Dunne, 1992; Robinson, 1993).

While tariffs may be relevant in the relations between the Central and East European countries (CEECs) and non-EU members, are they really an issue in CEECs – EU relations as indeed they have been phased out in the framework of the EAs? Patrick Messerlin who authored the special chapter on tariff protection in an ECE/UN volume (ECE/UN, 1996b, pp. 79–98) argues that they are, though the average level of CEFTA countries' tariffs (around 10 per cent in 1996) is very close to that of the EU (7.2 per cent) because the highest tariffs are concentrated in sensitive sectors such as agricultural and food processing goods, apparel, footwear, cars and engines, among others (*ibid.*, p. 87).

(c) As shown in Table 9.4, the more sensitive products, for which trade concessions are the lower, amounted to the dominant share in Central and East European exports to the West at the time the agreements were signed. These goods were typically produced in existing capacities. These capacities, in industry and agriculture, have immediately been mobilised in the shift from East to West. In most cases these are 'negative value added' activities, which *should* be scrapped in due course. Steel industry is the best, also the most controverted, example.

(d) Both parties may use *anti-dumping* and *safeguard* procedures. In fact from the outset it was clear that such procedures were to help the EC against a surge of low-price imports from the East. In the past, *anti-dumping* procedures have been extensively used against state trading countries, especially for chemicals. The transition countries are now considered as market economies, but their price structure and the operation of the state companies help the EU producers to prove that in some particular industries (especially steel) market rules do not yet work.

As for the *safeguard* clause, the conditions are very extensively defined. Safeguard measures are authorised whenever imports from any Central European country may cause 'serious injury to domestic producers of like or directly competitive products', or 'serious disturbances in any sector of the economy or difficulties which could bring about serious deterioration in the economic situation of a region' (quoted from the official text). This clause is very undetermined. What is a 'serious' deterioration, disturbance or injury? It is quite subjective, and even more so is the potential impact of the 'difficulties'. The clause may be invoked by domestic producers, by 'sectors', or by 'regions'. Finally, special safeguard clauses apply to agricultural, and textile and clothing trades.

(e) *Rules of origin* are rather strictly defined. Products which qualify for trade concessions must have been produced in the Central European countries, and must not have more than a 40 per cent import content (in per cent of the value of the output) from non-EC countries. This is a powerful disincentive to non-EC foreign investment. In particular, US or Japanese

Table 9.4 Trade in sensitive products between the EC countries and five countries in transition in 1992

Commodity groups (according to sections of EC Common Tariff)	Five CEECs	Poland	CSFR	Hungary	Romania	Bulgaria
– Agricultural goods (including processed): share in total exports to EC (in percent)	12.3	13.4	5.0	20.8	5.5	20.4
– balance of the CEECs (exports minus imports), in million ECU	+301	+28	–141	+602	–248	+59
Chemical products:						
– share in total exports to EC (in per cent)	5.7	5.6	6.2	5.5	4.1	7.7
– balance of the CEECs (exports minus imports), in million ECU	–1,012	–492	–175	–234	–67	–44
Textiles:						
– share in total exports to EC (in per cent)	16.5	15.7	12.0	16.5	35.2	22.1
– balance of the CEECs (exports minus imports), in million ECU	+749	+170	+244	+104	+170	+62
Base metals and articles:						
– share in total exports to EC (in per cent)	16.1	18.9	18.2	10.4	10.7	15.2
– balance of the CEECs (exports minus imports), in million ECU	+1,869	+886	+630	+178	+78	+99
Total sensitive products:						
– share in total exports to EC (in per cent)	50.6	53.6	41.4	53.2	55.5	65.3
– balance of the CEECs (export minus imports), in million ECU	+1,907	+592	+558	+650	–67	+176
Total trade:						
– total exports to EC (in per cent)	100.0	100.0	100.0	100.0	100.0	100.0
– total balance of the CEECs (exports minus imports), in million ECU	–2,541	–1,071	–728	–74	–452	–215

EC = European Community
CEEC = Central and Eastern European countries
Source: Calculations from D. Mario Nuti, 'The Impact of Systemic Transition on the European Community (Table 7), in Stephen Martin (ed.), *The Construction of Europe – A Festschrift in Honour of Emile Noel*, Berlin: de Gruyter, 1994.

computer manufacturers may find it very difficult to invest in Central Europe, as in this industry more than 40 per cent of the components are usually imported from non-EC countries. A similar statement has been made for the textile and clothing industry (Corado, 1994). In this industry, the provisions related to rules of origin in the particular framework of outward processing trade (OPT) were initially very stringent: when an EU producer sent intermediate goods abroad for processing, these goods and services (fabrics and design) had to originate in the EU. These rules have been alleviated since July 1997 (Temprano-Arroyo and Feldman, 1998). At the same time the Europe Agreements gave preferential treatment to textiles and clothing exported by the CEECs under OPT arrangements as compared with direct exports of textiles and clothing in terms of tariffs and quotas, so as to help EU producers subject to strong competition from developing countries. As a result, exports of garments from the CEECs under OPT arrangements strongly increased, and the share of the CEECs as non-EU suppliers of clothing and textile doubled, from 7 per cent in 1988 to over 13 per cent in 1994. Along with a positive impact (the quick modernising of the firms involved in OPT in Central and Eastern Europe), the preferential treatment for OPT exports along with stringent rules of origin has led to a quasi-collapse of the domestic textile industry which was prevented from supplying the OPT manufacturers (ECE/UN, 1995, special section 'Outward Processing Trade between the EU and the Associated members of Eastern Europe: the case of textiles and clothing', pp. 109–27).

(f) All facilities included in the Europe Agreements applied to trade in goods. As L. Alan Winters (1992) rightly stated, 'little as the EC desires CHP [Czechoslovakia, Hungary, Poland] goods, it desires their workers even less' (p. 23). True, both parties granted each other the national treatment in terms of establishment rights. However, exceptions were possible for up to ten years. Manpower movements are considered a matter of national legislation. Hence the principle of non-discrimination only applies to the workers already legally employed in the EC. No new facilities are granted, and the legal rules are defined exclusively by each member state. In fact the immigration laws are increasingly restrictive in all the EC countries, and the movements, from the East to the EC, of workers other than the highly qualified are bound to meet a growing resistance.

Some of the EA provisions were revised later at the Copenhagen (June 1993) and Essen (December 1994) EC (EU) Councils. The timetable of the concessions made to the Central and East European countries was modified so as to accelerate the implementation of the agreements (by six months on average). But the framework of the EAs remained unchanged. Between their signature and their ratification by the parliaments of the EU states there has been a period of at least three years when only the trade provisions, incorporated in Interim Agreements, were in force. Another component of the EAs, implemented following the ratification, was a political dialogue, concerning democracy, human rights and foreign policies. Since 1993 (i.e.since the conclusion of the agreements with Bulgaria and Romania) the EAs also incorporated a clause explicitly mentioning 'respect for democratic principles and human rights, and the principles of the market economy' (Laursen and Riishøj, 1996), which was very reluctantly accepted by the Czech Republic in the renegotiation of its EA (Nyssen, 1996). Finally the EAs include industrial, scientific and technical cooperation, as well as cultural cooperation (in particular in the television field) but not financial transfers provisions which remain monitored by the PHARE programme and the European Investment Bank (EIB). They are managed by an institutional framework of councils and committees. The EAs are thus complex constructions, whose implementation is spread over at least a decade taking into account lags between signature and ratification, and delays stipulated in the trade liberalising provisions.

Did the EAs improve market access to the EU? On the basis of a careful analysis of the EA provisions and of the actual situation in the CEECs, Drabek (1997) shows that 'the market openings provided by the EAs for the CEECs are estimated to be relatively small primarily during the first five years of the Agreement with some improvements in the sixth year and, mainly, thereafter' (p. 33) – that is, essentially, after 1997. The asymmetry built into the EAs is in fact an illusion. The EU presented this asymmetry as a generous act on its part, giving the associated countries longer delays to liberalise its trade with the EU than the delays stipulated for the EU itself. In fact, trade liberalisation conducted in the CEECs prior to the conclusion of the agreements had already largely dismantled trade barriers, so that there was little benefit to be expected from the declared asymmetry (Drabek, 1997, p. 36). For agricultural products, the high level of subsidisation of agriculture in the EU through the CAP, as compared with its relatively low level in the CEECs, creates an 'inverse asymmetry' (Inotai, quoted in Drabek, 1997, p. 37) (especially as the Commission decided in 1995 to limit to 5 per cent, instead of 10 per cent, the annual increase in tariff quota-levels for the next five years. See Halamska and Maurel, 1996, p. 51).

The first years of implementation of the EAs were marked by various conflicts over the surge in exports of sensitive goods. Among the most visible episodes, there was the anti-dumping case against steel-pipes exports of several East European countries, that was won by the Western European steel-makers in November 1992 (Messerlin, 1993; Hindley, 1993; Wang and Winters, 1993). Later, an agricultural 'war' erupted in 1993 when the EC Commission imposed a one-month ban on livestock, meat, milk and diary products imports from all East European countries, because a case of foot-and-mouth disease had appeared in Italy and had been traced to imports from former Yugoslavia. Hungary, Poland, and the Czech and Slovak Republics retaliated by banning imports (including transit) of the same goods from the EC, using the same pretext. Though the ban was lifted as scheduled, as well as the retaliatory measures, it left hurt feelings and was expected to trigger further protectionist measures (Weydenthal, 1993b). In the following years, periodically anti-dumping cases erupted (for steel tubes and pipes, some fertilisers, chemicals, etc.). There are also bans on agricultural imports for sanitary reasons (such as the ban on Polish milk imports in December 1997), that the CEECs are quick to interpret as disguised protectionism.

Was the initial export specialisation of the CEECs a rational one, or did it display a 'distress strategy' in which one sells what is at hand? Indeed the sectors which produce the 'sensitive goods' are declining. The chemical industry has developed on the basis of cheap Soviet oil and has no future at normal prices for fuels. The farm sector lacks finance and skills to imitate an efficient capitalist farming model. Textile and clothing look more promising, but basically as a sub-contracting workshop for EC producers: about two-thirds of the imports of clothing from the East by EC countries in 1992 were already due to OPT (Corado, 1994).

Are there more competitive export sectors in the long term? Following a much-referred-to study (Hamilton and Winters, 1992) it has been assumed that the East European countries had a comparative advantage in industries that are relatively intensive in human capital. Hughes and Hare (1992), using the DRC (domestic calculated costs) methodology, have shown that the most competitive sectors differ from one country to another, but that food processing (except in Bulgaria and to a lesser extent Poland and Hungary) is not competitive. Energy-intensive products tend to be uncompetitive. In general, the most competitive would be labour-intensive products included as sensitive in the EAs. Another author, using the revealed comparative advantage methodology (Neven, 1994), finds that the comparative advantage of Central and Eastern Europe lies in products that are both capital-intensive and unqualified labour-intensive. Actually the main factor of competitiveness is cheap labour. Using the composite index of exchange rate-adjusted unit labour costs (ULC) which expresses the combined effects of exchange rate movements and trends in productivity and wages one can see that the ULCs are still in 1997 less than half the Austrian level taken as a reference, except for Slovenia (Figure 9.1).

This may seem very disappointing for the East European countries in transition themselves. In the socialist past, they were always claiming that their future lay in high-technology exports, and that the unjustified West embargo on technology exports was preventing them from reaching this aim. Nowadays, while demanding to be integrated in the European Union, they hope to reach the Western European average level of technological development in a few years, provided there is market access for the products of their nascent advanced industries. These hopes will be dashed. Technological development is not just a matter of investments and skills, or even markets. It is also related to being part of industrial international

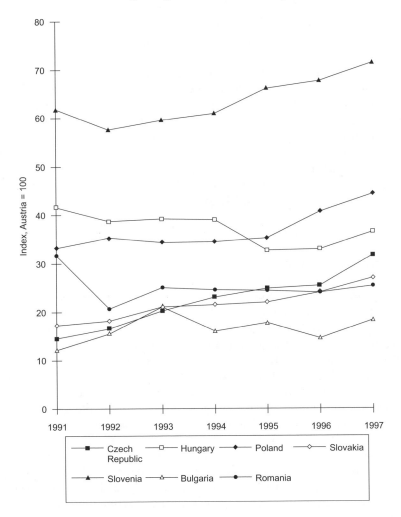

Figure 9.1 *CECCs: Unit labour costs, PPP-adjusted, Austria = 100, 1991–7*

Note: The unit labour cost (ULC) is the nominal wage deflated by productivity (estimated as the GDP per person employed at 1993 prices). The ULC were adjusted for each country for exchange rates change by dividing the ULC with the nominal exchange rate. The ULC level comparison with Austria was obtained from exchange-rate adjusted ULCs after multiplication with estimated PPP for the year 1996.
Source: Rosati *et al.* (1998); for the methodology, Havlik, Peter (1996).

cooperation, through the network of multinationals. At best Central and Eastern Europe may develop into the backyard or the assembly-line of such global firms (as the example of the car industry shows). Indeed, the increase in intra-industry trade of the CEECs since 1995 seems to be closely linked with the activities of multinational companies (ECE/UN, 1997b, p. 46). Exploring the opportunities of the service sector may be more promising, especially in its most advanced branches (such as business and computer services). Actually the structure of the CEECs' exports to the West is remaining stable. As a study by the ECE/UN (1997b, pp. 57 ff.) shows, the most remarkable change in the composition of trade is the increase in exports of machinery and equipment of the CEFTA countries, from 24 to 33 per cent between 1992 and 1996. These exports accounted for much less in the other CEECs' exports to the West (around 10–15 per cent) and its share did not change in 1992–6.

In any case, for the Central and East European countries, the immediate aim is to be integrated in the EU as soon as possible, which is supposed to solve all problems.

The Accession Process

Though not enthusiastic in the beginning to commit itself to enlargement, the European Community very early recognised the inevitability of the process. The European Council held in Copenhagen (June 1993) decided that the Associate countries could contemplate accession (without defining any time-table) provided several conditions were met. The Essen EU Council of December 1994 made a decisive step forward by defining a strategy of pre-accession. For the first time, six associated countries were invited to the Summit (the 'Visegrád Four' group, plus Romania and Bulgaria). Following the Council's decisions, the EU Commission was invited to draft a White Paper on the preparation of the associated countries for integration into the *internal* market, seen as 'the key element in the strategy to narrow the gap' between the applicants and the EU (CEC 1995a). In addition, the Essen Council decided to launch a 'Structured Dialogue' which would bring together all the associated countries together with all the EU states to discuss some specific matters – this did not however mean that the pre-accession process would be conducted *en bloc*; instead, there was an implicit preference for case-by-case negotiations in due time.

In 1995, the main concerns of the EU members were, first, the institutions and the agenda of the Intergovernmental Conference (IGC) meant to reform the EU institutions; second, the timetable of the introduction of a single currency. Both issues were discussed at the Madrid EU Summit in December 1995, with the enlargement issue remaining in the background. The IGC started in March 1996; it was then stated that the negotiations with the applicants would begin at least six months after 'successfully finalising' the IGC. By that time seven countries had officially applied for membership (Poland, Hungary, Romania, Slovakia, Latvia, Estonia, and the Czech Republic) while the three others were preparing to do so (Slovenia, pending the signature of the association agreement, Bulgaria, and Lithuania). In July 1997, despite the fact that the IGC had ended with the Amsterdam EU Summit in June without any 'successful finalising' on such crucial points as the number of commissioners, the weighting of votes in the Council and the scope of the decisions which might be taken with a weighted majority, the European Commission suggested opening negotiations in the beginning of 1998 with five Central European countries in view of their admission into the EU by the beginning of next century. These countries are Poland, the Czech Republic, Hungary (the hard core of the countries which have moved most successfully to the market), Slovenia and Estonia, to which one has to add Cyprus. Why just five? The five other applicants to membership, i.e. Bulgaria, Romania, Slovakia and the two remaining Baltic States, share the same ultimate aim; they apply, with more or less consistency and success, the same instruments, and should be admitted to negotiations as soon as their reform policies display better results. There is much resentment among these five countries about being put in the 'second circle'; there is also a feeling that the fatidic figure of five has been selected because in its present format, due to the non-completion of the IGC, the EU is not manageable beyond 20 members.

We shall first discuss the conditions that are imposed on the applicants (and also, because of the controversy surrounding them, the 'non-conditions'), and then turn to the costs and benefits of enlargement for both sides.

The conditions for accession

These conditions, which have been recalled by the European Councils of Copenhagen and Essen, are established by the Rome Treaty, as modified by the European Single Act (1986; art. 8) and by the Maastricht treaty, and follow from previous enlargements:

- any European country may apply to join the Union (art. 237 of the 1957 Treaty of Rome);
- politically the applicants must be stable pluralist democracies (this implying the existence of independent political parties) and be committed to the rule of law, to respect for human rights, and to the protection of minorities;
- economically they must have a functioning market economy;
- they must have the capacity to cope with competitive pressure and market forces within the EU;
- they must endorse the objective of political, economic and monetary union, and be able to assume the obligations of membership, in particular what comes under the 'acquis communautaire' (the 'Four Freedoms', free circulation of goods, services, capital and workers; the

Common Agricultural Policy; the competition policy rules; fiscal harmonisation; the commitments towards developing countries). This also means that the applicants must be able to comply with all the decisions and legal provisions of any kind implemented since the relevant Treaties have been in force.

These conditions of membership are so broad that they may be considered as met, by and large, and at the same time as unattainable in full for many years. It is impossible to spell out precise limits of non-compliance with, for instance, the criteria of 'respect for human rights' or of 'protection of minorities'. The definition of *a functioning market economy* is also a question of subjective judgement involving the whole of the transformation process. All the countries under review may be considered as being truly market economies as far as liberalisation of prices and trade is concerned, including the currency convertibility for current transactions. But the market environment is not yet in place. Privatisation is not completed, and the rules for corporate governance are not established clearly. The two-tier banking system is operating but the state enterprise indebtedness is not yet under control, and will not be until the bankruptcy procedures are implemented on a large scale. The tax system has moved closer to the Western format with the introduction of the VAT and of a standard income tax system, but a comprehensive reform of the fiscal system is yet to be completed, in particular so as to introduce more clarity in the subsidy procedures and to strengthen the tax generation. Capital markets are indeed operating and have been booming, but their base remains narrow. They are vulnerable both to external shocks such as spillovers from the South East Asian crises in 1997 or the Russian financial collapse in 1998, and to domestic mismanagement as in the Czech crisis of 1997. *The capacity to cope with competitive pressure and market forces* within the Union is, again, a very unclear concept. Everything that might enhance competitiveness comes under this heading. This may include measures or situations otherwise contrary to other requirements for accession, such as low environmental standards or inadequate safety and health protection in the workplace. As the main strength of the Central and East European countries lies in low labour costs, that are gradually increasing due to the appreciation of the national currencies (cf. Chapter 7), one might also assume that this particular condition means that competitiveness should not be secured, for instance, by competitive devaluations.

The present enlargement process is in many ways more demanding than the previous ones, which suggests that it is 'not "just another accession"' (Eatwell *et al.*, 1997). Daviddi and Ilzkovitz (1997, p. 21) stress for example that the new members will not be allowed to opt out on EMU and the social chapter. Political conditions were not so explicit in previous accessions, even for Greece or Spain and Portugal. To Michael Ellman, there is a danger that the whole process turns 'into a one-sided dictate that the applicants are obliged to accept' (Ellman, 1997b, p. 2).

Even the countries selected for the first round of negotiations have to do better in fields specified by the Commission in July 1997 (in its *avis* on each country (see below, p. 235). The remaining Five among the applicants are understandably bitter. Slovakia has been 'sanctioned' basically for short-comings on the first condition. Romania and Bulgaria are invited to go further on the reform path precisely at a time (1997) when their new governments have embarked on radical measures approved by the IMF. Lithuania and Latvia feel discriminated against, with the support of their Nordic partners. These recent developments strengthen the conclusions of Georges Mink and Gérard Wild to write in the special issue of the *Revue d'Etudes Comparatives Est-Ouest* devoted to EU enlargement: there is 'a kind of meritocratic logic in the integration mechanism . . . [which] increases the role of emotional, psycho-sociological parameters in the very process of the negotiations' (Mink and Wild, 1996, p. 9). To sum up, the applicants may have the impression that it is perfectly possible to decide first who is going to be admitted, and in what order, and second to grade the countries accordingly.

The conditions that are not required as accession prerequisites

As to the 'Maastricht (now *'Amsterdam'*, from the June 1997 EU Summit meeting and the signature of the Treaty on 2 October 1997) convergence criteria', contrary to a widespread view both in the East and in the West, these are definitely *not* conditions for accession, but for reaching the stage of the economic and monetary union within the EU. Indeed, art. 109 J of the Rome Treaty as modified by the Maastricht Treaty defines the 'convergence criteria' to be met for the evolution of the EU into an EMU (Economic and Monetary Union). When some countries (especially the Czech Republic, and Slovenia) claim that they are already meeting the convergence criteria better than some EU members, this is an irrelevant statement. First, even when the 'statistical' criteria of convergence are satisfied, the 'real' convergence is far from completed from the point of view of the functioning of the monetary, financial, budgetary and exchange rate mechanisms, as stated in a report prepared by the OFCE (Observatoire Français des Conjonctures Economiques; see OFCE, 1996, pp. 19 and 146). Second, it is impossible now to assess the extent of compliance of the CEECs with the convergence criteria, since the statistical measures of some indicators are not harmonised with the EU practice or simply do not exist (Table 9.5)

The new member countries acceding to the EU after the beginning of stage three of EMU (i.e. after 1 January 1999) will be treated under a different, derogatory regime (art. 109K of the Treaty). In principle, all present EU members are to become members of EMU sooner or later – they are called 'pre-ins' in EU parlance. The CEECs are to become 'pre-ins' as soon as they are members of the EU. The 'pre-ins', according to decisions reached at the Dublin Summit in December 1996 and at the Amsterdam Summit in June 1997, will be included, if they choose to do so (as Greece has done already in March 1998 when it joined the existing ERM), in an 'ERM-2' (a temporary Exchange Rate Mechanism on the model of the regime that was in force from 1979, with fixed but adjustable exchange rates with a central parity with the Euro and a fluctuation band). This regime is very attractive indeed. The 'pre-ins' will be able to choose whether they want to enter the ERM-2, and in this case accept monetary policy coordination and surveillance by the European Central Bank (ECB), or stay out of the ERM-2 and retain more flexibility, remembering that they too will be expected to adopt the *'acquis communautaire of the euro zone'* regarding their monetary policy, and will have to treat their exchange rate policy as a matter of common interest. In particular, they should avoid excessive fluctuations of their exchange rate, such as sudden devaluations. While the second, 'free-rider' attitude might have some advantages, insofar as it allows the country that opts for this solution to benefit from the constraints that the membership in EMU or ERM-2 imposes on its partners, participation in the ERM-2 might also have positive effects. It might give additional credibility to the participant countries, result in a lowering of risk premia in their international borrowing, and make FDI in these countries more attractive. Anyhow the applicant countries will soon be involved in euro-denominated transactions even before becoming 'pre-ins', in trade with the euro zone member states, in the management of investment portfolios, and also because global companies with subsidiaries in these countries will themselves use the euro (European Commission, 1998, pp. 17–18, 29 and 135).

An important point to be made is that the ERM-2, unlike the ERM, will not be multilateral but bilateral. The 'pre-in' currencies will be linked to the euro on the basis of an agreement between the EU and the applicant country, establishing a central rate against the euro with a fluctuation band of plus or minus 15 per cent, which the contracting party may wish to narrow also on the basis of an agreement with the EU.

Even before acceding to membership in the EU, and as soon as the euro replaces the national currencies in the EMU-member countries, the CEECs will have to make choices as to their exchange rate regime. Those whose currency is pegged explicitly or implicitly to the DM (which is the case for most of them) will have to replace the DM and logically might want to shift to the euro. Exchange rate regimes will have to be modified for countries with a floating rate regime (Romania) or for countries with pre-announced crawling pegs (Hungary and Poland), if they choose to join the ERM-2. The choice of the right exchange rate will then depend upon assumptions related to the expected exchange rate of the euro against the major currencies and to its evolution.

More generally, the economic policy of the applicant countries may be constrained by the prospects for EMU membership, especially as the requirements are in line with the stringent macroeconomic policies either imposed by the IMF or self-imposed in most of the CEECs. The White Paper unambiguously states: 'sound macroeconomic policies are essential to the success of the reform and of the pre-accession strategy . . . The immediate requirement is to adjust the sequence and pace of legislative approximation in each associated country so that it reinforces economic reform' (CEC, 1995a, vol. 1, p. 5). Thus convergence criteria are not pre-accession conditions, nor are the macroeconomic policies which would enable these criteria to be met, but the legislative framework that is determining for the implementation of these policies has to be enforced. More important is the fact that these criteria belong to a monetarist philosophy more or less enthusiastically endorsed by the Central and East European countries' governments and built into the stabilisation plans. Table 9. 5 recalls the compliance with the present 'convergence criteria' of the first round of EU applicants.

Checking the implementation of the conditions

The measuring of the degree of compliance with the accession conditions has been a very time-consuming and bureaucratic process. All of the applicant countries have already taken steps to comply with the 'acquis communautaire', and the Europe Agreements encompass some of them, such as the competition rules. The 1995 White Paper on the internal market states that it 'does not change the contractual relationship between the Union and the Associated Countries, which is based on the Europe agreements'. But though the 438-page Annex to the White Paper, broken into 23 chapters, clearly states for each item what belongs to key measures in each area and what belongs to 'stage II' measures to be implemented later, the mere list of Council directives is quite discouraging. What is required is not only a legal framework but also internal political credibility: 'The law must not only exist but it must also be applied and – *above all* [italics ours] – be expected to be applied' (CEC, 1995a, Annex, p. 51). In addition, the *acquis* itself is bound to evolve in the coming years, and this accession process will be the first one when the applying countries will be facing not just a set of precise rules, but new developments in the scope and content of these rules (see Fayolle in OFCE, 1996, p. 22).

How much of the detailed European rules on the internal market has to be implemented to allow for membership, from measures concerning the tar content of cigarettes, or to do with animal welfare, or hot boilers, to such broad areas as the free movement of capital or the competition policy? What weight is attached to these measures? The applicant countries all received in May 1996 a lengthy questionnaire which had to be returned by end-July

Table 9.5 *Convergence criteria for reaching Stage 3 of EMU and compliance by the CEEC*

Convergence criteria (art. 109J of the Maastricht Treaty, Appendix)	Compliance by the the CEEC in 1996–7
Public debt nor exceeding 60 per cent of the GDP.	The CEEC-10 all comply except Bulgaria (ratio over 100 per cent) and Hungary (ratio around 70 per cent). However statistics on public debt are not consistent with Maastricht coverage. The consolidation of the state-owned enterprises' and banks' indebtedness is not yet over, and its impact on the public debt is yet unclear.
A government budget deficit not exceeding 3 per cent of the GDP.	Only the Czech Republic, Estonia, Slovenia and Latvia would meet the criterion (see Appendix Table A.2). Even thus, it not clear whether the computation of the fiscal deficit is consistent with the criterion: some privatisation revenues may be included in the budget revenues; the budget may not be consolidated (it should include central, regional and local government budgets and all social security expenditures), while state-owned enterprises are for instance providing social benefits that are not included in the budget.
Inflation rates not exceeding 1.5 per cent and interest rate differentials not exceeding 2 per cent over the respective rates of the 3 member states characterised by the lowest inflation.	None of the CEECs meets the target of inflation (which is under 3 per cent for 1997–8). Not only do none meet the interest rate target, but as the long-term capital markets either do not exist or are so little developed the criterion is irrelevant.
A stable exchange rate (two years of participation in the ERM (exchange rate mechanism) without unilateral devaluations and while remaining within the authorised fluctuation band.	The 3 Baltic states and Slovakia would comply, if they were already ERM-members (which they may be only after accession, see text). Poland and Hungary would have to change their exchange rate regime (crawling peg). The Czech Republic and Bulgaria had devaluations in 1997. Romania had large fluctuations in 1996–7. Slovenia would be close to meeting the criterion.

Source: Macro-economic data, Appendix Table A.2 ; ECE/UN (1998); Daviddi and Ilzkovitz (1997).

1996. All complained about the short deadline, the frequent absurdity or irrelevance of the questions, and the scope of the task, which implied that the minimum length of the completed exercise amounted to about 2000 pages for each country (see Inotai, 1996, p. 80). There has been a follow-up period 'with new questions, answers and clarification' (Inotai, 1997, p. 204).

On the basis of all the answers, the EU Commission came up with '*avis*' on each country and recommendations, presented in July 1997 along with its '*Agenda 2000*' that contains, in addition to proposals for enlargement, also the impact of enlargement on the reform of the CAP and of the structural funds, and the EU budget for the period 2000–2006. (European Commission, 1997). The proposals for enlargement were endorsed at the Luxembourg Summit in December 1997. Negotiations were engaged in April 1998 bilaterally with each of the five applicants included in the first round. The negotiations were expected to last at least two years, and the accession treaties once signed must be ratified by the Parliaments of all the EU members and of the new members. Hence the actual integration of the applicants belonging to the first round will not take place before 2002 or 2003 – a deadline that might even be postponed until 2005–6. For all 10 applicants the EU Luxembourg Summit in December 1997 created a new instrument, called 'accession partnership', which is meant to centralise for each country all forms of EU pre-accession assistance (see below p. 250), and identify the measures that each country has to take to prepare for membership.

The way the enlargement process is conducted shows that the EU remains reluctant, though resigned, to the enlargement. The main problem is the EU's capacity to absorb new members. Unlike the three new members admitted as of January 1995 (Austria, Sweden and Finland), the new applicants are poorer (by comparison with the average EC income level) countries; structurally they have export specialisations that are potentially damaging to the EU (in particular in agriculture); they are thus likely to claim large transfers in the framework of the CAP on the one hand and the structural funds on the other.

Is the EU really ready to absorb new members?

The main issue would be that of *agriculture*. The agricultural potential of the CEECs and the present level of prices in these countries suggest that the present EU members would have to face increased competition, and very high costs arising from the CAP being extended to these new members, where agriculture has a much larger share in the GDP than on average in the EU. The average share for the EU is 2.3 per cent; it is 4.3 per cent in Slovenia, slightly less than 6 per cent in the Czech Republic, and around 7 per cent in Estonia, Hungary and Poland; in the countries of the 'second round' this share is 6 per cent in Slovakia, around 10 per cent in Latvia, Lithuania and Bulgaria, and 20 per cent in Romania. The differences in the share of agriculture in total employment are still more striking. This share is 5.3 per cent for the EU, and 22.5 per cent for the 10 CEECs as a whole. The integration of the 10 CEECs would more than double the present agricultural labour force in the Union; the integration of the 5 CEECs of the first round would increase it by 45 per cent.

A huge number of reports and studies devoted to reports have been issued in 1994–5 on the agricultural question (Nallet and van Stolk, 1994; House of Lords, 1994; CEC, 1995b). It is impossible to give a synthetic view of their conclusions as they diverge in their evaluation of the agricultural potential of the CEECs, of the policies conducted in these countries, and in the costs of the CAP once extended to Eastern Europe. There are also uncertainties stemming from the pending reform of the CAP and its consequences on the EU members, as well as from the inadequate statistical coverage of the agricultural production, productivity and prices in the CEECs before and after transition, which makes comparisons with the West very questionable. With all these caveats, the impact of enlargement in the agricultural field may be assessed as follows:

(a) Though the CEECs are much more depending on agriculture than the EU members, as may be seen from the shares of agriculture in their GNP and employment, the situation of the agricultural sector is rapidly deteriorating. Privatisation has been impeded in Hungary, and still more in Bulgaria and in the Czech and Slovak Republics, by the restitution and compensation procedures to the persons who had been expropriated by the communists. When de-collectivisation is achieved, it often amounts to splitting up large estates into a large number of small farms, not viable by Western standards. Small peasants do not have access to credit for modernising; credit is too expensive due to a stringent monetary policy, and anyhow not available. They could not really benefit from the increases in retail prices for food following the cuts in consumer prices subsidies. These increases mainly benefited state-owned wholesale distribution chains as privatisation has been slow in the downstream sector. Agricultural production resumed its growth only in 1995 for the region as a whole.

(b) Though agricultural production declined in the first years of transition, sales to the West increased due to the reorientation of domestic sales and of previous exports to the East (mainly to the USSR/Russia). But imports from the West increased still more, fuelled by the consumer demand for Western products. The imports from the EU are subsidised through the CAP. In 1993, for the first time, the EU moved into a surplus in food trade with Eastern Europe; it used to be in deficit in the past.

(c) Understandably, the farmers of Eastern Europe are requesting more protection from their governments. The farmers' parties have been in the ruling coalition in several countries, or have remained very influential. The requested support has moved from *ad hoc* measures to a more consistent policy, which borrows from a 'CAP for the poor' format, with guaranteed minimum prices and variable levies (Jackson and Swinnen, 1994, p. 64). But such a support, even at levels much lower than the EU level, is difficult to sustain by the CEECs due to the lack of finance. As a consequence, the real protection rates have increased from about 10 per cent in the beginning of the transition to almost double in the mid-1990s, still well below the EU average of 45 per cent (in terms of producer subsidy equivalent to prices) (Just, 1996, p. 233; Lucas, 1996 and 1997).

(d) But in such a situation the CAP itself is questioned. It would be quite unsustainable to ask the CEECs to refrain from introducing *their* CAP in the form of subsidised prices, and to go on subsidising EU agriculture on the same level as before. Thus a reform of the CAP seems unavoidable. The 'Agenda 2000' programme provides for such a reform, in line with the WTO negotiations to be started in 1999. EU agricultural prices (for grain and oilseeds crops) would be reduced by 20 per cent in 2000/2001, and the direct aids to farmers would compensate the price reductions by 50 per cent instead of 100 per cent. Meat and dairy product subsidies would also be reduced. As a consequence, the present gap between CEEC and EU agricultural prices, which is still significant (the gap differs according to countries and to products; the producer prices for wheat amounted in 1995 to 50–70 per cent of EU prices, for beef, to 30–44 per cent, for milk, to 28–65 per cent; see Le Cacheux, 1996b, p. 297), would shrink and entail less costs if the renewed CAP was to be extended to the CEECs. Higher inflation in the CEEC and the growth in domestic demand should also prop up CEEC prices. However the gap would still exist at the time of accession, which would limit the need for compensatory payments to CEEC farmers. During the pre-accession period, specific aid should instead be provided to future entrants for farm modernising and for improving food distribution channels (see the chapter on agriculture in Mayhew, 1998).

Another issue in the impending EU membership would be the qualification of all CEECs for receiving transfers from the *structural funds*. While the accession of the EFTA (European Free Trade Association) members has increased the income per capita level in the EU, the membership of the CEECs, even in the event of a continuing recovery, would decrease that level and ultimately jeopardise the situation of the less developed regions in the present EU (see Table 9.6). The complex system of the European structural funds pursues several aims: to assist the development of lagging regions (where GDP per capita is less than 75 per cent of the EU average) (Objective no. 1); to help the conversion of regions experiencing a decline in their industry (Objective no. 2); to reduce long-term unemployment (Objective no. 3); to promote the social insertion of young people (Objective no. 4); to help the restructuring of the agricultural sector (Objective no. 5); and since the 1995 enlargement of the EU there is an Objective no. 6 to help Arctic regions. Presently, under the criterion of GDP per capita, Greece and the Republic of Ireland qualify for the most important section (no. 1) for all their regions; so do half of the regions in Spain and Portugal, the Mezzogiorno in Italy, the new Länder in Germany, Corsica and the French West Indies, and Northern Ireland. To these regions have been added the Austrian Burgenland, and under a new 'basket' (Objective no. 6) the Arctic regions for the Scandinavian new members. The structural funds amounted to about one third of the EU budget in 1998. The CEEC applicants in the first round would all qualify for all their regions, though they would lower the average GDP per capita and thus evict some of the previous beneficiaries. If the system of the structural funds were to remain the same, this would mean larger contributions from the richest countries and would compel Greece, Portugal, Spain and Ireland to share some of the benefits with the newcomers. Spain has already expressed its reservation, claiming that its regions presently eligible to Objective no. 1 should not be immediately affected by enlargement (*Financial Times,* 18 November 1997) True, one may expect the CEECs to display higher growth rates than the EU incumbent members, but most of them have not yet regained their pre-transition level. Many estimates have been provided as to the duration of the catching-up period, the most optimistic put it at 20 years (see p. 277).

The *Agenda 2000* has estimated the EU budget expenditures for the period 2000–2006 taking into account the hypotheses of the Commission as to the enlargement, the CAP reform, and the structural funds disbursements. It also added the pre-accession expenditures to be supported for first-round and second-round applicants (Table 9.6). Is this a bad deal for the existing EU members? The conventional view is that the CEECs will gain more from accession than the existing members. In a provocative article, Baldwin, Francois and Portes (1997, p. 168) claim that indeed it is a bargain: 'Imagine how eager western Europe would have been in 1980 to pay ECU 8 billion a year in order to free central Europe from communism'. Leaving this uncheckable assumption to the authors, one may give more credit to the argument according to which EU enlargement, in addition to standard trade-creating effects, will promote investment in the CEECs by lowering the country-risk premia supported by Western investors (*ibid.,* p. 167).

Finally the problem of the European *institutions,* already substantial in the recent EFTA-members accession negotiations, will emerge as very acute. Namely, the 'big countries' of the EU-12 (France, Germany, Great Britain, Italy, and Spain) have a majority of votes in the Council of Ministers of the EU, with ten votes each for the first four, and eight for Spain. Thus they cannot be outvoted by a coalition of the smaller seven countries, which have four votes each. But the latter cannot be outvoted by the 'big five', because for important votes the blocking minority has been established at 23 votes. The admission of the three EFTA countries has already raised problems due to the fact that it increases the power of the smaller states. The integration of the new Five, not to speak of other associates, would add to this shift of power. The 9 'poorer countries' (Spain, Portugal, Greece and Ireland, plus the 5 new entrants) would then detain 40 per cent of the votes, all things

Table 9.6   *The costs of enlargement of the EU, 2000–6 (billion ECU, 1997 prices)*

Category of expenditures	1999	2000	2001	2002	2003	2004	2005	2006
1. CAP, total	43.3	44.1	45.0	46.1	47.0	48.0	49.0	50.0
of which: new members	0.0	0.0	0.0	1.5	2.0	2.4	2.8	3.3
applicants	0.5	0.5	0.5	0.5	0.5	0.5	0.5	0.5
2. Structural and cohesion funds, total	36.0	35.2	36.0	38.9	39.8	40.7	41.7	42.8
of which: new members	0.0	0.0	0.0	3.6	5.6	7.6	9.6	11.6
applicants	0.0	1.0	1.0	1.0	1.0	1.0	1.0	1.0
3. Other internal actions	6.1	6.1	6.4	7.3	7.5	7.7	7.9	8.1
4. External actions	6.6	6.6	6.8	7.0	7.1	7.3	7.5	7.6
5. Administrative expenses	4.5	4.5	4.6	5.1	5.2	5.3	5.4	5.5
6. Reserves	1.2	1.0	1.0	0.8	0.5	0.5	0.5	0.5
Total expenditures	97.8	97.5	99.8	105.1	107.1	105.9	112.0	114.5
of which: new members	0.0	0.0	0.0	5.8	8.2	10.8	13.3	15.7
applicants	1.3	3.0	3.0	3.0	3.0	3.0	3.0	3.0

Memorandum items:
GDP per capita of the CEEC 10 in per cent of the GDP per capita of the EU-15: 32 (1995).
GDP per capita of the poorest EU-15 (Greece, Spain, Portugal, Ireland) in per cent of the average GDP per capita of the EU-15 : 74 (1995).
Eligible population for Objective 1 assistance from structural funds, in per cent of total EU population: 25 per cent in 1995 (EU-15); 42 per cent in 2002+ (EU-26).

1.   CAP: Common Agricultural Policy
1 and 2. New members: 5 countries selected for first round of negotiations
            Applicants: 5 other CEEC.
3.   Funded priority programs (trans-European networks, research, education, environment protection, etc.).
4.   Includes pre-accession aid financed out of PHARE programme.
5.   Expenses linked with enlargement (use of new languages, bigger staff, etc.).

Source: Agenda 2000, from *Transition*, World Bank, vol. 8, no. 4, August 1997.

being equal, and have a blocking majority (this is the hypothesis offered by Baldwin *et al.*, 1997, p. 165). The reform of the EU institutions, which should have been solved by the Intergovernmental Conference (IGC), is still ahead.

The 'Outer' Circles

Countries that remain outside the enlargement process look at the Europe Agreements as a model. This is particularly obvious in the Russian case for the 'Partnership' agreement signed in 1994. The major contention of Russia in 1993 was that it should be treated not as a state trading country as was the case in the 'trade and cooperation agreement' signed in 1990, but as a market economy, even before its accession to GATT to which it applied in June 1993. The Partnership Agreement came into force in December 1997, allowing for the first meeting of an EU–Russia cooperation council that was to prepare the implementation of a free-trade zone (*Financial Times*, 28 January 1998). As in the Europe Agreements, there are tariff and quotas concessions, except for sensitive products such as steel, textiles, and uranium. The agreement also covers the sphere of services, with Russia easing the restrictions on foreign banks operating on Russian territory, and allowing them to accept deposits from Russian firms and persons.

A Partnership Agreement was also signed with Ukraine the same year (14 June 1994). Here the main concern of the EU members was to obtain the shutdown of the Chernobyl nuclear complex, against aid to build alternative nuclear reactors. Almost all CIS countries (except Tajikistan and Turkmenistan) had by the end of 1997 signed such agreements, but in most cases these agreements are not yet ratified, and only interim provisions covering trade-related matters are in force, including most-favoured nation treatment, abolition of quantitative restrictions on imports, and provisions on methods of payment and customs.

Many debates have focused on the issue of the Eastern border of Europe, in a geo-political perspective, also taking into account NATO membership which is in principle to be extended in 1999 to the Czech Republic, Hungary and Poland. Application to NATO by these three countries was accepted at the Summit of the organisation in Madrid in July 1997, while a few weeks earlier (end-May) a Founding Treaty on Mutual Co-operation was signed between NATO and Russia. EU and NATO enlargement to the East follow different schedules but a similar pattern: Russia is out, Central and Eastern Europe is to be in sooner or later; the Baltics belong to the economic space of Europe but not to its military–political space.

Integration into the world economy also involves membership in world economic organisations. Only three countries in transition – the Czech Republic, Hungary and Poland are members of the OECD (since 1995–6). Slovakia is negotiating accession. Romania, Bulgaria, Slovenia and Russia have specific cooperation programmes. Cooperation with the OECD and membership in this 'club of the rich' has a significant 'learning' impact through advice and consultation, and also generates harmonisation of legislation in such matters as legislation on foreign direct investment, financial services, tax matters, and environment protection.

Several countries in transition were GATT members, the oldest being Poland, since 1967 (if one does not take into account Czechoslovakia, a founding member which was also a silent partner during the communist regime); GATT membership was transformed into WTO membership in 1995 for the Czech and the Slovak Republics, Hungary, Poland, Slovenia and Romania, in 1996 for Bulgaria. All the former Soviet Union states, including the Baltics, have applied, except Tajikistan and Turkmenistan, which were in exploratory talks in 1997. Mongolia was the first country in transition to join the WTO as such in 1996. The main breakthrough will occur with the joining of Russia, which is expected in 1998, before the new round of negotiations within the organisation. In April 1998 the EU decided to abandon the classification of Russia (and China) as non-market economies, in anticipation of the WTO decisions. The main benefits of WTO membership, in addition to recognition as a full-fledged member of the international trade system, are the granting of the most-favoured-nation clause (which most of the countries had anyway with most of their partners, except the United States), and the opportunity for solving conflicts through the dispute settlement mechanism. For countries in transition it is also the sign that all remnants of state-trading are eliminated – that last point was a bone of contention between the GATT and the former centrally planned economies.

International Migration Issues

The Europe Agreements do not provide for opportunities of large East–West labour movements. The enlargement process has carefully postponed decision on this issue. It is remarkable, in this respect, that of the 'four freedoms' included in the internal market, only three are relevant in the pre-accession strategy. The fourth one, the free movement of persons, has been explicitly excluded from the Europe Agreements (which basically deal with the status of the workers from the East European countries already in the EU). The 1995 White Paper on the pre-accession strategy mentions that 'this part of the Community "acquis" cannot be considered as part of the present exercise of progressive alignment, although its importance for the establishment of the internal market *after accession* [italics mine. ML] is beyond doubt' (CEC, 1995a, vol. 1, p. 13). This wariness reflects concerns of the West. The beginning of the transition immediately fuelled fears of a massive emigration to the West. These fears now appear to have been largely exaggerated, especially in light of migration pressures originating from other regions of the world (Africa for Europe, Central America for the United States).

Does One Need To Be Afraid?

Several circumstances explain the 'migration psychosis' which seized Western Europe soon after the transition:

- There had been a strong migration drive just before the transition, in some cases quite dramatic, such as the flight of East German citizens to

the West through Czechoslovakia and Hungary in 1989, or the flight of Albanians to Italy in 1991.
- The Western media extrapolated from opinion polls made in the East that dozens of millions were potentially ready to emigrate.
- East European citizens quickly became very conspicuous in West European cities, as 'tourists' arriving in large parties, spending little and trying to earn some money through moonlighting or selling goods more or less legally.
- Cases of 'brain drain', especially for scientists from the former Soviet Union, were given much publicity.
- Information on unemployment in Eastern Europe, actual or potential, gave the impression that large numbers of migrants would seek jobs in the West.

The prospects for emigration from the East

It is very difficult to estimate the actual or future flows of migrants. The past flows do not provide any clue, as the right to leave was severely restricted, and strictly regulated for some categories of the population, such as Jews. Some estimates start from the South–North flows within Europe between 1950 and 1980 (Layard *et al.*, 1992, p. 17). Finding that during this period about 6 per cent of the South European population moved to richer countries, and retaining a very conservative percentage of 3 per cent in the case of Eastern Europe and the European part of the former USSR, the authors of the quoted study find that the likely flows of migrants should amount to a total of 10 million.

Other estimates take into account specific factors influencing migration, such as the present economic situation and the prospects for economic recovery in individual countries, the political situation including the state of civil war in some countries, and the Western response (ECE/UN, 1992, ch. 7: 'Migration from East to West: A Framework for Analysis'; ECE/UN and UNPF, 1996). Though no figures are offered, such studies suggest that the flows of migrants are to be much more diversified and on the whole much smaller than anticipated in the West:

- While the disparity in wages among Western and Eastern European countries should trigger emigration, it also limits permanent migration; to improve one's situation it is enough to work a few weeks in the West as a 'tourist'. With the increase in real wages in the East (see Table 7.3), the pressure toward emigration is lower.
- Unemployment is a pressure to emigrate. However the rates of unemployment are still either low (in the former USSR, in the Czech Republic) or manageable; unemployment affects specific categories (women, ethnic minorities).

- Poverty coupled with ethnic war or political trouble is a strong incentive to emigrate, but not necessarily to the West. Poland is unwillingly becoming an immigration country for Russians, Armenians, Romanian gypsies, Albanians.
- The Western response has to be taken into account. Though the US study quoted (Layard *et al.*, 1992) contends that Europe, which according to the authors admits virtually no refugees (p. 7), should take in an average of 300,000 people a year, this is wishful thinking. All European countries have indeed stopped entries on the basis of asylum-seeking, and entries on the basis of job permits are severely restricted.

Actual figures show that for the period 1990–5 net migration from the Central and East European countries amounted to 950,000 people, mainly from Poland and Romania, the two largest countries of the area (Chesnais, 1997, pp. 252–3). The case of Russia is more ambiguous. Since 1989 some 9 million people have moved 'within and among countries of the former Soviet Union' (Heleniak, 1997, p. 15). Russia, and also Ukraine and Belarus, have become net immigration countries (with a net migration of 2.8 million people over the years 1989–96). Most, but not all, of the migrants were ethnic Russians and Slavs fleeing discrimination in non-Slavic new independent states. Refugees from Transcaucasian states displaced by the civil war also contributed to the flow. The former Soviet Union has also generated a flow of migrants to the West, which amounts to about 2 million people between 1989 and 1996, with 'three countries, Germany, Israel, and the United States, receiving the bulk of this flow' (Heleniak, *ibid.*, p. 15). In the case of Germany, which has absorbed about 200,000 people annually migrating from the former Soviet Union over the years 1990–5, this reflects the policy of accepting ethnic Germans (mainly from Kazakhstan); in the case of Israel, the policy of resettlement of Jews. In addition, the former communist area has become a place of transit for migrants from Asia (especially from Afghanistan, Pakistan, Sri Lanka), and the Middle East, heading for the West. Crime is also moving West, with drug dealers, stolen-car traffickers, and smugglers of all kind. Poland is particularly affected as it has 1,300 km of borders with former Soviet states. The Polish government has been asked by the EU Commission to harden its entry requirements for citizens from borders countries, and is very reluctant to do so, fearing retaliation against Polish minorities in these states (*Le Monde*, 3 January 1998).

The alternatives to emigration

The initial frustration in the East about the controls on population movements have subsided. The citizens of the former communist world have quickly understood that economic liberalisation stops when labour movements are concerned. Are these disillusions creating a potential for a crisis? The West is afraid of the social and political impact of too large an imbalance in the standards of living between East and West. Economic theory shows that trade may be a substitute for migration (through exports of labour-intensive goods), as well as foreign direct investment (which would use the cheap labour resources in the Eastern countries). We have already seen that there are strong obstacles to a surge of labour-intensive exports (see Winters and Wang, 1993, for the footwear industry case) as such branches are sensitive sectors in the West; in addition there are competitors from the developing countries. Foreign direct investment is attracted by many factors of which low wages are only one component. Thus both solutions can only alleviate the problem. If low wages are due to low efficiency, itself the consequence of legacies of the past and of a slow transformation pace, then foreign investment will be deterred, and labour-intensive exports will perpetuate a wrong specialisation.

Integration in the global economy is not limited to trade, services or labour movements. It also implies capital movements. In the beginning of the transition, these were mainly understood as flows of Western assistance to transition. Gradually the countries in transition have become involved in world-wide capital movements. But they are not yet, by far, big players on the globalisation playing field.

PARTICIPATION IN THE GLOBAL ECONOMY

The first vehicle to reintegrate the countries in transition into the global economy has been Western assistance, by international financial institutions, the European Union, and governments. We shall review the build-up of Western assistance, its main forms, its difficulties and prospects.

The Initial Stage: Western Assistance to the Transition

Foreign assistance has followed the pace of transition in a gradual build-up. In July 1989, at the G-7 Summit in Paris, it was decided to help Poland and Hungary in their transition to a market economy and to democracy. The EC Commission was to ensure the coordination of the assistance undertaken by the G-24 (the 24 OECD members taking part in the initiative). The starting point was the setting up of PHARE (see p. 97). This aid programme was later extended to all the countries in transition except Croatia and the Federal Republic of Yugoslavia. For the CIS a special programme TACIS is applied (TACIS stands for Technical Assistance to the Commonwealth of Independent States).

In December 1989 the French President François Mitterrand proposed to set up the first post-cold war international financial institution, the EBRD (European Bank for Reconstruction and Development, so-called to correspond to the official name of the World Bank, the IBRD). The EBRD began to operate in April 1991. In 1997 it had 58 shareholder states (donors and recipients), including non-European developing countries such as Mexico, Morocco, Egypt, Israel, and Korea. It had also two international members, the EU represented by the European Commission, and the European Investment Bank, itself a lender to the European countries in transition for infrastructure projects especially in transport, telecommunications, and energy (Steinherr and Hurst, 1995, pp. 65–6). Its statutory aims were to promote democratic institutions and open market economies in Central and Eastern Europe, including the former USSR, through lending and investing, with 60 per cent funding at least being directed to private sector enterprises or to state-owned enterprises engaged in privatising.

Finally the international financial institutions became major actors in the assistance to transition. By 1992 all the Eastern and Central European countries were members of the IMF and the World Bank, as well as the Baltic States and the members of the CIS. Other institutional organisations involved in (mostly technical) assistance include the OECD, and the United Nations along with their specialised organisations such as UNIDO and the UNDP (detailed accounts of these organisations' role in transition may be found in special issues of journals: *Journal of Comparative Economics,* vol. 20, nos 1 to 3; *Moct-Most*, vol. 5 no. 2; see also Schönfeld (ed.), 1996).

The forms of assistance

It is very difficult to decide where to stop when identifying assistance to transition. From the most to the less obvious one can draw the following list:

- humanitarian aid, in the form of emergency supplies of food and medicine;
- technical assistance, such as training, and providing of consultancy and macro-economic policy advice;
- macroeconomic multilateral financing (including the drawings on IMF facilities);
- special balance of payments financing, which comprises debt write-offs, rescheduling and concessionary restructuring;
- financing of specific projects on concessionary terms;
- providing a stabilisation fund to help establish the currency convertibility;
- granting of export credits on concessionary or non-concessionary terms (the latter may be considered as assistance as many countries in transition would not be able to get credits on normal commercial terms due to their lack of creditworthiness);
- the provision of investment guarantees.

In a broader concept of assistance, private investment flows and trade arrangements also qualify as aid. Private investment and private finance flows are usually recorded separately from aid flows, but are intricately linked with the latter, because private finance is facilitated through specific assistance measures, and also because the global credibility of a country is enhanced by the seal of approval that it gets from the IMF. In addition, private finance and investment add to the overall external financing of the recipient country and reinforce the impact of assistance.

Are trade arrangements a form of aid or an alternative to aid? Improving the countries' market access to the West is undisputably a form of aid, and the most efficient one according to many political leaders in the East. Western experts do not deny the point but contend that the two questions must be separated; aid is granted precisely to allow the recipient countries to become internationally more competitive, and to turn into fully-fledged members of the international trade system.

The amount of assistance

Table 9.7 gives a very broad overview of the amounts of assistance granted in 1990–5. Table 9.8 itemises the aid packages specifically granted by the IMF. The figures are to be treated with extreme caution. Overall the assistance to transition is far from transparent. Information on bilateral assistance, and specifically on disbursements as opposed to commitments, is very patchy, not to say biased. It is available with great delay.

Table 9.7　*Assistance to Eastern Europe and to the former Soviet Union, 1990-5 (bnECU)*

	Assistance to the CEEC		Assistance to the CIS countries	
	(bn ECU)	(per cent)	(bn ECU)	(per cent)
European Union	13.3	15.3	5.1	4.1
of which PHARE aid	5.4	6.2		
Bilateral aid, of which	51.7	60.0	91.0	73.9
EU member countries	32.6	37.6	67.6	54.9
USA	10.1	11.6	17.1	13.9
Japan	5.0	5.7	6.3	5.1
Other members of G-24	4.0	4.6		
International financial institutions	21.4	24.7	27.0	22.0
Total	86.4	100.0	123.1	100.0

Sources:　G-24 and European Commission quoted in Remontet and Delbos, 1997; Mayhew, 1996.

Table 9.8 Borrowing from the IMF by the Eastern European countries and the CIS, 1990–5 (in million dollars; annual flows for disbursements; end-year for debt)

	1990	1991	1992	1993	1994	1995
Disbursements to:						
Eastern Europe	747	3717	1275	327	1895	253
CIS	–	–	1013	1839	2225	7457
Russian Federation	–	–	1013	1506	1514	5444
Baltic States	–	–	71	220	114	94
Total:	747	3717	2359	2386	4233	7804
Debt of:						
Eastern Europe	838	–	–	5272	5597	2991
CIS	–	–	–	2797	5220	12227
Russian Federation	–	–	–	2468	4198	9171
Baltic States	–	–	–	285	418	514
Total:	838			8354	11235	15732
Net disbursements to:						
Eastern Europe	65	3485	650	−1	−10	−2799
CIS	–	–	1013	1839	2225	7457
Russian Federation	–	–	1013	1506	1514	5444
Baltic States	–	–	71	220	144	94
Total:	65	3485	1733	2058	2329	4752
Share of transition economies in total IMF lending (not including exceptional lending to Mexico), in per cent	11.5	33.2	31.4	32.2	52.0	54.0

Memorandum: Financial flows to Eastern Europe, the Baltics, and the CIS combined, from official bilateral and multilateral sources (annual, in bn USD)

	1990	1991	1992	1993	1994	1995
Grants	0.6	6.5	5.9	4.8	4.6	4.3
Gross loans						
Bilateral	4.8	4.5	2.8	1.9	1.8	1.6
Multilateral (excl. IMF)	1.0	1.9	2.3	3.0	3.1	3.4
Net loans						
Bilateral	4.4	4.2	2.4	1.5	1.3	0.2
Multilateral (excl. IMF)	0.8	1.7	1.9	2.3	2.2	2.0

Sources: ECE/UN (1996a), EBRD (1996).

These gaps and delays in information explain why there has been a growing disappointment over assistance both in the East and in the West. The Western public knew about huge commitments to Eastern Europe and Russia. The Eastern population was very frustrated by the low share of the disbursements, and had the impression that only a trickle of the announced funding was actually available. Other frustrations added to the disappointment over the figures. The issue of assistance is however no longer high on the agenda. The CEECs are essentially getting assistance out of the PHARE programme as pre-accession (to the EU) aid. IMF aid is concentrated on the former Soviet Union countries and on low-income or crisis countries in Eastern and South Eastern Europe.

The drawbacks of assistance

We may sum up these drawbacks under four headings:

(a) *The very concept of assistance is ambiguous.* Even if a narrow concept is retained, excluding foreign direct investment, one may ask the question: who helps whom? Emergency food aid has been sensed as a way for the West to get rid of its surpluses, at the same time impairing the competitiveness of domestic producers (in the case of Poland) or enriching mafia networks (in the case of Russia). Technical assistance has largely been considered in the East as inadequate, supplied by individuals and institutions who generally lacked a serious knowledge of the countries in transition and at best only had some experience of the developing countries. It was perceived as providing funds to Western consultant firms or academic institutions, and allowing foreigners to learn about business opportunities in the East. Project finance has often been directed towards areas of interest to the West more than to the East (for instance, projects focused on nuclear safety or environmental protection) (for Eastern views, see Inotai, 1993; Kiss, 1994).

(b) *Assistance is tied or conditional.* There are different kinds of conditionality for the loans extended by the international financial institutions (IFIs). The *IMF* has a standard procedure linked with its stand-by and extended arrangements: there is first a letter of intent where the authorities of the recipient country state the measures they are to implement during the period of the arrangement; second, there is a list of economic policy measures to be taken before the arrangement is approved; third, there are quarterly or half-year targets to be met (on budget deficit as a percent of GDP, or on money supply) before the country may draw the current tranche of the loan; finally there are periodical reviews of the implementation of the programme (Schadler *et al.*, 1995). There are in addition concessional facilities such as the ESAF (Enhanced Structural Adjustment Facility) which has been extended to Albania and to less developed members of the CIS. Finally a Systemic Transformation Facility (STF) was granted in 1993–5 to countries where the process of transition was just beginning (it applied to most of the former Soviet Union countries, and to Eastern – as opposed to Central – European countries, including

Slovakia, Romania, Bulgaria, Croatia and Macedonia). The conditionality for ESAF and STF was slightly softer. The IMF conditionality is particularly crucial because the seal of approval by the IMF usually triggers agreements with other IFIs, inflow of private capital, and the conclusion of debts negotiations with official creditors in the framework of the Paris Club or with banks in the framework of the London Club. Sometimes the seal of approval is more important than the credit itself. For instance, Hungary signed a stand-by agreement with the IMF in March 1996, but did not draw on the loan, and said that the agreement was only needed to restore the country's image on the international financial markets. The project-related institutions, such as the *World Bank*, the *EBRD*, the *EIB* (European Investment Bank) have their own criteria linked with the viability of the investments financed, which leads them to recommend the freeing up of prices (such as energy prices, that have usually remained controlled in most of the countries in transition, at least in the beginning of the reforms), or the speeding up of demonopolisation. The World Bank has a significant share of its lending devoted to non-project-related loans (Wallich, 1995). It insists upon the drawing up of consistent reform blueprints in such areas as banking, social security, institutions-building, and environment protection, when negotiating its loans.

There is an implicit conditionality in private financing as well: the multinationals which make large investments in transition countries exert a pressure on the governments to obtain increased tariff protection, to force a devaluation, to keep domestic prices for the goods they manufacture low enough on the local market, all which may clash with the macro-economic policy recommended by the IMF and endorsed by the governments.

(c) *The grant element in assistance has been very low.* This is combined with the huge gap between commitments and disbursements. For the Central European countries, for instance, the grant component of the commitments amounted to 14 per cent in 1989–91. In addition, a large share of the assistance generates further indebtedness (Ners and Buxell, 1995).

(d) Even when assistance has actually been disbursed, its efficiency has been impaired by difficulties in *absorption*. The infrastructure was inadequate, the financial institutions in the East lacked experience, and the managers were unable to find the guarantees which trigger the delivery of the funds. This in turn created the impression in the West that the assistance was not really needed as the available funds often remained unused.

The early recommendations for more efficient assistance

Along with frequent appeals for a 'new Marshall Plan for the East', voiced in the first years following the collapse of communism, there have been many practical recommendations aiming at increasing the efficiency of aid.

Various proposals have been formulated to effect better *coordination* both among the donors and among the recipients (see Barre *et al.*, 1992a). Unfortunately all these proposals hit built-in obstacles. *Coordination among the donors* was fundamentally impossible due to the conflicts of interests among the donors and their institutions. Among the countries involved, the single biggest donor has been Germany, which had its own priority – to reconstruct Eastern Germany – and its own specific interests in a region, Central Europe, where it also controlled the flows of private finance. Among the international institutions, there has been an obvious overlapping between the coordinating functions of the EU and of the IMF. The EC (later EU) was the official coordinator for Central and Eastern Europe, but hardly went beyond monitoring and collecting information for all the assistance efforts outside the specific PHARE programme. The IMF, though not endowed with coordination functions, has in fact exerted an implicit governance of the assistance process.

Has *assistance been substantial enough?* It would be better to say that it has not been distributed evenly, and that the most attractive countries from the point of view of the trade and investment interests (Central Europe, Russia) got the lion's share. As the transition process is nearing completion, there is a feeling that gradually the recipient countries should need less multilateral or bilateral official help, and rely more on normal sources for investment.

Has it been adequately *geared to transformation needs?* In fact, it has been concentrated on macro-economic stabilisation. As the IMF was in fact the main controlling agency, it is not surprising that assistance was concentrated in the fields that the agency mastered best and for which it had a mandate. In addition, there is no worldwide experience in granting structural long-term assistance. The IBRD and the EBRD concentrate on project financing, with micro-economic criteria. There are no clear criteria by which to estimate and control the broader efficiency of this type of assistance.

The future of assistance

Is 'assistance to transition' still relevant? It is increasingly felt that as countries in transition are becoming 'normal' market economies, they no longer need assistance, except in some emergency cases. The main long-term problem is to ensure sustainable growth, which requires investments, mainly in the private sector. Foreign investment is the main vehicle here. International financial institutions can play a role for financing infra-structure projects (the World Bank, the European Investment Bank; see Steinherr and Hurst, 1995) or for co-financing private projects (the EBRD; Vuylsteke, 1995). The second line of assistance is linked with EU accession. It was decided in 1997 that grants from the EU's PHARE aid programme to Central and Eastern Europe would be tied to 'progress of and compliance with the programme for the adoption of policies designed to adapt the recipients to membership of the EU' (*Financial Times,* 24 December 1997). There is a growing perception that the benefits which are going to be made available to the applicants (pre-accession help, membership benefits such as access to the EU markets, structural funds, transfers originating from the Common Agricultural Policy) will reduce, if not simply annihilate, the need for other financial support. The Managing Director of the World Bank candidly states: 'it reduces the demand for World Bank financing per se and tilts its composition toward catalytic instruments such as guarantees' (Koch-Weser, 1996, p. 10). Finally the last remaining field for assistance is the crisis situation, where the assistance is required to prevent collapse or social unrest, especially when there might be spillovers outside the country or the region.

The involvement of the IMF in the countries in transition is thus changing. While the IMF has been the major inspiration source for transition packages, through the 'Washington consensus' (see Chapter 7) that has ultimately been endorsed by all the countries, it is no longer a major lender to Central and East European countries. Table 9.9 lists the countries still benefiting from IMF loans by 31 December 1997. In 1998, none of the Central European countries is financed by the IMF. In February 1998, the IMF ended the standby arrangement with Hungary on the grounds that the Hungarian economy was strong enough (*Financial Times,* 17 February 1998). Two Eastern European economies, Romania and Bulgaria, and two Baltic countries, Estonia and Latvia, were still on the IMF list in 1998.

For the countries that no longer need or solicit IMF's help, this does not mean that they are free from IMF evaluation. Hungary was warned in 1998 that its rate of inflation was too high. The Czech Republic had reimbursed the IMF by anticipation in 1994, and had declined to use the last tranche of the Stand-By Agreement concluded with the IMF in 1993. However the government had to welcome an information visit by an IMF delegation in April 1997, when the Czech currency crisis was developing. Following this visit, the first deputy director of the IMF Stanley Fisher wrote a letter to Vaclav Klaus, the Prime Minister, criticising the first package of measures adopted in mid-April 1997 and pressing the government for more radical measures.

The countries that still require IMF financing may be classified in three categories. First we have the developing countries of the former Soviet space (Central Asian and Transcaucasian countries), and the post-war reconstruction countries of the former Yugoslav space. Here assistance to transition is coupled with standard development assistance. The second group is made of the countries in transition experiencing serious macro-economic difficulties and at the same time lagging behind in the transformation process. Romania and Bulgaria were promised IMF loans in 1997 on the basis of such considerations. In both cases the agreement with the IMF was a present to

Table 9.9   *IMF involvement in some countries in transition by end-December 1997*

Countries	Date of agreement	Deadline	Total approved (in million SDR)	Not yet drawn
Stand-by agreements				
Bulgaria	11 Apr. 1997	10 Jun. 1998	371.9	124.5
Estonia	17 Dec 1997	16 Mar. 1999	16.1	16.1
Latvia	10 Oct. 1997	9 Apr. 1999	33.0	33.0
Romania	22 Apr. 1997	21 May 1998	301.5	180.9
Ukraine	25 Aug. 1997	24 Aug. 1998	398.9	217.6
Extended Financial Facility				
Azerbaijan	20 Dec. 1996	19 Dec. 1999	58.5	33.4
Croatia	12 Mar. 1997	11 Mar. 2000	353.2	324.4
Kazakhstan	17 Jul. 1996	16 Jul. 1999	309.4	309.4
Moldova	20 May 1996	19 May 1999	135.0	97.5
Russia	26 Mar. 1996	25 Mar. 1999	6901.0	3064.7
Enhanced Structural Adjustment Facility				
Armenia	14 Feb. 1996	13 Feb. 1999	101.3	33.8
Azerbaijan	20 Dec. 1996	19 Dec. 1999	93.1	38.0
Georgia	28 Feb. 1996	27 Feb. 1999	166.5	55.5
FYROM	11 Apr. 1997	10 Apr. 2000	54.6	36.4
Kyrgyzstan	20 Jul. 1994	31 Mar. 1998	88.2	0.0

Source: IMF Survey, 30 March 1998.

new governments that had expressed their commitments to radical reforms. *Bulgaria* indeed got a loan in April 1997 (see Table 9.9) when it decided to introduce a currency board (see Box 7.2 in Chapter 7). A new stand-by loan was being negotiated for 1998–2001 in the beginning of 1998. In *Romania*, the conditions for the loan agreed upon in April 1997 as well were to cut inflation to 2 per cent per month, to reduce by 40 per cent the budget deficit, and to increase foreign exchange reserves. The efforts of the government to meet this goal were praised by the IMF, but in the beginning of 1998 the fourth tranche of the loan was stalled because the government did not move quickly enough on privatisations (*Financial Times*, 16 January 1998). According to a familiar scenario, the appointment of a new prime minister in April 1998 was followed by a resumption of the talks with the IMF (*Financial Times*, 28 April 1998).

The third group of countries benefiting from IMF loans comprises two big recipients – Russia and Ukraine, large countries with a political bargaining power. Russia became in 1996 a major beneficiary of IMF lending, with a three-year 10.1 billion dollar extended funding facility. The disbursement was stalled in late 1996 and early 1997 because of poor rates of tax collection, insufficient efforts to curb corruption and failure to pay wages and pensions in the state sector. In April 1997 the IMF's managing director expressed his satisfaction regarding the course of the economic reform and promised to recommend a resumption of the delayed payments for the loan (*International Herald Tribune*, 3 April 1997; *Financial Times*, 4 April 1997). Later, in June 1997, the World Bank approved six big loans to Russia for a total of 885 million dollars, and declared its willingness to increase its lending in the future (*Financial Times*, 12 June 1997). However it is difficult to say that the macro-economics parameters significantly improved in a few months. In the Russian case, the Bretton Woods institutions are keen to send out signals rather than to exert outright pressure, because of the international political status of the country, expressed in the symbolic admittance of Russia in the G-7 group in June 1997 and in the Paris Club of the main creditor governments in September 1997.

In February 1998, the IMF extended the Russian loan until the year 2000 with the open aim of preventing Russia from developing an Asian-like crisis (*Financial Times*, 20 February 1998). When the financial crisis indeed erupted in April–May, a previously stalled tranche of the loan was promptly released. In July, alarmed by the mounting crisis in Russia, the Bretton Woods institutions agreed to provide Russia with a 22.6 billion dollar loan package (incorporating a part of previously agreed loans and a loan from Japan) of which 14.8 billion dollars would be disbursed in 1998 and 7.8 in 1999. The package was supposed to stabilise Russia's finances and help strengthen the ruble, and a first tranche of 4.8 billion was released. Despite this massive programme, and a brief recovery of Russia's financial markets, the ruble was devalued in August, and Russia asked for still more aid.

IMF funding was also made available for *Ukraine* in November 1997, after a freeze of several months, when it became obvious that the Ukrainian capital market was feeling the spillover of the Asian crisis. The loan was again stalled in the beginning of 1998 because Ukraine did not meet the macro-economic targets set by the IMF.

The master word in the new concept of assistance is *partnership*. It was put on the agenda at the Madrid 1994 meeting of the IMF's 24-member Interim Committee, and has been restated in October 1996 in Washington. What does 'partnership' mean exactly? We suspect that in addition to the honourable goal of associating the recipient countries to the definition of targets and instruments, the concept also means that the donors do not wish to increase their burden. Already in IMF circles one is ready to consider that 'dialogue' must become a substitute to direct assistance for the countries that are most advanced in transition (Central Europe for instance). The World Bank has less reason to walk out, as tasks stemming out of structural transformation are still on the agenda: financial sector reform, social security and pension reform, institutions-building (Wallich, 1995; Koch-Weser, 1996). However the World Bank itself is subject to pressure in a liberalising world. Its role in lending to the public sector is questioned when the main weight of lending shifts towards the private sector (Richardson and Haralz, 1995). Partnership here means increased links with the private sector and the non-governmental institutions, and developing the 'guarantee pipeline' of the Bank. All this amounts to solving the problem: how to do more with less means. The Russian financial crisis shatters these schemes, and the Bretton Woods institutions are caught in a dilemma. Either they stop assistance to Russia, which might precipitate the country in a political crisis with unknown consequences for the rest of the world, or they go on supporting a country which exemplifies the failure of IMF's recipes for a quick transition to the market.

Globalisation and the Countries in Transition

The withering away of assistance requires that other funding be found. Since 1990, the European countries in transition have received large capital flows in the form of foreign direct investment (FDI) and portfolio investment.

Foreign Direct Investment (FDI)

The main driving force of FDI into the countries in transition has been privatisation (see Chapter 8). We shall look at the main features and patterns of FDI, the motivations of the investors, and the impact on the host countries.

(1) *The features of FDI in the countries in transition* While the centrally planned economies were getting less than 1 per cent of the world FDI before 1989, the share of the European (including Russia) countries in transition amounted in 1995 already amounted to 5 per cent of the world total. Table 9.10 shows the net FDI inflows for the period 1990–7 together with the cumulated inflows and the inflows per capita. The data allow for the following assessments:

(a) There has been a very rapid growth. Overall the annual inflow (in current dollars) was multiplied by 4.8 between 1991 and 1996.

(b) The average ratio net FDI inflow/GDP was in 1996 and 1997 2.2 per cent in Central and Eastern Europe, 3.5 per cent in the Baltics, and less than 1 per cent in the CIS countries (0.8 per cent in 1997 for Russia). This compares with averages (for 1986–92) of 2–2.7 per cent for Spain and Portugal, 3.5 per cent for Belgium and Luxembourg, 0.8 per cent for the United States (Martin and Velásquez, 1997).

(c) In absolute terms, FDI has been concentrated on very few countries. In 1997, Hungary, the Czech Republic and Poland had cumulatively attracted 84 per cent of overall FDI in Eastern Europe, and Russia 85 per cent of FDI in the CIS area. In cumulated FDI per capita, Hungary is the

Table 9.10 *Foreign direct investment in countries in transition, 1991–7 (million US$)*

	1991	1992	1993	1994	1995	1996	1997	1989–97*	1989–97** FDI flows per cap. ($)	1997 FDI flows/GDP (in per cent)
Eastern Europe	2330	3120	4106	3479	9159	7573	9076	38403	354	2.4
Bulgaria	56	42	40	106	90	106	498	1000	121	5.6
Czech Rep.	513	1004	654	869	2562	1428	1300	7473	726	2.4
Hungary	1460	1471	2339	1146	4453	1983	2085	15403	1519	4.7
Poland	117	284	580	542	1134	2768	3077	8442	218	2.3
								19250**	497**	4.9**
Romania	37	73	94	341	419	263	1222	2389	106	2.9
Slovakia	82	100	134	170	157	206	161	912	169	0.8
Slovenia	65	111	113	128	176	185	321	1074	538	1.8
Baltic countries		101	236	471	457	684	1034	2708	396	5.0
Estonia		58	160	226	205	150	262	809	557	2.8
Latvia		42	46	214	180	382	418	1287	515	7.6
Lithuania			30	31	73	152	355	612	165	3.6
CIS, total	–100	830	1495	1603	3656	5637	10593	19990	70	1.2
Russia	–100	700	900	640	2016	2479	6241	9743	66	0.8
Ukraine			198	159	267	521	516	1661	36	1.4
Total	2230	4051	5837	5553	13272	13894	20703	61100	153	1.8

* Cumulated inflows.
** The EBRD provides a second series of data for Poland resulting from banking system data and surveys of foreign investment enterprises.
Source: ECE/UN, Economic Survey of Europe, 1998, vol. 2; for the three last columns, EBRD (1998), p. 12.

leader, having attracted twice as much FDI as the second in line, the Czech Republic. This may explain why the most detailed studies of the FDI have been realised on the Hungarian case (Csáki, 1997; Hunya, 1997; Inotai, 1995). Geography (distance from Western Europe) and size (for Russia) explain this concentration, along with other determinants. However the countries in transition are lagging behind the main host countries for FDI in emerging markets. An UNCTAD estimate for the accumulated FDI stock up to 1996 shows that all the countries in transition taken together (50.6 billion dollars) have received twice less than Brazil ($108.3 bn) and more than three times less than China (USDA, 1997, p. 3).

(d) The sectoral pattern is very different for Central and Eastern Europe, on the one hand, and for Russia, on the other. In Russia, FDI in the energy sector is dominant, with over 50 per cent of the cumulated flow. While this pattern is similar to that of investment flows into a developing country endowed with natural resources, some diversification is occurring, with an increase in the share of food processing, machine-building, and trade and catering. The involvement of foreign capital in Russia is very low considering the potential of the country. Investors are dissuaded by an unclear and fluctuating legislation, conflicts with regional authorities (which explains the high share – over 70 per cent in 1996 – of overall FDI located in Moscow and Moscow region), and lack of market infrastructure. It was expected that once the legal framework was stabilised, many projects could finalise, up to an amount of $50 bn for the oil sector alone. In particular, the crucial law on production sharing, adopted in December 1995, leaving ownership of natural resources to the state but allowing foreign partners to retain a share of the revenues, has been supplemented by limitative provisions that made it almost inapplicable. A presidential decree of November 1997 opened a new opportunity by allowing foreigners to buy up to 100 per cent of Russian oil companies (instead of 15 per cent as before) (*Financial Times*, 19 November 1997). The political and financial crisis in 1998 stalled these expectations. In the other Newly Independent States (NIS), FDI is concentrated in the oil and gas-producing states (chiefly Kazakhstan and Turkmenistan, and more recently Azerbaijan).The potential for oil and gas exploration and extraction deals might be greatly enhanced if intra-CIS and international conflicts about pipeline transportation from Central Asia and Caucasus could be solved.

FDI sectoral distribution in the Central and Eastern European countries is much more associated with the globalisation of production. The FDI flows were from the outset directed towards manufacturing industries, moving gradually from less to more value-added and skill-intensive sectors. Also, we have already seen that OPT has been an important component of FDI. The privileged sectors have been the car-making industry, food processing, pharmaceuticals, and hotels. The service sector is still promising, especially banking and insurance activities, and public utilities (power distribution, air and railways transportation, and telephone).

(2) *The determinants of FDI* We look separately on the determinants from the investors' side, and from the recipient countries.

(a) The determinants on the investors' side. The countries in transition soon became the target of multinational corporations (MNCs) and became integrated in their world-wide strategy. This is obvious for the big oil MNCs operating in Russia and the oil-extracting NIS, which aim at expanding both profits and control on world-wide supplies. The Russian big oil and gas companies were also the only ones to be ranked in the 1997 *Financial Times* 500 world companies: Gazprom (ranked 91st), Lukoil Co. (224) and United Energy Systems (225) represented the three energy sub-sectors (*Financial Times,* 20 January 1998). Among the 50 largest Eastern European (Russia included) companies in 1997 (*ibid*), the first 10 were Russian, all in the energy sector. Among the 40 following, 20 were Russian, again mostly from the energy sector. These Russian MNCs are already very active in entering world-wide networks of alliances, chiefly with US corporations (however Gazprom developed an alliance in 1997 with the Anglo-Dutch Shell).

What are the determinants for the investors into the CEECs, and particularly the three core countries, Hungary, the Czech Republic and Poland? There have been many case studies (for an overview of the main surveys since 1991, see Lankes and Venables, 1996, pp. 332–3). The usual motivations are listed: the market potential, low costs (especially cheap labour costs for a level of skills comparable to what is found in industrialised countries), and a geographical determinant is added, the proximity from the EU. Lankes and Venables also conducted a survey of their own, on the basis of an EBRD project but with interviews basically conducted by researchers from the IFO institute in Munich. Along with the market and cost determinants, the authors introduce an additional characteristic of the projects surveyed, i.e. the control mode (subcontracting, joint venture, or wholly owned subsidiary). Other variables are taken into account, such as country risk perceptions, tax regime (which is perceived as of little importance), and trade policy of the country (which is felt as important except in the Czech Republic and Hungary). The conclusions of the authors are as follows: one should expect an acceleration of FDI once a critical mass of investment is reached (the 'herding' effect); the share of cost-motivated and export-oriented FDI is likely to increase while the FDI mainly determined by the size of the domestic markets and the natural resource endowments is likely to recede; finally, the share of fully-owned subsidiaries is going to increase while the share of joint ventures, a more 'primitive' form of FDI, is bound to decrease (Lankes and Venables, 1997, pp. 563–4). The three conclusions taken together suggest that the most successful Eastern European countries in attracting foreign investment are also the most integrated into the globalisation process. First, these countries are selected as an export base even when the domestic market is narrow. Second, the cost considerations tend to become essential, and hence the host country cannot afford to let its real dollar wages increase in comparison with other countries, though this consideration tends to become less important once a critical mass of FDI is attained. Third, the most successful countries in attracting FDI are included into multinational companies' (MNCs) global networks – up to becoming sub-regional headquarters for MNCs as Inotai suggests for Hungary (Inotai, 1995, p. 119). Such an evolution implies that FDI should decreasingly be linked with the privatisation process which has initiated foreign investment in the region.

Before looking at the motivations of the host countries, one has to mention that foreign-owned companies pursue aims of their own, which may contradict the home country's policy objectives. Foreign firms have pressed the governments to provide them greater protection, through increased tariffs on imported competing goods (such as cars) or a more depressed exchange rate so as to encourage exports and prevent imports. These demands may contradict the willingness of the countries in transition to open their economies, so as to increase competition on the domestic market and to respond to the lowering of tariffs granted by the EC in the framework of the association or other agreements negotiated or in negotiation (see above, p. 221). Some clashes between national governments and multinational firms had great visibility, such as the cancellation in 1993 of an investment package by the German firm Volkswagen for its subsidiary the Czech car manufacturer Skoda, which strongly reduced the expectations raised in 1991 when the joint venture was concluded (*Financial Times*, 17 December 1993). The joint venture concluded in 1989 between the US General Electric and the Hungarian firm of lighting products Tungsram turned into a near 99 percent GE ownership in 1994 after several increases in the US company's stake, large lay-offs, and disputes with the Hungarian government about the rate of exchange of the forint when the increase in the real exchange rate threatened to wipe out the initial attractiveness of the deal to GE, namely low Hungarian dollar wages.

(b) *The motivations on the host countries' side.* The countries in transition were initially rather reluctant to accept foreign investment – this may be seen as a legacy of the former system, when FDI was associated with the harmful influence of capitalism. They soon however competed for FDI. The first determinant was the need for capital, in a situation when domestic investment fell still more steeply than output, and when foreign assistance could not match the huge investment needs of the region. How do we estimate the amount of these needs?

FDI as a source of finance. Gros and Steinherr (1995) recall (p. 456) the various estimated investment needs of Eastern countries. Their own calculations, based upon the hypothesis of an overall domestic savings rate of 20 per cent per year to the GDP over the next 10–15 years, suggest that one-fifth of an investment ratio of 25 per cent might be financed by foreign sources (p. 470).The assumption of a 20 per cent savings rate may be close to reality. An EBRD study has shown that while the domestic savings rate fell dramatically in the first years of the transition it had recovered by 1995 to a level of 18 per cent of the GDP (EBRD, 1996, p. 80). Estimates of annual external financing needs that were made in the first years of transition for the 10–15-year period ahead for Eastern Europe (including Poland, Hungary, Czechoslovakia, Romania and Bulgaria) ranged from $25 bn to $103 bn depending on the annual growth rate target, the capital/output ratio and the initial value of the capital stock (Gros and Steinherr, 1995, p. 458).

The estimates quoted above relate to the external financial needs for investment, of which FDI is only a part (foreign assistance, and other capital inflows, add to the total). On the other hand, FDI is not only used for investment. Governments receiving cash for a share in the equity of a privatised enterprise may use it for pressing needs such as the servicing of foreign debt or the financing of a trade deficit. As Inotai (1995, p. 10) states, there is nothing wrong in that, especially if FDI is financing a 'modernisation deficit' arising from high machinery imports. The flexibility in the use of FDI inflows is, however, bound to be limited in the future, as these inflows are decreasingly linked with privatisation and increasingly linked with greenfield investments or increases in stakes of already privatised companies. In Hungary and the Czech Republic, the potential of privatisations was nearly exhausted by 1997. Poland, which has delayed the privatisation process until 1995–6, has still large state enterprises to sell, including in the telecommunications sector, which is also to sustain FDI inflows in Romania, Bulgaria, and Lithuania (*Financial Times*, 8 January 1998).

FDI as a driving force for restructuring. Restructuring needs are generally considered as an essential motivation for FDI in the countries in transition. The foreign partner, even with a minority share, brings a managerial culture, especially in fields very much under-developed in the centrally planned economies (such as marketing or financial management) and fosters the development of new technologies. The benefits associated with FDI in this respect must not be exaggerated. They are associated with a high degree of exposure of the country to foreign business influences. Hungary is the country where foreign penetration is strongest (with over 60 per cent of export sales and about 40 per cent in investment: Hunya, 1997). However, even in this case, there are limits to the restructuring potential of FDI. This potential is hindered if the financial sector is not restructured at the same pace as the industrial sector. Research and development is not necessarily enhanced when the foreign partner relies on its own resources (for instance, in the car industry, the most technically advanced technologies, especially motorisation, remain controlled by the foreign multinational, and this was a major disappointment in the Volkswagen–Skoda venture in the Czech Republic). Foreign-controlled enterprises often use their own suppliers rather than involving local suppliers in their activities. The foreign-controlled sector becomes a part of the global strategy of the foreign owners, with little say from the local governments. In such sectors as food processing or clothing, local producers have been crowded out. Foreign enterprises may create new jobs, but often they reduce employment (a development that is seen as much less critical than in European industrialised countries, as downsizing linked with increased productivity is a policy priority in the countries in transition).

Here, too, the motivations of the foreign investors may contradict the long-term aims of the national governments. When the foreign investor primarily looks at his gains in terms of lower costs, an increase in these costs may prompt him to settle in another location, and here the competition between the developing countries and the countries in transition is high; the latter are exceedingly confident in their specific advantages (geographical closeness to Western Europe, skills of the labour force) which are easily eroded in a context of industrial globalisation: distances matter less, human technical skills matter less. When the investor looks at market expansion, often he tries to buy a monopoly position, at a time when the national governments try to de-monopolise (ECE/UN, 1993, chapter 5, 'Restructuring of state-owned enterprises in Eastern Europe').

There is thus a difficult balance to be maintained between the wish to be incorporated into the global economy and the desire to keep a control on national industrial and social policies (Martin, 1998, p. 23). But it is not a matter of choice for the CEECs. The preference of the MNCs for Hungary, which seemed challenged by the Czech Republic before the Czech crisis in 1997, suggests that only Hungary might be included into the global strategy of the MNCs with its positive and negative consequences.

Is there a relation between FDI and growth, on the one hand, and between FDI and advancement of reforms, on the other? Growth and FDI are not correlated. The country that has attracted the largest share of foreign investment in Central Europe, Hungary, has not displayed the highest rate of growth in the region, and FDI does not seem to have been attracted by high growth prospects. Other features, such as stability and market orientation, have played a more substantial role. Can one say that the scope, the speed, and the intensity of the reforms has been determining? This is certainly the case for official Western assistance as the World Bank (1996, p. 138) states. The argument is double-sided: good reforms have attracted assistance because the latter was conditional on the commitment to reforms, and on the actual implementation of the commitment. Again, Hungary has been singled out by investors though it was not among the best reformers, in the eyes of the international financial institutions. Micro-economics are determining for business. Non-investment capital inflows are much more sensitive to macroeconomics.

Portfolio investment and other capital inflows

Non-FDI capital inflow has accounted for roughly 50 per cent of the private capital inflows into the Central and Eastern European countries (Table 9.11, and Fischbach and Scattaglia, 1997). We have already seen the impact of such inflows on macroeconomic stability (Chapter 7) and the institutional development of capital markets in the countries in transition (Chapter 8). We are now looking at these flows from the point of view of the integration of these countries into the global economy. They consist in portfolio investment, and bank or non-bank lending, to which one may add short-term funds and unrecorded movements (errors and omissions) in a broader view. These flows have been driven by several determinants:

(a) The 'push' exerted by the structure of international interest rates. The low level of interest rates in developed countries since 1990 has 'pushed' capital to emerging markets, as analytical studies have shown (Fernandez-Arias, 1996, and Fernandez-Arias and Montiel, 1996). Developing countries, and later (since 1993) countries in transition benefited from such a push. By mid-1997 all countries of Central and Eastern Europe including the Baltics, plus Russia and Kazakhstan, had received international credit ratings, which added to their visibility, as well as their generally improving creditworthiness. The overall approval (despite occasional reservations for some countries) of the international financial institutions, and the normal-isation of the most indebted countries' relations with their official and private creditors, have added to this creditworthiness.

(b) Domestic factors have exerted a 'pulling' effect. Among these factors one finds the domestic macroeconomic stability (measured by the rate of inflation). The movement of the exchange rate also matters: while frequent devaluations suggest instability, a managed float or a crawling peg may be preferred (from the point of view of the investor) to a fixed exchange rate which suggests a risk of excessive appreciation of the real exchange rate and of deterioration of the current account. The impact of the fiscal policy is ambiguous (see ECE/UN, 1997a, special study on capital inflows into Eastern Europe). A strict fiscal policy is a sign of stability, but a lax fiscal policy, especially when fiscal deficits are financed by borrowing abroad or bond emissions, goes with high interest rates that attract capital inflows. Structural policies also matter, namely the scope, speed and forms of privatisation, which impact on the valuation of assets (in the case of portfolio investment). The opening and expansion of stock exchanges (Chapter 8) is an important feature of structural policies that attracts foreign capital.

Table 9.11 Net capital inflows into countries in transition, 1995–7

	1995	1996	1997*	1995	1996	1997**	1996		
		(in $ bn)			(in per cent of GDP)		(in per cent of capital inflows)		
							FDI	Portfolio Investments	Loans
Eastern Europe, total of which:	23.7	15.6	21.8	7.3	4.5	6.4	57	14	29
Bulgaria	0.3	−0.8	1.2	2.0	−7.8	9.0			
Czech Rep.	8.8	3.5	1.4	17.5	6.2	3.0	32	17	49
Hungary	7.0	0.2	0.8	15.7	0.5	2.0	63	29	8
Poland	2.7	5.3	8.9	2.3	3.9	6.6	57	4	42
Romania	1.5	2.8	4.2	4.3	7.9	11.4			
Slovakia	0.9	2.3	1.6	5.4	12.3	6.9			
Slovenia	0.3	0.5	1.6	1.4	2.9	9.1			
Baltic countries	1.1	1.7	2.1	8.0	10.0	13.0			
Estonia	0.3	0.5	0.6	8.1	12.0	13.0			
Latvia	–	0.5	0.5	–	9.3	9.5			
Lithuania	0.8	0.7	1.0	14.2	9.4	11.3			
CIS, total excl. Russia	2.4	2.8	3.2	5.0	4.7	5.0			
Ukraine	1.6	2.1	1.9	4.4	4.7	3.8			
Russia***	7.9	−7.4	10.0	2.2	−1.7	3.5			
Total all countries in transition	35.1	12.6	36.9	4.7	1.5	6.0			

* Preliminary figures for 1997.
** Extrapolation of January–September data.
*** For Russia, the data do not take into account errors and omissions. The overall figure uses the Russian data.

Source: Same as Table 9.10.

The case of Russia is quite atypical. Russia has been the most profitable emerging market in 1997. The financial crisis that erupted in 1998 was not a spillover from the Asian crisis. It was much more due to the vagaries in Russian politics, the inability of the government to pay wage arrears to miners and the resulting strikes, the failure to collect taxes, and the lack of credibility of the Russian state institutions. The country is faced with a huge debt, coupled with assets that are not easily recoverable in developing countries, an endemic capital flight which resulted in cumulated outflows probably higher by mid-1998 than the amount of the Russian debt, and a shrinking trade surplus. Are investors to return to Russia? This was an open question by end-1998.

The Czech Republic too was affected by a confidence crisis in the first semester of 1997, that was quickly likened to a Mexico-like crisis. In fact it was much more a transition crisis, as the collapse of the Czech currency and capital markets was not the burst of a speculative bubble, but was rooted in the lack of completion of structural reforms, with an unreformed state-owned banking sector, and an opaque governance of the privatised enterprises. This explains why the Czech crisis did not extend to the neighbour countries (but for a short-lived attack on the Polish zloty) and could be solved by a quick policy response that however generated a deep and long-expected political crisis. When the Asian crisis erupted later in 1997, East European countries appeared relatively little affected by the Asian crisis, if only because of the small size of their capital markets. Stock market indices, which fell strongly in the last quarter of 1997, soon recovered, especially in Hungary and Poland. Postponed equity emissions resumed in 1998. In addition the transition countries' policy of attracting capital inflows resulted into a build-up of foreign exchange reserves. International investors looking for portfolio diversification following the Asian crisis may be attracted by the markets of Central and Eastern Europe. The Russian crisis had an immediate impact on the Central European capital market, with equity prices falling by 30–40 per cent in August 1998. A modest recovery followed in the next months but the markets remained unstable, mainly because many banks in these countries had invested in Russian bonds.

In the future, the reintegration of the CEECs in the world economy via EU membership will protect them from external disturbances but also limit their role as independent players. Russia has the ambitions and means to become a global player if it succeeds in reforming – but this statement is still a bet by the end of this century.

10 When is Transition Over?

A few years after the Bolshevik revolution in Russia, neo-classical economists asked whether a socialist economic system was viable. They concluded that it could not operate rationally. Other economists, socialist-oriented, attempted to show that resource allocation could be rational in a socialist economy, even if the actual Soviet regime was not functioning that way. Thus emerged in the 1930s the debate on 'market socialism'.

When a number of countries became centrally planned economies after the Second World War, various theoretical approaches were developed. Many analysts, both economists and political scientists, considered that this system unduly called itself 'socialist', and thus marred a concept which encompassed a set of positive human values. They preferred to call it 'real socialism' (or 'really existing'). This triggered a debate on the real nature of the system (or the real nature of the USSR when this country was taken as an ideal type). Many authors contributed to the debate in the West, in a political economy or a systemic approach. In the East, the most significant contributor was the Hungarian economist Janos Kornai with his *Economics of Shortage* (1980), and later *The Socialist System: Political Economy of Communism* (1992). We shall start from these analyses which help us to understand what was the starting point in the transition process, then revert to market socialism, which could have been a post-transition model but failed to materialise.

What is, then, the model, and where do we stand now? A 'transition fatigue' has developed; the general public and Western policy-makers alike would like to look at the post-communist countries as 'normal' ones. Russia of course is still exotic – but then it always has been in its tsarist past as well. The main question is now the following: When is transition over – if ever?

TRANSITION FROM WHAT? THE REAL NATURE OF 'REAL' SOCIALISM

Many people object to the use of the phrase 'transition' because of its indetermination. A transition is a journey from one point to another. It is thus necessary to define where one comes from, and where one is heading to. This book explores systemic transition, that is, the departure from a socialist, centrally planned economy, towards a free market economy. One might also argue that at the same time transition leads from under-development to development. For some non-European countries the distinction is quite relevant. China is in transition from a command economy to a market economy, from a lower to a higher level of development, but not, for the time being, from socialism to democracy. The same could be said for some countries of Central Asia. The issue is simply avoided when discussing the Central and Eastern European case: here it is assumed that the catching-up process is meant chiefly to recover the pre-transition level, and later to gradually reach the average level of the Western European countries in the same way as Greece, Spain, and Portugal did after joining the EU. After all, the latter countries were never listed among third world countries. The European communist world was supposed to belong to a second world which had solved its development problems through socialist industrialisation. We shall come back to this in the last section. Let us just point here to the fact that the seminal article of 1943 by Rosenstein-Rodan, which actually founded development economics, was precisely devoted to the industrialisation of Eastern and South-Eastern Europe (Rosenstein-Rodan, 1943).

Let us now revert to the systemic departure point of the transition. What was the true nature of the socialist societies?

A number of analyses viewed *socialism as a kind of capitalism* (state monopolist, bureaucratic, etc.). One of the most systematic representatives of this view is the French economist Charles Bettelheim, who theorised the split between the formal collective ownership of the means of production, and the real appropriation of these goods. The workers could not realise a 'social appropriation', and instead a state capitalism developed with all its negative consequences: existence of a wage-earning class, capital accumulation, confiscation of the profit by the exploiting class, made up of the true owners of the means of production, i.e. the party *nomenklatura*, and reproduction of market mechanisms. Such an analysis is essentially Marxist (Bettelheim, 1977 and 1979). A number of French analysts developed related though not ideologically connotated in the same way theses, often using the framework of the French school of *la régulation* which may be defined with some approximation as one of the French branches of the institutionalist school (Andreff, 1993; Sapir, 1990).

One may also feel there is implicit acknowledgement of the capitalist nature of the socialist economies in many developments, especially in the 1980s, whereby concepts and tools of conventional macro-economics and new micro-economics were applied to Eastern economies. Richard Portes developed the macro-economic line (especially in his analysis of the impact of external disturbances in the West on the socialist economies: see Portes, 1980). Irena Grosfeld (1990) provided a survey of the second current. She very rightly stated that, interesting as these approaches may be, they presume a market system with private ownership of the means of production, non-existing in the East. Not surprisingly, as soon as this market environment emerged, such theories as the agency theory, the theory of incentives, the transaction costs theory, and the theory of information, were quickly tried on the cases of the countries in transition.

Other analyses insist on *the systemic specificity of socialism*. Marxists in the West, and the official theorists of the system in the socialist countries, supported this view. A large debate emerged in the late 1960s to account for the fact that the economic reforms were yielding disappointing results while the socialist countries were supposed to have built socialism proper and to be heading toward communism and the age of plenty according to Marx. The 'Political Economy of Socialism' then developed into a theory of the 'advanced socialist society' (analysed in Lavigne, 1978). With the same ideological references but with opposite conclusions Gorbachev offered a theory of 'stagnation', or 'standstill' (*zastoy*). Western Marxists spoke of 'perverted' socialism (Nagels, 1990). A sophisticated approach combining the analytical tools of Marxism with those of modern micro-economics may be found in Roland (1989).

A large body of sovietologists adhered to a systemic approach, identifying and discussing the specific features of the socialist or centrally planned economies using the framework of comparative economic systems analyses (Bornstein, Holzman, Grossman, among many others; see Bornstein, 1994, and Grossman, 1994, for the most recent developments).

The Hungarian economist Janos Kornai provided the only non-Marxist comprehensive approach of the socialist system elaborated in the East. He did so in two stages (1980, 1992). In his *Economics of Shortage* (1980) starting from micro-economics (and even 'infra'-microeconomics), and using a non-standard disequilibrium analysis, he disclosed the main difference between planned and market economies. In the latter, firms are demand-constrained because they are producing for a market and have a hard budgetary constraint. If their costs exceed their revenue they go bankrupt, without any economic agent or authority to rescue them. In centrally planned economies the enterprise works with a view to implementing and overfulfilling the plan. The plan itself is always taut, and anticipates a volume of output higher than the production capacities would allow for, because the planning authorities expect that the enterprise will find ways of under-reporting its capacities and over-reporting its output. Thus there is no 'slack' in the system. The enterprise hits a resource constraint. It thus tries to expand its capacities in hoarding labour, inputs, and investment goods, extracted from the central allocator-planner. It is not constrained by demand as it has a soft budgetary constraint: if it does not meet its financial indicators it is always rescued by the authorities. As all the producers have a resource constraint and as the plan is taut, all the agents are always in short supply for some resource while keeping other resources in excess of their needs. Shortage and surplus coexist and cannot be netted out; the surpluses cannot be used while the shortages are a permanent constraint.

Kornai's analysis of the consumer shows that contrary to the producer, the consumer has a hard budgetary constraint: he cannot spend more than his income. But he is also subject to the paternalistic behaviour of the state. The state decides on his consumption through explicit or implicit (through shortages) rationing, provides him with free (rationed) goods on a large scale, and with a very wide protection system including guaranteed jobs.

This analysis was immediately very appealing to the Western sovietologists because it integrated the basic stylised facts about the functioning of centrally planned economies into a coherent, simply formalised whole. However a link was missing, because Kornai never expanded on the political setting. This link was re-established in *The Socialist System. The Political Economy of Communism* (1992). In this book, the 'anatomy' of the classical communist system begins with power and ideology, which are the core of the system. Then the author looks at the property system, and finally discusses the coordination mechanism, thus considering the three foundations of the system before analysing how it worked. The discussion of the external economic relations and of the 'national variations' introduces the international and comparative aspects, which were only briefly mentioned in *Economics of Shortage*. A very important conclusion is drawn: the 'classical' socialist system had a built-in coherence and was viable – albeit at high cost. Changes that were meant to reform it resulted in contradictions which undermined its viability. But the collapse of the system was a political act, from which the transition started.

In the decade following the publication of *Economics of Shortage*, Kornai's work was widely used and referred to in the West, often supplementing the analysis with a political economy approach (see, for instance, Dembinski, 1991; Welfens, 1992), and emphasising on the distortions that led to the collapse.

A DEAD END: MARKET SOCIALISM

Almost a decade has elapsed since the fall of the Berlin Wall in 1989. Why did transition lead from central planning to standard market, and not to market socialism?

Marx believed that capitalism could only generate anarchy. In the Soviet literature on the political economy of capitalism this built-in anarchy (*stikhiya*) was opposed to the efficient, plan-regulated coordination of economic activities. However, the first theoretical questioning of a socialist economy was, on the contrary, putting market rationality in opposition to plan irrationality. Ludwig von Mises demonstrated in 1920 that in a complex socialist economy, with thousands of plants operating, it would be impossible to the government to efficiently allocate labour and producer goods. To Mises this impossibility was due to the original sin of socialism, which had been to abolish private ownership on producers' goods. Hence the only way to an efficient economy was to get rid of socialism itself.

Other economists spoke of a practical impossibility, claiming that to solve millions of equations on the basis of thousands of statistical data obtained from millions of estimates would prove unfeasible (Robbins, 1937). What, then, if it was possible to achieve such economic calculation without having to solve millions of equations, or if modern computing techniques allowed us to solve these equations almost instantly?

Oskar Lange and the Market Socialism Blueprint

Though Oskar Lange never used the phrase he is generally considered the father of market socialism theory, having developed the model in two large studies in 1936–7. The paternity of the term *Marktsozialismus* is attributed by Nuti (1992) to a German economist, E. Heimann (1922). Reduced to its essentials, the market socialism model operates as follows. Individuals may freely choose which goods and services they want to consume, and which job they want to do in which work-place. Prices of the consumer goods, as well as wages, are determined by the supply–demand mechanisms. The incomes are the sum of the wages paid by the enterprises and of a 'social dividend' allocated by the state; this yields the aggregate demand. The means of production are owned by the state. The Central Planning Board (CPB) is informed of the consumer preferences (through the demand prices), of the total amount of the productive resources (which it controls), and of the feasible technological combinations of factors. The managers of the public-owned enterprises are instructed to choose the combination of factors which minimises their average cost, and to increase their output to the point where marginal cost is equal to the price of the product. In doing so, they use market prices for goods and labour, and 'accounting prices' fixed for the means of production by the CPB.

Who is to ensure that these 'accounting prices' are rational? The Lange model provides for a trial-and-error procedure. Initially the CPB fixes prices at random. The enterprises then determine their production programmes. On the same basis, the CPB itself determines investment programmes (which it controls). Because in the beginning prices will not be correct, at the end of the first period or production cycle the CPB will be informed that for a number of goods supply and demand were not balanced: there will be shortages, or excess inventories. The CPB will then change the prices. Gradually the process will converge to the system of equilibrium prices. The CPB will replicate the market, so as to ensure the same coordination functions with the same initial information. The so-called 'parametric function of prices' also allows the state to impose its choices in consumption and production.

Objections and New Suggestions

Lange was criticised on many technical points but the main objection to his theory had already been formulated by Friedrich von Hayek in 1935, a year before the first of his two articles had been published. As editor of *Collectivist Economic Planning*, a collection of essays including the 1920 article by Ludwig von Mises, Hayek emphasised a crucial point. According to him, the difficulty was not just whether under socialism one could calculate rational prices, but mainly that an incentive was needed for the enterprises to obtain and use the information required for their decisions to conform to the wishes of the CPB. Such incentives only exist, he claimed, if there is a private ownership for producers' goods.

Following the war and the establishment of a command economy on a large scale in Europe, the debate re-emerged in the early 1960s when the first wave of reforms spread in Eastern Europe and in the USSR. The phrase 'market socialism' was taboo in the East. The closest version to it was the 'socialism with a human face' model conceived during the Prague Spring (1967–8) and crushed by the Soviet armed intervention in 1968. The authors of the 'new economic mechanism' introduced in Hungary in the same year, 1968, were very careful not to refer to anything that hinted of market socialism ideas. In official Soviet parlance, all the reforms aimed at 'improving the planning methods' by a large recourse to 'money-market mechanisms'; Western comments spoke of the 'combination' of plan and market.

Among the theoretical contributions of this period one should mention those by Wlodzimierz Brus (1961) and Alec Nove (1983). None of them specifically refers to 'market socialism' but rather to 'central planning with regulated market mechanism' (Brus) or 'feasible socialism' with a large decentralisation of decision-making and broad social guarantees (Nove). Brus later evolved toward a broader definition of market socialism where the market would include capital as well (Brus and Laski, 1989).

What do we learn from these debates and what is the point of discussing them now? Probably the main weakness of the model (which maybe was acknowledged later by Lange himself, when after the war he almost reneged on his pre-war model) was that it treated economic calculation under socialism as a technical problem, and did not take into account the political features of the communist regime. Party monopoly of political power supplemented and superseded state monopoly of ownership and central planning. The managers of the state enterprises were trained to obey party orders, explicit or implicit, and therefore decentralisation and introduction of market mechanisms, even extensively as in Hungary, could not radically alter their priorities and their ways of adjusting. This was also the case in the Yugoslav self-managed system, which had been likened as well to a kind of market socialism *sui generis*, or 'market syndicalism' (Ward, 1958). It has been very convincingly shown by Milica Uvalić (1992) that 'although the institution of social property could have implied the redistribution of property rights in favour of enterprises *vis-à-vis* the state, since the political authorities continued to be responsible for a number of fundamental issues, it was the state that was the effective owner of enterprise assets' (Uvalić, 1992, p. 207).

Market socialism was thus not feasible. What has been demonstrated through the Soviet and Eastern European experience was not that the market is incompatible with central planning or state ownership, but that it is incompatible with the overall political interference of the Communist Party.

This requires a footnote: what about the Chinese model? It is tempting and too easy to answer that this is an entirely different world, with different traditions and different social behaviour. Is China the proof that market socialism is possible under a communist regime? Different explanations are possible. One may argue that there is no market socialism at all but a kind of social pact whereby the regime bargains dictatorship against social welfare and growth performance (Brada, 1993). Most of the specialists look at China as a case for a semi-reformed planned economy. In the country collective farms still remain but the household-responsibility system emerging within them provides incentives similar to those of private farming; in the field of services and small industry responsibility capitalism is emerging; the township and village enterprises (TVE) are not only very efficient but have generated an enormous literature on their features and their merits, and also, in some cases, have been discussed as an alternative model of transition (Smyth, 1997). But the bulk of industry is still organised in large state-owned enterprises that display all the standard features of a command economy, the main one being the softness of the budget constraint (Knell and Yang, 1992; Lardy, 1991). The boom in the Chinese economy reflects several factors: genuine liberalisation and decentralisation in agriculture; the emergence of a new private sector; the opening up of the economy through quasi-convertibility of the currency; and the position of the country at the early stage of the take-off, in a Rostowian sense. Does all this mean that China is typically a Hayekian case in that a spontaneous order developed among individuals freely contracting in a market setting in agriculture? (McKinnon, 1992). If we follow this line, it would be to admit that China offers a case of coexistence between pure capitalism and standard socialism, and certainly not a case of market socialism. Richard Pomfret (1997a) defines the Chinese regime as the officials themselves do : a socialist market economy. He argues that China is not a case of transition from plan to market but from stagnation to growth, and hence its experience cannot be relevant to Eastern Europe or Russia because the initial political aims of transition were different.

Could Market Socialism Offer a Workable Post-Transition Model?

In 1988, debates were conducted on market socialism in Eastern Europe – perhaps the first and the last year when this was possible (*Market Socialism,* 1989). While some expectations assumed that the transition would strengthen social-democrat orientations in politics, especially in Hungary, the 1989 revolutions actually brought to power right-wing governments in Eastern Europe. Such governments could obviously not accept any 'third way' which, according to the minister of finance of the Czech and Slovak Federative Republic, Vaclav Klaus (1990), was the surest road to the Third World. Is market socialism, then, to be labelled as 'the model that might have been and never was' (Nuti, 1992)?

Actually the countries that first engaged in transition have displayed 'capitalist triumphalism', to use the phrase of Peter Wiles (1992). This may easily be explained both by political aversion to communism and by the lack of means to finance social expenditures on a large scale. Instead what we have is what Kornai calls 'a *"dual system"*, in which many elements of the socialist and capitalist societies exist side by side' (Kornai, 1992); what is labelled by Nuti 'a necessary stage of *forced market socialism* , during which the state sector cannot just disappear but must be commercialised rapidly, reorganised, undergo financial restructuring and as much capacity restructuring as feasible, and be treated equally with the private sector in its fiscal burden and access to credit' (Nuti, 1993); what Chavance calls 'the post-socialist transition mixed economy' (1994). Unlike the market socialism blueprint, this is not an ideal or desirable model, but rather the unfortunate consequence both of past inertia and present political bigotry as far as the state sector is concerned.

Should one regret that market socialism was never given a chance? In his book *Whither Socialism?*, Joseph Stiglitz shows that the market socialism model as expressed in the Lange blueprint was based on a wrong model of a market economy, assumed to be Pareto-efficient in conditions of perfect competition: 'market socialism took seriously the neoclassical model, and that was its initial flaw' (Stiglitz, 1994, p. 197). However, though socialism cannot provide for a workable economic model – either in its command economy version or according to the market socialism blueprint – the quest for a society more humane and egalitarian than standard capitalism remains. But then we are in the realm of politics. *Sozialmarktwirtschaft,* German style, is a market economy tempered by basic social policies, not a socialist model.

THE END OF THE JOURNEY: WHEN IS TRANSITION OVER?

Now the collapse of communism is behind us, and a new world is emerging. When shall we stop talking about 'countries in transition'? If words are meaningful, then transition should be transitory. But for how long? Should its temporary character absolve us from trying to analyse it theoretically? A second question is practical. If the countries in transition are not yet fully-fledged market economies, what still needs to be done in order for them to qualify as such, and when shall we know that transition is over?

Is Transition an Identifiable Stage, or State, or Process?

In the beginning of transition, it has been asked whether theory might help (see Aghion, 1993; Roland, 1993; Weitzman, 1993). Does transition deserve a Grand Theory indeed?

Various analytical frameworks have been used to account for the kind of market economy which is emerging in the countries in transition. Because transformation is obviously very much affected by political factors, one group of analysts used the framework of *public choice theory*, which applies the tools of the economist to non-market decision-making (see Murrell, 1991, and the whole issue of the *Journal of Comparative Economics,* June 1991, devoted to this topic). As enterprise is often viewed as the core element of the transformation process, the contemporary developments of the *theory of the firm* are called upon (property rights, transaction costs, industrial organisation theory, incentives theory, principal/agent, etc.; see Frydman and Rapaczynski, 1994; Yavlinsky and Braguinsky, 1994). Problems of decision-making within organisations in a context of bounded rationality are typically faced by Eastern European and Russian managers. Strategic behaviour, and asymmetric access to information are investigated through case studies (Charap and Webster, 1993) and are theorised (Mayhew and Seabright, 1992; Frydman *et al.,* 1993a; Wijnbergen, 1993), usually with policy recommendations.

The *institutional approach* takes a broader view (see Jackson, 1992a). Within this current, the *evolutionary theory* appears the most controverted, first because it already raises much argument within the capitalist context, and second because it is wrongly confused with a standard 'gradualist' approach. The evolutionary theory as applied to transition economy has been elaborated by Peter Murrell in numerous articles (1992; 1993 with Yijiang Wang; and, more polemical, 1995). This approach does not provide clear insights into what will happen next, once the market structures are established (probably because it assumes that these structures will allow for the market to operate as in standard developed market systems). What is going to happen during the supposedly rather long time when the state-owned enterprises will be in operation?

To this question, one may answer: a country in transition is a mixed economy, whether it likes it or not. Such an assertion is usually seen as insulting to these countries. Alternatively, it is a judgement over the uncompletedness of the process in the countries which have not yet wholly disengaged themselves from the old system (for example, Romania, Ukraine, the Central Asian states, etc.). The idea of a mixed economy is rooted in that of market socialism, which is seen as an unacceptable or unrealistic concept. However, one can hardly question the fact that for the time being these economies are 'mixed' in the sense that they carry on a specific inertia of the former system (Nuti, 1993), and also that they are 'mutant', which turns them into 'monsters' that are not coherent either with the logic of the former system or with the target system (Nuti, 1996b). Along with residuals from the past, there are missing pieces that should belong to a 'normal' market economy, such as market infrastructures and an efficient state administration, and there are also pathological features that developed so as to fill the vacuum left by the missing institutions. Such features include rent-seeking that is confused with sound profit-seeking, organised crime, and what Nuti calls 'employeeism', a kind of populism fuelled by the fact that privatisation has largely been based on shares distribution to the workers of the former state-owned firms and that insiders' control dominates.

A French economist, Bernard Chavance (1994), is rather pessimistic about what he calls 'the mixed post-socialist transition economy'. His 'grey scenario' foresees a rather inert state sector, with a stagnant production, low modernisation and continuous disinvestment. The government tries to avoid bankruptcies for fear of social explosion. The private sector is burdened by the existence of the public sector which crowds it out. Social expenditures are decreasing except for unemployment benefits. Investment is low and deterred by high taxes. International competitiveness is weakened. A more 'rosy' scenario should, according to the author, imply a more interventionist role for the state, with an active industrial and agricultural policy, a voluntarist employment and regional policy.

From all these studies it may be derived that transition is a transitory, rather unstable state, which may however last longer than expected if nothing is done – hence the normativist and voluntarist tone of a large part of the literature on transition. Scenarios are not neutral. In any case, one has to get out of the transitional state.

What Is To Be Done?

Policy advice is numerous, and authoritative when it is provided by institutions or organisations that detain access to money or to an upgraded status such as membership. For the applicants to the EU, the compelling requests of the Commission define what is to be done so as to successfully achieve the transition process. As the EBRD experts state in the 1997 *Transition Report*, 'the conditions for successful transition and for meeting the requirements of membership in the EU are similar' (EBRD, 1997, p. 7; also see Table 8.3 in Chapter 8). The conditionality of international financial institutions is also directly translated into instructions, and the 'Washington Consensus' may be seen as a recipe for good behaviour which should not only trigger grants or loans but also the delivery of a 'normality' label. When it comes to be admitted to 'clubs' such as the OECD or the EU the conditions are more detailed and there is a permanent follow-up of their implementation along with additional advice and critics.

We have already looked at these numerous conditions and recommendations in the three previous chapters. Beyond detailed advice on macro-economic policy, or micro-economic transformation rules governing international relations, is it possible to identify a set of more general, or systemic, tasks? An increasing number of authors – academics, experts, policy-makers – have been calling for a greater role for the state. More generally, the importance of institutions is underlined (Taylor, 1994), which leads to a more general 'political economy' approach to the reform (Ellman, 1997a; Williamson, 1994; Roland, 1994; Dewatripont and Roland, 1996). Dewatripont and Roland, after underlining that 'no pre-established theory of transition existed before the fall of the Berlin Wall' (1996, p. 1), see transition as 'a general process of large-scale institutional change' (p. 3). In the same vein, Shleifer (1997, p. 388) notes that not enough attention was paid 'to the basic element of transition: the transition of government from the communist police state to an institution supporting a market economy'. According to him, the inability of the Russian government to make this transition – at the local and central levels – contrary to what the Polish government did, explains the failures of Russia as compared with the Polish success.

Transitologists ride on the wave of the reassessing of the state. The World Bank, after devoting an issue of its *World Development Report* (World Bank, 1996) to the transition 'from Plan to Market', dealt with 'The State in a Changing World' in its next *World Development Report* (World Bank, 1997). True, in the report the state is chiefly meant to help to enhance the role of the market, through liberalisation, together with some regulation and 'walking the industrial policy tightrope' (World Bank, 1997, p. 74: 'implemented badly, activist industrial policy can be a disaster'). The recommendations to the countries in transition include 'the job of reorienting the state towards the task of 'steering, not rowing', . . . far from complete in Central and Eastern Europe' (p. 164). In fact, there are two quite different visions of the state, that develop from the same initial assessment of the 'state failure' (Ellman, 1995, p. 219) in a communist regime. In the neo-liberal, dominant view (as far as advice to countries in transition is concerned), the state is meant to build market institutions and to enforce the rule of law (e.g. to make people and enterprises pay taxes, avoid illegal ways of settling business conflicts, etc.). In a more interventionist approach, the state is also to conduct an active economic policy, and here the example of the East Asian countries in the early stages of their development is quoted (Ellman, 1994, p. 232), but immediately raises the objection that the East Asian model contradicts the requirements for democracy.

A specific requirement for the countries in transition is that they should fight corruption. The EBRD report (1997) bluntly asks why the transition countries exhibit such high levels of corruption in comparison with other countries (p. 37), and whether this is rooted in the transition process itself, or in the legacies from the past. The answer is that corruption of officials is 'a means of hedging against the risks associated with the instability of government policy' (p. 39), as was largely the case under central planning. In the IMF-World Bank journal *Finance and Development* a study underlines not only the motivations (declining civil servants' salaries, lack of an appropriate social safety net) but also the numerous opportunities to engage in corruption in countries with lax regulations. Again, the recipe would be economic liberalisation and privatisation along with the enforcement of prudential banking regulations and the reform of tax administration and of the civil service (Gray and Kaufmann, 1998). Is indeed privatisation an opportunity for increased corruption, or the best protection against it? The liberal view is that it is not privatisation per se, but the failure to privatise quickly, which breeds corruption (Kaufmann and Siegelbaum, 1996). Conversely, one may consider that privatisation offers many opportunities for corruption: here again, one may argue about the privatisation methods that are most conducive to corruption. Kaufmann and Siegelbaum argue that swift methods such as voucher privatisation prevent corruption much more efficiently than gradual privatisation in the form of direct sales or tenders. One could object that what matters is the final outcome of quick privatisation: the Czech and Russian examples show that corruption and outright crime emerge after voucher distribution. Philip Hanson, discussing 'the sort of capitalism [that] is developing in Russia' (1997), explains corruption as a result of the weak rule of law, the weak public administration and the lack of transparency of the new capital markets in Russia, that also go back to a 'deficit of "social capital" in Russian society', rooted in history not unlike the origins of the Mafia in Italy (Hanson, 1997, p. 39).

What is to be done, and how to do it, is by no means clear. The strength of the Washington consensus is that the policies which it recommends are translatable either in quantitative guidelines (for inflation, fiscal deficits, etc.) or in non-intervention (the government must deregulate, liberalise, and let the markets operate). As Joseph Stiglitz puts it, the ideas advocating a greater involvement of the state 'are not easy to articulate as dogma nor to implement as policy' (Stiglitz, 1998, p. z7). The duration of the process is not clear either. One may as well claim that it will take time (Ellman,1997a; Kozul-Wright and Rayment,1997), and that it is already over, at least in Central Europe.

When Is Transition Over?

A straightforward answer to the question would be: when a young German, or British, tourist walking in the streets of Budapest or Vilnius would never be reminded that once this was a different world. A more sophisticated way to put it is to say that transition will be over when developments in these countries 'erase the economic connotations of the adjective *western European*' (Murrell, 1996, p. 41). My personal answer would be that, as the European Union requires that its members be 'functioning market economies', all the countries admitted into the EU would have by definition completed their transition. But what about those left out of the accession process? There is a kind of unexpressed consensus on this issue. Russia is a great power and a heterogenous nation. Moscow (to a lesser extent, Saint Petersburg or Nizhny Novgorod) has been likened to a 'tiger', if not a 'dragon'; its businessmen are equal partners to their most sophisticated counterparts in the West. The remote provinces of Russia are ages behind. Central Asian states are closer to the Middle East region in terms of development and societal features. The former Yugoslavia and Albania are still a black hole.

What has been said above assumes that transition is a process leading from plan to market. Very few people have mentioned that it could also be a process leading from under-development to development (Matejka, 1997). Actually the much disparaged Walter Rostow was the first economist to our knowledge to use the word 'transition' in qualifying the preconditions for the take-off (the second of his five stages of economic growth) as the 'transitional stage' (Rostow, 1960), and indeed in the 1960s it was acknowledged that the LDCs (less developed countries, in the parlance of that time) were in a stage of 'transition'. Laski and Badhuri (1997, p. 103) ask whether the strategy advocated for Central and Eastern Europe would be identical if the collapse had happened 20 years earlier. In fact, a forgotten economist has asked the question, not about 20 years ago, but about 60 years ago. This economist, Rosenstein-Rodan, is considered as the father of development economics, a much discredited branch of economics now. He published in 1943 (Rosenstein-Rodan, 1943) the seminal article on development economics – which dealt with Eastern and South-Eastern Europe, 'the whole area between Germany, Russia and Italy'. He was concerned about what would happen in the region after the end of the war, which he assumed would be won by the Allies as he expected war reparations from Germany. He believed that this region would not follow the Russian way, either politically, or even economically (by developing heavy industries and aiming at self-sufficiency). He proposed a pattern of industrialisation based on labour-intensive industries and sustained by international funding through an 'Eastern European Industrial Trust'. The word 'transition' is to be found in the article – but here meaning the phase between end of war and establishment of peaceful conditions. What the article conveys is that this part of the world needed to be developed so as to fit into the international division of labour.

This requirement is still valid. But we have not been used to looking at the former socialist countries as developing countries, which they certainly were in the beginning of the transition. The transition embodied in the Washington consensus was indeed borrowed from the set of policies applied in the inflation-plagued Latin American countries in the 1980s. This package was, however, not meant to ensure growth. Growth concerns came later, after output had fallen much more dramatically than expected. They were soon dismissed by the assumption that sound macro-economic policies and commitment to the market would ensure sustainable growth. In fact, while transition from plan to market may be considered as more or less completed, transition from a low level and a distorted pattern of development to the average level and pattern of Western Europe is largely overlooked. Experts have tried to assess in how many years the various countries in transition, especially in Central and Eastern Europe, might reach the Western European level. The estimates range from at least twenty years to several decades. The Bretton Woods institutions usually link the duration of catching-up with two sets of variables. The first set of variables is related to the transformation process and assumes that the faster-growing countries are those who were quickest to complete stabilisation and liberalisation (Fisher *et al.*, 1996). The second set of variables is derived from standard neoclassical and endogenous growth models (investment ratio, government consumption in GDP, and human capital indicators). Using several such models Fisher *et al.* (1998) come to the conclusion that the CEECs would need on average 30 years to converge to the per capita income level of the three lowest income countries in the European Union, with annual rates of growth in the range of 4.5 to 6 per cent (assuming EU low-income countries would grow by an annual rate of 3 per cent). Such forecasts do not take into account external shocks, reversals in policies and other unforeseeable events as they are based on an 'all other things being equal' assumption. As the 1997 *World Development Report* (1997, p. 147) rightly states: 'long-term stagnation and rising poverty . . . cannot be ruled out for some countries'. In this sense, transition may well never be over.

11 Conclusion

Salt is good; but if the salt have lost his savour, wherewith shall it be seasoned?

(Holy Bible, King James Version, St Luke, 14:34)

What is the impact of the transition on *us*? Isn't it indecent to ask the question when the transition directly and direly affects millions of people in their everyday lives? But isn't it also an implicit question that goes beyond the assistance programmes to the countries involved, the moral support, and the interest of the general public? We have to reconsider our own system, our values, our future. It also leads to a reconsideration of the relations between the developed and the developing world. North–South (i.e. West–South) relations were simpler when communism ruled a part of the world. Inadequate as they were, it could always be pointed out that East–South relations did not bring about a better solution for enhancing development. The transition is the end of a war, which was described as 'cold'. A symposium in 1992 was aptly devoted to the *Economic Consequences of the East*, an allusion to the famous book by Keynes published in 1919, *The Economic Consequences of Peace* (CEPR, 1992a). How will the world look once transition is over, if it ever is? This a new story, no longer about transition, but about the future of capitalism. As Lester Thurow writes: 'With the end of communism . . . those already living under capitalism will find that digesting this mass of humanity and geography profoundly alters the shape of their economic world' (Thurow, 1996, p. 8).

A SMALL ECONOMIC IMPACT

The change of regime has had immediate *ideological* consequences (Chirot, 1991). It has discredited the Left all over the world, and turned socialism into a dirty world. While communism is still strong in some Asiatic countries and in Cuba, the African-type Marxist ideologies have promptly collapsed – true, the latter were a camouflage for personal or tribal dictatorship still very much alive. In the West, the communist parties had to adapt through restructuring and renaming, and could not avoid losing ground. The non-communist left lost credibility as well, though endorsing many of the right-wing policy schemes. The right-wing parties and ideas benefited in the short term, but quickly realised that the loss of their main opponent and scapegoat might entail some perils in the future.

In *international politics*, the transition has led to a reconsideration of the whole security system. It has weakened the defensive international organisations and first of all NATO, which has ultimately decided to expand to the East by offering membership to the Central European countries. The transition has shaken the military–industrial complexes in all big countries. The foreign policy schemes which had been developed with a view to fighting, deterring or containing communism were suddenly out of date. The new ethnic or nationalistic conflicts have taken the West by surprise and have not triggered an adequate response.

By comparison, the economic impact has been very weak. Prospects are dim, in terms of opportunities, threats or risks. Foreign investors expect large potential returns but have committed little capital in terms of overall world foreign direct investment. Exporters have lost their routines; those who were familiar with state-trading ways had to adjust and find new partners. New exporters, among them small and medium enterprises, found they could take advantage of new niches, and sometimes struck very good deals. As a whole the Western world has maintained surpluses in trade with the countries in transition, and has not been flooded with cheap Eastern goods. Assistance to transition did not hurt the Western taxpayer much except in Germany, which paid large amounts of money for recovering its unity. It benefited a host of suppliers of goods and services, non-profit institutions, advice-givers, and money-makers of all kinds. Losses from transition were small in the West. Some sectoral interests claimed they were hurt, such as farmers or steelmakers; in fact losses directly due to Eastern exports were compounded with the impact of global recession and growing structural inefficiencies in these sensitive sectors in the West itself. The West did not suffer from a large-scale influx of immigrants from the East despite its fears. The only exception is Germany, but in this case the first wave was migration from Eastern to Western Germany before and after reunification, and from 'ethnic Germans' from further East. The transition process only began to alter the balance between the three main countries, the United States, Germany and Japan, in terms of economic power.

Did the South ('Third World') lose from the transition? The 'crowding out' effect is dubious. It is not evidenced that assistance to the East reduced funding available to the South. The argument is used on both sides: by the developing countries, to support the claims for help, and by the donors, as an excuse for not granting enough assistance.

The international economic organisations got increased responsibilities in the process. The European Community was the most involved as an overall coordinator of assistance, and as a negotiator of new relations between its members and the countries in transition. It had to alter earlier visions about its own evolution in terms of deepening and enlargement. The IMF strengthened its role in economic governance of the world.

The main 'economic consequences of the East' are still ahead, and ambivalent. The optimists contend that the recession in the East has bottomed out. The market will be successfully implemented. The 'green shoots' of the private sector are visible everywhere and will soon be blooming. The pessimists see a protracted recession, little structural change, and seeds of conflict and disorganisation on top of open wars in some areas of the CIS and in Yugoslavia. Capitalism has won. Moreover, it is now largely free from critics, as the questioning of its failures, in terms of social injustice or inequality in income distribution, can immediately be discarded as a resurgence of communist ideology.

THERE IS ONLY ONE WORLD

The new post-communist world is divided among developed and developing countries. The countries in transition belong to the second group, though without readily acknowledging this reality. Some may grow into members of the first. For most, there is still a long way to go.

The global market economy is regulated by a small number of countries or groups of countries which influence the domestic developments in the others through the enforcement of adjustment programmes drafted on a similar model, under the guidance of the leading international economic organisations. Within the industrialised countries' governments, big business and big finance interact; among them conflicts are solved by the same decision-making forces through cooperative or non-cooperative strategies. Capitalism no longer has competitors from outside.

Global capitalism is, however, insecure. It is pervaded by economic crime, financial volatility, environmental deterioration, and social threats as sluggish growth fuels unemployment and poverty. Sometimes sudden crises erupt, such as the East Asian financial crisis in 1997 or the Russian crisis in 1998. Big countries and global fire-fighting institutions such as the IMF rush to put the flames out. All these threats suddenly loom very large now that the threat of global confrontation between communism and the free world has vanished. What if the limited (in time and space) transition in the East was but the prelude to a world-wide transition, or to the 'big one' (the earthquake that rocks the system) as Thurow (1996, p. 328) puts it? The countries in transition do know where they want to go. We are all now on the same boat; we know how to make it float but we don't know how to steer it.

Statistical Appendix

Table A.1   Eastern Europe and the USSR: Exports and Imports by Direction, 1975, 1980, 1986, 1989

	1975 *(values, billion US $)*	1975 *(per cent)*	1980 *(values, billion US$)*	1980 *(per cent)*	1986 *(values, billion US$)*	1986 *(per cent)*	1989 *(values, billion US$)*	1989 *(per cent)*
Bulgaria								
Total exports	4.7	100.0	10.4	100.0	14.1	100.0	16.0	100.0
East	3.5	74.6	6.9	66.4	11.3	79.6	13.3	83.0
West	0.6	11.7	1.9	18.5	1.1	7.8	1.3	8.2
Other	0.6	13.6	1.6	15.1	1.8	12.6	1.4	8.7
Total imports	5.4	100.0	9.7	100.0	15.2	100.0	15.2	100.0
East	3.7	68.7	7.3	75.4	11.3	74.1	10.9	71.5
West	1.4	25.0	1.8	18.5	2.5	16.4	2.7	18.1
Other	0.3	6.3	0.6	6.1	1.4	9.5	1.6	10.3
Czechoslovakia								
Total exports	8.4	100.0	14.9	100.0	‖ 12.2	100.0	14.5	100.0
East	5.5	65.4	9.5	63.4	6.7	55.1	7.8	53.7
West	2.0	23.6	3.8	25.6	3.8	30.6	5.0	34.4
Other	0.9	11.0	1.6	11.0	1.8	14.3	1.7	11.9
Total imports	9.1	100.0	15.2	100.0	‖ 12.4	100.0	14.3	100.0
East	5.9	64.4	9.8	64.8	7.2	58.3	7.8	54.8
West	2.5	27.7	4.2	27.7	3.9	31.3	4.9	34.2
Other	0.7	7.8	1.1	7.5	1.3	10.4	1.6	11.0
GDR								
Total exports	10.4	100.0	18.6	100.0	‖ 16.4	100.0	17.3	100.0
East	6.8	65.5	11.1	59.4	7.0	42.9	7.2	41.7
West	2.9	27.4	5.9	31.5	7.7	46.9	8.7	50.1
Other	0.7	7.1	1.7	7.1	1.7	10.2	1.4	8.2
Total imports	11.7	100.0	20.3	100.0	‖ 16.1	100.0	17.8	100.0
East	7.1	60.5	11.3	55.5	7.6	47.0	6.8	38.1
West	3.9	33.4	7.5	36.9	7.1	44.0	9.8	54.8
Other	0.7	6.0	1.5	7.6	1.5	9.1	1.2	7.0
Hungary								
Total exports	6.1	100.0	‖ 8.6	100.0	9.2	100.0	9.7	100.0
East	4.1	67.7	4.3	50.3	5.0	54.0	4.0	41.0
West	1.5	23.9	3.3	38.0	3.2	34.8	4.6	48.0
Other	0.5	8.6	1.0	11.7	1.0	11.3	1.1	11.1
Total imports	7.2	100.0	‖ 9.2	100.0	9.6	100.0	8.9	100.0
East	4.5	62.7	4.3	46.9	4.9	50.8	3.5	39.2
West	2.0	28.4	3.9	42.2	3.9	40.4	4.7	52.9
Other	0.6	9.0	1.0	11.0	0.9	8.9	0.7	7.8

Table continued overleaf

281

Statistical Appendix

Table A.1 continued

	1975 (values, billion US $)	1975 (per cent)	1980 (values, billion US$)	1980 (per cent)	1986 (values, billion US$)	1986 (per cent)	1989 (values, billion US$)	1989 (per cent)
Poland								
Total exports	10.3	100.0	17.0	100.0	‖ 12.1	100.0	12.9	100.0
East	5.8	56.6	8.9	52.3	5.6	46.1	4.5	34.8
West	3.5	33.9	6.2	36.5	4.6	37.7	6.8	52.7
Other	1.0	9.5	1.9	11.2	2.0	16.2	1.6	12.5
Total imports	12.6	100.0	19.1	100.0	‖ 11.2	100.0	11.3	100.0
East	5.5	43.4	12.1	63.2	6.1	54.3	3.6	32.1
West	6.3	50.3	6.9	36.2	4.1	36.4	6.4	56.5
Other	0.8	6.2	2.1	11.0	1.0	9.3	1.3	11.4
Romania								
Total exports	5.3	100.0	11.4	100.0	‖ 9.8	100.0	11.3	100.0
East	2.0	38.2	4.2	37.2	4.0	41.4	4.6	40.5
West	2.0	38.0	4.4	38.5	3.4	35.1	4.3	37.7
Other	1.3	23.8	2.8	24.3	2.3	23.5	2.5	22.0
Total imports	5.3	100.0	13.2	100.0	‖ 8.1	100.0	10.5	100.0
East	2.0	36.9	4.1	30.7	4.4	55.0	4.0	38.5
West	2.4	44.8	4.4	33.0	1.6	19.9	4.3	41.2
Other	1.0	18.5	4.8	36.3	2.0	25.1	2.1	20.2
Eastern Europe								
Total exports	45.2	100.0	80.9	100.0	74.7	100.0	81.1	100.0
East	27.8	61.5	44.9	55.5	39.6	52.9	40.8	50.4
West	12.3	27.3	25.5	31.5	23.7	31.7	31.0	38.2
Other	5.1	11.2	10.6	13.1	10.7	14.3	9.5	11.7
Total imports	51.2	100.0	86.7	100.0	72.6	100.0	75.9	100.0
East	28.6	55.7	46.8	54.0	41.5	57.1	37.0	48.8
West	18.5	36.1	28.6	33.1	23.0	31.7	29.6	39.0
Other	4.2	8.1	11.2	12.9	8.1	11.2	9.3	12.2
USSR								
Total exports	33.3	100.0	76.5	100.0	96.9	100.0	‖ 109.1	100.0
East	16.4	49.4	32.2	42.1	51.0	52.6	50.4	46.2
West	9.6	28.9	28.1	36.8	21.2	21.9	29.6	27.1
Other	7.2	21.7	16.1	21.1	24.8	25.5	29.2	26.7
Total imports	36.9	100.0	68.5	100.0	88.9	100.0	‖ 114.5	100.0
East	15.7	42.4	29.4	42.9	47.3	53.2	56.8	49.6
West	14.1	38.2	25.7	37.5	25.6	28.8	36.0	31.4
Other	7.2	19.4	13.4	19.6	16.0	18.0	21.7	18.9

It is usually said that Eastern European countries had an extremely large share of their total trade within the CMEA, expressing their 'block autarky' (see Lavigne, 1991, p. 14). The average usually quoted is 60 per cent of that total. Table A.1 shows that in 1989 the average share of the 'East' (mainly Comecon) for Eastern Europe was 50 per cent, and was still lower for the USSR. The only country with an overwhelming share (over 70 per cent) was Bulgaria. Also, the table shows that for most countries at some point the share of trade with the CMEA suddenly decreased (it would have been still more obvious over a continuous sequence of years).

The reason why it is so difficult to estimate the shares of the CMEA (hence the share of the West) and moreover to compare the countries from this point of view, is that trade was not measured in comparable units.

Non-socialist trade was conducted in convertible currencies. As socialist trade was mainly conducted within the CMEA, it was expressed in transferable rubles, a unit of account which one may, with some approximation, equate to the Soviet foreign trade unit of account, i.e. the 'devisa-ruble'. The devisa-ruble was linked to the dollar and other convertible currencies by an official exchange rate. This exchange rate was initially derived from the official gold parity of the ruble, an arbitrary figure last set up in 1961 in order to convey the idea that the ruble was 'stronger' than the dollar (in 1961, 1 'devisa-ruble' = 1.11 dollars). Later, when the official gold parity of the dollar was terminated, this official exchange rate was calculated on the basis of a basket of Western currencies. It had no relation to the domestic purchasing power of the ruble; it was a pure unit of account. As the official ruble/dollar rate was overvaluing the ruble, it follows that the share of the trade flows conducted in rubles was significantly overestimated.

Each socialist country had foreign trade statistics denominated in its own, non-convertible currency. These currencies also had official exchange rates against the Western currencies and against the ruble. Gradually Eastern European countries moved toward more 'realistic' exchange rates, calculated as the export purchasing power parity, i.e. the average amount of domestic currency (in domestic wholesale prices) which had to be spent in production costs in order to obtain one unit of a convertible currency, or a 'devisa' (transferable) ruble. These rates were fixed by the Eastern European countries without any coordination among them, which brought about increasing difficulties in comparing foreign trade statistics, as the resulting ruble/dollar cross-rates were widely diverging. In addition, these new rates were introduced at different periods. Their introduction immediately brought about a discontinuity in statistics, expressed by the sign ‖ in the table. The discontinuity is due to the fact that the new 'commercial rates' amounted to a strong 'devaluation' of the ruble against the dollar (and all other convertible currencies) which immediately led to an increase in the share of trade with the 'West' and a fall in trade with the 'East'. No attempt was made to correct the previous trade figures.

Source: Calculations from ECE/UN, Economic Survey of Europe in 1990–1991, appendix tables C.4 and C.5.

'East' refers to East European country members of the CMEA and the Soviet Union; 'West' refers to Western European countries, North America and Japan.

Table A.2   Macroeconomic indicators of countries in transition, 1989–1997

	1989	1990
Poland		
GDP (average annual rate of change, in per cent)	0.2	−11.6
GDP per capita in US$ (current rate of exchange)	—	1630
GDP per capita in US$ (in PPP)	—	n.a.
GDP index (1989 = 100)	100	88
Gross industrial output (index, 1989 = 100)	100	76
Gross investment (index, 1989 = 100)	100	75
Consumer prices (annual rate of change, end-year)	640.0	289.0
Number of registered unemployed, end-year, in thousands	—	1126
Unemployed in per cent of the labour force	—	6.5
Real wages, CPI-based, index (1990 = 100)	—	100
Budget balance (in per cent of GDP)	−6.1	0.7
Trade balance (in bn$)	1.7	5.7
Current account balance (in bn$)	—	0.7
Net debt in convertible currencies (bn$, end-year)	—	44.0
Hungary		
GDP (average annual rate of change, in per cent)	−0.2	−3.3
GDP per capita in US$ (current rate of exchange)	—	3179
GDP per capita in US$ (in PPP)	—	n.a.
GDP index (1989 = 100)	100	97
Gross industrial output (index, 1989 = 100)	100	91
Gross investment (index, 1989 = 100)	100	93
Consumer prices (annual rate of change, end-year)	17.0	33.4
Number of registered unemployed, end-year, in thousands	—	80
Unemployed in per cent of the labour force	—	1.7
Real wages, CPI-based, index (1990 = 100)	—	100
Budget balance (in per cent of GDP)	−1.3	−0.1
Trade balance (in bn$)	0.8	0.9
Current account balance in convertible currencies (bn$)	—	0.1
Net debt in convertible currencies (bn$, end-year)	—	20.2
Czech Republic		
GDP (average annual rate of change, in per cent)	1.4	−1.2
GDP per capita in US$ (current rate of exchange)	—	3126
GDP per capita in US$ (in PPP)	—	n.a.
GDP index (1989 = 100)	100	99
Gross industrial output (index, 1989 = 100)	100	97
Gross investment (index, 1989 = 100)	100	98
Consumer prices (annual rate of change, end-year)	1.4	18.4
Number of unemployed, end-year, in thousands	—	39
Unemployed in per cent of the labour force	—	0.7
Real wages, CPI-based, index (1990 = 100)	—	100
Budget balance (in per cent of GDP)	−2.4	−0.3
Trade balance (in bn$)	—	—
Current account balance in convertible currencies (bn$)	—	−0.1
Net debt in convertible currencies (bn$, end-year)	—	4.0

1991	*1992*	*1993*	*1994*	*1995*	*1996*	*1997* (preliminary)
−7.6	1.5	4.5	5.2	7.0	6.1	6.9
2037	2197	2234	2399	3055	3459	n.a.
n.a.	n.a.	n.a.	n.a.	5400	n.a.	n.a.
82	84	88	92	99	105	112
67	69	74	83	91	98	110
72	74	76	83	97	117	142
60.4	44.3	37.6	29.4	21.6	18.5	14.5
256	2509	2890	2838	2629	2360	1826
11.5	13.6	16.4	16.0	14.9	13.2	10.5
102.9	98.7	99.4	104.3	105.9	112.1	117.0
−3.5	−6.1	−3.4	−2.8	−3.6	−3.1	−4.0
−0.6	−3.0	−4.6	−4.3	−6.2	−12.7	−16.0
−1.4	−0.3	−2.3	−0.9	−2.5	(rev. after 1995)	
		(see note a)		5.5	−0.4	−4.3
44.8	43.1	43.3	36.4	29.2	22.8	17.7
−11.9	−3.0	−0.8	2.9	1.5	1.3	4.0
3242	3617	3748	4069	4286	4357	n.a.
n.a.	n.a.	n.a.	n.a.	6410	n.a.	n.a.
85	82	82	84	86	87	90
74	67	70	76	80	82	92
83	81	83	93	89	94	—
32.2	21.6	21.1	21.2	28.3	19.8	17.0
406	663	632	520	496	479	464
7.4	12.3	12.1	10.9	10.4	10.5	10.4
98.8	99.9	101.6	103.5	97.5	96.0	98.7
−4.6	−7.4	−7.5	−8.2	−6.5	−3.5	−5.0
−1.2	−0.4	−3.7	−3.9	−2.6	−2.4	−2.0
0.3	0.3	−3.5	−3.9	−2.5	−1.7	−1.0
18.7	17.1	17.9	21.8	19.7	17.9	14.4
−14.2	−6.6	−0.9	2.6	5.9	4.1	1.0
2466	2903	332	3853	4814	5340	n.a.
n.a.	n.a.	n.a.	n.a.	9770	n.a.	n.a.
87	85	85	87	93	96	98
73	67	64	65	71	72	74
81	88	81	95	116	126	—
52.0	12.7	18.2	9.7	7.9	8.6	9.0
222	135	185	167	153	186	269
4.1	2.6	3.5	3.2	2.9	3.5	5.2
74.3	81.0	82.2	87.3	94.7	102.3	106.1
−1.9	0.0	0.1	0.8	0.4	−0.2	−1.0
—	−1.6	−0.2	−1.2	−3.6	−5.8	−4.4
1.7	−0.5	−0.1	−0.7	−1.4	−4.3	−3.2
7.0	6.8	5.8	6.1	3.3	8.8	11.5

Table continued overleaf

Table A.2 continued

	1989	1990
Slovak Republic		
GDP (average annual rate of change, in per cent)	1.4	−2.5
GDP per capita in US$ (current rate of exchange)	—	2710
GDP per capita in US$ (in PPP)	—	n.a.
GDP index (1989 = 100)	100	98
Gross industrial output (index, 1989 = 100)	100	96
Gross investment (index, 1989 = 100)	—	100
Consumer prices (annual rate of change, end-year)	1.4	18.4
Number of registered unemployed, end-year, in thousands	—	37
Unemployed in per cent of the labour force	—	1.5
Real wages, CPI-based, index (1990 = 100)	—	100
Budget balance (in per cent of GDP)	−2.4	−0.3
Trade balance (in bn$)	—	—
Current account balance in convertible currencies (bn$)	—	−0.8
Net debt in convertible currencies (bn$, end-year)	—	1.9
Slovenia		
GDP (average annual rate of change, in per cent)	−0.5	−4.7
GDP per capita in US$ (current rate of exchange)	—	8706
GDP per capita in US$ (in PPP)	—	n.a.
GDP index (1989 = 100)	100	92
Gross industrial output (index, 1989 = 100)	100	90
Gross investment (index, 1989 = 100)	—	100
Consumer prices (annual rate of change, end-year)	1000.0	105.0
Number of registered unemployed, end-year, in thousands	—	—
Unemployed in per cent of the labour force	—	—
Real wages, CPI-based, index (1990 = 100)	—	100
Budget balance (in per cent of GDP)	n.a.	−0.3
Trade balance (in bn$)	0.2	−0.6
Current account balance in convertible currencies (bn$)	—	0.5
Net debt in convertible currencies (bn$, end-year)	—	1.9
Bulgaria		
GDP (average annual rate of change, in per cent)	−0.3	−9.1
GDP per capita in US$ (current rate of exchange)	—	1343
GDP per capita in US$ (in PPP)	—	n.a.
GDP index (1989 = 100)	100	91
Gross industrial output (index, 1989 = 100)	100	83
Gross investment (index, 1989 = 100)	100	100
Consumer prices (annual rate of change, end-year)	6.2	72.5
Number of registered unemployed, end-year, in thousands	—	65
Unemployed in per cent of the labour force	—	1.7
Real wages, CPI-based, index (1990 = 100)	—	100.0
Budget balance (in per cent of GDP)	−0.6	−4.0
Trade balance (in bn$)	−0.7	−0.4
Current account balance in convertible currencies (bn$)	—	−1.7
Net debt in convertible currencies (bn$, end-year)	—	10.9

1991	1992	1993	1994	1995	1996	1997 (preliminary)
−14.5	−6.1	−4.7	4.8	7.3	6.9	6.5
2046	2216	2258	2576	3230	3525	2596
n.a.	6396	6285	6712	7320	7970	n.a.
83	78	75	79	84	90	96
77	70	68	71	77	79	81
75	72	69	65	65	86	—
58.3	9.1	25.1	11.7	7.2	5.4	7.0
302	260	368	372	339	330	348
11.8	10.4	14.4	14.8	13.1	12.8	12.5
71.3	76.5	75.3	78.1	82.2	88.2	93.0
−1.9	−2.8	−5.5	−1.3	0.1	−1.2	−3.5
—	−0.4	−0.9	−0.1	−0.2	−2.3	−0.5
−0.8	0.2	−0.6	0.7	0.6	−2.1	−1.5
2.1	2.5	3.3	2.7	2.5	4.4	6.8
−9.3	−6.0	1.3	5.3	4.1	3.1	3.3
6330	6261	6336	7193	9372	9279	n.a.
n.a.	n.a.	n.a.	9946.0	10594	n.a.	n.a.
84	79	81	86	89	92	95
78	68	66	70	72	73	73
89	77	85	96	113	—	—
247.0	93.0	22.9	18.3	8.6	8.8	8.8
91	118	137	124	127	125	129
10.1	13.3	15.4	14.2	14.5	14.4	14.8
77.4	75.5	82.9	87.9	91.2	96.1	98.4
2.6	0.2	0.3	−0.2	0.0	0.3	−1.0
−0.3	0.5	−0.4	−0.5	−1.2	−1.1	−1.0
0.1	0.9	0.2	0.6	−0.0	0.0	0.1
0.8	1.0	1.1	0.8	1.2	1.7	1.0
−11.7	−7.3	−1.5	1.8	2.1	−10.9	−7.4
872	1012	1276	1157	1538	1038	n.a.
n.a.	4112	4193	4377	4588	4190	n.a.
80	74	73	75	76	69	63
65	54	49	53	57	53	49
80	74	61	62	72	56	—
338.9	79.4	63.9	121.9	32.9	311.0	591.5
419	577	626	488	424	478	524
11.5	15.6	16.4	12.8	11.1	12.5	13.7
62.8	76.5	68.6	53.8	52.3	45.7	41.2
−3.5	−6.1	−11.9	−5.8	−6.4	−13.4	−6.3
0.7	−0.5	−1.0	−0.2	−0.3	−0.2	−0.4
−0.1	−0.4	−1.1	−0.0	−0.0	0.0	0.4
11.5	12.1	13.2	10.4	9.3	9.1	7.9

Table continued overleaf

Table A.2 continued

	1989	1990
Romania		
GDP (average annual rate of change, in per cent)	−5.8	−8.2
GDP per capita in US$ (current rate of exchange)	—	1257
GDP per capita in US$ (in PPP)	—	n.a.
GDP index (1989 = 100)	100	94
Gross industrial output (index, 1989 = 100)	100	82
Gross investment (index, 1989 = 100)	100	64
Consumer prices (annual rate of change, end-year)	0.9	37.7
Number of registered unemployed, end-year, in thousands	—	—
Unemployed in per cent of the labour force	—	—
Real wages, CPI-based, index (1990 = 100)	—	100
Budget balance (in per cent of GDP)	8.2	1.0
Trade balance (in bn$)	2.2	−2.3
Current account balance in convertible currencies (bn$)	—	−1.7
Net debt in convertible currencies (bn$, end-year)	—	0.6
Estonia		
GDP (average annual rate of change, in per cent)	—	−8.1
GDP per capita in US$ (current rate of exchange)	—	n.a.
GDP per capita in US$ (in PPP)	—	n.a.
GDP index (1989 = 100)	100	92
Gross industrial output (index, 1989 = 100)	100	100
Gross investment (index, 1989 = 100)	—	—
Consumer prices (annual rate of change, end-year)	n.a.	n.a.
Number of registered unemployed, end-year, in thousands	—	—
Unemployed in per cent of the labour force	—	—
Real wages, CPI-based, index (1990 = 100)	—	100
Budget balance (in per cent of GDP)	n.a.	n.a.
Trade balance (in bn$)	—	—
Current account balance in convertible currencies (bn$)	—	—
Net debt in convertible currencies (bn$, end-year)	—	—
Latvia		
GDP (average annual rate of change, in per cent)	—	2.7
GDP per capita in US$ (current rate of exchange)	—	n.a.
GDP per capita in US$ (in PPP)	—	n.a.
GDP index (1989 = 100)	100	103
Gross industrial output (index, 1989 = 100)	100	101
Gross investment (index, 1989 = 100)	—	100
Consumer prices (annual rate of change, end-year)	n.a.	n.a.
Number of registered unemployed, end-year, in thousand	—	—
Unemployed in per cent of the labour force	—	—
Real wages, CPI-based, index (1990 = 100)	—	100
Budget balance (in per cent of GDP)	n.a.	n.a.
Trade balance (in bn$)	—	—
Current account balance in convertible currencies (bn$)	—	—
Net debt in convertible currencies (bn$, end-year)	—	—

1991	1992	1993	1994	1995	1996	1997 (preliminary)
−13.7	−8.8	1.5	3.9	7.1	4.1	−6.6
1187	859	1159	1324	1573	1437	n.a.
n.a.	3542	3698	3931	4312	4591	n.a.
82	75	76	79	85	88	82
63	49	50	52	57	62	59
44	49	53	64	69	73	—
223.0	199.0	296.0	62.0	28.0	57.0	152.0
337	929	1170	1224	998	658	881
3.0	8.2	10.4	10.9	9.5	6.3	8.8
71.3	76.5	75.3	78.0	82.2	88.2	93.0
−2.4	−4.8	−0.4	−1.9	−2.8	−3.9	−4.5
−1.5	−1.9	−1.6	−1.0	−2.4	−3.4	−2.7
−1.4	−0.5	−1.2	−0.4	−1.8	−2.6	−2.1
1.5	2.7	3.3	3.5	5.0	6.2	5.6
−10.0	−14.1	−8.6	−2.7	2.9	4.0	9.0
n.a.	632	1105	1553	2400	3000	n.a.
n.a.	3957	3785	3842	4138	4431	n.a.
83	71	65	64	67	69	75
93	60	49	47	48	49	56
—	100	110	121	—	—	—
304.0	954.0	36.0	42.0	29.0	15.0	12.0
—	15	34	35	34	37	31
—	1.9	5.0	5.1	5.0	5.6	4.6
73.6	41.9	42.7	49.5	51.6	51.9	55.7
5.2	−0.3	−0.7	1.3	−1.2	−1.5	n.a.
—	0.0	−0.1	−0.4	−0.7	−1.1	−1.5
—	0.2	0.0	−0.2	−0.2	−0.4	−0.3
—	−0.2	−0.2	—	0.1	−0.3	−0.4
−8.3	−34.9	−14.9	0.6	−1.6	2.8	6.0
n.a.	525	836	1459	1780	2010	n.a.
n.a.	3451	3070	3204	3291	3484	n.a.
92	60	51	51	51	52	56
100	66	45	40	39	41	43
36	26	22	22	24	28	—
262.0	959.0	35.0	26.0	23.0	13.0	8.0
—	31	77	84	83	91	85
—	2.1	5.8	6.5	6.6	7.2	6.7
75.1	50.0	50.6	60.7	60.3	58.9	65.2
n.a.	−0.8	0.6	−4.1	−3.5	−1.4	−0.9
—	0.0	0.4	−0.3	−0.5	−0.9	−1.0
—	0.2	0.4	0.2	−0.0	−0.3	−0.3
—	—	0.2	0.3	0.4	−0.2	−0.3

Table continued overleaf

Table A.2 continued

	1989	1990
Lithuania		
GDP (average annual rate of change, in per cent)	—	−6.9
GDP per capita in US$ (current rate of exchange)	—	n.a.
GDP per capita in US$ (in PPP)	—	n.a.
GDP index (1989 = 100)	100	93
Gross industrial output (index, 1989 = 100)	100	97
Gross investment (index, 1989 = 100)	n.a.	n.a.
Consumer prices (annual rate of change, end-year)	n.a.	n.a.
Number of registered unemployed, end-year, in thousands	—	—
Unemployed in per cent of the labour force	—	—
Real wages, CPI-based, index (1990 = 100)	—	100
Budget balance (in per cent of GDP)	n.a.	−5.4
Trade balance (in bn$)	—	—
Current account balance in convertible currencies (bn$)	—	—
Net debt in convertible currencies (bn$, end-year)	—	—
Russia		
GDP (average annual rate of change, in per cent)	1.6	−4.0
GDP per capita in US$ (current rate of exchange)	—	2554
GDP per capita in US$ (in PPP)	—	n.a.
GDP index (1989 = 100)	100	97
Gross industrial output (index, 1989 = 100)	100	100
Gross investment (index, 1989 = 100)	—	100
Consumer prices (annual rate of change, end-year)	n.a.	n.a.
Number of unemployed, end-year, in thousands	—	—
Unemployed in per cent of the labour force	—	—
Real wages, CPI-based, index (1991 = 100)	—	—
Budget balance (in per cent of GDP)	n.a.	n.a.
Trade balance (in bn$)	—	—
Current account balance in convertible currencies (bn$)	—	−6.3
Net debt in convertible currencies (bn$, end-year)	—	58.2
Ukraine		
GDP (average annual rate of change, in per cent)	5.0	−3.6
GDP per capita in US$ (current rate of exchange)	—	n.a.
GDP per capita in US$ (in PPP)	—	n.a.
GDP index (1989 = 100)	100	96
Gross industrial output (index, 1989 = 100)	100	100
Gross investment (index, 1989 = 100)	—	100
Consumer prices (annual rate of change, end-year)	n.a.	n.a.
Number of registered unemployed, end-year, in thousands	—	—
Unemployed in per cent of the labour force	—	—
Real wages, CPI-based, index (1991 = 100)	—	—
Budget balance (in per cent of GDP)	n.a.	n.a.
Trade balance (in bn$)	—	—
Current account balance in convertible currencies (bn$)	—	—
Net debt in convertible currencies (bn$, end-year)	—	—

— = negligible or non-pertinent; n.a. = not available.
(a) Since 1996 Poland includes net receipts from unrecorded cross-border trade in goods and services. Comparable data for 1995 have been recalculated

1991	1992	1993	1994	1995	1996	1997 (preliminary)
−13.1	−39.3	−30.4	1.0	3.0	6.4	5.0
265	511	754	1501	2099	2700	n.a.
n.a.	5174	4049	4203	4471	4766	n.a.
81	53	37	38	39	40	42
94.0	66	43	32	33	35	35
n.a.	n.a.	n.a.	n.a.	n.a.	n.a.	n.a.
345.0	1161.1	188.8	45.0	35.5	13.1	10.0
—	21	66	78	128	109	120
—	1.0	3.4	4.5	7.3	6.2	6.7
89.8	58.7	38.2	35.4	37.7	44.0	49.0
2.7	0.8	−3.1	−4.2	−3.3	−3.6	−2.8
—	0.3	−0.3	−0.3	−0.9	−1.2	−1.8
—	0.3	−0.1	−0.1	−0.6	−0.7	−0.6
—	—	−0.2	—	0.1	0.5	0.4
−14.3	−14.5	−8.7	−12.7	−4.2	−4.9	0.4
140	575	1239	1870	2455	2985	n.a.
n.a.	n.a.	n.a.	n.a.	4480	n.a.	n.a.
92	79	72	63	60	57	58
92	75	65	51	50	48	48
84	49	37	27	25	21	—
144	2501	837	27	132	22	14
—	—	4120	5478	6431	6788	6400
—	—	5.5	7.5	8.9	9.3	9.0
100	65.5	60.3	53.1	41.3	46.0	52.5
n.a	−21.6	−7.2	−10.4	−5.5	−8.3	−8.0
8.0	5.4	17.5	24.7	32.5	40.1	29.7
2.5	−5.7	2.7	10.7	10.0	11.6	3.0
66.5	80.8	78.7	89.6	89.5	88.1	112.1
−11.2	−13.7	−14.1	−22.9	−11.8	−5.0	−3.0
n.a.	404	269	445	723	864	n.a.
n.a.	n.a.	n.a.	n.a.	2400	n.a.	n.a.
88	79	68	53	46	42	40
95	89	82	60	52	50	49
82	69	48	28	20	—	—
161	2730	10155	40	182	40	15
—	71	84	82	127	351	637
—	0.3	0.4	0.3	0.6	1.5	2.8
100	116.2	57.6	49.2	51.9	59.7	—
n.a	−25.4	−16.2	−7.8	−4.9	−3.2	n.a.
—	1.6	0.6	1.7	0.7	0.5	1.7
—	—	−0.8	−1.2	−1.2	−1.2	−0.9
—	—	—	7.0	7.1	6.9	6.7

Source: Most of the data are taken from ECE/UN (1998) updated with ECE/UN (1998), *Economic Survey of Europe*, no. 2, New York and Geneva: United Nations. The real wages index has been calculated by the author using data on nominal gross wages and annual average consumer prices changes given in the same source. Data on GDP per capita in US$ at the current exchange rate and in PPP, consumer prices (end-year) and budget balance are taken from EBRD (1998).

Table A.3   Basic demographic and social data on the countries in transition

		Population, millions, 1995	Pop. growth percent/year 1985–95	Life expectancy at birth (years) 1990	1995
1.	Czech R.	10.33	0.0	71.3 (1992)	73
2.	Hungary	10.33	−0.3	69	70
3.	Poland	38.61	0.4	71.1	70
4.	Slovakia	5.37	0.3	70.9 (1992)	72
5.	Slovenia	1.99	0.1	n.a.	74
6.	Bulgaria	8.40	−0.6	73	71
7.	Romania	22.69	0.0	71	70
8.	Estonia	1.49	−0.3	69.3	70
9.	Latvia	2.52	−0.4	69.1	69
10.	Lithuania	3.72	0.5	70.4	69
11.	Albania	3.26	1.0	72	73
12.	Russia	148.20	0.3	67.9 (1992)	65
13.	Belarus	10.34	0.4	69.8 (1992)	70
14.	Ukraine	51.55	0.1	69.4 (1992)	69
15.	Moldova	4.34	0.4	67.6 (1992)	69
16.	Kazakhst.	16.61	0.5	69.6 (1992)	69
17.	Kyrgyzst.	4.52	1.2	69 (1992)	68
18.	Turkmen.	19.17	3.3	65 (1992)	67
19.	Uzbek.	22.77	2.3	69.2 (1992)	70
20.	Mongolia	2.46	2.5	63	65
21.	China	1200.24	1.3	70	69
22.	Vietnam	73.48	2.2	67	68
Cuba		11.00	0.9	76	76
North Korea		23.87	1.8	71	70

Infant mortality per 1,000 live births		*Share of population age 15–64*	*Gini coefficient*		* *HDI Index as computed by the UNDP*	
1991	*1995*		*1993*	*Change since 1987–88*	*1990*	*1995*
10	8	65	27	8	0.892	0.872
16	11	62	23	2	0.887	0.856
15	14	55	30	5	0.831	0.855
12	11	60	20 (1992)		0.892	0.872
10	7	56	28	4	n.a	n.a
17	15	66	34	11	0.854	0.796
27	n.a.	65	26 (1992)		0.709	0.696
14	14	59	39	16	0.872	0.862
16	16	60	27		0.868	0.857
14	14	55	34		0.881	0.769
28	30	60	n.a.		0.699	0.731
20	18	65	48	14–24	0.862	0.849
15	13	60	22		0.861	0.866
18	15	60	26 (1992)		0.844	0.842
23	22	60	34 (1992)		0.758	0.739
32	27	59	33 (1992)		0.802	0.798
40	30	55	50	9–33	0.689	0.715
56	46	55	36		0.726	0.717
44	30	55	n.a		0.695	0.703 (1993)
62	55	50	n.a.		0.578	0.578
29	34	67	38		0.566	0.609
39	41	57	34		0.472	0.523
14	9				0.711	n.a
25	26				0.64	0.714

* The HDI index is a composite index taking into acount three key indicators: life duration, educational level and income level. Life duration is measured through the life expectancy index. The level of education is assessed through the indicator of adult literacy and the number of years of education. The income level is estimated taking into account the decreasing marginal utility of income (Atkinson's equation, see methodological notes in UNDP reports).
Source:
World Bank Atlas, 1997 and 1991;
World Bank Development Report 1996, special issue 'From Plan to Market';
UNDP, Human Development Reports 1993 and 1996.

Suggestions for Further Reading

It may seem strange to provide suggestions for further reading as the bibliography includes almost 500 entries. However some guidance is in order to help the non-specialist reader to find his or her way in a huge amount of literature on transition. The indications that follow will deal separately with Part I and Part II, as the former relates to history, while the latter is concerned with the moving target of transition. What follows is by no means a comprehensive guide. Rather, this is a personal selection, reflecting my own experience as a teacher and a tutor.

PART I

For this section of the reading guidance I would first recommend as an *introduction* the last edition (and also the previous editions which are to be found in libraries) of Bornstein (1994), a classic in comparative economics, to which one should add Campbell (1991), which despite its title is more concerned with pre-transition systems, and is a very accessible text on the socialist economies as they were entering the path of transition. Both books also provide reading guidance.

On the *bases of the socialist system*, Kornai (1980 and 1992) presents the most coherent and comprehensive view as seen from the East. An easier but no less accurate introduction, however focused on the Soviet model, is Nove (1987). Wiles (1968) and Holzman (1976) approach these fundamentals through their impact on international trade.

For an introduction to the *history* of the system, Nove (1992) for the USSR and Kaser (1985, 1986) are classic references. Zaleski (1980) is an extremely comprehensive book on Stalinist planning. There are many books on the history of the socialist systems; Swain and Swain (1993) and White *et al.* (1993) look at this history from the viewpoint of transition in progress.

A large number of books have been devoted to the *reforms* within the socialist system. To orient oneself in the maze of these sources one may use the very convenient guide of Jeffries (1993), of which more than one half is devoted to the socialist past of the countries in transition. Another approach would be to refer to the series of volumes edited for the Joint Economic Committee of the Congress of the United States since the end of the 1960s, covering China, Eastern Europe and the USSR. The general bibliography quotes two of them (Hardt and Kaufman, 1989 and 1993); these volumes are an invaluable source as they cover both general issues and country cases, and as they have attracted over years all the significant experts in the field in the Western world. Since the 1950s the UN Economic Commission for Europe has devoted a large share of the annual *Economic Survey of Europe* to a systematic coverage of Soviet and Eastern European economies, always based on national statistical data (though discussing their inconsistencies and supplementing their lacuna when needed), in a scholarly approach combining cooperation with Eastern economists and a professional, unprejudiced treatment of the issues.

On the record of economic performance and growth, Bergson and Kuznets (1963) and Gregory and Stuart (1990) should be starting-points.

International trade issues have been best covered by Franklyn Holzman (see the references to his quoted books and articles). Also see Brabant (1980), Wolf (1988) and Brada (1991).

PART II

The chapters of Part II contain a large amount of bibliographical references. I have selected only a part of a very large literature. A convenient way to follow on is to refer to the *Journal of Economic Literature* (particularly section P, *Economic Systems*). Rather than repeating them I would like to provide a guidance to institutions, journals and series dealing with transition economies.

National Institutes

The institutes and centres that dealt with the socialist planned economies usually carried on, sometimes under different names. New ones emerged. It is impossible to mention them all. In addition, new centres appeared in the countries in transition themselves.

In the United Kingdom, the CEPR (Centre for Economic Policy Research) is undoubtedly the largest think-tank and contributor of discussion papers on transition (of which a significant part later appears in a more or less modified form in other publications). The Birmingham CREES (Centre on Russian and East European Studies) has been publishing papers both on economic history and on contemporary issues, and has in particular explored issues linked with foreign trade and technological progress. Non-academic institutions also provide very useful current information in the field, such as the country reports of the *Economist Intelligence Unit*, and of the *Daiwa Institute of Research Europe*.

In Belgium, the LICEES (Leuven Institute for Central and Eastern European Studies; Dutch acronym LICOS) has expanded since 1991 and has published a number of discussion and working papers, in many cases with the contribution of Eastern European scholars. In Brussels, *Criteme* (Centre de Recherches Interdisciplinaires sur la Transition vers l'Economie de Marché des pays de l'Est) is based at the Institut de Sociologie of the Université Libre de Bruxelles.

In Germany, the main specialised research institutes (BOIST in Cologne – the acronym of the Federal Institute for International and East European studies; the Ost-Europa Institut and the Sudosteuropa Institut in Munich) essentially publish in German. There is a similar situation in France, where the ROSES (Réforme et Ouverture des Systèmes Economiques (post)-Socialistes) and the IRSES (Institutions et Régulation dans les Systèmes Economiques (post)-Socialistes) issue working papers mainly in French.

In Austria, the WIIW (the acronym for the Vienna Institute for Comparative Economic Studies) is a major source of statistical information and research reports.

In the United States, the researchers in the field are organised in networks rather than in research centres. One should mention long-established institutions such as the Averell Harriman Institute at Columbia University in New York, the Davis Research Center (formerly Russian Research Center) at Harvard University and the Woodrow Wilson Center at the Smithsonian Institution in Washington which hosts the Kennan Institute (Russian and Post-Soviet Studies) and the East European Studies Center.

In Central and East European countries, and in Russia, there are a great number of institutes publishing working papers. It is impossible to list them all. A sample would include, for Hungary, the series of the Institute for World Economics of the Hungarian Academy of Sciences, *Trends in World Economy*, and the Working Papers of the same institute, as well as the *Discussion Papers* of the Kopint-Datorg Institute, and the *Research Summaries* of the GKI Institute; for the Czech Republic, the series of working papers of the CERGE/EI (Centre for Economic Research and Graduate Education of Charles University and Economics Institute of the Academy of Sciences), and the *Economic Trends* of the Komercní Banka; for Poland, the Working Papers of the Institute of Finance in Warsaw; for Russia, the Russian Economic Barometer of the Institute for World Economy and International Relations of the Russian Academy of Sciences.

International Organisations

The major international organisations became increasingly involved in research on the countries in transition. We have already mentioned the United Nations Economic Commission for Europe; to the annual *Economic Survey of Europe* one should add the *Economic Bulletin for Europe*, also annual, devoted to international economic relations issues (both have merged in 1998 to give birth to an *Economic Survey of Europe* issued three times a year). The IMF Survey and Staff Papers have increased their coverage of transition issues. The World Bank, often jointly with the IMF, has published a number of volumes (often conference papers) on transition issues. It also publishes a newsletter about reforming economies, *Transition*.

The OECD (Organisation for Economic Cooperation and Development) publishes country studies on member Central European countries, the Czech Republic, Hungary and Poland, and also for some non-members, Bulgaria, Romania, Slovakia, Slovenia and Russia (see bibliography, under the heading of OECD).

The Commission of the European Communities (now Union) has produced a large number of papers on the countries in transition, in many cases restricted. The Directorate General for Economic and Financial Affairs publishes a journal, *European Economy*, and also *Euro Papers*, which have devoted several special issues to the countries in transition. In addition, a great quantity of studies has been generated by the ACE (Action for Cooperation in Economics) programmes subsidised by the EU. Most of these studies are in mimeo form; some are published, especially when large Western institutes have been acting as coordinators of the programmes.

The EBRD (European Bank for Reconstruction and Development) has been publishing working papers since 1993, and a journal, *The Economics of Transition*. Its major publication is the annual *Transition Report* with its mid-year *Transition Report Update*.

Journals

Most of the academic journals in the field of economics have been devoting a growing space to articles dealing with transition issues. More generally, the economic and business magazines and newspapers have extended their coverage of these countries. In the personal view of the author the best source in the newspaper category is the British *Financial Times* in terms of frequency and accuracy of information. Among the magazines, one may mention *The Economist*.

The list below only includes the specialised journals, and does not pretend to be exhaustive. Most have been published for many years on planned economies; some have changed their titles. A few have been set up after the beginning of the transition.

Communist Economies and Economic Transformation, quarterly; 1989; edited by the Centre for Research into Communist Economies, London; Abingdon, Oxford: Carfax Publishing Co.

Communist and Post-Communist Studies; quarterly; 1991 under this name; Center for European and Russian Studies, UCLA; Exeter, UK: Elsevier Science Ltd.

Comparative Economic Studies, quarterly, 1958, Association for Comparative Economic Studies, East Lansing: Michigan State University.

Le Courrier des Pays de l'Est (summary in English); monthly; 1964; edited by the Centre d'Etudes et de Documentation sur l'ex-URSS, la Chine et l'Europe de l'Est; Paris: La Documentation Française.

Economic Systems (formerly *Jahrbuch der Wirtschaft Osteuropas*), quarterly, 1976, Munich: Osteuropa Institute (in association with the European Association for Comparative Economic Studies).

The Economics of Transition, quarterly, 1993, European Bank for Reconstruction and Development, Oxford: Oxford University Press.

Europe-Asia Studies (formerly *Soviet Studies*), quarterly, since 1993 published six times a year; 1949; Glasgow: The University of Glasgow.

Joice, Journal of International and Comparative Economics, quarterly, 1992, European Association for Comparative Economic Studies, Heidelberg: Physica-Verlag.

Journal of Comparative Economics, quarterly, 1976, Association for Comparative Economic Studies, San Diego: Academic Press.

Moct-Most, Economic Journal on Eastern Europe and the Soviet Union, three times a year, 1991; Bologna, Italy: Nomisma.

Problems of Economic Transition (formerly *Problems of Economics*), A Journal of Translations from the Russian, quarterly, 1958, Armonk, NY: M. E. Sharpe.

Revue d'Etudes Comparatives Est-Ouest (summary in English); quarterly; 1970; Paris: CNRS.

RFE/RL Research Report, 1992–4; publication stopped August 1994. Munich: Radio Free Europe, Radio Liberty Inc. (successor to separate research publications by Radio Liberty and Radio Free Europe); from January 1995, replaced by *Transitions* (Prague: Institute for Journalism in Transition), monthly, and by the electronic daily *RFE/RL Newsline*, < newsline@list.rferl.org >

Transition, monthly, since 1998, 6 issues per year, 1990, Newsletter about reforming economies published by the World Bank.

Transitions, successor to Revue des Pays de l'Est (partly in English), bi-annual; 1991; Brussels: Université Libre de Bruxelles.

Bibliography

Ábel, István and John P. Bonin (1992), *The 'Big Bang' versus 'Slow but Steady': A Comparison of the Hungarian and the Polish Transformations*. London: CEPR (Centre for Economic Policy Research, no. 626).

Aghion, Philippe (1993), 'Economic Reform in Eastern Europe: Can Theory Help?', *European Economic Review*, vol. 37, nos 2/3, pp. 525–32.

Aghion, Philippe and Olivier Jean Blanchard (1993), *On the Speed of Transition in Central Europe*. London: EBRD, Working Paper no. 6, July.

Aghion, Philippe and Wendy Carlin (1997), 'Restructuring outcomes and the evolution of ownership patterns in Central and Eastern Europe', in OECD (1997d) pp. 241–61.

Anderson, Robert E., Stijn Claessens, Simeon Djanko and Gerhard Pohl (1997), 'Privatization Effects in Central and Eastern Europe', in *Moct-Most* (1997) pp. 137–62.

Andreff, Wladimir (1993), *La Crise des conomies socialistes, La rupture d'un systme*. Grenoble: Presses Universitaires de Grenoble.

Artisien, Patrick, Matija Rojic and Marjan Svetlicic (1993), *Foreign Investment in Central and Eastern Europe*. London: Macmillan.

Åslund, Anders (1995), *How Russia Became a Market Economy*. Washington, DC: The Brookings Institution.

Asselain, Jean-Charles (1994), 'Convertibilité précoce et protection par le change: un premier bilan de la réinsertion internationale des pays de l'Est', *Revue Economique*, vol. 45, no. 3, pp. 833–44.

Bahro, Rudolf (1978), *The Alternative in Eastern Europe*. London: New Left Books.

Bakos, Gabor (1993), 'After Comecon: A Free Trade Area in Central Europe', *Europe-Asia Studies*, vol. 45, no. 6, pp. 1025–44.

Balcerowicz, Leszek (1994), *Eastern Europe: Economic, Social and Political Dynamics*. London: School of Slavonic and East European Studies, The Sixth M.B. Grabowski Memorial Lecture.

Balcerowicz, Leszek (1995), *Socialism, Capitalism, Transformation*. Budapest, London and New York: Central European University Press.

Baldwin, Richard E., Joseph F. Francois and Richard Portes (1997), 'The Costs and Benefits of Eastern Enlargement: The Impact on the EU and Central Europe', *Economic Policy*, no. 24, April, pp. 127–76.

Barre, Raymond, William H. Luers, Anthony Solomon and Krzysztof J. Ners (1992a), *Moving Beyond Assistance*, Final Report of the IEWS Task Force on Western Assistance to Transition in the Czech and Slovak Federal Republic, Hungary and Poland, New York and Prague: Institute for EastWest Studies.

Barre, Raymond *et al.* (1992b), '*La coexistence pacifique 20 ans après, La Transition des économies de l'Est à l'économie de marché*. Fondation F. Perroux. Paris: Editions de l'Epargne.

Begg, David (1997), 'Monetary Policy during Transition: Progress and Pitfalls in Central and Eastern Europe, 1990–6', *Oxford Review of Economic Policy*, vol. 13, no. 2, pp. 33–46.

Begg, David and Richard Portes (1992), *Enterprise Debt and Economic Transformation: Financial Restructuring of the State Sector in Central and Eastern Europe*. London: CEPR, Discussion Paper no. 695, June.

Bergson, Abram (1994), 'The Communist Efficiency Gap: Alternative Measures', *Comparative Economic Studies*, vol. 36, no. 1 (Spring), pp. 1–12.

Bergson, Abram and Simon Kuznets (1963), *Economic Trends in the Soviet Union*. Cambridge, Mass.: Harvard University Press.

Bergson, Abram and Herbert S. Levine (eds) (1983), *The Soviet Economy Toward the Year 2000*. London: George Allen & Unwin.

Berliner, Joseph (1976), *The Innovation Decision in Soviet Industry*. Cambridge, Mass.: MIT Press.

Berliner, Joseph (1983), 'Planning and Management', in Bergson and Levine (eds) pp. 350–90.

Bettelheim, Charles (1977 and 1979), *Class Struggles in the USSR (1917–23 and 1924–30)*, 2 vols. London: Harvester Press.

Blanchard, Olivier (1997), *The Economics of Post-Communist Transition*. Oxford: Clarendon Press.

Blanchard, Olivier, Rudiger Dornbusch, Paul Krugman, Richard Layard and Lawrence Summers (1991), *Reform in Eastern Europe*. Cambridge, Mass.: MIT Press.

Blanchard, Olivier, Kenneth A. Froot and Jeffrey D. Sachs (1994), *The Transition in Eastern Europe*. vol. 1 *Country Studies*, vol. 2 *Restructuring*. NBER, Chicago, University of Chicago Press.

Blaszczyk, Barbara, Marzena Borowiec and Malgorzata Antczak (1997), 'The Role of the State in the Economy: Policies, Institutions and their Effects', in UNDP, *National Report on Human Development, The Changing Role of the State, Poland '97*. Warsaw: UNDP, pp. 38–83.

Bobinski, Christopher (1992), 'West Hides Behind Polish tariff. Cars Makers Show Protective Instincts', *Financial Times*, 10 March.

Boeri, Tito (1994), 'Transitional Unemployment', *The Economics of Transition*, vol. 2, no. 1, March, pp. 1–25.

Boeri, Tito (1997a), 'Labour-Market Reforms in Transition Economies', *Oxford Review of Economic Policy*, vol. 13, no. 2, pp. 126–40.

Boeri, Tito (1997b), 'Learning from Transition Economies: Assessing Labor Market Policies across Central and Eastern Europe', *Journal of Comparative Economics*, vol. 25, no. 3 (December), pp. 366–84.

Bofinger, Peter (1993), *The Output Decline in Central and Eastern Europe: A Classical Explanation*. London, CEPR, Discussion Paper no. 784, May.

Bofinger, Peter and Daniel Gros (1992), *A Payments Union for the Commonwealth of Independent States: Why and How*. London: CEPR, Discussion Paper Series, no. 654.

Bofinger, Peter, Eirik Svindland and Benedikt Thanner (1993), 'Prospects of the Monetary Order in the Republics of the FSU', in CEPR (1993), pp. 9–33.

Bofinger, Peter, Heiner Flassbeck and Lutz Hoffmann (1997), 'Orthodox Money-Based Stabilization (OMBS) Versus Heterodox Exchange Rate-Based Stabilization (HERBS): The Case of Russia, the Ukraine and Kazakhstan', *Economic Systems*, vol. 21, no. 1 (March), pp. 1–33.

Bornstein, Morris (1992), 'Privatisation in Eastern Europe', *Communist Economies and Economic Transformation*, vol. 4, no. 3, pp. 283–320; revised in Bornstein (1994), pp. 468–510.

Bornstein, Morris (ed.) (1994), *Comparative Economic Systems, Models and Cases*, 7th edn. Burr Ridge and Boston: Irwin.

Bornstein, Morris (1997), 'Non-standard methods in the privatization strategies of the Czech Republik, Hungary and Poland', *Economics of Transition*, vol. 5, no. 2, pp. 323–38.

Bossak, Jan W. (ed.) (1994), *Poland, International Economic Report 1993/94.* Warsaw: World Economy Research Institute, Warsaw School of Economics.

Brabant, Jozef van (1980), *Socialist Economic Integration, Aspects of Contemporary Economic Problems in Eastern Europe.* Cambridge: Cambridge University Press.

Brabant, Jozef M. van (ed.) (1991), *Economic Reforms in Centrally Planned Economies and Their Impact on the Global Economy,* in association with the United Nations. London and Basingstoke: Macmillan.

Brabant, Jozef M. van (1993), 'Economic Recession in the East: The Impact of Changing External Regimes', *Joice,* vol. 2, no. 3, pp. 165–89.

Brabant, Jozef M. (1994), *Industrial Policy in Eastern Europe, Governing the Transition.* Dordrecht: Kluwer Acedemic Publishers.

Brabant, Jozef M. (1998), *The Political Economy of Transition, Coming to Grips with History and Methodology.* London and New York: Routledge.

Brada, Josef C. (1988), 'Interpreting the Soviet Subsidization of Eastern Europe', *International Organization,* vol. 42, no. 4 (Autumn) pp. 639–58.

Brada, Josef C. (1991) 'The Political Economy of Communist Foreign Trade Institutions and Policies', *Journal of Comparative Economics,* vol. 15, no. 2 (June), pp. 211–38.

Brada, Josef C. (1993), 'The Transformation from Communism to Capitalism: How Far? How Fast?', *Post-Soviet Affairs,* vol. 9, no. 2, pp. 87–110.

Brada, Josef C., Ed A. Hewett and Thomas A. Wolf (eds) (1988), *Economic Adjustment and Reform in Eastern Europe and the Soviet Union,* Essays in Honor of Franklyn D. Holzman. Durham and London: Duke University Press.

Brada, Josef C and Arthur E. King (1992), 'Is There a J-Curve for the Economic Transition from Socialism to Capitalism?', *Economics of Planning,* January.

Brada, Josef C., Inderjit Singh and Adám Török (1994), *Firms Afloat and Firms Adrift: Hungarian Industry and the Economic Transition,* series 'The Microeconomics of Transition Economies', vol. 1. Armonk, New York: M.E. Sharpe.

Brezinski, Horst (1991), 'Economic Reforms in Asia and Europe and Co-operation With the Less Developed Centrally Planned Economies', in Brabant (ed.) (1991) pp. 243–65.

Brown, Bess (1994), 'Three Central Asian States Form Economic Union', *RFE/RL Research Report,* vol. 3, no. 13 (1 April), pp. 33–5.

Bruno, Michael (1992), 'Stabilization and Reform in Eastern Europe: A Preliminary Evaluation', *IMF Staff Papers,* vol. 39, no. 4 (December), pp. 741–77.

Bruno, Michael (1993), *Crisis, Stabilization and Economic Reform. Therapy by Consensus.* Oxford: Clarendon Press.

Bruno, Michael and William Easterly (1995), 'Inflation Crises and Long-Term Growth', NBER Working Paper, no. 5209.

Brus, Wlodzimierz (1961), *Ogólne Problemy Funkcjonowania Gospodarki Socjalistycznej* (General problems of fuctioning of a socialist economy). Translated as *The Market in a Socialist Economy* (1972). London: Routledge & Kegan Paul.

Brus, Wlodzimierz (1987), 'Market Socialism', entry in *The New Palgrave, A Dictionary of Economics,* ed. by John Eatwell, Murray Milgate and Peter Newman, vol. 3. London: Macmillan.

Brus, Wlodzimierz and Kazimierz Laski (1989), *From Marx to the Market: Socialism in Search of an Economic System.* Oxford: Clarendon Press.

Budina, Nina and Sweder van Wijnbergen (1997), 'Fiscal Policies in Eastern Europe', *Oxford Review of Economic Policy,* vol. 13, no. 2, pp. 47–64.

Calvo, Guillermo A. (1991), 'Are High Interest Rates Effective for Stopping High Inflation?', in Commander (ed.) (1991), pp. 247–59.

Calvo, Guillermo and Fabrizio Coricelli (1992), 'Output Collapse in Eastern Europe: The Role of Credit', IMF Working Paper.

Calvo, Guillermo A. and Fabrizio Coricelli (1994), 'Credit Market Imperfections and Output Response in Previously Centrally Planned Economies', in Caprio *et al.* (eds), pp. 257–94.

Calvo, Guillermo A. and Jacob A. Frenkel (1991), 'From Centrally Planned to Market Economy: The Road from CPE to PCPE', *IMF Staff Papers*, vol. 38, no. 2 (June), pp. 268–99.

Campbell, Robert W. (1991), *The Socialist Economies in Transition: A Primer on Semi-Reformed Systems*. Bloomington and Indianapolis: Indiana University Press.

Caprio, Gerard, David Folkerts-Landau and Timothy D. Lane (eds) (1994), *Building Sound Finance in Emerging Market Economies*, proceedings of a conference held in Washington, DC, June 10–11, 1993. Washington, DC: IMF and World Bank

Carlin, Wendy and Colin Mayer (1992), 'Restructuring Enterprises in Central and Eastern Europe', *Economic Policy*, vol. 15 (October), pp. 311–52.

Carlin, Wendy and Michael Landesmann (1997), 'From Theory into Practice? Restructuring and Dynamism in Transition Economies', *Oxford Review of Economic Policy*, vol. 13, no. 2, pp. 77–105.

Carlin, Wendy, John Van Reenen and Toby Wolfe (1995), 'Enterprise Restructuring in Early Transition: The Case Study Evidence from Central and Eastern Europe', *Economics of Transition*, vol. 3, no. 4 (December), pp. 427–59.

Carrère d'Encausse, Hélène (1979), *Decline of an Empire: The Soviet Socialist Republics in Revolt*. New York: Newsweek Books.

CEC (Commission of the European Communities) (1995a), 'White Paper, Preparation of the Associated Countries of Central and Eastern Europe for Integration into the Internal Market of the Union', Brussels, 3 May 1995, COM (95) 163 final, 2 vols.

CEC (Commission of the European Communities) (1995b), 'Study on Alternative Strategies for the Development of Relations in the Field of Agriculture between the EU and the Associated Counties with a View to Future Accession of These Countries', Brussels, November 1995, CSE (95) 607.

CEPR (1992a), *The Economic Consequences of the East*, Proceedings of a conference organized by the Centre for Economic Policy Research and hosted by the Deutsche Bundesbank in Frankfurt-am-Main, March 1992. London: CEPR.

CEPR (1992b), *Is Bigger Better? The Economics of EC Enlargement*. London: A CEPR Annual Report, Centre for Economic Policy Research.

CEPR (1993), *The Economics of the New Currencies*. London: Centre for Economic Policy Research, June.

CEPR and IEWS (1996a), *Banking Sector Development in Central and Eastern Europe*, contributions by Ronald W. Anderson, Erik Berglöf and Kálmán Mizsei, Forum Report of the Economic Policy Initiative no. 1. London: Centre for Economic Policy Research; New York: Institute for East-West Studies, March.

CEPR and IEWS (1996b), *Coming to Terms with Accession*, contributions by Jürgen von Hagen, Andrzej Kumar and Elżbieta Kawecka-Wyrzykowska, Forum Report of the Economic Policy Initiative no. 2. London: Centre for Economic Policy Research; New York: Institute for East-West Studies, October.

CEPR and IEWS (1997), *Fiscal Policy in Transition*, contributions by Fabrizio Coricelli, Marek Dibrowski, Urszula Kosterna, Forum Report of the Economic Policy Initiative no. 2. London: Centre for Economic Policy Research; New York: Institute for East-West Studies, May.

Charap, Joshua and Leila Webster (1993), 'Constraints on the Development of Private Manufacturing in St. Petersburg', *Economics of Transition*, vol. 1, no. 3 (September), pp. 299–316.

Charap, Joshua and Alena Zemplinerova (1993), *Restructuring in the Czech Economy*, London: EBRD, Working Paper no. 2, March.

Chavance, Bernard (1994), *La Fin des Systèmes Socialistes. Crise, Réforme et Transformation*. Paris: L'Harmattan.

Cheikbossian, Guillaume and Mathilde Maurel (1996), 'Le coût de la désintégration du CAEM et les perspectives du commerce intra-PECO', in Le Cacheux (1996), pp. 239–89.

Chesnais, Jean-Claude (1997), 'La mondialisation des migrations', in *RAMSES'98*, ed. by Thierry de Montbrial and Pierre Jacquet. Paris: IFRI, pp. 247–65.

Chirot, Daniel (ed.) (1989), *The Origins of Backwardness in Eastern Europe: Economics and Politics from the Middle Ages Until the Early Twentieth Century*. Berkeley: University of California Press.

Chirot, Daniel (ed.) (1991), *The Crisis of Leninism and the Decline of the Left. The Revolutions of 1989*. Seattle and London: University of Washington Press.

Christoffersen, Peter and Peter Doyle (1998), 'From Inflation to Growth: Eight Years of Transition', *IMF Working Paper*, 98/100, July.

Citrin, Daniel, Jonathan Anderson and Jeromin Zettlemeyer (1995), 'The IMF's Approach to Stabilization in the Baltics, Russia and the Countries of the Former Soviet Union', in *Moct-Most* (1995), pp. 85–100.

Clement, Hermann (1997), 'Integration in Osteuropa vor dem Hintergrund der Osterweiterung von NATO und EU', Osteuropa Institut München, *Working Paper* 208, December.

Collins, Susan M. and Dani Rodrik (1991), *Eastern Europe and the Soviet Union in the World Economy*, Institute for International Economics, Policy Analyses in International Economics, no. 32, Washington, DC, May, 152 pp.

Commander, Simon (ed.) (1991), *Managing Inflation in Socialist Economies in Transition*. Washington DC: The World Bank, Economic Development Institute (EDI) seminar series.

Connelly, Daniel A. (1994), 'Black Sea Economic Cooperation', *RFE/RL Research Report*, vol. 3, no. 26 (1 July), pp. 31–8.

Cooper, Julian (1991), *The Soviet Defence Industry: Conversion and Economic Reform*. London: Royal Institute of International Affairs.

Corado, Cristina (1994), *Textiles and Clothing Trade With Central and Eastern Europe: Impact on Members of the EC*. London: CEPR, Discussion Paper no. 1004, August.

Corbett, Jenny and Colin Mayer (1991), 'Financial Reform in Eastern Europe: Progress with the Wrong Model', *Oxford Review of Economic Policy*, vol. 7, no. 4, pp. 57–75.

Csaba, László (1990), *Eastern Europe and the World Economy*, Soviet and East European Studies, vol. 68. Cambridge: Cambridge University Press.

Csaba, László (1995), 'Hungary and the IMF: The Experience of a Cordial Discord', in JCE (1995), vol. 20, no. 2 (April), pp. 211–34.

Csáki, György (1993), *Recent Improvements in Hungarian Banking*. Budapest: Institute for World Economics, Working Paper, no. 27, December.

Csáki, György (1997), 'L'investissement direct étranger en Hongrie', *Revue d'Etudes Comparatives Est-Ouest*, vol. 28, no. 2, pp. 39–69.

Dallin, Alexander and Gail Lapidus (eds) (1991), *The Soviet System in Crisis: A Reader of Western and Soviet Views*. Boulder: Westview Press.

Daviddi, Renzo and Fabienne Ilzkovitz (1997), 'The Eastern Enlargement of the European Union: Major Challenges for Macro-economic Policies and Institutions of Central and East European Countries', *European Economic Review*, vol. 41, nos 3–5, pp. 671–80. (Enlarged version in Salvatore Baldone and Fabio Sdogati (eds) (1997), *EU-CEECs Integration: Policies and Markets at Work*. Milano: FrancoAngeli, pp. 15–40.

Davies, Robert W. (1980), *The Socialist Offensive: The Collectivisation of Soviet Agriculture*. London: Macmillan.

De Melo, Martha and Alan Gelb (1997), 'Transition to Date: A Comparative Overview', in OECD (1997d), pp. 59–78.

Dembinski, Pavel H. (1991), *The Logic of the Planned Economy. The Seeds of the Collapse*. Oxford: Clarendon Press.

Desai, Padma (1986), 'Is the Soviet Union Subsidizing Eastern Europe?', *European Economic Review*, vol. 30, no. 1, pp. 107–16.

Dewatripont, Mathias and Grard Roland (1996), 'Transition as a Process of Large-Scale Institutional Change', *Economics of Transition*, vol. 4, no. 1, pp. 1–30.

Drábek, Zdenek (1995), 'IMF and IBRD Policies in the Former Czechoslovakia', in *(JCE) Journal of Comparative Economics*, Papers of the Symposium on the Role of International Financial Institutions in Central and Eastern Europe: Part II, vol. 20, no. 2 (April) pp. 235–64.

Drábek, Zdenek (1997), 'Regional and Sub-Regional Integration in Central and Eastern Europe: An Overview', in Teunissen (ed.) (1997), pp. 11–77.

Dunne, Nancy (1992), 'Polish Tariffs Biased to the EC, Says US', *Financial Times*, 15 August 1992.

Earle, John S., Roman Frydman and Andrzej Rapaczynski (eds) (1993), *Privatization in the Transition to a Market Economy: Studies of Preconditions and Policies in Eastern Europe*, in association with the Central European University, New York: St. Martin's Press.

Easterly, William and Stanley Fisher (1994), *The Soviet Economic Decline: Historical and Republican Data*, World Bank Working Paper no. 1284. Washington: World Bank.

Eatwell, John, Murray Milgate and Peter Newman (eds) (1990), *Problems of the Planned Economy*, reprinted entries from *The New Palgrave: A Dictionary of Economics*. London and Basingstoke: Macmillan.

Eatwell, John, Michael Ellman, Mats Karlsson, D. Mario Nuti and Judith Shapiro (1997), *Not 'Just Another Accession', The Political Economy of EU Enlargement to the East*. London: Institute for Public Policy Research.

EBRD (1993) *Annual Economic Review 1992*. London: European Bank for Reconstruction and Development. (Special reports included, namely: bankruptcy legislation; voucher privatisation).

EBRD (1996), *Transition Report 1996, Infrastructure and Savings*. London: European Bank for Reconstruction and Development.

EBRD (1997), *Transition Report 1997, Enterprise Performance and Growth*. London: European Bank for Reconstruction and Development.

EBRD (1998), *Transition Report Update*. London: European Bank for Reconstruction and Development, April.

ECE/UN (1955), *Economic Survey of Europe in 1954*, Economic Commission for Europe, New York: United Nations.

ECE/UN (1991), *Economic Survey of Europe in 1990–1991*, Economic Commission for Europe, New York: United Nations.

ECE/UN (1992), *Economic Survey of Europe in 1991–1992*, Economic Commission for Europe, New York: United Nations.

ECE/UN (1993), *Economic Survey of Europe in 1992–1993*, Economic Commission for Europe, New York: United Nations.

ECE/UN (1994a), *Economic Bulletin for Europe*, vol. 45 (1993). New York and Geneva: United Nations.

ECE/UN (1994b), *Economic Survey of Europe in 1993–1994*. New York and Geneva: United Nations.

ECE/UN (1995), *Economic Bulletin for Europe*, vol. 47 (1995). New York and Geneva: United Nations.

ECE/UN (1996a), *Economic Survey of Europe in 1995–1996*. New York and Geneva: United Nations.

ECE/UN (1996b), *Economic Bulletin for Europe,* vol. 48 (1996). New York and Geneva: United Nations.

ECE/UN (1997a), *Economic Survey of Europe in 1996–1997*. New York and Geneva: United Nations.

ECE/UN (1997b), *Economic Bulletin for Europe*. vol. 49 (1997). New York and Geneva: United Nations.

ECE/UN (1998), *Economic Survey of Europe*, no. 1. New York and Geneva: United Nations.

ECE/UN and FAO (1997), *The Role of Agriculture in the Transition Process Towards a Market Economy*. Economic Studies no. 9. New York and Geneva: United Nations.

ECE/UN and UNPF (United Nations Population Fund) (1996), *International Migration in Central and Eastern Europe and the Commonwealth of Independent States*. Economic Studies no. 8. New York and Geneva: United Nations.

Eichengreen, Barry (1993), 'A Payments Mechanism for the Former Soviet Union: Is the EPU a Relevant Precedent?', *Economic Policy*, no. 17, pp. 309–54.

Eichengreen, Barry and Marc Uzan (1992), 'The Marshall Plan: Economic Effects and Implications for Eastern Europe and the Former USSR', *Economic Policy*, vol. 14 (April) pp. 13–76.

Ellman, Michael (1992), 'Shock Therapy in Russia: Failure or Partial Success?', *RFE/RL Research Report*, vol. 1, no. 34 (28 August), pp. 48–61.

Ellman, Michael (1994), 'Transformation, Depression and Economics: Some Lessons', *Journal of Comparative Economics*, vol. 19, no. 1 (August), pp. 1–21

Ellman, Michael (1995), 'The State under State Socialism and Post-Socialism', in Ha-Joon Chang and Robert Rowthorn (eds), *The Role of the State in Economic Change*. Oxford: Clarendon Press, pp. 215–36.

Ellman, Michael (1997a), 'The Political Economy of Transformation', *Oxford Review of Economic Policy*, vol. 13, no. 2, pp. 23–32.

Ellman, Michael (1997b), 'EU Accession Should Be a Partnership, Not a Dictate', *Transition* (World Bank), vol. 8, no. 4, pp. 1–2.

Erlich, Alexander (1960), *The Soviet Industrialization Debate, 1924–1928*. Cambridge: Harvard University Press.

Estrin, Saul (ed.) (1994), *Privatization in Central and Eastern Europe*. London and New York: Longman.

Estrin, Saul, Alan Gelb and Inderjit Singh (1995), 'Shocks and Adjustment by Firms in Transition: A Comparative Study', *Journal of Comparative Economics*, vol. 21, no. 2 (October), pp. 131–53.

European Commission (EC), DG II (1998), 'The Euro: Explanatory Notes', *Euro Papers*, no. 17, February.

European Commission (1998), *Agenda 2000, For a Stronger and Wider Union*. COM (97) 2000 final, and *Avis* for each of the 10 applicants, COM (97) 2001 to 2010.

Fallenbuchl, Zbigniew (1988), 'Present State of the Economic Reform', in P. Marer and W. Siwinski (eds), *Creditworthiness and Reform in Poland*. Bloomington: Indiana University Press, pp. 115–30.

Fayolle, Jacky (1996), 'L'intégration des pays d'Europe centrale et orientale à l'Union Européenne: un processus à construire', in OFCE (1996), pp. 21–53.

Fernandez-Arias, E. (1996), 'The New Wave of Private Capital Inflows: Push or Pull?', *Journal of Development Economics*, vol. 48, no. 2.

Fernandez-Arias, E. and P. Montiel (1996), 'The Surge in Capital Inflows to Developing Countries: An Analytical Overview', *The World Bank Economic Review*, vol. 10, no. 1.

Fischbach, Mireille and Maria Scattaglia (1997), 'Financial Flows to Eastern Erope: Determinants, Volatility and Sustainability Issues', in *Moct-Most*, special issue (1997), pp. 67–99.

Fisher, Stanley, Ratna Sahay and Carlos A. Végh (1996), 'Stabilization and Growth in Transition Economies: The Early Experience', *Journal of Economic Perspectives*, vol. 10, no. 2 (Spring) pp. 45–66.

Fisher, Stanley, Ratna Sahay and Carlos Végh (1998), 'How Far is Eastern Europe from Brussels?', *IMF Working Paper*, 98/53, April.

Frydman, Roman, Edmond S. Phelps, Andrzej Rapaczynski and Andrei Shleifer (1993a), 'Needed Mechanisms of Corporate Governance and Finance in Eastern Europe', *Economics of Transition*, vol. 1, no. 2 (June) pp. 171–207.

Frydman, Roman and Andrzej Papaczynski (1993b), 'Insiders and the State: Overview of Responses to Agency Problems in East European Privatization', *Economics of Transition*, vol. 1, no. 1, pp. 39–59.

Frydman, Roman, Andrzej Rapaczynski, John S. Earle *et al.* (1993c), *The Privatization Process in Central Europe*, Budapest, London and New York: Central European University Press.

Frydman, Roman and Andrzej Rapaczynski (1994), *Privatization in Eastern Europe: Is the State Withering Away?*. Budapest, London and New York: Central European University Press.

Frydman, Roman, Cheryl W. Gray and Andrzej Rapaczynski (eds) (1996), *Corporate Governance in Central Europe and Russia*. 2 vols: vol. 1, *Banks, Funds and Foreign Investors*; vol. 2, *Insiders and the State*. Budapest, London and New York: Central European University Press.

Girard, Jacques (1992), 'De la récession à la reprise en Europe centrale et orientale: bilan et perspectives', *Cahiers de la Banque Européenne d'Investissement*, no. 18, (novembre) pp. 9–22.

Goldman, Josef and Karel Kouba (1967), *Economic Growth in Czechoslovakia*. Prague: Academia.

Gomulka, Stanislaw (1991), 'The Causes of Recession Following Stabilization', *Comparative Economic Studies*, vol. 33, no. 2 (Summer), pp. 71–89.

Gomulka, Stanislaw (1992), 'Polish Economic Reform, 1990–91: Principles, Policies and Outcomes', *Cambridge Journal of Economics*, vol. 16, pp. 355–72.

Gomulka, Stanislaw (1994), 'Economic and Political Constraints During Transition', *Europe-Asia Stuidies*, vol. 46, no. 1, pp. 89–106.

Granick, David (1954), *The Red Executive*. New York: Columbia University Press.

Gray, Cheryl W. and Arnaud Holle (1996), 'Bank-led Restructuring in Poland: The Conciliation Process in Action', *Economics of Transition*, vol. 4, no. 2 (October), pp. 349–70.

Gray, Cheryl W. and Danial Kaufmann (1998), 'Corruption and Development', *Finance and Development*, March, pp. 7–14.

Gregory, Paul and Robert Stuart (1990), *Soviet Economic Structure and Performance*. 4th edn. New York: Harper & Row.

Gros, Daniel and Alfred Steinherr (1995), *Winds of Change, Economic Transition in Central and Eastern Europe*. London and New York: Longman.

Grosfeld, Irena (1990), 'Reform Economics and Western Economic Theory: Unexploited Opportunities', *Economics of Planning*, vol. 23, no. 1.

Grossman, Gregory (1994), 'What Was – Is, Will Be – the Command Economy?', *Moct-Most*, vol. 4, no. 1, pp. 5–22.

Halamska, Maria and Marie-Claude Maurel (1996), 'L'agriculture polonaise et la question de l'intgération européenne: regards croisés', *Revue d'Etudes Comparatives Est-Ouest*, vol. 27, no. 4 (December), pp. 45–78.

Hamilton, C.B. and L. Alan Winters (1992), 'Opening up Trade in Eastern Europe', *Economic Policy*, no. 14.

Hanke, Steve H., Lars Jonung and Kurt Schuler (1993), *Russian Currency and Finance: A Currency Board Approach to Reform*. London and New York: Routledge.

Hanson, Philip (1982), 'The End of Import-Led Growth? Some Observations on Soviet, Polish and Hungarian Experience in the 1970's', *Journal of Comparative Economics*, vol. 6, no. 2, pp. 130–47.

Hanson, Philip (1992), *From Stagnation to Catastroika: Commentaries on the Soviet Economy, 1983–91*. Centre For Strategic and International Studies, in cooperation with Radio Free Europe, The Washington Papers, no. 155. New York: Praeger.

Hanson, Philip (1997), 'What Sort of Capitalism is Developing in Russia?', *Communist Economies and Economic Transformation*, vol. 9, no. 1, pp. 27–42.

Hardt, John P. and Richard F. Kaufman (eds) (1989), *Pressures for Reform in the East European Economies*, 2 vols, Study Papers, Submitted to the Joint Economic Committee, Congress of the United States. Washington, DC: US Government Printing Office.

Hardt, John P. and Richard F. Kaufman (eds) (1993), *The Former Soviet Union in Transition*, 2 vols, Study Papers Submitted to the Joint Economic Committee, Congress of the United States. Washington, DC: US Government Printing Office.

Hardt, John P. and Richard F. Kaufman (eds) (1994), *East-Central European Economies in Transition*, Study Papers Submitted to the Joint Economic Committee, Congress of the United States. Washington, DC: US Government Printing Office.

Havlik, Peter (1996), 'Exchange Rate, Competitiveness and Labour Costs in Central and Eastern Europe', Vienna, WIIW, *Working Papers*, no. 231, October.

Hayek, Friedrich von (ed.) (1935), *Collectivist Economic Planning: Critical Studies on the Possibilities of Socialism*. London: Routledge & Sons.

Heimann, E. (1922), *Mehrwert und Gemeinwirtschaft*. Berlin: H.R. Hengelmann.

Heleniak, Timothy (1997), 'Mass Migration in Post-Soviet Space', *Transition*, vol. 8, no. 5, pp. 15–17.

Hewett, Ed A. (1974), *Foreign Trade Prices in the Council for Mutual Economic Assistance*. Cambridge: Cambridge University Press.

Hewett, Ed A. (1989), 'Eastern Europe and the International Economy: an Overview', in Hardt and Kaufman (eds) (1989), pp. 1–6.

Hindley, Brian (1993), *Helping Transition Through Trade? EC and US Policy Towards Exports From Eastern and Central Europe*. London: EBRD, Working Paper no. 4, March.

Hoen, Herman W. (1996), '"Shock versus Gradualism" in Central Europe Reconsidered', *Comparative Economic Studies*, vol. 38, no. 1, pp. 1–20.

Holzman, Franklyn D. (1962), 'Soviet Foreign Trade Pricing and the Question of Discrimination: A "Customs Union" Approach', *Review of Economics and Statistics*, vol. 44, no. 2 (May), pp. 134–47.

Holzman, Franklyn D. (1965), 'More on Soviet Bloc Trade Discrimination', *Soviet Studies*, vol. 17, no. 1, pp. 44–65.

Holzman, Franklyn D. (1974), *Foreign Trade Under Central Planning*. Cambridge, Mass.: Harvard University Press.

Holzman, Franklyn D. (1976), *International Trade Under Communism, Politics and Economics*. New York: Basic Books.

Holzman, Franklyn D. (1985), 'A "Trade-Destroying" Customs Union?', *Journal of Comparative Economics*, vol. 9, no. 4 (December), pp. 410–23.

Holzman, Franklyn D. (1986), 'The Significance of Soviet Subsidies to Eastern Europe', *Comparative Economic Studies*, vol. 28, no. 1 (Spring), pp. 54–65.

House of Lords (1994), *The Implications for Agriculture of the Europe Agreements*. House of Lords Select Committee on the European Communities, June, 2 vols. London: HMSO.

Hrnkxř, Miroslav (1997), 'The Global and Regional Outlook in Eastern Europe', in Teunissen (ed.) (1997), pp. 93–126.

Hughes, Gordon and Paul Hare (1991), 'Competitiveness and Industrial Restructuring in Czechoslovakia, Hungary and Poland', *European Economy*, special issue no. 2, pp. 83–110.

Hughes, Gordon and Paul Hare (1992), 'Industrial Policy and Restructuring in Eastern Europe', CEPR Discussion Paper, no. 653.

Hunya, Gábor (1993), 'Frictions in the Economic Transformation of Czechoslovakia, Hungary and Poland', *WIIW Forschungsberichte*, Vienna Institute for Comparative Economic Studies, no. 190, February.

Hunya, Gábor (1997), 'Large Privatisation, Restructuring and Foreign Direct Investment', in OECD (1997d), pp. 275–300.

IMF (1992), *World Economic Outlook*, Washington, D.C., September.

Impavido, Gregorio (1997), 'Pension Reforms and the Development of Pension Funds and Stock Markets in Eastern Europe', in *Moct-Most* (1997), pp. 101–35.

Inotai, András (1993), *Western Economic Support for Central and Eastern Europe: A Hungarian View*. Budapest: Institute for World Economics, Working Paper Series, no. 25.

Inotai, András (1995), 'Foreign Direct Investment in Hungary: Experience, Critical Crossroads and Strategic Options', in Tamás Ferenczi (ed.), *The Path to Economic Development*. Budapest: Institute for World Economy of the Hungarian Academy of Sciences, no. 77, pp. 107–22.

Inotai, András (1996), 'Sur le chemin de l'intégration: un point de vue hongrois', *Revue d'Etudes Comparatives Est-Ouest*, vol. 27, no. 4, pp. 79–107.

Inotai, András (1997), 'Prospects for Joining the European Union', in Teunissen (ed.) (1997), pp. 200–35.

Inotai, András and Magdolna Sass (1994), *Economic Integration of the Visegrád Countries: Facts and Scenarios*. Budapest: Institute for World Economics, Working Papers, no. 33, May.

Iwasaki, Teruyuki, Takeshi Mori and Hiroichi Yamaguchi (eds) (1992), *Development Strategies for the 21st Century*. Tokyo: Institute of Development Economics.

Jackson, Marvin (1992a), 'Constraints on Systemic Transformation and Their Policy Implications', *Oxford Review of Economic Policy*, vol. 7, no. 4, pp. 16–25.

Jackson, Marvin (1992b) 'Company Management and Capital Development in the Transition', in Lampe (ed.), pp. 57–74.

Jackson, Marvin (1997), *Perspectives for the CEEC Entering the EU*. Leuven: Lycos.

Jackson, Marvin and Johan Swinnen (1994), *A Statistical Analysis and Survey of the Current Situation of Agriculture in the Central and Eastern European Countries*. Report to to DGI, European Commission, mimeo. Leuven: Licos.

JCE (Journal of Comparative Economics) (1995), special issues on the *Symposium on the Role of International Financial Institutions in Central and Eastern Europe*, vol. 20, nos 1 to 3.

JCE (Journal of Comparative Economics) (1997), 'Bank Privatization in Central Europe and Russia', special issue, ed. by Jan Svejnar, vol. 25, no. 1 (August).

Jeffries, Ian (1993), *Socialist Economies and the Transition to the Market. A Guide*. London and New York: Routledge.

Just, Flemming (1996), 'The Common Agricultural Policy and the Adjustment to the East', in Laursen and Riishøj (eds), pp. 217–37.

Kantorovich, Leonid (1959), *Ekonomicheskiy raschet nailuchshego ispol'zovaniya resursov*. Moscow: Gosizdat.

Kantorovich, Leonid (1965), *The Best Use of Economic Resources*. Oxford: Clarendon Press; Cambridge: Harvard University Press.

Kaser, Michael (ed.) (1985, 1986), *The Economic History of Eastern Europe 1919–1975*. Oxford: Clarendon Press.

Kaser, Michael (1995), *Privatization in the CIS*. London: The Royal Institute of International Affairs.

Katsenelinboigen, Aron (1977), 'Coloured Markets in the Soviet Union', *Soviet Studies*, vol. 29, no. 1 (January), pp. 62–85.

Kaufmann, Daniel and Paul Siegelbaum (1996), 'Privatisation and Corruption in Transition Economies', *Journal of International Affairs*, Winter.

Kenen, Peter B. (1991), 'Transitional Arrangements for Trade and Payments Among the CMEA Countries', *IMF Staff Papers*, vol. 38, no. 2 (June), pp. 235–67.

Keuschnigg, Mirela (1997), 'Banking in Central and Eastern Europe', in *Moct-Most* (1997), pp. 7–35.

Khanin, Gregoriy and Vassiliy Selyunin (1987), 'Lukavaya tsifra' ('Wicked Figure'), *Novyi Mir*, no. 3.

Kimura, Tetsusaburo (1989), *The Vietnamese Economy 1975–86, Reforms and International Relations*. Tokyo: Institute of Developing Economies, IDE Occasional Papers Series, no. 23.

Kimura, Tetsusaburo (1992), 'Economic Reform in Vietnam: Coming to the Crucial Point', in Iwasaki, Mori and Yamagushi (eds), pp. 248–69.

King, Timothy (1991), 'Requirements for Participation in the International Monetary Fund and the World Bank', in Brabant (1991), pp. 279–300.

Kiss, Judit (1994), *Who Pays the Piper? Financial Resource Mobilization for Transformation and Development*. Budapest: Institute for World Economics, Working Papers, no. 29, February.

Klaus, Vaclav (1990), *A Road to a Market Economy (Selected Articles, Speeches and Lectures Held Abroad)*. Prague: Top Agency.

Knell, Mark and Christine Rider (eds) (1992), *Socialist Economies in Transition. Appraisals of the Market Mechanism*. Aldershot: Edward Elgar.

Knell, Mark and Wenyan Yang, 'Lessons From China on a Strategy for the Socialist Economies in Transition', in Knell and Rider (eds), pp. 216–35.

Koch-Weser, Caio (1996), 'Agenda for Transition, Second Phase', excerpts, *Transition*, vol. 7, no. 11–12, pp. 10–11.

Kodrzycki, Yolanda K. (1993) 'Tax Reform in Newly Emerging Market Economies', *New England Economic Review*, November–December, pp. 3–17.

Koen, Vincent and Steven Phillips (1993), *Price Liberalization in Russia, Behavior of Prices, Household Incomes and Consumption During the First Year*. Washington, DC: International Monetary Fund, Occasional Paper, no. 104, July.

Kolodko, Grzegorz W. (1993), 'Stabilization, Recession and Growth in a Post-Socialist Economy', *Moct-Most*, Nomisma, January, no. 1, pp. 3–38.

Kornai, János (1980), *Economics of Shortage*. Amsterdam: North Holland, 2 vols.

Kornai, János (1990), *The Road to a Free Economy. Shifting from a Socialist System: The Example of Hungary*. New York: W.W. Norton.

Kornai, János (1992), *The Socialist System. The Political Economy of Communism*. Oxford: Clarendon Press.

Kornai, János (1994), 'Transformational Recession: The Main Causes', *Journal of Comparative Economics*, vol. 19, no. 1 (August), pp. 39–63.

Köves, Andras (1983), ' "Implicit Subsidies" and Some Issues of Economic Relations Within the CMEA (Remarks on the Analyses Made by Michael Marrese and Jan Vanous)', *Acta Oeconomica*, vol. 31, no. 1–2, pp. 125–36.

Köves, Andras (1992), 'Shock-Therapy versus Gradual Change: Economic Problems and Policies in Central and Eastern Europe (1989–1991)', *Acta Oeconomica*, vol. 44, no. 1–2, pp. 13–36.

Kozul-Wright, Richard and Paul Rayment (1997), 'The Institutional Hiatus in Economies in Transition and its Policy Consequences', *Cambridge Journal of Economics*, vol. 21, no. 5, pp. 641–61.

Lampe, John R. (ed.) (1992), *Creating Capital Markets in Eastern Europe*. Washington, DC: The Woodrow Wilson Center Press.

Lange, Oskar (1936), 'On the Economic Theory of Socialism', *Review of Economic Studies*, vol. 4, no. 1, pp. 53–71.

Lankes, Hans-Peter and Tony Venables (1996), 'Foreign Direct Investment in Economic Transition: The Changing Pattern of Investment', *Economics of Transition*, vol. 4, no. 2, pp. 331–47.

Lankes, Hans-Peter and A. J. Venables (1997), 'Foreign Direct Investment in Eastern Europe and the Former Soviet Union: Results From a Survey of Investors', in Salvatore Zecchini (ed.) *Lessons From the Economic Transition, Central and Eastern Europe in the 1990s*. Paris: OECD, pp. 555–65.

Lapidus, Gail (1991), 'State and Society: Towards the Emergence of Civil Society in the Soviet Union', in Dallin and Lapidus (1991), pp. 130–50.

Lardy, Nicholas R. (1991), 'Is China Different? The Fate of Its Economic Reform', in D. Chirot (ed.) (1991), pp. 147–62.

Laski, Kazimierz and Amit Badhuri (1997), 'Lessons to be Drawn from Main Mistakes in the Transition Strategy', in OECD (1997d), pp. 103–21.

Laursen, Finn and Søren Riishøj (eds) (1996), *The EU and Central Europe: Status and Prospects*. Esbjerg: South Jutland University Press.

Lavigne, Marie (1974), *The Socialist Economies of the Soviet Union and Europe*. London: Martin Robertson.

Lavigne, Marie (1978), 'The Advanced Socialist Society', *Economy and Society*, vol. 7, no. 4 (November), pp. 367–394.

Lavigne, Marie (ed.) (1988), *East-South Relations in the World Economy*. Boulder and London: Westview Press.

Lavigne, Marie (1991), *International Political Economy and Socialism*, Cambridge: Cambridge University Press.

Lavigne, Marie (1995), 'Market Economies as Project and Practice', pp. 93–119, in Jack Hayward and Edward C. Page (eds), *Governing the New Europe*. Cambridge: Polity Press.

Layard, Richard, Olivier Blanchard, Rudiger Dornbusch and Paul Krugman (1992), *East West Migration. The Alternatives*. Cambridge, Mass. and London: The MIT Press.

Le Cacheux, Jacques (ed.) (1996a), *Europe, La nouvelle vague, Perspectives économiques de l'élargissement*. Paris: Presses de la Fondation Nationale des Sciences Politiques.

Le Cacheux, Jacques (1996b), 'Scenarios d'intégration des PECO à l'UE: la politique agricole commune', in OFCE (1996), pp. 55–68.

Leeds, Eva Marikova (1993), 'Voucher Privatization in Czechoslovakia', *Comparative Economic Studies*, vol. 35, no. 3 (Fall), pp. 19–37.

Lemoine, Françoise (1986), *L'économie chinoise*. Paris: La Découverte, Repères, no. 39.

Lemoine, Françoise (1994), *La nouvelle économie chinoise*. Paris: La Découverte.

Lhomel, Edith (1990), 'Les mutations des structures agricoles à l'Est', *Le Courrier des Pays de l'Est*, no. 347 (February), pp. 3–32.

Linotte, Daniel (1992), 'The Fall in Industrial Output in Transition Economies: A New Interpretation', Working Paper, Leuven: Leuven Institute for Central and East European Studies.

Liska, Tibor and Antal Marias (1955), 'Optimal Returns and International Division of Labour', in ECE/UN (1955).

Long, J. Bradford de and Barry Eichengren (1992), 'The Marshall Plan: History's Most Successful Structural Adjustment Program', *CEPR Discussion Paper Series*, no. 634; also published in R. Dornbush, W. Nolling and R. Layard (eds), *Postwar Economic Reconstruction and Lessons for the East Today*. Cambridge, Mass.: The MIT Press.

Lucas, Zdenek (1996), *Die Landwirtschaft der Oststaaten 1995*, WIIW, Vienna Institute for Comparative Economic Studies, *Forschungsberichte*, no. 164 (September).

Lucas, Zdenek (1997), *Die Landwirtschaft der Oststaaten 1996*, WIIW, Vienna Institute for Comparative Economic Studies, *Forschungsberichte*, no. 169 (October).

Malle, Silvana (1985), *The Economic Organisation of War Communism*. Cambridge: Cambridge University Press.

Marer, Paul (1985), *Dollar GNPs of the USSR and Eastern Europe*, Baltimore: The Johns Hopkins University Press.

Market Socialism (1989), special issue of *Acta Oeconomica*, vol. 40 (3–4), pp. 179–283.

Marrese, Michael (1992), 'Hungary Emphasizes Foreign Partners', *RFE/RL Research Report*, special issue on Privatisation, vol. 1, no. 17 (24 April), pp. 25–33.

Marrese, Michael and Jan Vanous (1983), *Soviet Subsidization of Trade With Eastern Europe: A Soviet Perspective*. Berkeley: University of California, Institute of International Studies.

Martin, Carmela and Francisco J. Velásquez (1997), 'The Determining Factors of Foreign Direct Investment in Spain and the rest of the OECD: Lessons for the CEECs', CEPR, Discussion Paper Series, no. 1637, London: CEPR (June).

Martin, Roderick (1998), 'Central and Eastern Europe and the International Economy: The Limits to Globalisation', *Europe-Asia Studies*, vol. 50, no. 1, pp. 7–26.

Matejka, Harriet (1994), 'La dégradation des statistiques commerciales des pays de l'Europe de l'Est et sa signification pour l'analyse de l'évolution de leurs échanges', *Revue Suisse d'Economie Politique et de Statistique*.

Matejka, Harriet (1997), 'La transition est transitoire', in Marie Lavigne (ed.), *Almanac(h)*, Pau, pp. 232–3.

Matejka, Harriet (1998), 'L'élargissement de l'UE à la République tchèque: quelles consésequences pour la Slovaquie?', *Le Courrier des Pays de l'Est*, Paris: La Documentation Française, no. 430, June, pp. 30–7.

Matolcsy, György H. (1997), 'Privatization and Transition in Central and Eastern Europe', *Cuadernos del Este* (Universidad Complutense de Madrid), no. 20, pp. 165–77.

Maurel, Marie-Claude (1991), 'Les agricultures d'Europe centrale face au défi européen: la transition peut-elle se résoudre à un transfert de modèle?', in *Les défis de l'an 2000*, Proceedings of a symposium organized at the University of Warsaw, June 1991.

Mayhew, Alan (1996), 'L'assistance financière l'Europe centrale et orientale: le programme PHARE', *Revue d'Etudes Comparatives Est-Ouest*, vol. 27, no. 4, pp. 135–58.

Mayhew, Alan (1998), *Recreating Europe. The European Union's Policy Towards Central and Eastern Europe*. Cambridge: Cambridge University Press.

Mayhew, Ken and Paul Seabright (1992), 'Incentives and the Management of Enterprises in Economic Transition: Capital Markets Are Not Enough', *CEPR Discussion Paper Series*, no. 640.

McKinnon, Ronald I. (1991a), *The Order of Economic Liberalization: Financial Control in the Transition to a Market Economy*. Baltimore: Johns Hopkins University Press.

McKinnon, Ronald I. (1991b), 'Liberalizing Foreign Trade in a Socialist Economy: The Problem of Negative Value Added', in John Williamson (ed.), *Currency Convertibility in Eastern Europe*. Washington: Institute for International Economics, pp. 96–115.

McKinnon, Ronald I. (1992), 'Spontaneous Order on the Road Back From Socialism: An Asian Perspective', *The American Economic Review*, vol. 82, no. 2 (May), pp. 31–6.

Mendershausen, Horst (1959), 'Terms of Trade Between the Soviet Union and Smaller Communist Countries, 1955–1957', *Review of Economics and Statistics*, vol. 51, no. 2 (May), pp. 106–18.

Mendershausen, Horst (1960), 'The Terms of Soviet-Satellite Trade: A Broadened Analysis', *Review of Economics and Statistics*, vol. 52, no. 2 (May), pp. 152–63.

Menshikov, Stanislav (1994), 'State Enterprises in Transition', *Transitions*, vol. 35, no. 1, pp. 125–48.

Messerlin, Patrick (1993), 'The EC and Central Europe: The Missed Rendez-Vous of 1992?', *Economics of Transition*, vol. 1, no. 1, pp. 89–109.

Mihályi, Péter (1993), 'Property Rights and Privatization, The Three-Agent Model (A Case Study on Hungary)', *Eastern European Economics*, vol. 31, no. 2 (Winter 1992–3), pp. 5–64.

Mihályi, Péter (1997), 'On the Quantitative Aspects of Hungarian Privatisation', *Comparative Economic Studies*, vol. 39, no. 2 (Summer), pp. 72–93.

Minassian, Garabed (1994), 'The Bulgarian Economy in Transition: Is There Anything Wrong With Macroeconomic Policy?', *Europe-Asia Studies*, vol. 46, no. 2, pp. 337–51.

Mink, Georges and Gérard Wild (1996), introduction to the special issue on the Eastern enlargement of the European Union of the *Revue d'Etudes Comparatives Est–Ouest*, vol. 27, no. 4, pp. 5–14.

Mises, Ludvig von (1920), 'Economic Calculation in the Socialist Commonwealth', in Hayek (ed.) (1935), pp. 87–130.

Moct-Most (1995), 'The Role of the International Organisations in the Transition: Economic Challenges, Financial Support and Targets', special issue, vol. 5, no. 2.

Moct-Most (1997), 'Financial Issues and Catching-up in Eastern Europe', special issue ed. by Alfred Steinherr, vol. 7, no. 3.

Mundell, R. A. (1995), 'Great Contractions in Transition Economies', paper prepared for the First Dubrovnik Conference on Transition Economies, Dubrovnik, June.

Murrell, Peter (1990), *The Nature of Socialist Economies: Lessons From Eastern European Foreign Trade*. Princeton: Princeton University Press.

Murrell, Peter (1991), 'Public Choice and the Transformation of Socialism', *Journal of Comparative Economics*, vol. 15, no. 2 (June), pp. 203–10

Murrell, Peter (1992), 'Conservative Political Philosophy and the Strategy of Economic Transition', *Eastern European Politics and Societies*, vol. 6, no. 1, pp. 3–16.

Murrell, Peter (1995), 'The Transition According to Cambridge, Mass', *Journal of Economic Literature,* vol. 33 (March), pp. 164–78.

Murrell, Peter (1996), 'How Far Has the Transition Progressed?', *Journal of Econmic Perspectives*, vol. 10, no. 2 (Spring), pp. 25–44.

Murrell, Peter and Yijiang Wang (1993), 'When Privatization Should be Delayed: The Effect of Communist Legacies on Organizational and Institutional Reforms', *Journal of Comparative Economics*, vol. 17, no. 2, pp. 385–406.

Nagels, Jacques (1990), *Du socialisme perverti au capitalisme sauvage*. Bruxelles: Université Libre de Bruxelles.

Nallet, Henri and Adrian van Stolk (1994), *Relations Between the European Union and the Central and Eastern European Countries in Matters Concerning Agriculture and Food Production*. Brussels: European Commission, 15 June.

Ners, Krzysztof and Ingrid T. Buxell (1995), *Assistance to Transition, Survey 1995*. New York: IEWS.

Neuberger, Egon and Laura d'Andrea Tyson (eds) (1980), *The Impact of International Economic Disturbances on the Soviet Union and Eastern Europe, Transmission and Response*. New York: Pergamon Press.

Neven, Damien (1994), *Trade Liberalization with Eastern Nations: How Sensitive?* London: CEPR, Discussion Paper no. 1000, July.

Newbery, David M. (1997), 'Reforming Tax and Benefit Systems in Central Europe: Lessons from Hungary', in OECD (1997d), pp. 413–43.

North, Douglass (1990), *Institutions, Institutional Change and Economic Performance*. Cambridge: Cambridge University Press.

Nove, Alec (1964), *Was Stalin Really Necessary? Economic Rationality and Soviet Politics*. London: George Allen & Unwin.

Nove, Alec (1983), *The Economics of Feasible Socialism*. London: Allen & Unwin. (Revised edition in 1991: *The Economics of Feasible Socialism Revisited*.)

Nove, Alec (1987), *The Soviet Economic System*. London: Allen & Unwin.

Nove, Alec (1992), *An Economic History of the USSR 1917–1991*. Harmondsworth: Penguin Books.

Nove, Alec (1994), 'A Gap in Transition Models? A Comment on Gomulka', *Europe-Asia Studies*, vol. 46, no. 5, pp. 863–9.

Nuti, D. Mario (1986), 'Hidden and Repressed Inflation in Soviet-Type Economies: Definitions, Measurements and Stabilisation', *Contributions to Political Economy*, vol. 5, pp. 37–82.

Nuti, D. Mario (1991), 'Stabilization and Reform Sequencing in the Reform of Central Eastern Europe', in Simon Commander (ed.), *Managing Inflation in Socialist Economies in Transition*. Washington: EDI-World Bank, pp. 155–74.

Nuti, D. Mario (1992), 'Market Socialism: The Model that Might Have Been but Never Was', in Anders Åslund (ed.), *Market Socialism or the Restoration of Capitalism?* Cambridge: Cambridge University Press, pp. 17–31.

Nuti, D. Mario (1993), 'Economic Inertia in the Transitional Economies of Eastern Europe', in M. Uvalić, E. Espa and J. Lorentzen (eds), *Impediments to the Transition in Eastern Europe,* Florence: European University Institute, pp. 25–49.

Nuti, D. Mario (1994), *Mass Privatisation: Costs and Benefits of Instant Capitalism.* London: London Business School, CIS – Middle Europe Centre, May.

Nuti D. Mario (1996a), 'Inflation, Interest and Exchange Rates in the Transition', *Economics of Transition*, vol. 4, no. 1, pp. 137–58.

Nuti, D. Mario (1996b), 'Transition or Mutations: For a New Political Economy of Post-Communist Mutations', *Emergo, Journal of Transforming Economies*, no. 7 (Winter), pp. 7–15.

Nuti, D. Mario and Richard Portes (1993), 'Central Europe: The Way Forward', in R. Portes (ed.) (1993), pp. 1–20.

Nyssen, Lars (1996), 'L'Ostpolitik de l'Union Européenne à la lueur de l'Accord d'association avec la République Tchèque', *Revue d'Etudes Comparatives Est–Ouest*, vol. 27, no. 4, pp. 15–44.

OECD (1993), *Employment and Unemployment in Economies in Transition: Conceptual and Measurement Problems.* Paris: Center for Co-operation with European Economies in Transition (CCET), OECD.

OECD (1994), *Unemployment in Central and Eastern Europe: Transient or Persistent?* Paris: CCET.

OECD (1995), *Hungary*. Economic Survey. Paris: CCET.

OECD (1996a), *The Czech Republic*. Economic Survey. Paris: CCET.

OECD (1996b), *The Slovak Republic*. Economic Survey. Paris: CCET.

OECD (1997a), *Bulgaria*. Economic Survey. Paris: CCET.

OECD (1997b), *Russian Federation*. Economic Survey. Paris: CCET.

OECD (1997c), *Sloveni*a. Economic Survey. Paris: CCET.

OECD (1997d), *Lessons from the Economic Transition, Central and Eastern Europe in the 1990s.* Edited by Salvatore Zecchini. Dordrecht: Kluwer Academic Publishers.

OECD (1997e), *The New Banking Landscape in Central and Eastern Europe. Country Experience and Policies for the Future.* Proceedings. Paris: CCET.

OECD (1998), *Romania*. Economic Survey. Paris: CCET.

OFCE (1996), *L'élargissement de l'Union Européenne aux pays d'Europe centrale et orientale: une analyse prospective des conséquences économiques et budgétaires,* annexe au rapport Badré, Paris: Les rapports du Sénat, 1995–96, no. 228.

Pinto, B., M. Belka and S. Krajewski (1993), *Transforming State Enterprises in Poland: Microeconomic Evidence on Adjustment.* Washington, DC: Brookings Papers on Economic Activity, no. 1993/1.

PlanEcon (1993a), 'Results of Czechoslovak Voucher Privatization', 'Part I: Overall Review and Statistical Data', 25 January (dated 31 December 1992), 'Part II: Sectoral and Industry Branch Reviews', 16 February, *PlanEcon Report*, vol. 8, nos 50–51–52, vol. 9, nos 3–4.

PlanEcon (1993b), 'East European Stock Market Report: Polish, Hungarian and Czech Stock Markets Outperform Most Other Emerging Markets By a Wide Margin', *PlanEcon Report*, vol. 9, no. 40–41 (19 November).

PlanEcon (1994), 'Czech Stock Market Review: The Market Collapses, Returning Many Czech Stocks to Bargain Levels', *PlanEcon Report*, vol. 10, no. 12–13 (7 June).

Podkaminer, Leon *et al.* (1998), *Transition Countries: 1997 External Deficits Lower Than Feared, Stability Again a Priority.* WIIW, Vienna Institute for Comparative Economic Studies, *Forschungsberichte*, no. 243 (February).

Pomfret, Richard (1997a), 'Growth and Transition: Why Has China's Performance Been So Different?', *Journal of Comparative Economics*, vol. 25, no. 3, pp. 422–40.

Pomfret, Richard (1997b), 'The Economic Cooperation Organization: Current Status and Future Prospects', *Europe-Asia Studies*, vol. 49, no. 4, pp. 657–67.

Portes, Richard (1980), 'Effects of the World Economic Crisis on the East European Economies', *The World Economy*, no. 3, pp. 13–52.

Portes, Richard (1992), 'The Contraction of Eastern Europe's Economies', IMF-World Bank Conference, 4–5 June, mimeo.

Portes, Richard (ed.) (1993), *Economic Transformation in Central Europe. A Progress Report.* London: CEPR; Luxembourg: Office for Official Publications of the European Communities.

Pryor, Frederic L. (1985), *A Guidebook to the Comparative Study of Economic Systems.* Englewood Cliffs: Prentice Hall Inc.

Remington, Thomas (1991), 'A Socialist Pluralism of Opinions: *Glasnost* and Policy-Making Under Gorbachev', in Dallin and Lapidus (1991), pp. 97–115.

Remontet, Catherine-Anne and Marcel Delbos (1997), 'L'évolution de la politique économique de l'Union européenne envers les PECO et l'ex-URSS', *Le Courrier des Pays de l'Est*, no. 412 (August), pp. 3–19.

Revue du Marché Commun et de l'Union Européenne (1993), special issue, 'Les Relations CEE-Europe centrale: problématique de l'adhésion', no. 369, June.

Richardson, Richard W. and Jonas H. Haralz (1995), *Moving to the Market: The World Bank in Transition*, Policy Essay no. 17. Washington, DC: Overseas Development Council.

Richter, Sándor (1997), *European Integration: The CEFTA and the Europe Agreements.* WIIW, Vienna Institute for Comparative Economic Studies, *Forschungsberichte*, no. 237 (May).

Robbins, Lionel (1937), *Economic Planning and International Order.* London: Macmillan.

Robinson, Anthony (1993), 'Tariffs Creeping Back in Poland', *Financial Times*, 13 January.

Robinson, Anthony and Nicholas Denton (1993), 'Clean-Up Prior to Going on Sale', *Financial Times*, 15 September.

Rodrik, Dani (1992), *Making Sense of the Soviet Trade Shock in Eastern Europe: A Framework and Some Estimates.* CEPR, Discussion Paper, no. 705.

Roland, Gérard (1989), *Economie politique du système soviétique.* Paris: L'Harmattan.

Roland, Gérard (1993), 'The Political Economy of Restructuring and Privatization in Eastern Europe', *European Economic Review*, vol. 37, no. 2/3 (April), pp. 533–40.

Roland, Gérard (1994), 'The Role of Political Constraints in Transition Economies', *Economics of Transition*, vol. 2, no. 1 (March), pp. 27–41.

Roland, Gérard and Thierry Verdier (1997), 'Transition and the Output Fall'. London: CEPR, Discussion Paper, no. 1636, May.

Rosati, Dariusz (1993), 'East European Trade in the Post-CMEA Era', Uvalic *et al.*, pp. 66–103.

Rosati, Dariusz (1996), 'Exchange Rate Policies during Transition from Plan to Market', *Economics of Transition*, vol. 4, no. 1, pp. 159–83.

Rosenstein-Rodan, P. N. (1943), 'Problems of Industrialisation of Eastern and South-Eastern Europe', *Economic Journal*, June–Sept., pp. 202–11.

Rostow, Walt Whitman (1960), *The Stages of Economic Growth. A Non-Communist Manifesto*. Cambridge: Cambridge University Press.

Rusinow, Dennison (1989), 'Yugoslavia: Enduring Crisis and Delayed Reforms', in *Pressures for Reform in the East European Countries*, Study papers submitted to the Joint Economic Committee, Congress of the United States, vol. 2, Washington, DC: USGPO, pp. 52–69.

Russo, Massimo (1998), 'The Transition Countries of Central and Eastern Europe: Why EMU Matters', paper prepared for the 53rd Session of the ECE/UN, 20 April, mimeo.

Sachs, Jeffrey D. and David Lipton (1991), ' "Shock Therapy" and Real Incomes', *Financial Times*, 29 January.

Sachs, Jeffrey D. and A. Warner (1996), 'Achieving Rapid Growth in the Transition Economies of Central Europe', Development Discussion Paper no. 544. Harvard Institute for International Development, Harvard University, July.

Sapir, Jacques (1990), *L'économie mobilisée, essai sur les économies de type soviétique*. Paris: Agalma – La Découverte.

Scalapino, Robert A. (1992) 'Asian Politics and Economics: The Challenges of the 1990s', in Iwasaki, Mori and Yamagushi (eds), pp. 229–47.

Schadler, Susan *et al.* (1995), 'IMF Conditionality Review: Experience Under Stand-By and Extended Arrangements, Part I: Key Issues and Findings, Part II: Background Papers', *IMF Occasional Papers*, nos 129 and 130. Washington, DC.

Schiavone, Giuseppe (1992), *International Organizations, A Dictionary and Directory*, 3rd edn. London and Basingstoke: Macmillan.

Schmitter, Philippe C. and Terry Lynn Karl (1994), 'The Conceptual Travels of Transitologists and Consolidologists: How Far to the East Should They Attempt To Go?', *Slavic Review*, vol. 53, no. 1 (Spring), pp. 173–85.

Schönfeld, Roland (ed.) (1995), *The Role of International Financial Institutions in Central and Eastern Europe*. Munich: Südosteuropa Gesellschaft, vol. 56.

Schönfeld, Roland, with Josef C. Brada and Ben Slay (1995), *Die Rolle der Internationalen Finazorganisationen in Ostmittel- und Südeuropa*, Südosteuropa-Studien Band 56. München: Südosteuropa Gesellschaft.

Schroeder, Gertrude (1979), 'The Soviet Economy on a Treadmill of "Reforms" ', in *The Soviet Economy in a Time of Change*, Joint Economic Committee, Congress of the United States, Washington, DC: USGPO, pp. 312–40.

Schuller, A. and H. Hamel (1985), 'On the Membership of Socialist Countries in the International Monetary Fund', *Acta Oeconomica*, vol. 34, no. 1–2, pp. 113–30.

Senik-Leygonie, Claudia and Gordon Hughes (1992), 'Industrial Profitability and Trade Among the Former Soviet Republics', *Economic Policy*, vol. 15 (October), pp. 353–86.

Sereghyova, Jana (ed.) (1993), *Entrepreneurship in CentralEast Europe*. Heidelberg: Physica Verlag.

Shleifer, Andrei (1997), 'Government in Transition', *European Economic Review*, vol. 41, nos 3–5, pp. 385–410.

Slay, Ben (1993), *The Polish Eonomy: Crisis, Reform and Transformation*. Princeton: Princeton University Press.

Smyth, Russell (1997), 'The Township and Village Enterprise Sector as a Specific Example of Regionalism – Some General Lessons for Socialist Transformation', *Economic Systems*, vol. 21, no. 3, pp. 235–64.

Sobell, Vlad (1984), *The Red Market, Industrial Co-operation and Specialisation in Comecon*. Aldershot: Gower.

Sorsa, Piritta (1997), 'The Global and Regional Outlook in the Baltics', in Teunissen, ed. (1997), pp. 142–80.

Steinherr, Alfred (1997), 'Banking Reforms in Eastern European Countries', *Oxford Review of Economic Policy*, vol. 13, no. 2, pp. 106–25.

Steinherr, Alfred and Pier-Luigi Gilibert (1994), 'Six Proposals in Search of Financial Sector Reform in Eastern Europe', *Moct-Most*, vol. 4, no. 1, pp. 101–14.

Steinherr, Alfred and Christopher Hurst (1995), 'Investment in Eastern Europe: The Role of Multinational Organisations', *Moct-Most*, special issue, pp. 65–83.

Stiglitz, Joseph (1994), *Whither Socialism?* Cambridge, Mass.: MIT Press.

Stiglitz, Joseph E. (1998), 'More Instruments and Broader Goals: Moving toward the Post-Washington Consensus', *WIDER Annual Lectures 2*, The United Nations University, January.

Sutela, Pekka (1994), *Socialism, Planning and Optimality. A Study in Soviet Economic Thought*. Helsinki: The Finnish Society of Sciences and Letters, vol. 25.

Sutela, Pekka (1997), 'Privatization in the Countries of Eastern and Central Europe and of the Former Soviet Union', UNU/WIDER Project, *Transition Strategies, Alternatives and Outcomes*. Helsinki: UNU/WIDER, May.

Svejnar, Jan and Miroslav Singer (1994), 'Using Vouchers to Privatize the Economy: the Czech and Slovak Case', *Economics of Transition*, vol. 2, no. 1 (March), pp. 43–69.

Swain, Geoffrey and Nigel Swain (1993), *Eastern Europe since 1945*. London and Basingstoke: Macmillan.

Szamuely, László (1993), *Transition from State Socialism: Whereto and How?* Budapest: Kopint-Datorg Discussion Papers, no. 12.

Szpringer, Zofia (1993), *Assessment of Price Liberalization Effects in Selected Post-Socialist Economies*. Warsaw: Institute of Finance, Working Papers, no. 34, 28 pp.

Taylor, Lance (1994), 'The Market Met Its Match: Lessons for the Future from the Transition's Initial Years', *Journal of Comparative Economics*, vol. 19, no. 1 (August), pp. 64–87.

Temprano-Arroyo, Heliodoro and Robert A. Feldman (1998), 'Selected Transition and Mediterranean Countries: An Institutional Primer on EMU and EU Relations', *IMF Working Paper*, 98/82, June.

Teunissen, Jan Joost (ed.) (1997), *Regionalism and the Global Economy. The Case of Central and Eastern Europe*. The Hague: FONDAD.

Thurow, Lester C. (1996), *The Future of Capitalism*. New York: William Morrow & Co.

Tinbergen, Jan (1961), 'Do Communist and Free Economies Show a Convergent Pattern', *Soviet Studies*, vol. 12, no. 4, pp. 333–41.

Trzeciakowski, Witold (1978), *Indirect Management in a Centrally Planned Economy: Systems Constructions in Foreign Trade*. Amsterdam: North Holland.

USDA (United States Department of Agriculture) (1997), *Newly Independent States and Baltics Update, Spotlight on Foreign Direct Investment*. Washington, DC: USDA Economic Research Service.

Uvalić, Milica (1992), *Investment and Property Rights in Yugoslavia. The Long Transition to a Market Economy*. Cambridge: Cambridge University Press.

Uvalić, Milica, Espa, Efisio and Jochen Lorentzen (eds) (1993), *Impediments to the Transition in Eastern Europe*. Florence: European University Institute, European Policy Studies, no. 1.

Vacic, Aleksandar M. (1992), 'Systemic Transformation in Central and Eastern Europe: General Framework, Specific Features and Prospects', in 'Transition en Europe de l'Est: les nouveaux rivages du marché', *Economies et Sociétés*, série G 'Economie Planifiée', special issue, vol. 44.

Vintrová, Růžena (1993), 'Macroeconomic Analysis of Transformation in the CSFR', WIIW, Vienna Institute for Comparative Economic Studies, *Forschungsberichte*, no. 188, January.

Visegrad (1991), Visegrad Summit Declaration, *Report on Eastern Europe*, Radio Free Europe/RL Research Institute, 1 March 1991, pp. 31–2.

Vuylsteke, Charles (1995), 'The EBRD: Its Mandate, Instruments, Challenges and Responses', in *Moct-Most*, special issue, pp. 129–55.

Wallich, Christine (1995), 'What's Right and Wrong with World Bank Involvement in Eastern Europe', in *JCE* (1995a), pp. 57–94.

Wang, Zhen Kun and L. Alan Winters (1993), *EC Imports from Eastern Europe: Iron and Steel*. London: CEPR Discussion Paper Series, no. 825, October.

Ward, Benjamin (1958), 'The Firm in Illyria: Market Syndicalism', *American Economic Review*, vol. 48, no. 4 (September), pp. 566–89.

Weitzman, Martin L. (1993), 'Economic Transition: Can Theory Help?', *European Economic Review*, vol. 37, no. 2/3 (April), pp. 549–55.

Welfens, Paul J. J. (1992), *Market-Oriented Systemic Transformations in Eastern Europe: Problems, Theoretical Issues and Policy Options*. Berlin: Springer Verlag.

Weydenthal, Jan B. de (1993a), 'Controversy in Poland Over "Euroregions"', *RFE/RL Research Report*, vol. 2, no. 16, 16 April.

Weydenthal, Jan B. de (1993b), 'The EC and Central Europe: A Difficult Relationship', *RFE/RL Research Report*, vol. 2, no. 21, 21 May.

White, Stephen, Judy Batt and Paul G. Lewis (eds) (1993), *Developments in East European Politics*. Basingstoke and London: Macmillan.

Wijnbergen, Sweder van (1993), 'Enterprise Reform in Eastern Europe', *Economics of Transition*, vol. 1, no. 1 (January), pp. 21–59.

Wiles, Peter (1968), *Communist International Economics*. Oxford: Basil Blackwell.

Wiles, Peter (ed.) (1982), *The New Communist Third World*. London: Croom Helm.

Wiles, Peter (1992), 'Capitalist Triumphalism in Eastern Europe, or the Economics of Transition: An Interim Report', in A. Clesse and R. Tökes (eds), *Preventing a New East–West Divide: The Economic and Social Imperatives of the Future Europe*. Baden-Baden: Nomos Verlagsgesellschaft.

Williamson, John (ed.) (1991a), *Currency Convertibility in Eastern Europe*. Washington: Institute for International Economics.

Williamson, John (1991b), *The Economic Opening of Eastern Europe*. Washington: Institute for International Economics, May, vol. 31.

Williamson, John (1992a), *Trade and Payments After Soviet Disintegration*. Washington: Institute for International Economics, June, vol. 37.

Williamson, John (1992b), 'Why Did Output Fall in Eastern Europe?', Paper prepared for the Arne Ryde Symposium on 'The Transition Problem', Denmark, Rungsted Kyst, 11–12 June.

Williamson, John (ed.) (1994), *The Political Economy of Policy Reform*. Washington, DC: Institute for International Economics.

Winiecki, Jan (1993a), *Post-Soviet-Type Economies in Transition*. Aldershot: Avebury.

Winiecki, Jan (1993b), *'Heterodox' Stabilisation in Eastern Europe*. London: European Bank for Reconstruction and Development, Working Papers no. 8, 29 pp.

Winters, L. Alan (1992), 'The Europe Agreements: With a Little Help from our Friends', in *The Association Process: Making it Work, Central Europe and the European Community*, CEPR Occasional Paper no. 11, November 1992.

Winters, L. Alan (1994), *The Liberalization of European Steel Trade*. London: CEPR, Discussion Paper no. 1002, August.

Winters, L. Alan and Zhen Kun Wang (1993), *Liberalizing EC Imports of Footwear From Eastern Europe*. London: CEPR Discussion Paper series, no. 836, September.

Wolf, Thomas A. (1988), *Foreign Trade in the Centrally Planned Economy*, New York: Harwood Academic Publishers.

Wolf, Thomas, Warren Coats, Daniel Citrin and Adrienne Cheaty (1994), *Financial Relations Among Countries of the Former Soviet Union*. Washington, DC: International Monetary Fund, IMF Economic Reviews, February.

World Bank (1996), *From Plan to Market, World Development Report 1996*. Washington DC: World Bank and Oxford: Oxford University Press.

World Bank (1997), *The State in a Changing World, World Development Report 1997*. Washington DC: World Bank and Oxford: Oxford University Press.

Yavlinsky, Grigory and Serguey Braguinsky (1994), 'The Inefficiency of *Laissez-Faire* in Russia: Hysteresis Effects and the Need for Policy-Led Transformation', *Journal of Comparative Economics*, vol. 19, no. 1 (August), pp. 88–116.

Zaleski, Eugene (1980), *Stalinist Planning for Economic Growth, 1933–1952*. London: Macmillan and Chapel Hill: University of North Carolina Press.

Zoethout, Tseard (1993), 'Financing Eastern Europe's Capital Requirements', *RFE/RL Research Report*, vol. 2, no. 7, 12 February, pp. 38–43.

Index

Abalkin, L., 95, 126
Abel, I., 119
accession, of the Eastern European
    countries to the European Union,
    228–9, 276; 'Agenda 2000', 237,
    238, 239; conditions, 229–30;
    'Maastricht criteria', 140, 231–2
administration, economic, 5, 23, 30–3
Afghanistan, 28, 60, 65, 80, 82, 83
Aghion, P., 176, 178, 179, 184, 272
agriculture, forms of ownership in, 8–10;
    privatisation in, 197–8;
    restructuring in, 199; statistics for,
    47; under the NEP, 20–1
Albania, 15, 25, 26; and Comecon, 72;
    party, 4; under transition, 159,192,
    198, 218
anchoring, 115, 117, 130–3, 136
Anderson, R.E., 178
Andreff, W., 265
Andropov, Y., 18, 23
Angola, 80
arenda, 18
Asselain, J.-C., 142, 144, 157
assistance, from East to South, 79–81; to
    transition, 244–54
Association agreements, *see* Europe
    Agreements
autarky, 65–72, 84

bad debts in the transition period, 136,
    187–9
Badhuri, A., 276
Bahro, R., 3
Bakos, G., 207
balance, *see* material balance
Balcerowicz, L., 101, 118, 154
Baldwin, R.E., 238, 239
Baltic States, 113, 115, 139, 159, 167,
    181, 196, 198, 209–10, 234, 247,
    255, 261; *see* Estonia, Latvia,
    Lithuania

bank, central, 13, 117, 140, 186; state,
    17, 31, 186; commercial, 117, 187
banking system, reform of, 117, 186–91
bankruptcy, 150, 180–1
Barre, R., 207, 250
barter trade, 69
Begg, D., 187
Belarus, 109–10
Bergson, A., 93, 315
Berlin Wall, 91, 96, 274
Bettelheim, C., 265
big bang, 113, 118–20, 165
Black Sea Economic Cooperation, 212
Blanchard, O., 150, 157, 158, 176, 178,
    179
Blaszczyk, B., 173, 193
Bobinski, C., 221
Boeri, T., 150, 197
Bofinger, P., 115, 157, 215
bolshevik, 16, 19
Bornstein, M., 163, 176, 266, 315
Brabant, J.M. van, 207, 315
Brada, J.C., 78, 157, 182, 207, 270, 315
Braguinsky, S., 272
branch ministries, 31, 33, 168
Brezhnev, L., 18, 23, 76
Brown, B., 211
Bruno, M., 115, 118, 152, 157
Brus, W., 269
budget deficit, 114, 137–140, 148
Budina, N., 143
Bukharin, N.I., 20
Bulgaria, 15, 24, 27; agricultural policy,
    198; banking reform, 186, 189, 190;
    growth strategy under socialism,
    51–3, 58; international economic
    relations, 209, 220, 223, 225, 227,
    228, 229, 231, 234, 235, 236, 251,
    252, 255, 259, 262; privatisation,
    167, 174, 175, 201–2; reforms, 31,
    41; stabilisation policy in, 115, 117,
    120, 123, 121, 129, 131, 135, 141–2,